HADRIAN'S WALL

ARCHAEOLOGY AND HISTORY AT THE LIMIT OF ROME'S EMPIRE

HADRIAN'S WALL

ARCHAEOLOGY AND HISTORY AT THE LIMIT OF ROME'S EMPIRE

Nick Hodgson

ROBERT HALE

First published in 2017 by
Robert Hale, an imprint of
The Crowood Press Ltd
Ramsbury, Marlborough
Wiltshire SN8 2HR

enquiries@crowood.com

www.crowood.com

This impression 2019

British Library Cataloguing-in-Publication Data
A catalogue record for this book is available from the British Library.

ISBN 978 0 7198 1815 8

Typeset by Servis Filmsetting Ltd, Stockport, Cheshire
Printed and bound in India by Parksons Graphics

Contents

THIS IS NOT A GUIDE BOOK TO THE REMAINS of Hadrian's Wall, but (I hope) a simple explanation of how it came to be built, the major events in its history, what purpose it was intended to serve, what life was like for the people who lived on the Wall and in its shadow, how archaeologists know these things, and the limits to what they can know.

One of the curious things about Hadrian's Wall is that, although they all rely on the same evidence for what happened in the past, archaeologists approach it from different perspectives. There is much disagreement between experts, and not a little misunderstanding. I hope that by producing a straightforward and up-to-date account of the Wall, based on modern archaeological and historical research, I can show readers that there is more than one way of interpreting the Wall, but at the same time offer a factually reliable and interesting account for visitors, general readers, students and archaeologists.

This version of the Wall story gives more emphasis than most to the indigenous population of Britain and the way the Wall affected them, something we have only recently begun to learn more about. It also reflects my concern that archaeologists are getting less and less confident about trying to draw general historical conclusions from the evidence. Historical narrative is increasingly 'out', and the social history of what people wore and ate, increasingly 'in': but I try to show that there is room for both, and that we can begin to obtain a clearer picture of how the experience for those who lived with the Wall changed from one century to another.

This book may seem unusual because I have deliberately not named any modern archaeologist or historian in the text (with rare exceptions). This is to make for accessibility and readability, and to avoid getting bogged down in debates between personalities. It is also because I feel that sometimes we can only look at a problem afresh by stepping away from it, looking at it from a different angle, and forgetting for a moment the accretion of thought around it. This means I inevitably describe ideas and arguments without crediting their authors in the text, but I have tried always to acknowledge them in the endnotes. I apologise if I have inadvertently failed to do this at any point.

I thank all colleagues who have supplied information or discussed the problems of Hadrian's Wall over the years. They are too many to name individually, but I am particularly grateful to David Breeze for his friendly encouragement, and for agreeing to read and comment on the text. Paul Bidwell has also read the text and offered valuable suggestions. James Bruhn has provided invaluable discussion and practical assistance. None of these is responsible for any errors in the book, or necessarily agrees with any of the views advanced.

I must thank three people to whom I feel especially indebted. The late Cliff Davies, an inspiring tutor who was unflagging in his help to me as an undergraduate, can never have dreamt that his training in the use of modern historical evidence would one day be applied to Roman times. The late Charles Daniels, my PhD supervisor, first encouraged my move into archaeology and placed his wide knowledge of the Roman frontiers at my disposal. Above all, I have been privileged to work for nearly thirty years with Paul Bidwell, at once a teacher and a friend, and to benefit from his generosity and extraordinary insights. Many of the ideas in this book are his, and I offer it to him in gratitude.

Newcastle upon Tyne
2016

WHAT IS HADRIAN'S WALL?

MOST PEOPLE HAVE HEARD OF THE GREAT wall built by the Roman Emperor Hadrian in northern Britain. It has been a World Heritage Site since 1987, and year by year is more aggressively marketed to tourists. Of the hundreds of thousands who make the pilgrimage to see it, many are thrilled by the sight of Hadrian's Wall in the wildest of Northumbrian settings. The Elizabethan antiquary William Camden (one of the first to give an archaeological description of the Wall, in 1599) was similarly moved: 'Verily I have seen the tract of it over the high pitches and steep descents of hills, wonderfully rising and falling.' Many of the modern visitors to the best known parts of the Wall rise above the relentless retail opportunity of the soulless souvenir shops and the corporately branded information panels, and when they get amongst the lichen-covered Roman stones feel – an unmistakable feeling – that they stand among the abandoned ruins of a vanished civilization. The questions are soon triggered: who exactly were these Romans? Why did they come to this remote island and raise such

Fig. I.1 'Verily I have seen the tract of it over the high pitches and steep descents of hills, wonderfully rising and falling': the Wall as it appears today, west of Housesteads.

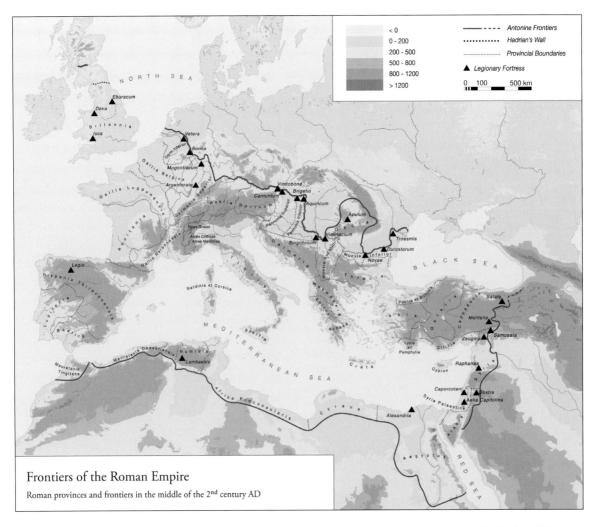

Frontiers of the Roman Empire

Roman provinces and frontiers in the middle of the 2nd century AD

Fig. I.2 Hadrian's Wall did not stand alone as a fortification line at the edge of the Roman Empire: this map shows the frontiers of the Roman Empire in the second century AD. FRONTIERS OF THE ROMAN EMPIRE CULTURE 2000 PROJECT/D. J. BREEZE

massive structures here? And where did they go? Why was this most impressive and enduring phase in the archaeological record of northern Britain abandoned, leaving traces of a Mediterranean-based culture, still visible in the remote countryside of Northumberland and Cumbria after 1,600 years?

A smaller number of enthusiasts are rapidly hooked and begin to wonder what archaeological secrets are held in the parts of the Wall that now lie wholly buried, whether under sheep-cropped grass or beneath the urban landscapes of Tyneside or Carlisle. This book sets out to answer those questions, and to explain what modern archaeology tells us about the reality of events and life on Hadrian's Wall over the three centuries of its operation.

It is important at the outset to see Hadrian's Wall in its context: the Wall did not stand alone as a fortification line at the edge of the Roman Empire. Not many visitors to Hadrian's Wall know that only 160km (100 miles) north there was an equally elaborate Roman frontier work, the Antonine Wall in Scotland. This was built only twenty years after work had begun on the much better known wall of Hadrian, and superseded Hadrian's barrier for a brief twenty-year period. Fewer still appreciate that the remains of another great series of Roman barriers can be traced for nearly 500km (300 miles) through modern Germany, along the land frontier of the empire from near Koblenz on the Rhine to the area of Regensburg on the Danube.

All these barriers were built and manned by the Roman army, an institution that, like Hadrian's Wall, has been the subject of much popular fascination. This is partly because the imperial army seems at first sight so sophisticated, so modern, in its organization. It is also because of the sheer scale of its achievements, both in conquest and building. The Roman army, and its changing character over the centuries, takes a central role in this story. However, the army was always surrounded by a civilian galaxy of wives, girlfriends, children, suppliers, traders, priests, slaves, and its own retired veterans, and we shall see that these people outnumbered the soldiers on Hadrian's Wall and have left their archaeological mark. Only in recent years have archaeologists begun to get a clearer idea of the natives – the indigenous Iron Age people who lived in the area of the Wall and whose northern neighbours constituted the rebellious external peoples who posed a threat to the areas of Britain under direct Roman government.

Any account of what Hadrian's Wall was for, how it worked, and its ultimate fate, must include these people, practically invisible, archaeologically speaking, until recently: they play a major part in our story, in contrast to previous accounts that have ascribed them little meaningful role, claiming that the comings and goings of the Romans in north Britain were more to do with the personal agendas of Roman emperors and competing priorities on the continent than resistance on the ground. For many historians it has been hard to believe that the will of the invincible Roman army could be frustrated by mere barbarians. We will return to these fundamental issues, but first it is time to set the scene and introduce the Wall, and describe what it consisted of, and the landscape through which it was constructed.

The Course of the Wall

Hadrian's Wall crosses the narrow isthmus between the Tyne, in the Newcastle area, and the Solway estuary, which indents the western coast just north

Fig. 1.3 Hadrian's Wall and other Roman forts in northern Britain.

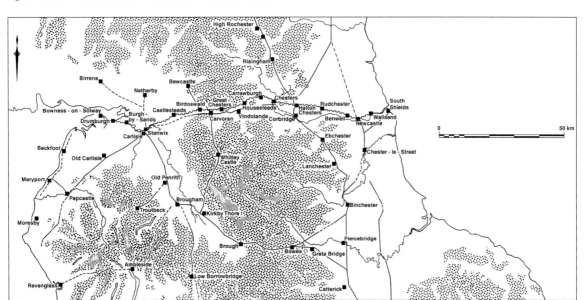

of the Lake District, near Carlisle. Here Britain is only 127km (78 miles) wide. As we shall see, the Roman mind seized upon such narrow necks of land as having potential for defence by long walls: subsequently, the narrowest isthmus of all in Britain, between the Forth and the Clyde (only 60km – 37 miles), would be chosen for the Antonine Wall in Scotland.

It is traditional to describe the Wall from east to west, the direction adopted in most of the accounts by pioneer archaeologists in the eighteenth and nineteenth centuries – 'the antiquaries'. The Romans also 'read' the Wall from east to west: this direction is used in two surviving ancient Roman lists of all the forts along the Wall. In this sense, then, the Wall 'begins' on the north bank of the River Tyne at Wallsend, now a suburb of eastern Newcastle. This point is actually 8km (5 miles) inland: the river was deemed wide enough to substitute for the Wall in the few miles between Wallsend and the sea. From Wallsend the Wall runs directly to the point where a Roman bridge crossed the Tyne to Newcastle. From Newcastle the course is west-north-west and follows the northern lip of the broad Tyne and South Tyne valleys.

From Newcastle to the beginning of the crags in the central sector, the Wall was laid out in long straight stretches. Throughout this eastern sector there was no obvious ridge or high commanding line for the Wall to seize. Therefore it ran from high point to high point through an uneven, rolling landscape, having to cross a number of denes and river valleys that dramatically serrated the landscape as they ran into the Tyne, particularly in the Newcastle area. At 43km (27 miles) from Wallsend the Wall crossed a major river, the North Tyne, by means of a bridge.

In the central sector the Wall followed the precipitous basaltic ridge known as the Great Whin Sill. It ran a different kind of course here, weaving to maintain the crest of the crags. As it descended from the Whin Sill at Carvoran, the Wall resumed a course of predominantly straight stretches. It crossed the turbulent Irthing by another major bridge, to run along the well-defined narrow east/west-running ridge north of the river. Between Castlesteads and

Carlisle there was again no obvious feature for the Wall to follow so it cut arbitrarily through the landscape, and once again it adopted straight stretches surveyed over a long distance.

From Carlisle to the Solway the Wall was laid out partly in long curving sectors, and partly in straight stretches. There was no elevated contour for the Wall to follow, and its curving course immediately west of Carlisle suggests that it may have been sited to overlook the River Eden. Further west it ran in short, straight stretches overlooking the marshes that merged into the coastline. The Wall ended its course of 80 Roman miles at Bowness-on-Solway, where once it could be traced running far into the sea beyond the present village.

What the Wall Consists of

The Wall was measured in Roman feet (for which the abbreviation RF is used below), and the distances in between structures on the Wall in Roman miles. A Roman mile was a notional 5,000 Roman feet, that is, a thousand 'paces' of five feet each; from the Latin *milia passuum* – a thousand paces – comes our word 'mile'. Roman miles and feet were somewhat shorter than the modern imperial units. Since Roman measuring rods and rulers were not all made to a standard as in modern times, and as there was more than one 'kind' of Roman foot, it is impossible to give a simple conversion into modern units. Many books give 296mm for the standard Roman foot or *pes Monetalis*, and the feet used on Hadrian's Wall never vary greatly from this. The equivalent in modern inches would be 11.64. Using a Roman foot of this length, a Roman mile is approximately 1,480m or just under 1,620 yards, which compares to the 1,760 yards of a modern statute mile.

The Wall itself varied in its materials and width according to time and place. It seems to have been originally envisaged as a stone barrier a massive 10RF thick, with a wall walk and parapet taking it to a total height of perhaps 20RF. Originally the western 31 miles were of turf construction (the 'Turf Wall' of

Fig. I.4 Cross-section of the Wall as reconstructed at Wallsend to the minimum likely dimensions. This is the 2.4m (8ft) wide 'Narrow Wall'. The reconstruction stands 3.7m (12ft) high to the wall walk, with a further 1.5m (5ft) for the parapet.

Hadrian), though soon replaced in stone. Changes in the course of construction mean that for most of its course the Wall was completed to lesser widths, and probably correspondingly lesser height than in the original scheme, but still on a daunting scale and constituting the most formidable of frontier barriers in the Roman Empire. At 6m (20RF) in front of the Wall ran a great V-shaped ditch, generally over 8m wide and up to 3m deep.

At every Roman mile or 1,620m was a small fort ('fortlet') that functioned as a fortified gateway through the Wall. For obvious reasons these have become known as 'milecastles'. There are some minor adjustments to their regular spacing for local reasons, but on the whole in the provision of the milecastles we see the orderliness and unswervability of the Roman military mind at work. The regularity of the system descends to even smaller structures, for between every two milecastles were two watch-towers ('turrets' in the time-honoured terminology special to Hadrian's Wall), spaced, therefore, at every third of a mile. On the Turf Wall the milecastles were made of turf, but even there the turrets were originally built in stone.

West of Bowness, down the Cumbrian coast, a system of milecastles and turrets (known there as 'milefortlets' and 'towers') continued for at least 40km (25 miles). The milecastles are numbered from east to west, and the turrets in each Wall-mile have the number of the preceding milecastle with the suffixes A and B. So, for example, between Milecastles 48 and 49 we find Turrets 48A and 48B. The Cumbrian coast structures are numbered similarly from north to south. This is not a Roman system of numbering, and we have no idea how the Romans referred to the individual structures. The system of notation was devised in the 1920s: it is the basic means archaeologists have of distinguishing structures and referring to their location, and they would be lost without it.

Major garrison forts for full Roman army units also occur along the Wall, in various relationships to it; there are some fifteen in number, spaced on average around 11 or 13km (7 or 8 miles) apart. A further system of full-scale forts was built along the Cumbrian coast. Detached from the east end of the Wall, a fort at South Shields defended a sea-port at the mouth of the Tyne. The forts do not have numbers, and are conventionally and properly referred to, in archaeological literature, by their modern names ('Chesters', 'Housesteads' and so on) and not their ancient ones, about which there is often considerable uncertainty. Vindolanda, a name that has been in use for a long time and for which there is cast-iron evidence, is the exception to this rule. 'Chester(s)', which is such a common element in modern fort names (but only in Northumberland, not in Cumbria), is derived from the

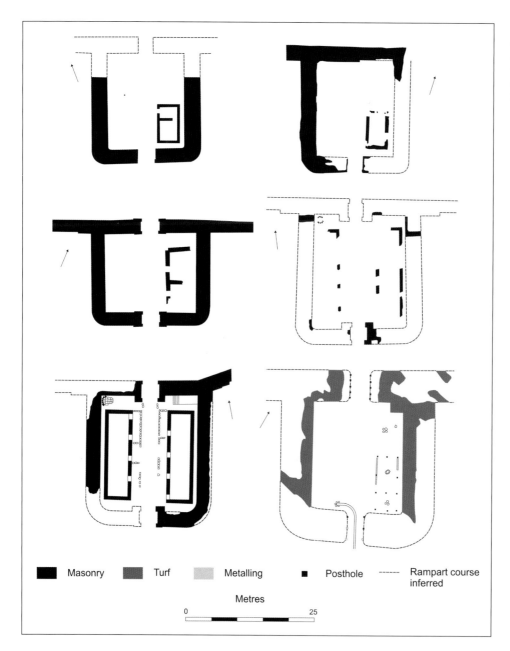

Fig. I.5 A selection of milecastle plans. Bottom right is a Turf Wall milecastle.

M. A. SYMONDS

Masonry   Turf   Metalling   ■ Posthole   ----- Rampart course inferred

Metres

0   25

Old English *ceaster*, and ultimately from the Latin *castra* (meaning 'a camp'), and was applied in Saxon times to Roman forts and walled towns in Britain.

The Wall did not mark the limit of Roman military control, for there were also garrison forts in the zone to the north. The pattern and number of these varied over time: they lay in a zone between 15 and 80km (10 and 50 miles) north of the Wall. The Wall

forts were not used occasionally or episodically, but became the permanent homes of particular military units and their attached civilian communities. Their archaeology is therefore deep and complicated, reflecting centuries of occupation.

To the rear of the Wall, between Newcastle and Bowness (and therefore not running all the way to Wallsend), is found a linear earthwork, the so-called

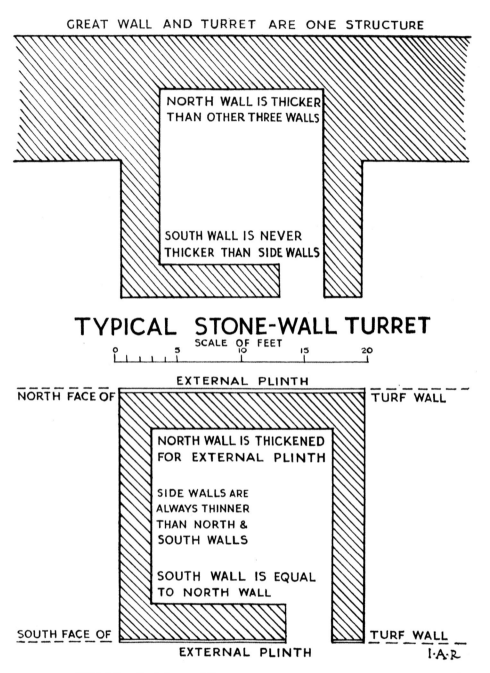

GREAT WALL AND TURRET ARE ONE STRUCTURE

NORTH WALL IS THICKER
THAN OTHER THREE WALLS

SOUTH WALL IS NEVER
THICKER THAN SIDE WALLS

TYPICAL STONE-WALL TURRET

SCALE OF FEET

0   5   10   15   20

EXTERNAL PLINTH

NORTH FACE OF   TURF WALL

NORTH WALL IS THICKENED
FOR EXTERNAL PLINTH

SIDE WALLS ARE
ALWAYS THINNER
THAN NORTH &
SOUTH WALLS

SOUTH WALL IS EQUAL
TO NORTH WALL

SOUTH FACE OF   TURF WALL

EXTERNAL PLINTH   I·A·R

TYPICAL TURF-WALL TURRET

Fig. I.6 I. A. Richmond's diagram of typical turret plans.

Vallum. This was a flat-bottomed ditch, 6m (20RF) wide and 3m (10RF) deep, with a substantially built mound to cither side, set 9m (30RF) from the lip of the Vallum ditch. This formidable obstacle demarcated and secured the southern edge of the military zone associated with the Wall fort's milecastle and turrets. Along this corridor, between the Wall and the Vallum, there runs a Roman road, the main means of communication and supply between the forts and lesser installations, known as the 'Military Way' (like

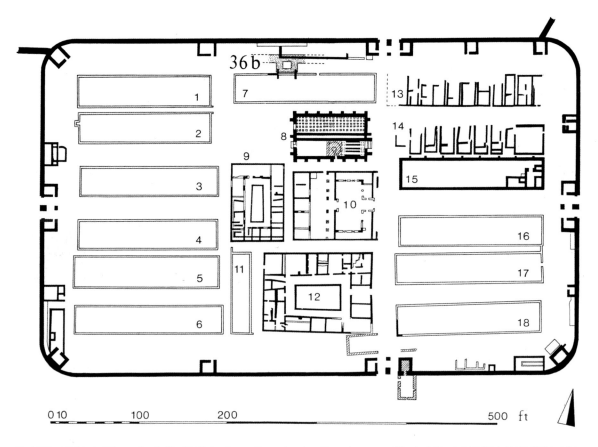

Fig. I.7 The Wall fort of Housesteads. The Wall joins the north-west and north-east corners of the fort. The original line of the Wall can be seen lying slightly further south, along with Turret 36B, destroyed to make way for the fort.

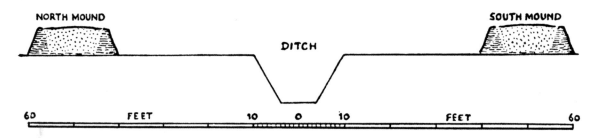

Fig. I.8 Profile across the ditch and flanking mounds of the Vallum.

'milecastle', and 'turret', a term used since the eighteenth century).

Not all elements of the Wall described above were built at one time. But the basic package described above is what was recognizable to the antiquaries and earliest twentieth-century archaeologists who studied the Wall, before modern survey and excavation began to reveal the complicated sequence by which the frontier was built under Hadrian, and modified under subsequent emperors.

This ensemble of works is still visually apparent in the remote central areas where the Roman works are

Fig. I.9 The earthworks of the Vallum in Wall-mile 41 (Cawfields). Looking south-east, the central ditch and flanking mounds can be seen, and behind the head of the figure, the later 'marginal mound' on the south lip of the ditch.

Fig. I.10 Milecastle 39 in the central sector. In contrast to most of the Wall, which in this area was unscientifically exposed 150 years ago, the stretches of the Wall to either side were excavated in the 1980s.

Fig. I.11 The Wall
in its unexcavated
natural ruined state
as a stony grass-
covered mound in
Wall-mile 39. The
excavated Wall
can be seen in the
distance.

preserved as upstanding monuments; but today the Wall is no longer visible for much of its course. For the most part there is now only buried archaeology, invisible until contacted by excavation or remote sensing techniques. The eastern 16km (10 miles), where some of the most intriguing recent archaeological discoveries have been made, are buried beneath urban Tyneside. For 37km (23 miles) west of this conurbation, the Wall itself lies beneath a modern road (the B6318), a legacy of the construction of a new military road between Newcastle and Carlisle in the aftermath of the Jacobite uprising of 1745, which utilized the line of the Wall and levelled it for hard-core. Only in Wall-mile 33 do the two lines diverge, the eighteenth-century road taking a low-level route and the Wall ascending to the high crags.

From this point, where (in the words of Hutton's description of 1802) we 'quit the beautiful scenes of cultivation and enter upon the rude of Nature, and the wreck of Antiquity', for some 27km (17 miles) the Wall and its works are substantially visible to the walker across the backbone of England, largely, in the case of the stone structures, as the result of unscientific nineteenth-century excavations; in their natural ruined state the Wall and its milecastles appear as grass-grown stony mounds. Beyond the crags, west of the River Irthing in Cumbria, the Wall is subsumed in a low-lying agricultural landscape (and the city of Carlisle), and hardly anything is now visible in the western 50km (30 miles). Of the structures running down the Cumberland coast, with a handful of exceptions, very little is visible to the modern visitor.

A wholly unexpected discovery in 2001 was a system of emplacements for obstacles in the space between the Wall and its frontal ditch (termed 'the berm'). These were found at Shields Road, Byker (Wall-mile 2), and later in the same year over a 1km (0.6 mile) length between Throckley and Heddon

Fig. I.12 Emplacements for obstacles on the berm between the Wall and ditch, discovered at Byker (Wall-mile 2) in 2001. The Wall foundation can be seen to the left; the dark area to the right of the pits is the Wall ditch.

(Wall-miles 10 to 11). They have since been found at several other points in the eastern 18km (11 miles) of the Wall, and have also been recognized at five sites along the easternmost third of the Antonine Wall in Scotland.

Not man-traps (*lilia*), these rectangular and vertical-sided pits were most probably emplacements for an impenetrable entanglement of forked branches, closer in appearance and function to what Caesar described as *cippi*. The frequent description of the emplacements in archaeological literature as 'pits' or *lilia* is therefore misleading, for although they survive archaeologically as pits, in fact they denote the presence of a substantial above-ground structure. The obstacles seem to have been accompanied by a mound raised on the south lip of the Wall ditch.

These obstacles represent the first discovery of a new element in the repertoire of regular Wall works to be made in modern times. Whether they extended along the whole length of Hadrian's Wall is doubtful: the obstacles were not found in a recent excavation at Black Carts (Wall-mile 29), nor at Appletree on the Turf Wall (TW), 95m (104yd) west of TW Turret 51B. At Black Carts the natural surface was rock, and even the Wall ditch had not been excavated to the usual full size. Most probably it will be found that the obstacles were provided widely throughout the lowland areas to the east and west (where the construction of the wall itself had been prioritized), but were perhaps thought unnecessary in much of the upland central sector. That they are a Hadrianic provision and were originally *envisaged* everywhere is shown by the width of the berm of both Hadrian's Wall and the Antonine Wall. At some 6m (20RF) – unusually great by the standards of Roman military design – this is governed by the width of the strip of emplacements.

There is obviously much more to be learned about

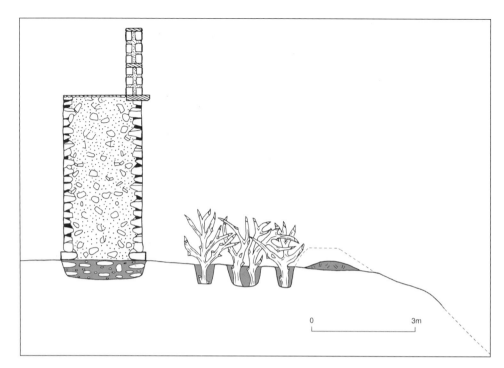

Fig. I.13 The obstacles restored as *cippi*, consisting of sharpened branches. The Wall cross-section shows the dimensions of the 8RF-wide Narrow Wall between Wallsend and Newcastle. Note to the right the beginning of the Wall ditch, at least 8m (26ft) wide and 3m (10ft) deep.
TYNE & WEAR ARCHIVES & MUSEUMS

these previously unsuspected elements of the Wall. What has emerged so far is evidence for a primary design that, whether or not implemented everywhere, binds together the functions of the Wall, berm, ditch and turrets in a unitary whole. The obstacles on the Antonine Wall have been found through dogged research, but on Hadrian's Wall our knowledge of them is due largely to the system, in place since 1990, by which developers and utilities firms fund archaeological work on threatened sites.

Research on the Wall

The Wall attracted antiquarian interest from the sixteenth century onwards. Roman inscriptions, coins and other finds came to light, which had a profound meaning for educated men whose learning was rooted in texts transmitted from classical antiquity. The first really detailed accounts and surveys of the remains came after 1700. Excavation was not conducted on any scale until the nineteenth century, and only towards the end of that century did excavations become scientific, in the sense of trying to obtain evidence for the history and significance of a site, or even to answer specific questions.

The most important nineteenth-century contribution to the subject was John Hodgson's argument (buried in the 1840 volume of his *History of Northumberland*), based on the inscriptions found at milecastles, that the Wall was the work of Hadrian; previously it had been ascribed to the later Emperor Severus on the strength of misleading late Roman sources. The term 'Hadrian's Wall' only became commonly used in the course of the twentieth century, and for many local people it remains simply 'The Roman Wall'.

In both Britain and Germany the foundations of modern archaeological knowledge of the Roman frontier works were laid between the 1890s and 1930s. On Hadrian's Wall this was done by pioneer explorers attached to local archaeological societies and universities, among whom F. G. Simpson and Ian Richmond were foremost. By the 1930s they had worked out the basic structural sequence by which

Hadrian's Wall was constructed, a sequence that still holds true in its basic essentials today.

From about 1930 the history of the Wall was divided into a series of 'Wall periods', based on historical dates for supposed episodes of destruction and rebuilding (thought to have taken place in the years 197, 296 and 367), derived from interpretations of the literary sources and inscriptions found at the Wall fort of Birdoswald in 1929, and supposedly apparent at every site on the Wall. This was a universally accepted and unquestioned orthodoxy for a generation, with its most literal expression being found in the writings of Ian Richmond and of Eric Birley, one of the best known and most influential Wall authorities of the mid-twentieth century.

The 'Wall period' system was abandoned in the course of the 1960s and 1970s, when it became generally accepted that things could not be that simple, and that different sites on the Wall probably had different histories. As far as the function of the Wall is concerned, one legacy of the 'Wall periods' era still holds sway: the belief, first advanced by R. G. Collingwood and strongly supported by Eric Birley, that the Wall curtain controlled unauthorized movement and regulated economic traffic, rather than being a military fortification line.

Although the pace of investigation slowed in all areas after World War II, it has picked up again in recent times, and the 1980s and 1990s saw more excavation and survey on Hadrian's Wall than in any previous twenty-year period. The large-scale excavations of recent decades have rarely been carried out merely for the sake of pure research, but have tended to have been triggered or justified by heritage management considerations, the pace of building development, and schemes to attract tourists and regenerate run-down areas: in a way a return to the large-scale pioneering work of the nineteenth century, but usually with much more sophisticated techniques. Nevertheless, the knowledge gained since the 1970s has been immense, and controversies and questions that by the 1960s seemed settled, have been reopened.

There is now an immense specialist literature concerning the Wall and its archaeology. Arguably we have a greater knowledge than thirty years ago of distinct archaeological characteristics belonging to different chronological periods of the Wall. It is one of the basic purposes of the present book to use this recently gained knowledge to explain how the Wall changed over time. This will return us to what may be thought of as a series of Wall periods, but they will be very different from those of the 1950s.

One would think that with this great tradition of research there would not be much left to find out about the Wall, and one of the questions most frequently asked by visitors is: 'Surely it has all been excavated by now?' In reality, however, archaeological excavation has barely scratched the surface of the resource offered by the buried remains. Some 92 per cent of the Wall itself is now buried and invisible and hardly researched; just over 1 per cent has been destroyed; and the remaining 7 per cent is visible either in its natural ruined state, or as exposed and displayed at various times since the mid-nineteenth century, but very rarely with any accompanying formal archaeological study. The vast majority of the fort interiors are unexcavated.

As a result, there is much that is poorly understood or simply unknown. The fact that an entirely new element of the basic anatomy of the Wall, the frontal obstacles, was not discovered until 2001 illustrates this. If this arrangement could go wholly unsuspected through all the explorations of the nineteenth and twentieth centuries, what other elements of the Wall might await discovery? I hope this book demonstrates that the idea that the archaeology of Hadrian's Wall has been 'done to death' is a fatal error, and that rather, our understanding has a long way to go.

Also, despite all that has been written about the Wall, there is still a fundamental disagreement about how the Wall really functioned. Intuitively the Wall has been seen as the defensive frontier of an empire that had ceased to expand, acquiring a poetic resonance as the means by which Roman civilization held the barbarians at bay, for a time at least. This romantic view has had its critics ever since Collingwood in the 1920s (and before that), and the currently fashionable interpretation of the Wall, and of Roman frontiers in general, is a very different one. This counter view – now an orthodoxy – does not see the Roman Empire as on the defensive, but stresses the economic relationship between the empire and the peoples beyond the frontiers, seeing the two as interdependent.

According to this view the army units on the Wall defended the province from attack, and projected Roman power aggressively, but the Wall itself was a mere border, a means of regulating, even facilitating, economic movement in and out of the empire. Some modern archaeologists still prefer to see the Wall itself as having had a military purpose in preventing raids or invasions from outside the province. Unexpected discoveries such as the berm obstacles have reopened and sharpened these debates.

How do Archaeologists know about Hadrian's Wall in the Past?

The intelligent visitor will often ask questions about the day-to-day operation of the Wall, such as: 'How often was it attacked?' or 'How many men were stationed in a milecastle?', assuming that there are surviving documents that tell us about such things. But somewhat shamefacedly the archaeologist has to tell the enquirer that there are no such documents, and the simple fact is that not a single Roman document bearing on the operation of the Wall now exists. They will have existed once, for the Roman army kept voluminous records, as we know from very rare survivals of documents in conditions of exceptional preservation, such as the dry deserts of Egypt and the Middle East, which have occasionally preserved archives of papyri.

From the Hadrian's Wall area there comes one of these great exceptions, a mass of ink-written wooden writing tablets preserved because of water-logged and anaerobic ground conditions at the fort of Vindolanda, found at intervals since the early 1970s and now extensively published, the most extensive collection of new Latin writing from anywhere in the western empire (a smaller number of writing tablets of the same period have also been found at Carlisle).

The Vindolanda archive sheds light on many details of military life: unit strength reports, requests for leave, duty rotas, accounts, lists of supplies, domestic arrangements in the commanding officer's household, letters to and from overseas relatives of soldiers. They play a regular role in television documentaries and books about Hadrian's Wall, and assuredly are a prime source for day-to-day social and economic life as it would have been experienced in the early years of Hadrian's new frontier. Yet what is not often clearly stated is that the vast majority of the tablets date to the years before Hadrian came to Britain in 122, and before the Wall was conceived of and built. They do not make any mention whatsoever of Hadrian's Wall and therefore cannot possibly shed light on its practical function or day-to-day operation. On the other hand, as near contemporary documents, they provide valuable insights into diet, supplies and aspects of everyday military routine that are unlikely to have changed much when soldiers were manning the Wall twenty or thirty years later.

If there are no routine daily documents of the sort that a historian would normally use, how do archaeologists construct their picture of what happened on the Wall? There is some written evidence. We have the writings of historians and other authorities from the ancient world, which for one reason or another were copied and preserved through the centuries between the end of the Roman Empire and the dawn of modern Europe in the renaissance. These provide the basic background knowledge, but the texts that bear directly on events in northern Britain or on the Wall can be collected in a booklet no bigger than a parish magazine. They are unspecific, sketchy and sometimes of questionable reliability.

Then we have inscriptions. The majority of these are carved in stone: these include commemorative slabs put up when military buildings are completed, tombstones and milestones, and religious dedications on altars or temples. Inscriptions can sometimes be dated by their inclusion of the emperor's titles or the names of governors. The Romans did not give the current year a number – the concept of having years 'BC' and 'AD' did not exist in Roman Britain – and the closest to this sort of dating we get is when the names of the consuls in office during the year the inscription was erected are given. There are other kinds of stone inscription, but not many, and stone inscriptions only occur in useful numbers for a very limited part of the Roman period. Inscriptions on materials other than stone can contain significant historical information, such as the bronze certificates ('diplomas') awarding citizenship to auxiliary soldiers, but such examples are extremely rare.

Sometimes important evidence for events in Britain occurs on inscriptions from outside the island, for example inscriptions detailing the careers of Italian senators or provincial aristocrats who in their younger days were governors or military officers in Britain. There is a scattering of other local documents (we have already discussed those from Vindolanda), but hardly any with direct bearing on the Wall. Writing tablets are preserved only in deeply buried, waterlogged conditions, and therefore are not only rarely found, but are almost never from the higher, dry archaeological layers that relate to the second, third and fourth centuries, the bulk of the time when the Wall was functioning. The same, incidentally, applies to timbers that can be dated to an exact year of felling by dendrochronology – tree-ring dating. This technique has had spectacular results at the early end of the Roman period, demonstrating, for example, that the pre-Hadrianic fort at Carlisle was founded in AD72/73, but suitable timbers have never been found in the later levels of the archaeological sequence of the Wall.

Otherwise, what do archaeologists rely on? The excavated remains of structures and the finds associated with them – predominantly pottery, animal bone, coins and metal items, architectural stonework – and so on. This combination of structural and artefactual archaeology is the bread and butter of Wall archaeologists in our time. The scientific identification and statistical study of animal bones and plant remains recovered in excavation offer important insights into the ancient diet, sources of supply, and the appearance of the ancient environment. This is essentially an insight into social and economic history, but drawing a narrative of events out of the archaeological evidence is complicated and difficult. The coins are sometimes closely datable and can be used to date structural phases, while fine samian-ware pottery can be closely datable: the coarse pottery is not inherently datable, but its typology can be dated by its occurrence in phases on sites dated by coins, inscriptions or other evidence.

With this kind of artefactual evidence it is often a dry statistical study comparing the amounts of coins or pottery from a given site with the amounts recorded at other sites that will give most information about when and how intensively a site was occupied, or perhaps show up odd patterns that may suggest that some unusual or interesting personnel were present. From all this it should be clear that even on the biggest dig, what is revealed and found does not tell a straightforward story, and it can very rarely be directly integrated with any kind of written record. There is the additional problem that the majority of excavations on the Wall were carried out before the careful techniques of modern stratigraphic digging and recording were developed.

That means it can often be difficult to give a straightforward answer to some of the commonest questions that visitors ask. For example, was Hadrian's Wall painted white, presenting a dazzling statement of Roman power and superiority to the world beyond? At present there is no simple 'yes' or 'no' answer to this. At two or three points on the Wall evidence for different kinds of decoration has recently been found. This includes traces of whitewash on a block from the north side of the Wall at Peel Gap (Wall-mile 39), and from the south side of the Wall at Denton (Wall-mile 7), a plaster rendering over the joints between stones, which was scored with lines imitating the joints between ashlar blocks. It seems likely that the latter was part of an overall rendering that would

Fig. I.14 One of the highest surviving parts of the Wall, at Highshield Crag, Wall-mile 39, exposed in the 1980s, when traces of possible whitewash were found.

have been completed with whitewash and red paint in the lines; however, not enough survived for this to be certain.

For all the excavation on the Wall over the years these isolated incidences are the only ones that have been recorded: such evidence was simply not looked for in earlier excavations, and in any case, most clearance of the Wall up to the 1970s was unarchaeological. We have no way of knowing how representative of the Wall in general either of these observations is, and neither need belong to the original Hadrianic construction of the Wall, which might have been rendered in different ways in different times and places. Judgement also has to be influenced by our knowledge of building in the wider Roman world, where it would be routine and usual to give a structure like the Wall an overall rendering and ornamental painting, for practical and aesthetic reasons.

This illustrates the point that, despite the fragmentary nature of the evidence, the Roman archaeologist has the advantage that he or she can sometimes understand what is going on by comparing structures of finds from other parts of the Roman Empire: Roman Britain is part of a bigger picture, and archaeological and historical information from other Roman provinces and their frontiers offers clues to how we might fill the great gaps in the evidence from Britain. Caution is needed in doing this, but we are helped by the fact that surviving structures from different ends of the empire suggest that there were *sometimes* strong similarities in the way that the army was organized and did its building: there was an empire-wide military culture.

So far we have been talking about the evidence from Roman sites, and if it seems patchy and difficult, this is nothing compared to the problems offered by the archaeology of the native Britons in the area of

Hadrian's Wall and to the north. This was a culture without a written language, so all our historical and political knowledge comes from Roman sources. There are no finds, other than the Roman ones, from these settlements that are directly and closely datable, and in any case, these finds occur in such low numbers that they can rarely provide a representative and meaningful sample.

Large numbers of radiocarbon dates and other scientific dating techniques offer the only means of tracing the history of these settlements, and these methods have become increasingly practical to use as they become less expensive and are increasingly funded by developers, as planning guidance now demands, during the process of rescue archaeology on threatened sites. Such scientific dating is in general too imprecise to compete with coins and pottery as the main method of dating on Roman sites, but it comes into its own at the end of the Roman period, in the fifth century, when datable coins and pottery ceased to be made or imported. In these circumstances radiocarbon dating can be the only means of determining how long a Roman site continued in occupation.

This may sound a rather depressing assessment of the information available to us, but it is only fair to admit that occasionally really dramatic and surprising finds come to light, which instantly transform our knowledge or change our understanding. The Vindolanda documents have already been mentioned. An outstanding recent discovery (not on the Wall, but in Staffordshire) has been that of a bronze vessel of a type already known, which gives the names of the forts at the western end of the Wall – part of a souvenir set for the soldiers that had served there. Astonishingly, the inscription, on the most probable reading, confirms for the first time what the Wall was called by contemporaries: *Vallum Aelium*, which translates as 'Hadrian's Wall' (*Aelius* was Hadrian's family name). Like the developer funding that revealed the berm obstacles, this discovery is very much a product of our times, for the vessel was found, near Ilam, by metal detector, and it is thanks to the finder and the Portable Antiquities Scheme that it has come to the notice of students of the Wall.

Having seen what the Wall is, and looked at the evidence with which we have to work, it is time to meet the main characters in the story – the Roman army and its opponents in north Britain – and to see how the faltering of once unstoppable Roman military expansion ended with the decision to build frontier walls in Britain and elsewhere. ❖

Chapter 1

HOW THE ROMANS CAME TO BUILD A WALL IN BRITAIN

The Limits to Roman Power

THE CITY OF ROME ACHIEVED COMPLETE military domination over the Italian peninsula by 272BC and embarked on a seemingly ineluctable whirlwind of external conquest. By 146BC the North African Empire of Carthage was eliminated, and Greece and Macedonia were Roman possessions. All of Spain except the far north-west of the peninsula was conquered by 133BC. By 121BC southern Gaul had been acquired and the province of Gallia Narbonensis created. The pace was ratcheted up again in the late republic, as ambitious nobles, theoretically acting in the interests of the state, used military power and conquests to buttress their own political positions: most famously, Julius Caesar overran Gaul north of Narbonensis in 58–50BC, in the process taking a Roman army to Britain for the first time and bringing the island into the Roman orbit.

The civil wars between such over-mighty magnates were finally brought to an end in 31BC when Octavian eliminated his last rival and became unopposed master of the Roman world. In 27BC he took the title Augustus and thus became the first *princeps*, or Roman emperor. So began the period of imperial government that lasted until late in the third century AD, which historians know as 'the Principate'.

Now that the armies that had once followed this or that dynast were all brought together under the control of Augustus, they could resume their mission of war against foreign enemies. The idea of an empire without end (*imperium sine fine*) was trumpeted in Augustan propaganda. Augustus genuinely believed that the whole of the globe could in his time be brought under Roman domination (the Romans knew that the Earth was a sphere, although of course they did not know of the existence of the American or Australian Continents). At this stage the Romans did not think in terms of fixed frontiers and permanent limits to the empire. There were lands that were not in practice under their control, but that was a situation that would be remedied by further conquest, and Augustus renewed the process with gusto.

As Augustus entered the thirty-third year of his principate (AD6), the final pacification of the whole of northern Europe must have seemed just within reach. In Germany beyond the Rhine a Roman province was being formed under P. Quinctilius Varus – but it was not to be. In AD6 a serious revolt broke out in the recently 'pacified' Pannonia (the Balkan area south of the Danube), and this took three years of bitter fighting to subdue. In AD9, just when the situation seemed to have been recovered, the aged Augustus received the news of the destruction of three entire legions by the Germans beyond the Rhine. At a stroke the assumption that conquest could be carried on indefinitely was dead.

Augustus, shattered and disillusioned by the disaster, stipulated in his will that his successors should keep the empire within its existing limits. He was succeeded by Tiberius (AD14–37), whose son Germanicus carried out punitive campaigns in Germany in 12–16 in an attempt to restore the honour of the annihilated legions. But these failed to have a decisive outcome, and in the end Tiberius recognized the pointlessness of further ambitious offensives beyond the Rhine.

From the time of Augustus a series of legions was

permanently stationed along the left (west) bank of the Rhine. It would be a little longer before legions were permanently placed on the Danube, but from the reign of Tiberius (14–37), successor to Augustus, it is certain that detachments of troops were stationed on and patrolling that river, and that it must have been regarded as a boundary. The basic pattern of the Roman imperial frontier in north-west Europe was set. There would eventually be further (though strictly circumscribed) expansion beyond the two great rivers, but no Roman would ever again seriously contemplate the conquest of the whole of Germany. It was in this period, by a murkily understood process, that the regularly planned forts to house permanently stationed army units evolved: these units are a consistent and conspicuous feature of the imperial frontier lines, and therefore familiar from Hadrian's Wall. But to understand these military bases we need to understand the organization of the Roman army.

An Introduction to the Roman Army

The Roman army was organized into the famous legions. These were basically heavy infantry units, all Roman citizens. Originally these citizen-soldiers had been recruited on a temporary basis to serve in particular campaigns, but Augustus reformed the legions left over from the civil wars into a professional standing army. During the Principate a legion consisted of something over 5,000 men, and there were around thirty legions to meet the military needs of the whole empire.

Even before Augustus, legionary units had been supplemented by so-called *auxilia* – that is, allied, non-citizen troops. These 'auxiliaries' were originally raised from the very peoples that Rome found itself subjugating in its wars of expansion. Augustus also seems to have been responsible for organizing them into permanent standing units, and new units continued to be raised after his time. Often we see them supplying specialist military skills that the heavy infantry legions could not provide: notably fighting on horseback. Auxiliary cavalry 'wings' (*alae*) were essentially formations of mounted warriors from Celtic and Germanic societies that could be deployed against people very like themselves, but they would go on to become some of the most prestigious and formidable units in the Roman army.

In Augustus' day the citizen-soldiers of the legions (known as *legionaries* in the English-speaking world, and never, ever 'legionnaires') would still have been largely Italian in origin, and for two hundred years they maintained a strongly Mediterranean character, though the number of actual Italians declined sharply over the first century. The auxiliaries must have cut very different figures, to begin with at least. On the reliefs of Trajan's Column in Rome, carved in the early second century, legionaries are depicted building, manoeuvring and fighting in orderly fashion. In the same scene two auxiliary cavalrymen ride past, thrusting a pair of recently severed heads into the view of the emperor. Even allowing for cosmopolitan prejudice and artistic convention, this tells us a lot about the Roman perception of the contrast between legionaries and auxiliaries.

Originally auxiliaries were probably forcibly conscripted, but in the course of the first century a deal emerged by which after twenty-five years of service they were awarded Roman citizenship upon discharge. Citizenship and the legal and financial privileges it brought with it would be passed on to sons and daughters, so this was a powerful incentive that ensured a flow of voluntary recruits into the auxiliaries in the first two centuries.

Each legion consisted of ten cohorts, each of which consisted of six centuries of eighty men: so the whole was 10 times 480. Around AD70–80 the Senior, or First Cohort, was enlarged in size, to number 800 (ten centuries), although the size and structure of the first cohort in later times may have varied and is not well understood. The legion contained only a very small amount of cavalry, numbering 120. Individual auxiliary units seem to have been modelled on the legionary cohort: so a simple auxiliary unit of infantry (*cohors peditata*) consisted of six centuries and totalled 480 men. A 480-strong auxiliary

Fig. 1.1 Trajan's Column in Rome illustrates the difference between legionaries and auxiliaries in the early second century AD; the legionaries (left), wearing plate armour, move in orderly fashion, while the mounted auxiliaries (right) present severed heads to the emperor.

cavalry unit was termed an *ala* ('wing') and was made up of sixteen *turmae* ('troops'), each of thirty horsemen. Most common among auxiliary units was the part-mounted *cohors equitata*: 480 foot soldiers (six centuries) and 120 horse (four *turmae*). Larger, 1,000-strong (*milliaria*) versions of the *ala* and *cohors equitata* appear after around AD70, the *ala milliaria* having twenty-four larger *turmae* of forty-two horsemen each (in total 1,008), and the *cohors milliaria equitata* ten centuries of eighty, and eight thirty-strong *turmae* (800 infantry and 240 cavalry, therefore 1,040 men in total).

These 'paper strengths' are based on fragmentary evidence and have been the subject of much controversy; they may also have varied according to time and place. Auxiliary units of the various types occupied the Hadrian's Wall forts; so, for example,

we find *cohors IV Lingonum equitata* (the Fourth Cohort of Lingones, raised in eastern France – part mounted) at Wallsend; *cohors I Tungrorum milliaria* (the First Cohort of Tungrians, raised in Belgium – 'one thousand strong') at Housesteads; and *ala II Asturum* (the Second Cavalry Unit of Asturians, from Spain) at Chesters.

Although the Roman army had existed for centuries, before the early first century AD, we have very little archaeological trace of any kind of military bases or forts. Before this the army had only ever possessed temporary accommodation in the form of seasonal camps. Nowadays archaeologists reserve the term 'camp' to refer to encampments without permanent buildings, which the army had always used in earlier times and which it continued to use when on campaign or on the move. In shape these 'marching camps' (to use another term from archaeological literature) can look, superficially, like the permanent bases. Typically in imperial times they might have had the same rectangular shape with rounded corners, but they came in a much greater variety of sizes, had much slighter defences, and inside, rather than any kind of buildings, were pitched rows of tents, made of leather.

Permanent military bases only appear clearly in the continental archaeological record in the early first century. A fair amount is known about the legionary bases built during the German campaigns of Augustus and Tiberius. These sites were still in the process of evolution from the temporary encampments that Roman armies used when on campaign, but already they contained massive buildings, their plans based on Mediterranean prototypes but constructed entirely of timber. By the reign of Nero (54–69) a more familiar fortress type for a single legion was emerging. Only under Claudius (41–54) do we see the first examples of smaller forts for auxiliary units or detachments of legionaries with auxiliaries, but these still have highly irregular layouts, still not well understood. It is only under the Flavian emperors (after AD70) that we see, in Britain and on the continent, the first classic plans of auxiliary forts that have the developed form familiar in the century and a half that ensued.

The types and sizes of units are reflected in the permanent bases they constructed. So a legion was accommodated in a great base some 20ha (50 acres) in area. This is conventionally referred to as a 'fortress' in English. The stupendous area covered by a legionary fortress can only really be appreciated by walking the perimeter of one where its outlines can still be made out, whether in the pattern of medieval streets or surviving earthworks, as at the British fortresses of York and Inchtuthil respectively. Just as an auxiliary unit was modelled on one tenth part of the legion, so its base was a microcosm of the great legionary fortress, often covering around a tenth of its area, typically around 2ha (5 or 6 acres). The auxiliary sites are known as 'forts' to English-speaking archaeologists.

Fortresses and forts had a rectilinear shape and an internal plan laid out according to standard principles that must have developed rapidly in the first century. But despite this, the plans of no two are exactly alike. The army did all its building itself. In the early days the legionaries, not the auxiliaries, were the builders – on Trajan's Column the legionaries do the building while auxiliary soldiers stand guard. The materials used in forts and fortresses were mostly earth, clay, turf and timber, and it was only around the turn of the first and second centuries AD that stone came into more general use for defences and buildings, and then only very gradually.

It has probably not escaped your notice that the firming up of forts and fortresses in the archaeological record coincides with the flagging of the imperial project to conquer the world, and Tiberius' recognition that advance had halted on the Rhine and Danube. A permanent frontier begets more permanent, more easily recognizable archaeological remains, and some of the legionary bases founded by Augustus on the Rhine would be occupied by the army for centuries to come.

So much for the army that made possible the hothouse growth of empire, and which, in some areas, had still further to advance. But what kind of peoples did the Romans encounter in their conquest of north-west Europe and, in particular, Britain?

The Pre-Roman Inhabitants of Britain

The peoples of the later Iron Age of north-west Europe were divided into two broad groups with different languages and customs, and these are still usually known as the Celts and the Germans. In the Celts of Gaul, Spain and Britain, the Romans were dealing with peoples of a common culture, although within this there were countless regional groups with their own peculiar characteristics and dialects of the 'Celtic' language. The Celts had no written form of their language. To generalize brutally, these Iron Age people lived in extended family groups in individual farming settlements rather than villages or towns,

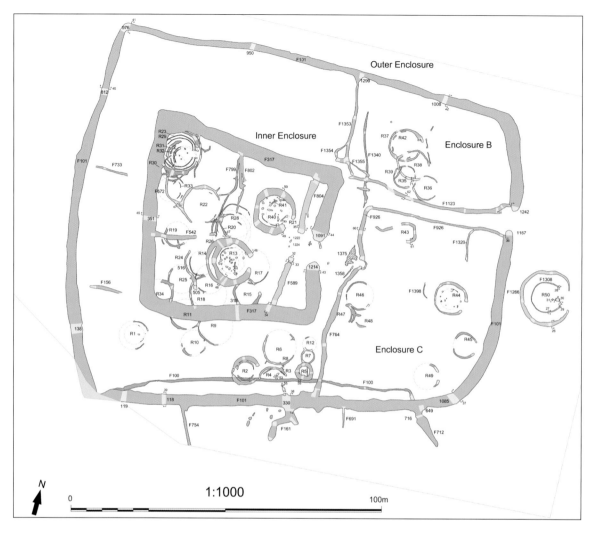

Fig. 1.2 A typical enclosed settlement of the pre-Roman Iron Age in the fertile lowlands north of the eastern part of Hadrian's Wall.
TYNE & WEAR ARCHIVES & MUSEUMS

and operated an economy based on both arable farming and livestock rearing. They were divided into 'tribes' or 'peoples', though these did not cover extensive areas or have any significant degree of centralization – in 15BC the Romans recorded over forty-six named tribes living in the Alpine region alone.

In the lowland parts of Britain, including those transected by Hadrian's Wall, the Roman army invaded a landscape that was already predominantly cleared of woodland, cultivated and densely settled,

at least in the lower lying and more fertile areas. Settlements typically took the form of ditched and banked enclosures containing timber roundhouses, evenly and tightly distributed over the landscape: typically around 900m (980yd) separated neighbouring farmstead enclosures. The economic basis of society was a mixture of wheat cultivation (spelt 'wheat' in lowland north-east England, the poorer 'emmer wheat' further north in Scotland) and cattle rearing. In north-east England especially, this intensively used pre-Roman landscape has become known

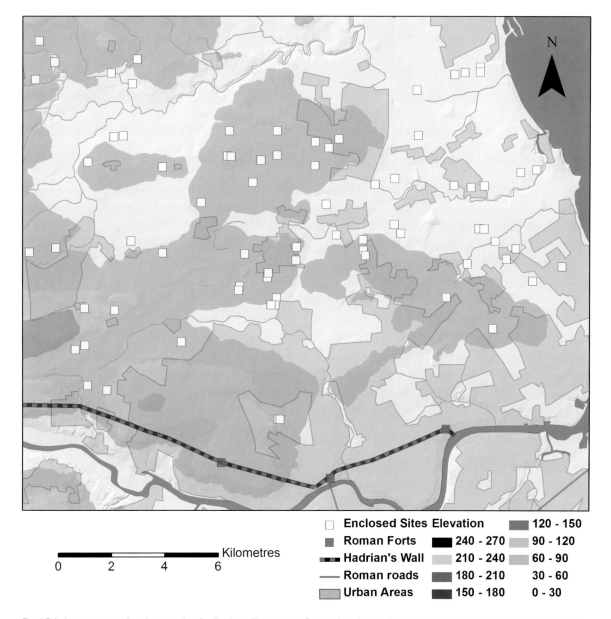

Enclosed Sites **Elevation**
☐ Enclosed Sites
■ Roman Forts
▬■▬ Hadrian's Wall
─── Roman roads
▦ Urban Areas

Elevation	
240 - 270	120 - 150
210 - 240	90 - 120
180 - 210	60 - 90
150 - 180	30 - 60
	0 - 30

Kilometres
0   2   4   6

Fig. 1.3 A dense pattern of settlement: the distribution of known pre-Roman Iron Age settlements north of the Wall in the Newcastle area.
JAMES BRUHN

to us in much greater detail in recent years, as rescue archaeology in advance of development now routinely discovers and investigates these unglamorous and formerly invisible rural sites.

In north-west England and Scotland the picture is less clear, but there is little doubt that the lowland parts of these regions were also populous societies practising mixed agriculture. In the dales and upland areas of the Pennines, and in the lowland hills and highlands of Scotland, there was obviously a much more marginal pattern of small dispersed settlements, and much less is understood about the economic basis or the dates of individual sites.

From the finds made at their settlements the

people of Iron Age Britain come across as farmers first and foremost, but occasionally there are finds of weaponry, usually in hoards away from the settlement sites – a recently discovered example is a magnificent hoard of swords and spearheads from South Cave in the East Riding of Yorkshire, concealed at the time of the Roman conquest. These are a reminder that there was warfare between Iron Age peoples, and for the purposes of this, or resistance to the Romans, they were capable of raising armies, and the social élite was presumably a warrior élite. We have seen how Iron Age warriors were reconstituted into Roman auxiliary units: Spain, noted for its mounted warriors, was the recruiting ground for a series of cavalry *alae*, and in parts of northern Britain chariots really were used in warfare, as Tacitus describes and as is confirmed by occasional burials of these vehicles. From the Roman sources we see how warriors from these highly dispersed societies could be united under a leader, perhaps specially elected in time of emergency, to wage war.

How Iron Age People were Absorbed into the Empire

The peoples north of the Mediterranean world who did not have cities or towns must have appeared in striking contrast to the urban civilization of Rome. In acquiring Gaul and Spain, however, the Romans found that, if military victory could be achieved – a centuries-long struggle in the case of Spain – it was possible to forge a tolerably 'Roman' provincial society. This meant having an aristocratic élite in charge (often the descendants of the pre-Roman Iron Age élite), the cities and country houses in which they displayed their wealth, and a developing market economy, leading to the growth of small market towns in the countryside.

The principle of Roman imperial rule was actually self-government by local élites. Iron Age societies conquered by Rome were organized into areas of local government, based at least theoretically on tribal units. These units of government are known

as *civitates* (this is the plural of the singular form *civitas*). Our word 'city' is derived from the Latin *civitas*, and indeed at the centre of each of these units was a town where the governing council of the territory sat. Besides the 'native' *civitates* there were other territories with urban centres of higher rank or privilege, such as *municipia* and settlements of Roman citizens (*coloniae*).

This is the method of provincial administration that the Romans imposed on the part of Iron Age Britain that was militarily subjugated. To give an idea of the size of these administrative units, that part of Britain south of Hadrian's Wall, in its heyday as a Roman province, had around twenty-four such city territories, a figure that might be compared to the thirty-nine historic counties of England.

It was easier to effect conquest rapidly where there were pre-existing centres of political control that the Romans could take over. In lowland south-east Britain there were pre-Roman centres of élite power ('*oppida*'), with kings and minted coinages, which had developed because of their proximity to, and relations with, the Roman Empire. These were obvious candidates for *civitas* capitals. The pre-Roman Iron Age centre at Silchester (Hampshire), for example, became a Roman city, *civitas Calleva Atrebatum* – 'Calleva, city of the Atrebates'. As with a modern concept such as 'Iraq' or 'Syria', the Atrebates and other *civitates* were probably the administrative creations of imperial officials, glossing over a much more complicated reality of pre-Roman tribal identities.

It was easier to move towards local self-government on the *civitas* model if there were strongly defined local élites to take charge, but throughout much of northern and western Britain there were simply no pre-existing visible centres of élite power. There was less social stratification, and a much more numerous, broadly based warrior élite. Agricultural economies were more subsistence based and poverty stricken. In the north the general lack of easily controllable élite power centres, compounded by the more dispersed pattern of upland settlement, meant that the Roman army was faced with a long task of occupation and pacification before invaded areas could be handed over to civil administration. The Romans seem to have invaded Scotland on the assumption that with perseverance the task could be completed, but because of problems elsewhere the army was never to get the opportunity to finish the job.

The Invasion of Britain

For the Romans, at least, the disaster of AD9 beyond the Rhine was a horrific setback – but the Roman Empire still had a hundred years of expansion ahead of it. But conquest was no longer as constant, and no longer had the dizzying pace of the first century BC, and it fell to the Emperor Claudius (AD41–54) to invade Britain in AD43. The ostensible aim of this late addition to the Roman portfolio was the annexation of the kingdom of the late Cunobelinus, a ruler who had close ties with the Rome of Tiberius. On Cunobelinus' death around AD40, both Gaius (37–41) and Claudius (41–54) preferred the policy of winding up this long-standing client kingdom. Claudius in particular was anxious for some military glory and the chance to emulate the great Julius Caesar. But once in Britain the Roman army was immediately sent to conquer more of the island beyond the immediate target of Colchester, Cunobelinus' capital. The commitment to Britain was major: four of the thirty precious legions that ringed the Roman world (over 20,000 men), and as many non-citizen auxiliary troops. The conquest of lowland Britain following the invasion of 43 took place rapidly, but was marred by an early setback: the devastating revolt of Boudicca, leader of the Iceni of East Anglia (60), delayed the pace of advance for a decade.

Following the civil war that convulsed the empire after the assassination of Nero in 68, a new ruling family emerged to replace the Julio-Claudians descended from Augustus. The new dynasty gives its name to the Flavian period (AD69–96). Under the first of the Flavian emperors, Vespasian

(69–79), the British advance was resumed. Wales was finally completely overrun, and northern Britain invaded wholesale for the first time. In 79 Vespasian's governor, Julius Agricola (77/8–83/4), penetrated as far as the River Tay in Scotland. Agricola has a special place in the study of Roman Britain, for his exploits were immortalized in a eulogy written by his son-in-law, the historian Tacitus. There is nothing remotely comparable for any other Roman official who served in Britain, so naturally this text has been closely examined for centuries. However, although once hallowed as an impeccable authority, the *Agricola* is no longer regarded as a literal historical account.

Agricola and his predecessors established a dense network of forts over the newly acquired lands of the north. Domitian, emperor from 81 to 96, authorized Agricola to press home his war in Britain to final victory, which he seemingly achieved at the battle of Mons Graupius, somewhere in Scotland in 83 (less probably 84). Immediately after this victory, building work started on a legionary fortress at Inchtuthil (near Blairgowrie) and a network of forts ringing the Highlands.

Gradually, then, the legacy of Augustus had become forgotten and ignored, and we see under the Flavians a cautious revival of expansionist ideas. By 85 Britain had been completely overrun and was ripe for transformation into a quiescent Roman province. Some at least must have considered that this process could be taken further: Tacitus lamented in 98 that 'the conquest of Germany is taking such a long time'. The historian also tells us that even before reaching the end of Britain, his father-in-law Agricola had Ireland in his sights.

All these possibilities evaporated, and advance on the British and German fronts was suddenly halted, as a result of unexpected news from outside the region. Attention switched to the Lower Danube, where the Roman province of Moesia was attacked by the Dacians (from the area of modern Romania) in 85–6. The governor of Moesia was killed, and a legion (V Alaudae) destroyed. Despite Roman counter attacks there followed other invasions by Germanic peoples from beyond the river. A further war broke out after 89 on the Lower Danube, with an invasion of Pannonia by the Suebi and the Sarmatians. Again a whole legion (XXI Rapax) was destroyed. Domitian gathered troops to mount a campaign against the invaders in 92, gradually managing to contain the problem.

Retreat from Conquest in Northern Britain

These incursions from the barbarian world were serious: the disappearance of two legions from the historical record indicates the direness of the emergency. For our purposes the important thing is the immediate impact these events had on the north-west frontiers.

We have no written records that give details about the history of the Roman frontier in Britain in these years, but the presence or absence at excavated fort sites of certain types of the ubiquitous, well studied and closely datable pottery known as samian – a lustrous fine tableware imported from Gaul – and the dates of the coins found at fort sites, allow us to trace the stages by which the army gradually fell back from its conquests in Scotland.

The legionary fortress at Inchtuthil was abandoned shortly after 86 while still incomplete, and the northern Scottish conquests were given up. Almost certainly the explanation is that troops had to be withdrawn from Britain in order to be sent to the more

Fig. 1.4 Roman forts in north Britain between about AD86 and AD105: for around twenty years the northernmost Roman military dispositions were arranged along this axis, the major military centres at each end of this baseline being at Newstead and Dalswinton on the Nith. FRONTIERS OF THE ROMAN EMPIRE CULTURE 2000 PROJECT/D. J. BREEZE

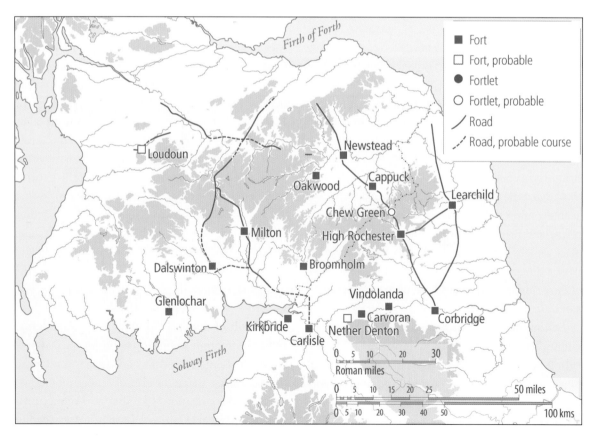

urgent theatre of operations on the Lower Danube. In the case of one unit this is known to be the case: an inscription shows that the legion II Adiutrix, still in Britain in 86, was operating on the Lower Danube by 92. Legions in Britain were therefore reduced from four to three – hence the impossibility of keeping a legion in Scotland.

In the new arrangement, all forts north of Newstead, near Melrose on the Tweed, were evacuated, and the army fell back to a front line close to the modern political border between England and Scotland. For around twenty years the northernmost Roman military dispositions were arranged along this axis, the major military centres at each end of this baseline being at Newstead and Dalswinton on the Nith. It is to this period that most of the documents found at Vindolanda, on the Tyne–Solway isthmus, belong: it was in these years, between about 92 and 105, that the fort was occupied successively by the First Cohort of Tungrians and the Ninth Cohort of Batavians, details of whose day-to-day affairs are preserved in the writing tablets.

The bulk of the tablets therefore belong to a time when Vindolanda was not on the front line, and there were still considerable dispositions to the north, in Scotland. The documents include a description of the fighting characteristics of the *Brittunculi* ('despised little Brits') – perhaps a report on military activity far north of the Vindolanda base, or a description of recruits being conscripted from the part of recently conquered Scotland that was still held.

So events a thousand miles away precipitated a dramatic retreat from recent gains in Britain. But it was the personality and policies of the Emperor Trajan (98–117) that sealed the fate of north-west Europe as a scene of never completed conquest. Trajan liked pursuing wars of conquest, but his interests lay elsewhere, and he embarked on a revengeful war against the Dacian kingdom (101–2). Resistance was more vigorous than expected, however, and it took a second war to subdue Dacia (105–6).

The Stanegate Frontier

The requirements of Trajan's second Dacian war led indirectly to the removal of more troops from Britain, sent to the continent to plug gaps created by the movement east of other units, as we see from a detachment made up of troops from Britain (*vexillatio Britannica*), attested on tile-stamps from Nijmegen on the lower Rhine and argued to date to the period around 105–20. No doubt as a result of troop withdrawals from the island in around 105 the Roman army withdrew completely from southern Scotland. Newstead and the other forts there were abandoned. A linear arrangement of forts was now

Fig. 1.5 'The Stanegate': after AD105 a linear arrangement of forts was now intensified on the isthmus between the Tyne in the east and the Solway in the west, along the narrow neck of north Britain where Hadrian's Wall would eventually be built. The Devil's Causeway Road leaves Dere Street just north of Corbridge to run north-east across Northumberland, possibly forming the eastern extension of the 'Stanegate frontier'. FRONTIERS OF THE ROMAN EMPIRE CULTURE 2000 PROJECT/D. J. BREEZE

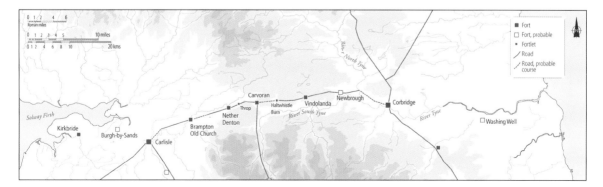

intensified on the isthmus between the Tyne in the east and the Solway in the west, along that narrow neck of north Britain where Hadrian's Wall would eventually be built.

'The Stanegate' is the term used in recent times for a Roman road that runs east–west across the isthmus, a short distance to the south of the line that would later be taken by Hadrian's Wall. Physically the Stanegate road has only been traced between Corbridge, on the Tyne, and Carlisle, in the west. At both of these places the earliest in a series of important military bases had been founded in the seventies of the first century, each lying on the river crossing of a major invasion route leading north. By the eighties of the first century, the interval between Corbridge and Carlisle was broken by the addition of forts at Vindolanda and Nether Denton.

Excavations at all but the last of these three forts have shown that they have varying and complex histories, with much alteration in the nineties, but they all fall into line in being completely rebuilt around 105. This is best explained as a reconstitution of the line of forts at the limit of Roman control following the withdrawal from southern Scotland. The abandonment of the Scottish sites must have led to much redistribution of units into new bases: at Vindolanda the Ninth Cohort of Batavians left the site (they were transferred abroad as part of the troop movements for Trajan's second Dacian war) and the First Cohort of Tungrians returned to garrison the new fort built around 105.

This also seems to be the most likely time for the addition of various other sites along the road, including full-sized forts for auxiliary units at Carvoran and Old Church, Brampton. There were also some small forts – around 0.35ha (0.86 acres) in area – that are too small to have held a complete unit, and must have been intended for detachments outposted from larger forts: such small sites are referred to as 'fortlets'. At least three are known, at Haltwhistle Burn, Throp and Castle Hill, Boothby. The first of these was excavated in 1908, and there is a plan, though not very well understood. Significantly

it made extensive use of stone construction, hitherto rare: recognition that the emerging frontier line was a permanent one, and that conquest was not going to be resumed. Finally, a number of stone watchtowers, some on the high ground to the north of the road that would later be seized by Hadrian's Wall, have been identified.

The general impression is of an intensification of surveillance along the Stanegate route, and a dispersal of troops into smaller groups to maintain a close watch at all points along the line – a preclusive cordon that would detect any attempt at infiltration, raiding or invasion, and which would be able to trigger a response in strength: effectively a line of military defence. Not all have been convinced, however, and particularly in the 1970s and 1980s some archaeologists argued that there was insufficient evidence that all the Stanegate sites were of the same date, or that they formed a regular frontier 'system'. Rather it was felt that they merely marked the limit of Roman occupation, with the road held no more strongly than others in northern Britain. In this view the function of forts and fortlets was concerned with safeguarding river crossings and securing convoys on an important route.

However, the Stanegate can be rehabilitated as a preclusive frontier line by the study of similar and exactly contemporary arrangements of military sites on the frontier of Roman Germany. Here, arrangements of forts of varying size, and fortlets, were strung out along lines where there was no road or route, and where the formation of a screen or cordon controlling access to the empire can have been their only function. In the German cases, as on the Stanegate, there was no regular spacing or easily recognizable system: the sites are irregularly sized and spaced to suit local circumstances.

It has also been argued that the engineered road that we call 'the Stanegate', far from having been built by Agricola in the first century, as traditional belief would have it, is probably an addition of late Trajanic or even Hadrianic date, because its alignment seems to post-date the siting of fortlets such as Haltwhistle

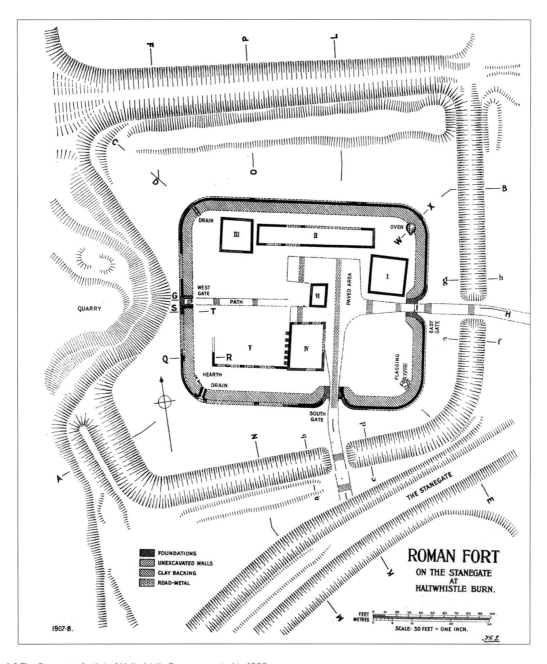

Fig. 1.6 The Stanegate fortlet of Haltwhistle Burn, excavated in 1908.

Burn and Throp. Although there must always have been a negotiable route between Corbridge and Carlisle, the chain of sites along the isthmus cannot have been primarily intended as road stations, as they were probably in place before the road itself was built. On balance, then, the military sites along the Stanegate should be regarded as forming a preclusive chain of forts belonging to the years following *c.* 105.

To make any sense, this system of preclusion would have to extend west of Carlisle, to the Cumbrian coast, for although the Solway estuary forms a natural barrier between south-west Scotland and northern Cumbria, it is easily fordable. A Trajanic fort that might be at the western end of 'the Stanegate' is known at Kirkbride, at the mouth of the river Wampool, just over 5km (3 miles) south of the later western end of the Wall. Halfway between here and Carlisle, a fort (Burgh I) lies nearly a kilometre (half a mile) south of the later Wall fort at Burgh-by-Sands. Burgh I is possibly pre-Hadrianic on the basis of excavated pottery, and overlies a circular ditch that has been interpreted as a Roman watchtower.

Very slight linear ditches have been found running away from the fort at Burgh I to the east and west, associated with a slight fence-like row of post-holes seen in a small excavation. 5km (3 miles) west, at Fingland Rigg, another slight running ditch was found, with a possible road running parallel to its south. These features have been claimed as elements of a frontier system, barriers ('*clausurae*') not forming a continuous line, but blocking access on disconnected ridges of land that rose from the marshes, which made much of the ancient Solway impassable. Other ditched enclosures have been interpreted as associated watchtowers.

Unfortunately none of these features has produced conclusive evidence of Roman military origin, and there is a danger of confusion with native enclosures and agricultural boundaries. Most archaeologists reserve judgement on whether these are really remains of a preclusive barrier on 'the Western Stanegate'. Having said that, circumstantially a route between Carlisle and Kirkbride must have existed, and the expectation of a pre-Hadrianic road accompanied by running barriers is in itself entirely reasonable. Ditches or fences do not occur on the central sector of the Stanegate, between Corbridge and Carlisle, but there is no reason why arrangements on the low-lying land of the Solway should have been the same: it is a characteristic of the contemporary frontiers in Germany that various kinds of barrier were provided intermittently, in isolated stretches, only where required. More intensive fieldwork on the Solway is needed.

A continuation of the Stanegate east of Corbridge has never been found, and this is a notable problem.

With the exception of an undated fort at Washing Well, Whickham, and possible early occupation at South Shields, no military sites of this period, and emphatically no road, have ever come to light between Corbridge and the North Sea. There are many suggestions, and further evidence may come to light. But there is an alternative: at intervals since the 1930s it has been suggested that the Trajanic Stanegate frontier might have run along the Devil's Causeway, a Roman road that runs north-east across Northumberland north of Hadrian's Wall, from near Corbridge to Berwick-on-Tweed. It is a suggestion that deserves to be taken seriously.

Excavation at the one known fort along this road line, Low Learchild (others must await discovery), showed that occupation ran down to the construction of Hadrian's Wall, and that the fort was enlarged in its second and final phase. This would accord with this line effectively becoming part of the northern frontier of the province in the period *c.*105 to *c.*122, and would fall in with the rebuilding at Corbridge, Vindolanda and Carlisle. The Trajanic frontier line, in other words, might not have run all the way across the Tyne–Solway isthmus at all, but may have included and protected the Northumberland coastal plain, taking in an area that would be abandoned with the building of Hadrian's Wall.

This would make sense, because we now know that the coastal plain was intensively settled and farmed by a populous and politically stable pre-Roman Iron Age people. They would constitute a valuable tax base, and the lack of Roman forts within their territory has long led to suggestions that these people were Roman allies. The course of the Devil's Causeway seems to be dictated by the line separating the fertile coastal plain from the less hospitable uplands of North Tynedale, Redesdale and the Cheviots. Looked at in conjunction with the Stanegate west of Corbridge, it is easy to see how the Trajanic frontier line may have been to protect lowland and friendly areas from the upland zone where, with the abandonment of sites such as Newstead, control had been relinquished – essentially a frontier line facing north-west rather than north.

Whatever the truth about the arrangements east of Corbridge, we can conclude that Hadrian inherited from his predecessor a preclusive chain of forts already on the isthmus, which had perhaps proved inadequate to prevent attacks from the north.

The Unravelling of Trajan's Conquests

Towards the end of his reign (AD114–17) Trajan embarked on a far from necessary war against the Parthian Empire (modern Iran), a regional superpower that rivalled Rome in administrative sophistication and military organization. Trajan's victory over the Parthians was short-lived, and the vast territorial gains in Mesopotamia unsustainable, but the whole costly exercise shows how far from north-west Europe his mind strayed. It is hard to escape the conclusion that more troops might have been withdrawn from British units to contribute to this war, but we have no direct evidence. It is often suggested that much or all of the IX Legion was withdrawn from Britain at this time, reducing the island to a two-legion province: the last dated record of the legion is an inscription of 108 at its fortress at York. Inscriptions from Nijmegen (the Netherlands) on the Lower Rhine suggest that the legion was there in the early second century, but these cannot be closely dated – as we shall see, a later date is possible. On the whole it seems unlikely that the legion closest to the northern frontier in Britain would have been removed wholesale in 114.

Hadrian

Hadrian (AD117–38) was left to pick up the pieces after the disastrous failure of the glory-seeking wars of his predecessor. Facing rebellion across the east, he abandoned Trajan's conquests there. He also ditched an extension of Moesia north of the Danube, which Trajan had established after the Dacian conquest, and was forced to negotiate with the Roxolani who were threatening this area. Unlike Trajan, Hadrian was to pay very close attention to the problems of the north-west European provinces, visiting them in person.

Hadrian, forty-six years old when he visited Britain, was an experienced soldier, a lover of Greek culture and an enthusiastic amateur architect. He was a moody activist who imposed strongly held personal beliefs in a number of areas: he promoted military discipline, restlessly toured the provinces, and it was evidently his vision that the Roman model of government would prosper best if the civil development of the frontier provinces was secured from external threats.

Britain was one of some forty-four provinces that made up the Roman Empire at its height in the early second century AD. It was governed for the emperor by an ex-consul of the highest senatorial rank (*legatus* – the usual English term is governor) who also commanded the armed forces in the island. As with all the north-western provinces he visited, Hadrian found the lowland area of Britain, where Roman-style civil administration had begun to take hold, transformed beyond recognition since the days of the conquest eighty years earlier. The provinces of Gaul, Germany and Britain had acquired a distinctive

Fig. 1.7 Coin portrait of the Emperor Hadrian. TYNE & WEAR ARCHIVES & MUSEUMS

identity and enjoyed a burgeoning economy. This meant an unarmed and peaceable rural population, and urban centres of conspicuous size.

There is some reason to believe that Hadrian deliberately encouraged the process of urbanization in other provinces, paying for buildings out of his own purse. At the same time he must have been aware that the cities of Britain lay very close to the untamed expanse beyond Roman control and, as we shall see, they may very well have been directly threatened by the war that raged in Britain early in his reign. Hadrian's great contribution was to recognize that this problem could not be solved by attempting further expansion into the unconquered parts of Britain and Germany. This had been shown to be impossible: the thirty legions thinly stretched around the frontiers could never be concentrated sufficiently for such a venture without leaving the Danube fatally vulnerable. The weakness of this theatre had been demonstrated under both Domitian and Trajan.

Hadrian evidently saw the need to avoid unsustainable military expansion and to consolidate the frontiers in order to protect the developing provincial societies from the world outside that could not be conquered. The zone of military control at the edge of the empire had already started to congeal into fixed lines of forts before Hadrian. From Hadrian's time onwards the legions around the empire became permanently fixed in their existing fortresses, rooted to the spot and closely identified with the frontier provinces in which they were based. At Hadrian's accession the bases for the remaining three of the four legions that had come over to Britain at the conquest were now irredeemably fixed at Caerleon, near Newport, South Wales (*Legio II Augusta*), Chester, close to north Wales (*Legio XX Valeria Victrix*) and York (*Legio IX Hispana*). The constant movement of legions, and the foundation of new fortresses that had signalled an age of expansion, was now at an end (with a very few exceptions). Henceforth detachments ('vexillations') were shuffled between legionary bases as required.

Through most of Continental Europe the obvious line along which to consolidate the Roman frontier forces ran along the two great rivers, the Rhine and the Danube, communication routes as well as obstacles to raids and unwanted movement into the empire. During the first century AD there evolved chains of forts along these rivers, but the area beyond their upper stretches, in the re-entrant formed by the Upper Rhine and Upper Danube, was also absorbed into the provinces of Upper Germany and Raetia, and towns and civil society developed there.

To protect these areas beyond the great rivers, chains of watchtowers were gradually erected along the land border at the outer edge of Roman-controlled territory, it is now thought starting in the period 105–115. Garrison forts were spaced at roughly 7 to 8 miles (11 to 13km), as on Hadrian's Wall, and interspersed with smaller posts, not unlike the milecastles of the Wall, but irregularly spaced as required. Under Hadrian himself, in 120–1, the upper German line was sealed by a massive timber palisade. Later, probably in the late second or early third century, the palisade was to be superseded by a great earth bank and ditch '(the *Pfahlgraben*)', and in places by a narrow stone wall. Raetia was also fortified with a palisade (by the 160s), also replaced by a narrow stone wall (the *Teufelsmauer* or Devil's Wall), some 1.20m (4ft) wide and at least 3m (10ft) high, shortly after AD200. Chains of towers, forts and some running barriers also surrounded the province of Dacia north of the Danube, conquered by the Emperor Trajan in 105–6.

Substantial barriers as they were, the continental palisades and walls differed in one key respect from Hadrian's Wall: they were too narrow to carry a patrol walk, and did not command frontal ditches (although the Pfahlgraben did). In other respects the arrangements of forts, small fortlets and towers, and their use with running barriers, is highly reminiscent of the frontier lines we see in Britain – Hadrian's Wall and the Antonine Wall in Scotland. Hadrian's Wall was to be simply the largest and most elaborate expression of a kind of military fortification line to be found throughout Europe.

In 121, just before coming to Britain, Hadrian had inspected the timber palisade that had been erected

Fig. 1.8 In Germany a frontier line was already marked by forts and watchtowers and a substantial timber palisade, seen here in a modern reconstruction, by the time of Hadrian's visit there in 121.

along the military frontier line of Upper Germany. Tree-ring dating now suggests that in one place its timbers were felled beginning in the winter of 119–20, before his arrival. We know that Hadrian went on to visit Britain in person, the date usually being given as 122, although an arrival as early as 121 cannot be absolutely ruled out.

Events in Britain Early in Hadrian's Reign

We have no recorded detail of events in Britain in the few years before the building of Hadrian's Wall. In the near absence of historical evidence, historians and archaeologists can only use very fragmentary clues to piece together theories of what course of events ensued in Britain in the years following Trajan's death.

One source says that the Britons could not be kept under control when Hadrian became emperor in 117, suggesting rebellion and warfare in the island in the early years of his reign. The governor of Britain from around 118 to 122 is known to have been an experienced and formidable general – Pompeius Falco, succeeded in 122 by a friend and trusted general of Hadrian, Aulus Platorius Nepos, who had previously

governed Lower Germany. A legion – *Legio VI Victrix* – was transferred to Britain from the province of Lower Germany, either with Nepos or very shortly after.

At some point in Hadrian's reign there was a great war in Britain. We must envisage insurgency and attacks on the settled part of the province emanating from the area north of the military-controlled Tyne–Solway line, of such scale and ferocity that even the Roman army could not easily control it. The war is not directly mentioned in any historical source, but we hear of it on the career inscriptions of two officers who were sent on an *expeditio Britannica* – a military campaign in Britain – under Hadrian. One of them, the senior centurion Pontius Sabinus, brought reinforcements of 3,000 legionaries from the continent: there had clearly been serious Roman losses in Britain.

The scale of the Roman casualties is indicated by various other strands of evidence. Forty years later, the Emperor Marcus Aurelius' tutor, Fronto, reminded him, 'When your grandfather Hadrian was emperor, how many soldiers were killed by the Jews, how many by the Britons!' A tombstone dating from around this time, found in 1997 at the Stanegate

Fig. 1.9 Evidence for warfare in north Britain under Trajan or Hadrian? A cavalryman from the *ala Petriana*, with plumed helmet and standard, rides down a hirsute barbarian. This unit was based at Corbridge, near the Wall, in this period. The barbarian is not realistic but a stock image borrowed from archetypes in classical art. The stone can be seen in Hexham Abbey.

fort of Vindolanda, records the death of an auxiliary centurion '*in bello*' – 'in the war'. A recently excavated workshop in the Hadrianic fort at Carlisle contained a cache of body armour that had seen heavy use in battle, and which was being prepared for further recycling and reuse.

It was long believed that the *expeditio Britannica*

was commemorated on a coin issue thought to date to 119 (although the coin type is strictly only datable to 119–128), and that the campaign must have been a response to a major uprising at the outset of Hadrian's reign, in which the Ninth Legion was destroyed, explaining its subsequent disappearance from history. But the romantic story of the Ninth disappearing into the Scottish mists was spoiled when a closer look was taken at the inscriptions recording the careers of some of its officers, which suggested that their service in the legion cannot have been earlier than the 120s. Also, the Pontius Sabinus who was sent on the 'British expedition' had also been centurion in three separate legions between his service in the Parthian War of 114–17 and being sent to Britain, suggesting that the *expeditio* cannot have taken place as early as 119.

All this means that the great British war of Hadrian's reign must have occurred later than 117–19. The response of some historians has been to place it late in Hadrian's reign, long after the building of the Wall, around AD130, when the formidable General Julius Severus was sent to Britain. But there is no evidence for war in Britain at this time: it is simply that it has been difficult to place this war elsewhere.

The one part of Hadrian's reign that historians have not, up until now, seen as the likely time of the British war, has been that of his own visit, in 122 or just possibly 121–2. The basic reason for this is that the only available historical source merely says that Hadrian 'set out for Britain. There he put many things right and was the first to build a Wall, 80 miles long, to separate the barbarians and the Romans'. There is no hint of military crisis or active campaigning against an enemy: but the source in question, the late fourth century *Augustan History*, is a 'hasty compilation' of good source material riddled with curious omissions and repetitions. Moreover, recent research has suggested that the term *expeditio* followed by the name of an enemy – as in *expeditio Britannica* – almost invariably means that the emperor himself was present and took part in the military campaign. This has convinced an increasing number of (though not all) British historians that the *expeditio Britannica* and Hadrian's visit to Britain have to be one and the same thing. This would certainly be the neatest solution, accommodating all the evidence.

But historians have perhaps not yet seen the full implications of dating the war to the time when, or immediately before, the emperor arrived on the scene in 121/2. Given that the arrival of Pontius Sabinus' 3,000 reinforcements cannot predate 122 by any significant interval, a hot northern frontier war was either very recently concluded or still raging when Hadrian arrived in Britain. This might tell us something about the climate in which the Wall was conceived, and something of its intended function. In the older version, where war in Britain is concluded long before Hadrian makes his measured tour of the frontier provinces, the building of the Wall could be seen as an unhurried phase in a long-term policy of keeping the empire within its bounds.

But if the *expeditio Britannica* dates to 122, this forces us to consider whether the Wall might have been urgently constructed in the face of severe hostility, perhaps checked by the time of Hadrian's advent, but still a perceived threat. One theory even has it that the Wall was begun as early as 120, provoking the revolt that resulted in the emperor's expedition to Britain. Nor can we rule out a flaring up of war again after the emperor's departure. Several historians have placed the *expeditio Britannica* in the years 124–6, but that removes the link between the *expeditio* and the emperor's presence.

The shifting of the war to 122, or shortly after, might at first sight leave the way open to the Ninth legion having been lost or irreparably damaged in the conflict. None of the officers whose career inscriptions we have need *necessarily* have served in *IX Hispana* after this year. But the specialists who know the inscriptions best feel that they indicate that the legion was still in existence later in the 120s, and its sojourn at Nijmegen on the Rhine has been argued by archaeologists in the Netherlands to date to the years after 120 rather than before.

The Ninth had ceased to exist when a list of the legions around the empire was drawn up shortly after

161. The most favoured solution has been to see the legion transferred from Britain entirely, first to the Lower Rhine (in 114–7), and then on to be destroyed finally either in the Jewish War of 132–5, or as late as 161 on the Eastern frontier. Indeed, this non-British explanation of the fate of the legion has gained such common currency that it is sometimes stated as if it were a known fact. But there is no record either of the legion or of any known base it could have occupied in the eastern provinces. The fact that *Legio VI* was brought over to Britain and permanently replaced the Ninth Legion at York is difficult to explain unless the Ninth was permanently out of the picture. But why swap these two legions around – *VI Victrix* was transferred to Britain from Xanten, the next fortress up the Rhine from Nijmegen – unless the Ninth was no longer capable of garrisoning York?

Perhaps the possibility should not be dismissed out of hand that the Ninth suffered such severe casualties during the Hadrianic war in Britain that the Sixth and other reinforcements were brought in to replace it, and its remnants were sent to Nijmegen – not necessarily in disgrace – where eventually the legion was disbanded and its survivors transferred to other units. That it was reformed and lost at some later date remains a possibility, but if so it has left no trace of its movements.

The war, or at least one phase of conflict, was presumably over by 17 July 122 when soldiers were honourably discharged with the promised citizenship from no fewer than fifty auxiliary units then serving in Britain – this we know from the surviving bronze tablet certifying citizenship ('diploma') issued to one of the veterans. It was customary to make such discharges after the conclusion of campaigns, rather than in their midst. The discharge had actually been carried out by Platorius Nepos' predecessor as governor, Pompeius Falco, but Nepos had taken over by this time.

With the war brought to a conclusion, Hadrian and his friend Nepos could turn their attention to the great project of the Wall. ✣

Chapter 2

THE WALL IS BUILT

The Scale of the Task

EVEN BY THE STANDARDS OF THE ROMAN Empire, the construction of Hadrian's Wall was an impressive achievement. The 117km (73-mile) line of the Wall had to be accurately surveyed and marked out, and the positions of over 240 structures – milecastles, turrets, bridges – chosen. The project called for forty-five stone milecastles, each an imposing structure with walls some 20m (66ft) long and up to 3m (10ft) thick, towering to the same height as the curtain wall, and with monumental gates in the north and south sides, each a 3m- (10ft) wide arched portal. A multi-storey tower stood

Fig. 2.1 Reconstruction of the Wall with frontal ditch (right), a turret (centre) and in the distance, a milecastle. This depicts the Narrow Wall in Wall-mile 2. TYNE & WEAR ARCHIVES & MUSEUMS (DRAWING BY PETE URMSTON)

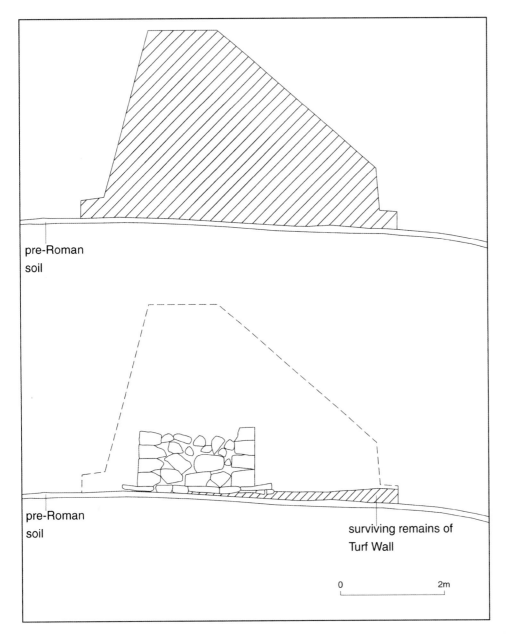

Fig. 2.2 Profile of the Turf Wall, showing how it had a near-vertical north face (left) and a more battered rear (right). The top would have been finished with a timber walkway and parapet. The lower illustration shows how the Turf Wall was later replaced in stone, usually on the same alignment.

pre-Roman
soil

pre-Roman
soil

surviving remains of
Turf Wall

0   2m

above the north portal, and possibly above the south also. Milecastle walls were constructed of coursed rubble – roughly dressed squared stones – but the gates and their arches contained massive blocks, lifted into position by crane. The timber Turf Wall milecastles were identical in scale, and although they would have been simpler to construct, the programme called for no fewer than thirty-one of these.

Along the stone and turf walls some 160 stone turrets were required – a remarkable figure when it is considered that each was a sturdy tower perhaps 12m (40ft) high, with walls over 1m (3.2ft) thick, with two upper storeys and either a battlemented roof platform or some other complicated roofing arrangement.

Broadly speaking, the continuous stone wall itself (often referred to as the 'curtain wall' or 'the curtain') was started at 10 Roman feet (RF) in width (the 'Broad Wall'), but was completed to a narrower width (the 'Narrow Wall'), 6RF to 8RF wide. The detailed dimensions are more complex and varied: the Broad Wall superstructure was 2.80m (9ft 3in) wide above a wider offset placed on the 10RF wide foundations; the 'standard' Narrow Wall is actually 2.29m (7ft 6in) wide, above an offset course 8RF wide. The 10RF-wide foundation of the Broad Wall consists of massive stone slabs, boulders or whinstone fragments (depending on the area) laid directly on the ground or in a shallow construction trench, and it runs with very little interruption over 71km (44 miles). Where completed, in the eastern sector, the Broad Wall was built up from the foundation with faces of distinctive, square-faced sandstone rubble (sometimes with the sparing use of mortar) and a core of clay mixed with large stones or sandy soil.

The Narrow Wall also used mortar sparingly or not at all. Its core has rarely been seen, but where it has (as in a recent excavation at Wallsend) it is more carefully constructed than the interior of the Broad Wall, with hewn sandstones or boulders placed in courses interspersed with layers of soil or clay. The volume of the Broad Wall as planned would have been something like 36 million cubic feet. The Narrow Wall, which was usually laid on the pre-prepared Broad foundation, involved a saving of only 15 per cent in materials and manpower, and less than that if its foundations had to be built from scratch, as they had to be in some areas. The intended height of the Wall was probably between 3.60m (12RF) and 4.60m (15RF) to the walkway, with a parapet taking the total height to some 5 to 6m (17 to 20ft). The evidence for the walkway and parapet will be discussed in Chapter 6. Scaffolding would be required for building once the Wall had risen above a height of about 1.5m (5ft).

The rampart of the Turf Wall was 6m (20RF) wide at its base and probably rose to a walkway at a height of 3.60m (12RF), protected by a timber or hurdle breastwork; it was built of sods of turf, laid directly on the pre-existing ground or, as has been seen at one point, on a foundation of cobbles and boulders. As

with its stone equivalent, the material inside the Wall varied in detail from place to place: there was much use of earth, and 'Turf Wall' is a term of convenience. An excavation at Crosby-on-Eden (Wall-mile 61) has shown that a strip *at least* 25m (82ft) wide north and 20m (65ft) south of the Wall was de-turfed to provide the material (a minimum stripped area of over 200ha or 500 acres over the whole length of the Turf Wall), with the turf beneath the Wall left in place.

The frontal ditch, excavated apparently quite early in the sequence of construction, had to be surveyed and constructed with fine precision along the entire length of the Wall, except against the precipitous crags of the central sector. It was often cut through solid rock. In one famous instance at Limestone Corner (Milecastle 30) the task was left incomplete – a steep slope to the north offers natural protection here – and the holes cut by the Roman engineers to insert wedges to split the rock can still be seen. Close by, at Black Carts, the ditch was never cut to full size through the same intractable dolerite, but these are rare abdications.

This enormous building programme developed to include twelve forts, at least six of which were built of stone at the outset. A typical stone fort covered an area equivalent to two or three stadium football pitches, needed ten arched gate portals of the sort already discussed at the milecastles, around twenty towers, surrounding walls and ditches, and an array of architecturally ambitious internal buildings. With the forts came the Vallum, itself a meticulously surveyed and complex structure of built mounds, maybe 2m (6.6ft) high flanking an almost vertically sided, flat-bottomed ditch relentlessly cut to a full 3m (10ft) depth, even through solid bedrock where this was encountered. In addition to all this, there was a need for the rapid provision of specialist structures, such as the four multi-arched river bridges at Newcastle, Chesters, Willowford and Carlisle, and road building and improvement would certainly have formed part of the whole package.

Finally, the recently discovered system of obstacles on the berm between Wall and ditch would

Fig. 2.3 The surviving base and individual turves of the Turf Wall, seen in a section cut at Appletree (Wall-mile 50).

Fig. 2.4 Work in progress in the 1970s on a reconstruction at Vindolanda shows the landscape dramatically cleared of turf for the building of the Turf Wall, for which a strip *at least* 25m (82ft) wide north and 20m (65ft) south of the Wall was de-turfed by the Roman builders.

have entailed the procurement and installation of seventy-two separate upright timber elements per 15m (50ft) of Wall, or 7,200 per Wall-mile. So how was this vast programme of work organized, and who actually did the work?

Who Built the Wall and Where did the Stone come from?

The Roman army built the Wall, as shown by building inscriptions erected to record the work of the soldiers. These inscriptions record that the British legions *II Augusta*, *XX Valeria Victrix* and *VI Victrix* were the builders of the Wall and its forts. The army had always built roads and bridges, its own fortifications and architecturally ambitious buildings within forts, so all the necessary skills and craft specialities, from architectural design and surveying to stonemasonry and carpentry, existed within the ranks of the legions. On Trajan's Column legionaries are seen gathering materials and building as often as they are shown fighting, often with auxiliary soldiers standing guard as they work.

This is what made the Roman army distinctive and formidable as a force: it was capable of transforming the environment to its advantage, throwing up fortifications at a moment's notice, bridging rivers, cutting down forests, and building supply routes through previously impenetrable areas. The army carefully nurtured the skills that made this possible. Hadrian's Wall is one such dramatic alteration to the environment, intended to put Rome's northern foes at a disadvantage, and it was only natural that the legions, once supplied by the provincial governor with a specification of what was required, should set to the work. It is possible that impressed or prisoner labour was used, perhaps in the laborious tasks of digging the Wall ditch and Vallum or transporting materials, but given the degree of precision required and the difficulties of supervision that this would entail, it is unlikely. Legionaries were proud of their ability to carry out such works at speed, and they

Fig. 2.5 Trajan's Column: legionaries build while auxiliaries stand guard.

would not have found them below their dignity. We also find auxiliaries building alongside legionaries on the Vallum, and even the *classis Britannica*, the fleet of Britain, makes an appearance, building at Benwell Fort.

Visitors to the Wall often ask where the stone was obtained, expecting the answer that it was transported from some distant source. In fact the opposite is true, and once again reflects long-standing traditions in Roman military building. The army on the frontiers of the empire always built using whatever materials were close to hand. Although the procurement and transport of stone and especially other materials, such as timber for scaffolding, limestone for mortar and foodstuffs for the workforce, was often complicated and organized over considerable distances, the basic principle was that building materials were sourced as locally as possible. The crudely squared facing stones of the Wall are mostly of local sandstone, quarried

reasonably close to the building sites, dressed in the quarry and apparently transported in a finished state to the Wall. Very few quarries in the Wall area can be identified as having Roman origins with certainty, but many are likely to have had, and in some cases, for example at Fallowfield Fell (600m (660yd) south of Wall-mile 25) it is certain: here a soldier humorously inscribed the quarry face '*petra Flavi Carantini...*': 'My very own rock – signed Flavius Carantinus.'

However, even where quarries by the Wall can be shown to be Roman, this does not necessarily mean they were used in the original Hadrianic building. Some of the stone could have been obtained from the Wall ditch and Vallum, where these were cut through rock. Building in sandstone was possible in the western sector, for the Turf Wall was eventually replaced in stone, but for the initial building, once again we see that a conveniently obtainable local material, turf, was used.

Fig. 2.6 Victorian engraving of an inscribed Roman quarry face near the Wall at Fallowfield (Wall-mile 25), 'The rock of Flavius Carantinus'. It is now at Chesters Museum.

Where were the Troops Accommodated while they were Building the Wall?

The legions were not moved permanently and wholesale into the northern frontier area to build the Wall. Movement between the north and the legionary bases at Caerleon, Chester and York was probably constant, with many troops leaving their seasonal camps close to the building project to return to their fortress during the winter months. Their temporary accommodation in the Wall zone is one of the most poorly understood aspects of the Wall. The earthwork ramparts of numerous Roman army camps are known in the Wall corridor, and many are still clearly visible on the ground, but they come in a range of sizes and there is no regular pattern or spacing to their distribution. This contrasts with the Antonine Wall in Scotland, where a series of camps 2–2.5ha (5–6 acres) in area are spaced along the Wall and presumably accommodated the legionary detachments carrying out the construction work.

On Hadrian's Wall the bulk of the known camps lie in remote moorland in the central sector; far fewer are known in the lowland areas, and none at all in the farmed and industrialized eastern 47km (29 miles) of the Wall, where presumably camps once existed. There is a remarkable concentration around Haltwhistle Burn, near the centre of the Wall. Some camps are so small they were probably built for practice; others are large enough to represent the movement of campaigning armies in pre-Hadrianic times. There is a group of camps between 1 and 2ha (2.5 and 5 acres) in area, which might have accommodated detachments of troops between 500 and 1,000 strong engaged in quarrying or building, or both.

Although their distribution sheds no light on the way building gangs moved and operated, their areas hint at the sizes of detachments at work. One was recently discovered at Shield-on-the-Wall (Wall-mile 32), 1.4ha (3.5 acres) in area and clearly associated with stone quarrying and the layout of the Vallum and perhaps the Wall itself. The camp might have held something over 600 men. The site was found by airborne laser scanning (LiDAR), a new technique with the potential to reveal many more previously invisible camps (and other kinds of site) in the Hadrian's Wall corridor.

The Sequence of Construction

To understand how the Wall was built, we need to look first at the sequence of construction, gradually worked out by archaeological research during the first half of the twentieth century.

• The initial plan called for the Wall to be constructed in stone between Newcastle and the River Irthing to a width of 10 Roman feet. The line of

Fig. 2.7 Hadrian's Wall as planned, without forts on the line of the Wall (individual milecastles and turrets are not shown).
FRONTIERS OF THE ROMAN EMPIRE CULTURE 2000 PROJECT/D. J. BREEZE

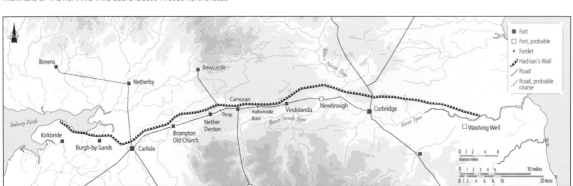

Fig. 2.8 Turret with Broad wing walls and its relationship to the Broad and Narrow Wall.

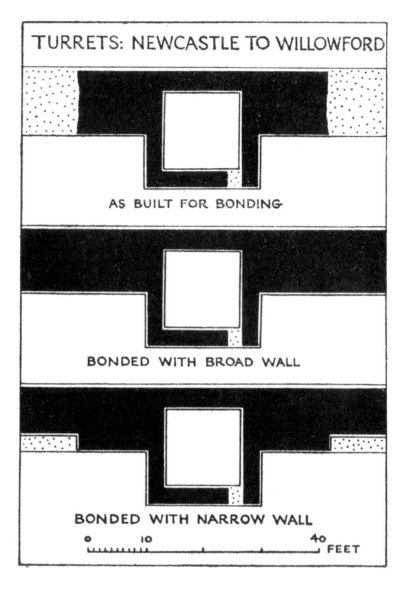

TURRETS: NEWCASTLE TO WILLOWFORD

AS BUILT FOR BONDING

BONDED WITH BROAD WALL

BONDED WITH NARROW WALL

0   10   40 FEET

the Wall was surveyed – and presumably marked out on the ground with poles or similar – and foundations for the 3m (10RF) 'Broad Wall' were laid between Newcastle and Milecastle 39. West of that the Broad foundation was only intermittently provided, until resuming continuously for the last 5km (3 miles) (46–48) of the stone Wall.

• Building began on the structures, the milecastles and turrets, first. These were built with 'wing walls' on either side, for the Broad Wall to be bonded into when it arrived. Some milecastles have been identified as being earlier than others because of the great thickness of their side walls and sometimes their south walls – almost the same thickness as the Broad Wall. Very early in the building it seems to have been accepted that the walls did not have to be this thick, so many milecastles have narrower walls. The potentially early milecastles occur just west of Newcastle (4, 9, 10 and 14) between Milecastle 22 and the North Tyne (23–27) and immediately east of the Irthing (47 and 48). Note that we only have measurements for twenty-five out of forty-eight stone milecastles.

- Some Broad Wall was built on the foundation provided west of Newcastle. Possibly it was completed to full height in the whole stretch between Newcastle and Wall-mile 22.

- Between Milecastles 22 and 27 some stretches of Broad Wall were built, again possibly to full height, but these completed lengths are interspersed with a Narrow Wall, only 2m (6ft) wide, built above the Broad foundation. Here we have the easternmost clearly documented evidence of a major change of plan: an order had evidently gone out to build the Wall to a narrower width. Because the structures and their 'wing walls' had already been built, this led to an obvious mismatch where the Narrow Wall met a Broad wing wall. The north face of the Narrow Wall was always kept flush with Broad wing walls, the change in gauge only being visible on the south side.

- West of the North Tyne (Wall-mile 27) there is no curtain superstructure built to broad gauge, *apart from* in the area east of the Irthing, where up to four courses of offset footings were placed above the foundation. The Wall is narrow on Broad foundation and meets Broad wing walls awkwardly on either side of the pre-existing milecastles and turrets. In the craggy central sector there are places where the Narrow Wall takes a different course to the Broad foundation – suggesting there was a considerable interval before the Narrow Wall was completed on the remote heights. It is notable everywhere that the south edge of the Broad foundation was never completely removed, and the Narrow Wall was always placed so that its north face was flush with the Broad foundation: the awkward mismatch was *always* left on the south side, so a viewer from the north would see only seamless neatness.

- Milecastles and turrets west of the North Tyne were in various stages of building, and a few not even begun, when the news came through that the Wall was to be narrow gauge. It is impossible to tell from the surviving remains how many had been built to full height, but some could have been completed.

- West of the River Irthing (Wall-miles 49–80) the Wall was built of turf, with turf and timber milecastles and stone turrets, which were free-standing towers (with no wing walls) abutted by the turf rampart. The scheme of regular spacing of milecastles and turrets is carried seamlessly through from the Broad Wall in the east to the Turf Wall in the west, demonstrating that stone and turf walls were planned contemporaneously – the western sector is not built of turf because it is earlier than the rest of the Wall. A different explanation must be sought for the use of a different building material in the west.

- While work was still in progress on the stone curtain, building work began on a series of full-size forts for auxiliary units on the actual line of the Wall. Those in the stone sector were built of stone, those on the Turf Wall (except perhaps Birdoswald) of turf and timber. The original series was intended to be about twelve in number, spaced out at roughly 11km (7-mile) intervals. In all investigated cases it has been found that the Wall, the Wall ditch, and sometimes a turret or milecastle had already been built on the chosen site, and these structures had to be demolished and the ditch filled in to make way for the fort. Thus, Halton Chesters is built over the infilled Wall ditch, Chesters Fort overlies the remains of Turret 27A, Housesteads overlies 36B, Great Chesters overlies Milecastle 43 and Turf Wall Turret 49A had to be demolished before Birdoswald could be built.

- This structural evidence that the forts were secondary to the Wall was first found in the 1930s, and since then it has been generally accepted that the auxiliary units, the fighting army of the Wall, were intended in the original scheme to remain stationed in their old bases on the Stanegate frontier line. It was only after a change of plan after the Wall had been

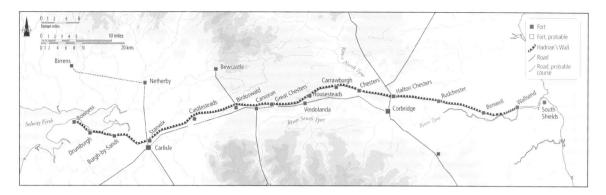

Fig. 2.9 Hadrian's Wall as built, after the decision to add forts (individual milecastles and turrets are not shown). FRONTIERS OF THE ROMAN EMPIRE CULTURE 2000 PROJECT/D. J. BREEZE

begun – usually referred to as 'the fort decision' – that they were moved up on to the Wall itself. At Housesteads the fort was built free-standing over the Broad Wall structures, and only later incorporated in the Narrow Wall when that was built at a later stage in this area.

• The Vallum was dug to the south of the Wall, all the way along the stone and turf walls. The Vallum is intimately linked to the provision of the forts: it seems to have been surveyed in straight alignments out from certain of the fort sites. At the forts where the relationship has been investigated, the Vallum makes a diversion around the fort, and an undug causeway across it gives access to the south gate of the fort.

• From Newcastle for the 6.5km (4 miles) east to Wallsend there is no Broad foundation, and the narrow-gauge Wall here has generally been taken to be an extension to the original Broad Wall scheme (some believe that the Wall was *planned* to end at Wallsend from the very beginning). The Narrow Wall between Newcastle and Wallsend differs from the Broad Wall in having a vertically sided foundation trench packed with stone and clay. The fort at Wallsend has been shown to be of one build with this Narrow Wall. There is no Vallum in the Newcastle–Wallsend section.

• The series of milefortlets and towers running down the Cumbrian coast must have been built close in time to the similar structures (milecastles, turrets) on the Wall, but there are no physical relationships to tie them into any part of the Wall-building sequence; the same applies to the forts at Beckfoot and Maryport.

The Organization of the Building

How was all this organized? Specialist division of labour would be typical in any building project, and with the Wall it is likely that different gangs carried out the tasks of foundation laying, milecastle building, turret building, ditch digging and so on – so we see that those charged with the more rapid tasks of laying foundation and building structures forged far ahead of those building the actual curtain. There would be no single unit completing part of the works wholesale and moving on to start a new section. It is most likely that there was activity at many points along the Wall from the outset, with different specialist gangs interacting in a complex fashion.

On the other hand, we would also expect discrete parts of the Wall to be allotted to the sole responsibility of a particular legion. The group of inscriptions of *Legio II Augusta* from milecastles in one particular area (37, 38 and 42; the last inscription is incomplete but the legion's name can be restored, as the fragment is from an identical inscription to the others) supports this principle, suggesting that at one point in time this legion was responsible for that batch of structures and whatever other building had been ordered along a particular length of the Wall which included them.

During the course of the twentieth century, Wall specialists have developed the theory that certain recurring structural features along the stone Wall may characterize three different groups of builders. These 'building signatures' are seen in particular combinations of milecastle gateway types, milecastle laying out lines and orientation (the long or short axis perpendicular to the curtain), the position of turret doorways (to the east or west), and the number of projecting ('offset') courses at the base of the Wall.

In the fifteen Wall-miles 7 to 22 the structures that have been seen (nine out of fifteen milecastles, fifteen out of thirty turrets) are broadly consistent (there are exceptions) with there being three distinct combinations of these characteristics, each occurring in a block 8km (5 miles) long. Since this involves the structures, the first things to be built, this must have been at the outset of building.

Not unnaturally the three 8km (5-mile) 'blocks' in Wall-miles 7–22 have been linked with the three legions that *might* have been (we do not know for sure) engaged in the building of this part of the Wall. For a long time milecastles with a short axis and a certain gate type ('Type 1') were confidently assigned to *Legio II Augusta*, on the basis of the inscriptions of that legion that occur at three milecastles (37, 38 and 42) with those characteristics. There are no unambiguously Hadrianic building inscriptions from any of the structures in this sector to identify the other two legions involved. Nowadays even the identification of *II Augusta* with the building plans of Milecastles 37, 38 and 42 is doubted, as it has been claimed that there was an interruption in the building of these structures, and that it is possible that *Legio II* signed them, having merely completed work that another legion might have started.

Some archaeologists are sceptical about the idea of 8km (5-mile) legionary 'blocks': they do not dispute that the various structural combinations denote the work of different building parties, but suggest that the variants are more numerous and more complicated than the simple three 'types' defined, and that the same legion could contain different building parties

Fig. 2.10 One of the Second Legion building inscriptions from milecastles in the central sector (RIB 1638, Milecastle 38), naming Hadrian and Platorius Nepos. SOCIETY OF ANTIQUARIES OF NEWCASTLE UPON TYNE AND GREAT NORTH MUSEUM: HANCOCK

building in different styles. This could explain hybrids such as Milecastle 18, which has the 'wrong' kind of gate for the 'legionary block' 17–22. In this way of looking at it, the Wall was possibly divided into much longer legionary lengths – one legion responsible for the Turf Wall and Cumberland coast, and one for the stone Wall, say – within which we find the stylistic variations of different gangs within the same legion.

However, it is more likely that the neat 8km (5-mile) lengths, which do seem to have a reality, denote different legions at work. Such short and specific work allotments are also found on the Antonine Wall, as we know from inscribed slabs that identify the particular lengths with legions – a rich seam of evidence that is entirely absent from Hadrian's Wall. On the Scottish wall there was a recurrent legionary building length of 3⅔ Roman miles (5.3km). At its western end legions were allotted lengths of only 3,000–4,411 Roman Feet, probably to speed up the work. The apparent 8km (5-mile) blocks in Wall-miles 7 to 22 on Hadrian's Wall suggest that this was started with a similar system. Presumably speed of building was crucial, and the division into short legionary blocks meant that competition between the legions to be the fastest builder would be encouraged. The Turf Wall would lend itself to division into similarly short legionary lengths.

The picture that emerges is of the building of the Wall being organized in large sectors defined by the rivers crossed by the barrier. The Turf Wall extended from the Solway to the Irthing. The first stone structures seem to have been built from the Newcastle end westwards and from the North Tyne eastwards, and a start was made on a few structures at the west end of the stone Wall, working from the Irthing eastwards until the crags were reached. There, the large Milecastles 47 and 48 and Turrets 48A and 48B have odd characteristics that do not occur elsewhere, suggesting early, experimental structures: the turrets have thin north walls and resemble Turf Wall turrets, perhaps indicating that builders freed up from the Turf Wall moved straight on to these stone structures.

Work on filling in the Wall itself between the structures was prioritized in, and at first confined to, the Turf Wall sector and the lowland area east of the North Tyne, although work on Broad Wall foundation and structures extended into the central sector before the Broad Wall east of the North Tyne was completed. Within these broad areas defined by the rivers it remains on balance probable that the work was divided into the 'legionary blocks' we have discussed. These are the east end of the Wall, from the bridge at Newcastle to Milecastle 7 (5.3km (3⅔ miles), a work length found on the Antonine Wall), with four blocks running 7–12, 12–17, 17–22, 22–27 (the North Tyne). Then comes a longer legionary block (27–36B), a block associated with the *II Augusta* inscriptions (37–42), and a final allotment (42–49), which brings us to the Irthing. That, at least, was how the work might have been organized at the outset of building, although the work allotments were probably reorganized when the order came to change to narrow gauge.

The Change to Narrow Wall

Two kinds of reason have been put forward to explain this decision. The first is to do with economy of labour: either because of a general need to speed things up, or a particular need for manpower to be transferred to the fort-building programme, a reduced specification was introduced. The second suggestion is that the Broad Wall had been found to be structurally unstable, especially on the steep hills that had to be built on in the central sector. Perhaps all these factors played a part.

At some stage it was apparently decided that it was more efficient for one legion to be assigned the task of completing the Wall between the North Tyne and the Irthing. The initial organization of building into 8km (5-mile) blocks would have been good from the point of view of competition and of involving every legion in the emperor's pet project, but would have wastefully hampered centralized procurement and delivery of materials, and might have duplicated many processes. Also, in completing the central sector, a unified approach would allow vulnerable gaps through the crags to be prioritized according to a centrally directed plan, which would be difficult if legions were working on small individual blocks.

So the point is that whatever the truth of the initial 'legionary' blocks in which the structures and Broad foundation had been built, it was a different legion, assigned a much more extensive block of work, that raised the superstructure of the Narrow Wall on the Broad foundation between the North Tyne and the Irthing, and which built those structures there that had never been started during the Broad Wall phase.

The legion given this task was *XX Valeria Victrix*, two of whose centurions, Julius Florentinus and Flavius Noricus (both of the Tenth Cohort), named their legion on inscriptions in Wall-miles 44 and 45. Centurions Maximus Terentius and Ferronius Vegetus, also building in Wall-mile 45 (and in the latter case 48), appear on inscriptions at Chester, which was the base of *XX Valeria Victrix*. Rufius Sabinus, building near Milecastle 42, is found on an inscription from the works depot of the legion at Holt, near Chester. The century of Claudius Augustanus is found building at possibly four points on the Wall between Turrets 25A and 47B. His name occurs on a leaden die at the Chester Fortress. Other centurions working in the same area, and therefore almost certainly of the same legion, are found on centurial stones, presumably all belonging to the same narrow time-frame, distributed at many different points between Wall-miles 28 and 48. The most industrious was Lousius Suavis of the Sixth Cohort, for whom we have no fewer than six building records, all from the Wall curtain, in Wall-miles 27, 28, 42, 46 and 48 (twice).

This strongly suggests that *Legio XX* was the sole legion charged with completing the Wall between North Tyne and Irthing. If a different legion was given sole responsibility for any outstanding works east of the North Tyne, that might explain why in miles 23–27 gaps in the Broad Wall were plugged with a distinctive 2m (6ft) Narrow Wall, whereas in our XX Legion sector the Wall was built at the 'standard' narrow gauge throughout.

The Narrow Wall decision had reached the central sector before the XX Legion took over the whole job: Milecastle 37 was apparently completed to the narrow gauge by *Legio II Augusta*, which also built Milecastle 38, which there is no reason to believe had not been completed entirely to the broad gauge. As we have seen, it has been suggested that these milecastles might have had been started by a different legion to that – the Second – which put up the finishing building inscriptions, but here a straightforward view is taken that it is most probable that they were erected and largely completed in one go by a single legion. There is no compelling evidence for a long interruption in the building of these milecastles, and it is most likely that *Legio II* was working on Milecastle 37 when the order to narrow the Wall gauge came through, and adapted the work accordingly.

If the building inscriptions of these milecastles had really been erected by a legion finishing off work that someone else had begun, we would expect them to be signed by the XX Legion because of its role in the completion of the central sector. There are very occasional building records of other legions than the Twentieth in the central sector (*II Augusta* left a stone in Wall-mile 34), but on the high crags, where the Wall was hardly a priority, completion of the continuous curtain may have been left to later, even post-Hadrianic, building campaigns.

The Forts on the Wall

It is usually assumed that the XX Legion shouldered the burden of completing the Wall curtain because *II Augusta* and *VI Victrix* had been given the job of building the Wall forts. It is difficult to be sure about that, as we only have a single Hadrianic legionary building inscription from a fort: from Halton Chesters, and it is indeed of the Sixth.

The original vision for the forts on the Wall was that they should be twelve in number. This is the series as initially planned; not all were actually built straightaway, and others, as we shall see, were added at a slightly later date. Great Chesters, for example, although planned, was not built as part of the initial series, and a smaller fort than originally intended was built here some years later. The *intended* series was fairly regularly spaced, as follows:

Wallsend
Benwell
Rudchester
Halton Chesters
Chesters
Housesteads
Great Chesters
Birdoswald
Castlesteads
Stanwix
Burgh-by-Sands
Bowness

The average spacing between forts was therefore meant to be 12km (7–8 miles). Here we have taken the straightforward view that Wallsend was included in the original series of forts, and was contemporary with the decision to add forts to the Wall and to change to narrow gauge.

We shall hear more of how these forts were laid out and operated in Chapter 3. For now, it should be noted that they were full size forts for various different kinds of auxiliary units, ranging in size from 1.76ha (4.4 acres) – Halton – to 3.72ha (9.32 acres) – Stanwix. East of the North Tyne all the forts of the initial series were built straddling the Wall, so that half of the fort, and three out of four of its principal gates, lay on the north side of the barrier. Wallsend, on the added stretch on the Narrow Wall east of Newcastle, was also built to project. Housesteads, in the central sector, did not project, perhaps because topography made this impossible. This fort was built before any work on the Narrow Wall superstructure began in this area.

On the Turf Wall, Birdoswald was probably built as a projecting stone fort, like those on the stone Wall, but further west, all the forts seem to have been detached from the Wall and built of turf and timber, like the Wall to which they belonged. There is no clear evidence that any of these turf forts were built to project north of the Wall: at Stanwix and Bowness this has been explained by a steep slope on the north side. At Castlesteads the fort was built detached wholly to the south of the Wall.

Somewhat later – we do not know by how much, but it was within the reign of Hadrian – the fort at Great Chesters was built, but seemingly to a smaller size than was originally planned. Significantly, it was not built as a projecting fort but merely attached to the back of the Wall. A fort at Great Chesters had been part of the original plan, because an undug causeway across the Vallum had been left in readiness for the fort. A fort already existed at Burgh-by-Sands and was bypassed by the Wall and excluded by the Vallum, but it was probably *intended* to have a Wall fort here eventually. Like Great Chesters it was not actually built until later: Burgh was moved up on to the line of the Wall itself either late in Hadrian's reign or around AD160.

A true afterthought was a fort at Carrawburgh, which halved the rather long distance between Chesters and Housesteads. This had not been planned at the outset, for it overlay the Vallum. The date is usually given as the early 130s, but it is not really clear. Like the late fort at Great Chesters, it was attached to the rear of the Wall: the idea of the projecting forts had had a short life. Finally, a fort at Drumburgh early in the life of the Wall is implied by the sequence of names on the recently found Ilam Pan, which names Drumburgh but not Burgh-by-Sands. Drumburgh was perhaps a special provision to overlook the Solway marsh from the west side.

With these last forts to be added to the curtain, Hadrian's Wall was substantially complete.

The Direction and Method of Building: Centuries at Work

Most people imagine the Wall being started at one end and 'rolled out' progressively in one direction,

CHESTERS

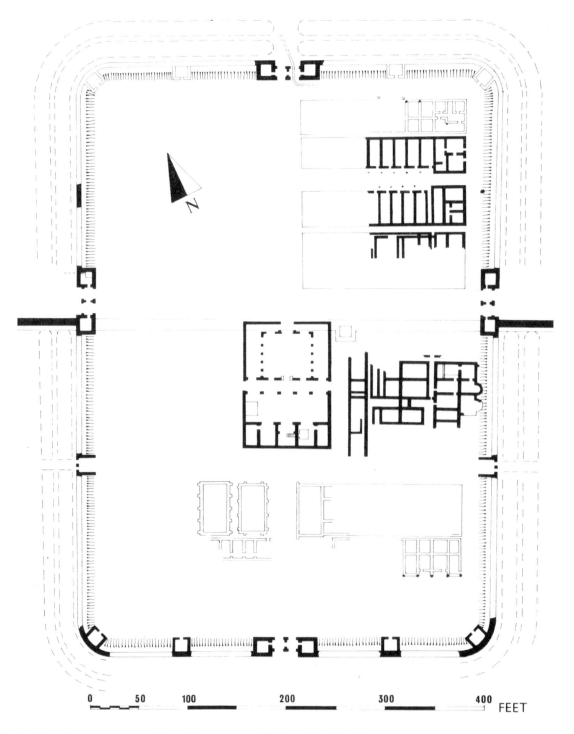

Fig. 2.11 Chesters, a typical projecting fort added so that three of its four principal gates lie north of the Wall. The line of the Wall and Turret 27A, cleared to make way for the fort, can be seen.

or at each end and working inwards. The Broad Wall foundation reached the central sector long before any Wall superstructure was placed on top of it, broadly showing an east-to-west direction of movement. However, the actual distribution of building work at any one time would have been far more complicated. Work would have started simultaneously in each of the 'legionary blocks' we have discussed, and within each of those there is no reason why building of the actual curtain might not have run from west to east – so for example the building of the Broad Wall curtain *might* have started at the Portgate (Milecastle 22) and progressed towards the east simultaneously with building being commenced close to Newcastle. Building parties finishing their work on foundation and structures in these areas and moving west would have started work at many different points simultaneously. The only overriding restriction is that they would have to be in a length that had been allotted to their particular legion. Presumably the Turf Wall was divided into legionary blocks that were advanced simultaneously, the whole thing (as will be suggested below) being thrown up in a single season.

The most numerous building inscriptions from the Wall are the so-called centurial stones, which marked the completion of a particular length of Wall curtain by an individual legionary century (nominally eighty men, but we must imagine that maybe half were elsewhere on other duties). Sometimes they state the legionary cohort to which the century belonged. They were presumably erected at either end of a completed piece of work, as evidence for what the century had achieved. They seem to have been placed on the south side of the Wall – they were a system of internal record-keeping, and like the untidiness of the Broad/ Narrow Wall junctions, were not to be seen from the north. They are not without problems: for various reasons they have been found in clusters in certain particular areas, and are lacking from much of the Wall. In themselves they are undated, but they have a very simple, recognizable style (again, they were internal records of work completion, not commemorative inscriptions for display), which makes it reasonably certain that the bulk are Hadrianic and not to do with later repair or rebuilding – there are some inscriptions recording such later work which are in a noticeably different style.

There are over 200 of these stones from various parts of the stone Wall, and they comprise one of the most extensive documentary records of a building project from anywhere in the Roman world. One would think that they might hold the key to understanding in detail how the building of the Wall curtain was organized. Elaborate theories of how the Wall was built have in fact been founded on the centurial stones, but these have never found acceptance. A new study of the centurial stones could be very revealing, but in the meantime they do give us some basic hints

Fig. 2.12 A typically crude and simple centurial stone from the central sector, recording the work of the century commanded by Gellius Philippus.

about how the building of the Wall was organized. In some ways the most important point about the centurial stones is that they hardly ever name the legion in question, and this is because it must have been unnecessary to do so, because only one legion was ever working at one time in a given sector. This supports the idea that the Wall was divided into lengths, for each of which a single legion was responsible.

We are lucky to have a sketch plan of part of Wall-mile 24, made by an antiquarian visitor in 1807, when the remains of the Wall, now obscured by the modern road surface, were still visible in the dust of the eighteenth-century Military Road. This sketch shows alternating Broad and Narrow superstructures in Wall-mile 24, implying that a stretch of Wall 119m (130yd) long was divided into three completed Broad and two Narrow sections, each about the same length and therefore some 25m (80ft) long. Perhaps lengths of variously 25, 30 or 37m (80, 100 or 120ft) were assigned to cohorts, and subdivided into centurial lengths. The gaps in Wall-mile 24 at least indicate the length of work allotments in this area, and suggest that lengths of 25 to 30m (80 to 100ft) were being scaffolded as a unit (by the cohort?) so that the superstructure could be built. Dividing this length by six gives a remarkably short 'centurial' allotment, but the number of centuries building presumably varied from cohort to cohort, sometimes being less than the full six, and short centurial stints are directly attested. Two possibly Hadrianic centurial stones from the central sector record centurial lengths of 7m (22ft), and 9m (30ft) are stated on centurial stones from the later replacement of the Turf Wall in stone between Birdoswald and the Irthing.

When the smallest of the building units, those individual centuries, marked their completed lengths – of 6m (20ft) or whatever it was – with centurial stones, what work had they done, and how? One school of thought has it that the curtain would be rolled out in horizontal layers: foundation first (we know this to be the case); then the curtain itself up to the height – about 1.5m (5ft) – where scaffolding becomes necessary for those placing the stones; then

the Wall was left for a time at that height until the scaffolding arrived, along with a potentially different set of builders who built up the next 1.5m (5ft) stage; then potentially the scaffolding was moved down the line, and the Wall was left until the next scaffolding gang and another lot of builders arrived to complete the final stage.

This view assumes that limited amounts of scaffolding were available, and that the Wall stood incomplete for long periods until it arrived. It means that in a given stretch of the Wall you might find up to three sets of centurial stones recording the work of three different centuries which had contributed the different layers – and that the divisions between centurial lengths might not coincide vertically.

This method of building seems unlikely, because, assuming enough scaffolding could be made available, it would be grossly wasteful to erect scaffolding, take it down and then re-erect it, rather than erecting it once (over a 30m/100ft length?) and simply building the Wall to full height. Also, if the first stage of Broad Wall were built up to 1.5m (5ft) without scaffolding and just left, we would expect to find evidence of Narrow Wall set on top of Broad Wall at some height above the foundations. This phenomenon is not seen anywhere – where Narrow Wall is set on Broad foundation it is always at ground level, implying that was where it was started, Broad Wall was immediately carried up to full height, and where Narrow Wall is built it is in those gaps where Broad Wall superstructure had not begun before the order came to narrow the gauge.

The 1807 sketch already mentioned showing alternating Broad and Narrow superstructure in Wall-mile 24 was recorded in the surface of the eighteenth-century road overlying the Wall, not far above foundation level – so it is clear that in the 'gaps' in Broad Wall superstructure the infilling Narrow Wall was built up from foundation level – as we see in the nearby visible remains at Planetrees. In this area it seems more likely that Broad Wall superstructure was raised in discrete blocks of regular length, and this suggests that they were scaffolded and taken straight up – there is no continuous layer of the first 1.5m of

Fig. 2.13 A length of Broad Wall (right) meets Narrow Wall built on Broad foundation (left) at Planetrees (Wall-mile 26).

Broad Wall rolled out across the landscape without scaffolding. Broad Wall, progressing westwards, does not simply stop at one point, to be replaced by Narrow Wall. At Planetrees we have a shift from Broad wall (east) to Narrow wall (west). But west of this, Broad Wall picks up again, and west of *this*, Narrow wall picks up again (east of Turret 26B). West of the turret it is Broad Wall again. Between Milecastle 27 and the bridge across the North Tyne it is Narrow Wall again. In each case Narrow Wall is found at foundation level. Broad Wall interspersed with 2m (6ft) Wall effectively disproves the notion of building in horizontal layers.

It is more likely, then, that the Wall was scaffolded and immediately built to full height in lengths of around 30m (100ft) in the 22–27 area – although of course these 'cohort lengths' might have varied

greatly from place to place along the Wall. Within such 'cohort' allotments individual centuries raced to build 'their' portion of Wall (*pedatura*) to full height. The vertical joints that would result are not a problem – they can be clearly seen in Roman building works, such as the walls of the Saxon Shore fort at Pevensey.

West of the North Tyne we no longer have alternating Broad and Narrow Wall to shed light on the way the Wall was being built: the Wall superstructure is all Narrow, and it can only be an assumption that the building was divided into short lengths in a similar fashion. The stretch of stone Wall that replaced the Turf Wall between Milecastle 49 and Birdoswald Fort later in Hadrian's reign contains one of the richest concentrations of centurial stones known, several of which are still visible *in situ*. All the *in situ* stones are on the south side, mostly in the seventh to tenth courses of stone up – at convenient eye level for inspection. Three of them specifically mention that a length of 30RF (9m) was built by a given century, and another stone implies 7.5RF (2.5m) – a quarter of this. Given these extremely short building lengths, it seems unnecessary to conclude from the close proximity of stones of different centuries, as has been done, that they mark different 'layers' of horizontal construction.

For the closing stages of the Wall curtain in the central sector we must again envisage work starting simultaneously in different places, and progressing according to local priorities – such as gaps and openings blocked off before high precipices. Immediately east of the Irthing, where, although the structures and foundation had been built early, the Wall superstructure is universally narrow, a centurion called Libo of the Second Cohort left an inscription; he is also recorded near Milecastle 48, on Walltown Crags (45A-B), and further east – but by the time these stones were inscribed, Libo had been promoted to the First Cohort. This shows that the Narrow Wall was built eastwards from the Irthing into the central sector.

This is confirmed by changes in the status of two other centurions building in this area, Socellius and Flavius Noricus. Noricus was in the Tenth Cohort when he was building on Walltown Crags (45A-B), but had been promoted to the Ninth Cohort by the time he was building near Milecastle 42. The century of Socellius also moves from west to east. If we are right in seeing the Twentieth Legion taking on the task of building the central sector Narrow Wall, it looks very much as if they started simultaneously from the Irthing eastwards and from the North Tyne westwards.

The Timetable of Building

What evidence do we have as to when the Wall was started, and how long it took to build? The *only* firm dating is provided by building inscriptions that, as well as naming Hadrian himself, also named his friend, the Governor Aulus Platorius Nepos, as being in Britain by July 122, still there in September 124, and replaced by summer 127 at the latest. The inscriptions come from three milecastles in the central sector (37, 38 and 42) and from two forts: Benwell and Halton Chesters. A fragment of a wooden inscription from Turf Wall Milecastle 50 bears Nepos' name on a reasonable reconstruction. It was clearly within his governorship that parts of the Wall were overlain by forts: at Halton Chesters, the west gate bearing Nepos' inscription was given extraordinarily deep foundations because it was built over the infilled Wall ditch.

The Platorius Nepos inscriptions prove that the Wall had not been completed before Hadrian arrived. However, the inscriptions allow for uncertainty about whether the Wall was begun by Hadrian and Nepos, or whether it had been ordered from a distance and begun, before Hadrian's arrival, by the Governor Pompeius Falco. This earlier start date has been championed by various writers from time to time. Those who favour the earlier date see Hadrian and Platorius Nepos arriving to inspect a work in progress and, seeing the need for a change of plan, deciding to narrow the Wall gauge and add the forts. Those who prefer a start in 122 suggest that the most important decision – to build the Wall – would have been taken while the emperor was present, and that the various dislocations occurred later in Nepos' governorship, possibly after the emperor had left.

So, how long would it have taken to assemble the materials and build the various elements? A calculation by the present writer based on experimental work building a turf rampart at the Lunt Roman Fort, Coventry, in the 1970s, taking into account factors such as procurement and transport of materials, arrived at a figure of some 800,000 man days for the whole of the Turf Wall and its structures. Another quantity survey in a recent PhD thesis has put this at 1,393,909 man days.

Figures for a single stone milecastle and turret, again calculated by the writer (*see* Quantity Survey appendix), come out at 4,375 and 1,407 man days. These may be compared with figures of around 6,137 and 534 in the same PhD thesis. Obviously no close reliance can be placed on figures such as this, but there is some broad agreement here, and they do give a general sense of the relative time and resources required. Both, especially the PhD one, will exaggerate the labour requirements because they are based on modern practice and do not fully take account of the experience and competitive speed with which the Roman army will have built. They also assume that the army did all the work, without recourse to captives or slaves. On the other hand, that may be counterbalanced by elements that are omitted, such as building roads and construction camps, organizing the food supply, and soldiers defending those doing the building (as auxiliaries are seen to do on Trajan's Column).

All attempts at quantity survey agree that the completion of the stone curtain was proportionately a much greater task than anything else, and would have taken many more man days than the milecastles or turrets, or even the full-sized forts in a given section of the Wall. A rough quantity survey suggests that an 8km (5-mile) block of Broad Wall, structures and ditch will have taken 329,420 person days (the PhD quantity survey suggests a broadly similar total). The three 'legionary blocks' of Wall-miles 7–22 will therefore have required close to a million man days (988,260), even though this was less than half the length of the Turf Wall, which had a broadly similar requirement.

It seems unlikely, given all the other things there were to do in the province, that a single legion could have devoted much more than half of its 5,600 strength to Wall building. One recent estimate is 2,400, which is perhaps too generous: besides building the Wall, the legions had to supply the governor's official staff, organize the delivery of supplies and materials to the Wall zone, and (with their auxiliaries) maintain the military occupation of the province and deal with whatever resistance continued to emanate from the North. The available legionary building force would be soaked up by building the Turf Wall in a season, or by building three 8km (5-mile) blocks of stone Wall in a season. Three legionary contributions of 1,743 might have built the Turf Wall in 200 days, or three of 1,647 have built the Broad Wall in miles 7–22 in the same time – but they could not have done both in the same year. There seem to be two basic alternatives: either the builders from the legions worked piecemeal on all areas of the Wall simultaneously over several years, or they were concentrated on getting particular chunks of the Wall completed rapidly, one by one, prioritizing the sectors seen as most urgent.

The widely cited 'timetable' in Breeze and Dobson's *Hadrian's Wall* suggests a little building on the Broad Wall in 122, and the first main drive there in 123, and on the Turf Wall in 123–4, with the fort decision in 124 and the Narrow Wall decision in 126. In this model the building does not get going in earnest until 123, the first full season of work. This seems questionable, given the building traditions of the Roman army, and the likelihood, to which we shall return, that the Turf Wall was intended as a temporary expedient to get a Wall up and running rapidly in the most endangered western sector of the frontier.

Given a unit of work like this – a turf barrier 50km (31 miles) long – it would not be in the character of the Roman army to work on it piecemeal over a number of years. The army could build at an astonishing pace, timed by their commanders and with fierce competition between rival units or work gangs. The historian Josephus witnessed four legions surround the entire city of Jerusalem with a stone siege wall and build thirteen forts in only three days. He also describes how a detachment of infantry and cavalry built 10km (6 miles) of road in just four days. In his speech to the African army in 128, Hadrian praised the III Legion: 'Work that others have spread out over several days, you took only one day to finish. You have built a lengthy [stone] wall... in nearly as short a time as if it were built from turf...'

This culture of fanatical competitive labour to satisfy the vigour and excellence (*virtus*) of a unit and to win praise from the commander must be borne in mind when estimating how quickly the army might have built. On the other hand, any quantity survey will show that however quickly the army could build, the stone Wall will have taken longer than the Turf Wall, and the legions are unlikely to have had the resources to complete much more than 24 to 30km (15 to 20 miles) of the stone curtain in a given building season.

Dissipating the entire building strength of a given legion over a whole third of the Wall, as some who are doubtful about the 8km (5-mile) legionary lengths would have it, or having the three legions building along the whole length – Turf Wall and Broad Wall – simultaneously, would have delayed the completion of any given part for several seasons. The basic solution may have been to concentrate the available manpower of all three legions on the Turf Wall in season one, and on the Broad Wall – where we see the evidence for this in the three 8km (5-mile) legionary blocks from 7 to 22 – in season two. There is no indication that this triple block of Broad Wall and structures was not completed to full height (it has been argued that it might not have risen beyond the first few courses before the fort/Narrow Wall decision), and the view taken here is that it would have been completed in a single year.

This order of construction would also allow for the procurement and stockpiling of resources for the stone Wall during season one, and no doubt the reality was more complicated than the simple shift from Turf Wall to stone Wall suggested here. Whatever resources could be spared from the exercise of throwing up the Turf Wall in a single season will have been used to start work on the stone Wall, perhaps building a trial length from Newcastle to Milecastle 7, and the Broad foundation and milecastles and turrets immediately east of the Irthing. It is possible that much of the Turf Wall and these beginnings on the stone Wall could have been accomplished in a single year.

If a trial length of the Broad Wall had been built immediately west of Newcastle in the first season – say, from the bridge to Milecastle 7 (6km (3⅔ miles)), then 24km (15 miles) of curtain would need to be completed in the second season to take the Wall to the beginning of more elevated ground west of the Portgate (Milecastle 22), or 30km (20 miles) to the North Tyne. If any credence is given to the orders of magnitude suggested by the quantity survey, these allotments do broadly fit with the available manpower. If the first season had included the Turf Wall and the stone Wall up to Milecastle 7 (6km (3⅔ miles) of Broad Wall, three milecastles and five turrets), and allowing for a start on the Wall bridges, the total of legionary man days required would have been 1,045,721. If we allow a 200-day building season, each legion would have to supply 1,743 men. A shorter building season – say, 150 days with 2,324 from each legion – would allow time for the preliminary survey to have taken place in the same year.

With at least the bulk of the Turf Wall completed, work could go all out on the stone Wall in the second season. To complete the Broad Wall between Milecastle 7 and the Portgate (by Milecastle 22) and for the foundation-laying gangs and milecastle and turret specialists to move to carry out their Broad Wall work in the central sector, will have taken some 1,310,400 man days, or a contribution of 2,184 from each legion. The exactitude of the figures is immaterial – the important point is that they would not have been able to do significantly more than this in a single season.

The switch to Narrow Wall was decided on either at the end of this season, perhaps as the curtain builders managed to move into the 8km (5-mile) stretch 22–27, or early in the next. The following, third season would see the first main drive by the Twentieth Legion to construct Narrow Wall on Broad foundation in the central sector, probably working east from the Irthing and west from the North Tyne simultaneously. If the Twentieth Legion were really working alone, it would have needed two seasons, the third and fourth, to make serious progress towards completing the Wall in miles 27–48.

Thus seasons three and four saw the fitting into place of the last and central of the three big jigsaw pieces of the Wall curtain, effectively completing the

Wall as a barrier, although completion of parts of the curtain on the precipices of the high crags might have been deferred to a later stage – there is evidence from a number of points on the crags that vegetation and soil accumulated between the laying of the Broad Wall foundations and the eventual construction of the Narrow Wall. The building of the twenty-two turf-and-timber fortlets and forty-four stone towers along the Cumbrian coast must also be fitted into the schedule: but without a running barrier to build, this was a relatively minor task (an estimated 89,958 man days), perhaps achievable by 500 men in a season, and perhaps carried out in more than one stage.

While *Legio XX* devoted itself to the Wall in the central sector, the other two legions may have concentrated on the programme of fort building that was surely in full swing by now. My own quantity survey estimate for building the walls, gates and towers of a stone fort comes out remarkably close to the quantity survey PhD figure, at around 33,862 man days. A doubling of this figure to allow for internal buildings gives 67,724, so the initial seven stone forts would have required something like 474,068 man days, just about one and a half times the requirement for an 8km (5-mile) block of Broad Wall and structures. So these forts, and three to four Turf Wall forts (which would have taken a fraction of the time of the stone ones – say, 100,000 man days for all), could have been accomplished in 200-day seasons by around 1,435 men contributed from each of two legions over two years. In reality, of course, the basic structures would be rapidly supplied, but work completing internal buildings might have dragged on over several years.

The Vallum (where auxiliaries were involved in the work) was presumably constructed at the same time as the forts, requiring by my estimate 949,620 man days (similar in the PhD thesis, at 1,078,137). Spread across two 200-day seasons, this would require 2,374 men in a year, which might have been supplied by perhaps twelve auxiliary units – most likely those that were to take up residence in the new forts on the Wall.

What is proposed here is that the Wall, as an imperial building project, would have been raised as quickly as was humanly possible: the very speed with which it arose out of the landscape was part of the spectacle that was aimed at, and which was wholly characteristic of such exceptional Roman construction projects. An attempt at quantity survey suggests that the basic elements of the work could have been executed over four years. The programme suggested here does not drastically shorten the building time usually proposed, but it offers a different sequence of building, based on the idea that the Romans would wish to complete one piece of Wall wholesale at a time, prioritizing the parts most urgently needed, with work falling into four main phases or seasons: 1: the Turf Wall and some trial Broad Wall; 2: the completed 24km (15 miles) of Broad Wall; 3: Narrow Wall, forts and Vallum I; 4: Narrow Wall, forts and Vallum II.

In reality the work was probably not divided neatly and simply into building seasons: for the mortar work of the structures and forts a winter break would have been necessary, but the greatest part of the project, the Broad and Narrow curtain, made minimal or no use of mortar (as recently seen in the Narrow Wall at Wallsend), and this work could have been progressed in the winter months. Also, it is possible that work on the Narrow Wall curtain was suspended until after the forts had been completed, or even that the change to narrow gauge was not decided on until the forts were well advanced, which might have extended the fort/Narrow Wall phases over more than the two years illustrated here. Nevertheless, taking into account the proportion of the legions likely to be available for building, the other things the legions had to do, and the procurement of materials and supplies not included in the quantity survey calculations, the 200-day building seasons illustrated here probably do give a fair impression of what could be achieved year by year.

Can we attempt to anchor this sequence to actual dates? The following table sums up the possibilities:

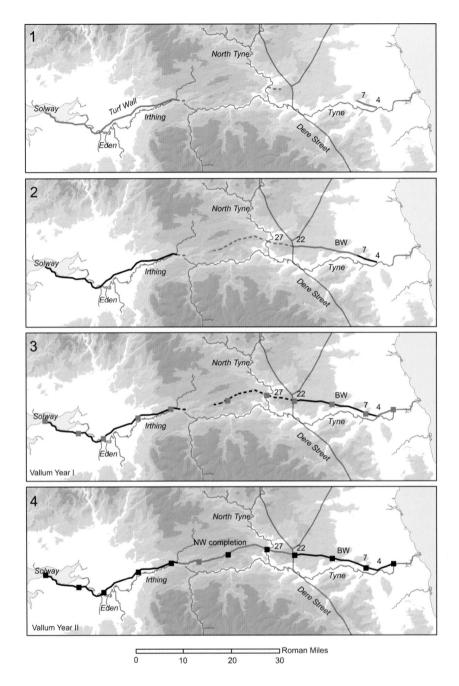

Fig. 2.14 Suggested stages of construction of Hadrian's Wall, year by year.

1. Year 1: Turf Wall is built, and perhaps some Broad Wall in miles 47. Some work begins on Broad Wall foundations and structures east of the Irthing and east of the North Tyne.

2. Year 2: Broad Wall and structures are begun and completed in miles 7–22, and a start made on the Broad Wall superstructure between 22 and 27. Some work on structures and Broad Wall foundation laying in the central sector west of the North Tyne.

3. Year 3: Work on Broad Wall between 22 and 27 and on the foundations and structures in the central sector is left incomplete as the decision to add forts to the Wall is made and the forts and the Vallum are begun.

4. Years 4–5 and possibly 6: The forts and Vallum are completed. The XX Legion completes the Narrow Wall and structures between the North Tyne and the Irthing, at least two years of work. Completion of the Narrow Wall may not have begun until the forts were completed, so the work illustrated in 4. may have taken place over some three years.

BUILDING PHASE	Option 1	Option 2	Option 3	Option 4	Option 5
Turf Wall and trial Broad Wall	120	120	121	122	122
Broad Wall miles 7–22	121	121	122	123	123
Fort/Narrow wall decision	—	122 **British war?**	—	—	124 **British war?**
Forts, Narrow Wall I	122	123	123	124	125
Forts, Narrow Wall II	123	124	124	125	126

Building Phase Options

At first sight a start as early as 120 (Option 1) seems impossible, if we accept the rapid pace of construction argued for here. If Wall building really began as early as *c.* 120, as has been argued, then the Turf Wall and much of the Broad Wall should have been completed long before Hadrian came to Britain. But if its building inscription is correctly restored, Turf Wall Milecastle 50 was probably being built under Platorius Nepos – no earlier than spring/summer 122 – suggesting that the Wall cannot have been begun much before. Some have argued that the Turf Wall was built from west to east, and that the Nepos inscription marks a late stage in its building – but this is to adhere to an implausibly long building programme for an earthen barrier that was probably built as one entity very rapidly by legionaries working simultaneously and in competition in their allotted 'blocks'.

However, it could be argued that a building programme of 120 and 121 was interrupted by warfare and the *expeditio Britannica*, and that the project was resumed in its modified form in 123, with the Nepos inscriptions at Milecastles 50TW and 38 marking the finishing touches being put to structures that had been begun much earlier (Option 2). Such an early start would mean that one of the three legions building the Turf Wall and Broad Wall in miles 7–22 would have to be the Ninth; there is no inscription of this legion from Hadrian's Wall, but then neither is there any inscription that links the replacement Sixth (or indeed any other) Legion to this stretch of Wall.

A start in 121, presumably ordered by Hadrian from a distance, is a possibility (Option 3). The idea of the Upper German palisade does seem to have been implemented before Hadrian's arrival there, so in principle such great fortification lines could be ordered from a distance and at least begun before the emperor got to the province. A Turf Wall mostly constructed in 121 might still have been fitted with inscriptions as late as summer 122, when Nepos arrived. The Broad Wall scheme would still have been current in the first months of Nepos' governorship, as implied by the most straightforward reading of the inscriptions from Milecastle 38. The completed Broad Wall in miles 4–22 might have been inspected by Hadrian, and the decision taken to narrow the gauge and add the forts while the emperor was present. The disadvantage of this model is that it takes no account of the war that may have occurred in 121–2. It is hard to believe that such a war would not have caused some disruption to the building programme, and it is precisely disruption that we see in the archaeological record. But if the Wall was not started until 121 there is not enough time to fit in both the completed Turf and Broad Wall before the proposed war.

The date most often favoured for the start of the project is 122 (Option 4), with Nepos and Hadrian present at the outset; this allows the inscriptions from Turf Wall Milecastle 50 and Milecastle 38 to be taken at face value, as indicating that the Turf Wall and the Broad Wall were building under Nepos. The 122 start also has the virtue of simplicity: the Wall would be conceived and built at the conclusion of the war placed in 121–2. In this scheme, however, the decision to narrow the Wall and add the forts can only have been taken after Hadrian had left the province late in 122. But there is no compelling reason why Hadrian had to be present on the ground to approve these modifications. To build the Wall in the first place, and the choice of its line, were equally momentous decisions. A rare use of the genitive case in the Hadrian/Nepos milecastle inscriptions, effectively describing the Wall as the personal work of the emperor, might suggest that its conception arose out of his visit to Britain.

What if the association of the *expeditio Britannica* with the emperor's visit of 122 is incorrect, and the war occurred at a later date? This would make a start in 121 possible, with Hadrian's visit the following year being in time to initiate the changes to the scheme (Option 3). If the Wall were begun in 122, a war starting in 123–4 would have been at exactly the right time to disrupt the original plan and trigger the addition of forts to the Wall (Option 5). It is even possible that *Legio VI Victrix* was brought across to Britain in 123–4 rather than with Platorius Nepos, as is usually assumed. The Ninth legion might have been in Britain up until 124, and have participated in the building of the Turf and Broad Walls in building phases I and II. Such a scheme allows the Nepos building inscriptions to be accepted at face value. But such a dating for the Hadrianic war loses the neat link with the emperor's visit and the term *expeditio*, which implies an imperial presence – nevertheless it is a possibility for all that.

In conclusion, it is possible to establish that the start date for the Wall must have occurred within a narrow frame of years, 120–2, but within that there is uncertainty, and although we can estimate how many years it would have taken to build the Wall, the actual programme might have been interrupted by a war whose date is itself unclear. The simplest solution is for Hadrian's visit and the *expeditio Britannica* to have occurred in 121–2, and to have been followed by the building of the Wall (Option 4) – but all the other possibilities should be borne in mind, and the question must remain open until more evidence comes to light.

The Building of the Wall in Perspective

The completion of the Wall was commemorated on a dedicatory inscription, probably on a monument at the very east end of the Wall where it ran out into the waters of the Tyne at Wallsend. The surviving pieces were found in 1782, reused in the Saxon church of Jarrow, just 3km (2 miles) from Wallsend. The text, though highly fragmentary and maybe restored after Hadrian's time, is perhaps based on a speech that Hadrian himself gave to the army in Britain. Parts can be reconstructed along these lines:

> Hadrian, son of all the deified emperors, was told by the Gods that it was necessary to keep the empire within its limits... the barbarians were scattered and the province of Britain recovered... he added a Wall between either shore of the Ocean... built by the army of the province...

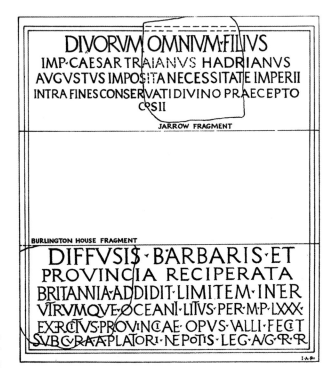

Fig. 2.15 I. A. Richmond's conjectural restoration of the inscription from a Hadrianic memorial at the eastern end of the Wall, probably at Wallsend. SOCIETY OF ANTIQUARIES OF NEWCASTLE UPON TYNE

This supports the idea that the *expeditio Britannica* coincided with Hadrian's visit to Britain in 122 and was immediately followed by the building of the Wall, and tends to confirm the difficult and war-afflicted circumstances in which the Wall was planned.

The Wall was an imperial building project, personally ordered by, and closely associated with the emperor. There can be no doubt that having once decided on the Wall, its builders would want it to be progressed urgently. On the most urgent timetable possible, detachments from all three legions might have built the Turf Wall in the west and a trial section in the east in season one, and completed most of the Broad Wall in the remaining eastern sector in the second. The approach was perhaps changed in the third season, with one legion devoted to the less urgent curtain in the central sector and the others to the forts.

The general sense of urgency helps explain the odd difference of building materials – turf in the west, stone in the east – and also the very unusual and unparalleled design of the Broad Wall itself, with its great width but minimal use of mortar; this was perhaps an invention to allow rapid all-year building with the immediately available materials, but which led to in-built structural instability. Urgency also explains the absence of forts at the outset, whether through oversight or deferment. Much is explained if we see these odd mixes of materials, innovations and disjunctures as stages of progression towards the intended fulfilment of ideal overall plans.

But however neat and uniform the finished product envisaged by the designers, the Romans realized they could not do it all at once – the scale of the task meant it could only be accomplished over a period of years. On the other hand, the most urgently required lengths of frontier Wall had to be up and running as quickly as possible. Those parts of the Wall in lowland areas, especially in the west, were required to function immediately. So the builders decided to prioritize, introducing temporary stopgaps and deferring some elements to a later stage.

The perplexing variation in building material offered by the Turf Wall still troubles archaeologists. Nobody now believes the old geological explanation – shortage of freestone quarries and limestone (to make mortar) west of the Red Rock fault – the critical point being that the Romans did manage to build the Wall here in stone, a generation later. But the relative difficulty in winning stone *did* mean that it would take longer, and more manpower, to build a stone Wall than it would take in the east. The most likely explanation is that the Turf Wall was, in the words of a recent writer, 'a quick fix'. In other words, the ideal plan called for a stone wall here, just like that in the east, but the urgency of having a functioning Wall in the west dictated the use of a temporary stopgap, which could be replaced in stone when convenient.

One objection to this is that it makes the Wall seem defensive and reactive: if there was an immediate threat from the north-west, would the Roman army not have marched north to defeat it? But this is to assume that the Romans were unstoppable and to forget the attested military setbacks of the period: it is equally possible that the Roman army did not have the leeway to launch an aggressive campaign instead of protecting the province by building the Turf Wall.

The use of a temporary structure destined to be superseded by a fully realized building project was a practice ingrained in the Roman military mind. There is a good example in Britain, in the legionary fortress of Inchtuthil, where a timber headquarters building (itself an ambitious and elaborate structure) was built first, but carefully designed to fit within the courtyard of an intended larger stone-built successor. Once the latter had been built, Russian doll-like, around it, the small temporary headquarters would be demolished. On the Turf Wall it was probably calculated that the turrets could be built in stone at the outset, as relatively simple, quick-to-build structures that could easily be incorporated into the replacement stone Wall when it came. As we have seen, the Turf Wall could have been erected in a single year. A stone wall could not have been built so rapidly.

The 'fort decision', which radically altered an original plan in which no forts on the actual barrier had been envisaged, was probably made after only two seasons of building. It has been suggested that the forts, and the Vallum that came with them, should be seen as a delayed implementation of an intention that was there from the very beginning. The Wall without forts would indeed have had grave functional difficulties. In the west and the central sector, the pre-existing forts on the Stanegate could support the fortless Wall, which generally had good visual communication with the Stanegate line, but east of Corbridge there were no pre-existing forts on the north side of the Tyne, which would have cut the Wall off from the army to the south, and in miles 49–58 the Irthing severs the Wall from the Stanegate. There is not a trace of archaeological evidence that the Broad Wall or the Turf Wall anticipated yet-to-be fort sites, and it is hard to believe that if forts had been intended from the beginning, their sites would not have been chosen and incorporated into an overall design, even if actual construction was deferred.

It seems significant that the regular spacing of the forts as finally sited and built does not relate to the end of the Broad Wall at the bridge at Newcastle, but rather falls in with Wallsend, at the end of the Narrow Wall eastern extension. This suggests that the sites of the forts were chosen at the same time as the Narrow Wall decision. Although it could be argued that this extension was itself a delayed implementation of an original intention, this would not be supported by it apparently having its own system of milecastle spacing, which does not integrate with that west of Newcastle. It seems most likely on balance that the original designers made the assumption that the Wall could be supported by the existing fort network (in the east Corbridge, and a putative fort at Gateshead, perhaps supplemented by an intended but never built fort in between), but that after only two years of building the need for forts on the line itself was felt.

The first forts to be built, and their relationship to the Wall and Vallum, betray something of an ideal design in the minds of those modifying the original vision for the Wall. The initial series of forts on the stone Wall – and Birdoswald, west of the Irthing – were built to a highly idealized architectural plan, unique in the Roman Empire. The placing of half of the fort and three out of four of the principal gates on the north side of the Wall seems to have been to allow the rapid deployment of troops to engage an enemy north of the Wall: but the apparent defensive weakness of having so many openings – six portals in total – on the north side was compensated for by making the gate portals proportionally squatter than they would normally have been, and indeed were, in milecastles.

The placing of the side gates on the north side of the Wall meant that those travelling east–west behind the Wall, whether for routine business or military reinforcement, could not enter there, so extra single portal gates were provided south of the Wall, showing that a lateral road or 'Military Way' behind the Wall was planned. These minor side gates (*portae quintanae*), themselves substantial portals surmounted by towers, are a unique invention in the planning of Roman forts and fortresses. The envisaged road was protected and enclosed by the Vallum, which formed a southern boundary to the corridor along which troops moved laterally to whatever fort needed to respond to a threat from the north.

So we have a package where the whole is greater than the parts, an ideal conception of a defensive Wall and its garrisons, which looks like a product of the study or the drawing office, a theoretical approach to design clearly imposed from outside the normal military ambit by an intellectual – an emperor, say, with ambitions to be an architectural and military theorist? It is attractive to detect the hand of the emperor himself in the idealized design that introduced the modifications, but he need not have been present in person. High-powered architects sent out by the emperor may have worked with the military on the ground, and the emperor himself would at the very least have been consulted.

The principle of stopgap and delayed implementation may also explain why the distinctive projecting style of Wall fort is not found on the Turf Wall (except at Birdoswald). As with the Turf barrier itself, speed may have been the uppermost consideration. The forts were presumably rapidly built with the Vallum and the stone forts further east in 124–5 (on the 122 start model), or even earlier; they were of turf and timber, and not built to project, but were attached to the rear of the barrier or, in the case of Castlesteads, built detached from the Wall. Yet the topography near Castlesteads, in the vicinity of Turret 56A, would easily allow a projecting fort on the Wall itself. It is hard to believe that the ideal projecting fort arrangement was not intended for the whole length of the Wall; but in the Turf Wall sector its implementation may have been deferred until such time as the Wall was built in stone. The priority for now was to get a set of forts rapidly up and running with the new Turf barrier.

We can therefore see how the original design for a fortless Wall evolved into an ideal plan for an entirely stone Wall with projecting forts and Vallum, but also that the Romans knew that they would have to live with interim arrangements while they worked towards the completion of the ideal plan. This indicates two things. First, there must have been real military requirements driving the urgency about getting an interim version of the Wall to function. We have seen that work on the Wall curtain prioritized the lowland areas to east and west, more vulnerable to raids and penetration, and the intention was probably to get the west blocked off by the Turf Wall in the first season (50km/31 miles), and the stone Wall in the east in the second. When it came to the addition of the forts, this was prioritized in areas (the east, and Birdoswald) where there were no pre-existing support forts in easy communication with the Wall; and for speed, the forts in the Turf Wall sector were built in turf. Second, the army could not roll out the idealized version of Hadrian's Wall just as it wished, according to a rigid step-by-step building programme, because it was hindered by shortage of manpower, and presumably by active threats.

On the spot, work often began to a very high standard, but the quality of the masonry dropped away as the structures rose above the first few courses – this has been noted especially at certain fort and milecastle gates. Rather than indicating a general abandonment and resumption of work (a 'dislocation'), we see again an anxiety to speed up the process, and a move away from perfectionism once the emperor and his governor were off the scene.

If this is accepted, it leads to an important question: why was the Wall not eventually completed either to its original specifications (Broad Wall at 10RF), or to the modified scheme of a Wall with projecting forts and Vallum? The answer is probably twofold: over the life of the extended building programme, many of the bright ideas of the study proved to be useless and were quietly dropped, like projecting forts with three double-portalled gates on the north side of the Wall. The later forts of Great Chesters and Carrawburgh were built entirely behind the curtain. At the projecting fort of Chesters all but one of the six portals north of the curtain were eventually blocked up. The 3m (10ft) wide Broad Wall perhaps simply did not work on the slopes of the central sector; here a Narrow Wall proved structurally best.

Secondly, military difficulties meant that manpower and resources remained scarce. The intended conversion of the Turf Wall in stone surely took longer than originally intended. Work did begin on this under Hadrian, although probably not until late in his reign. This could point to continuing warfare and difficulties following the effective completion of the Wall by about 126. One could simply put it down to lack of imperial interest, but the presence of Julius Severus, a formidable general who governed Britain in the early 130s, suggests a backdrop of continuing warfare and close interest in events on the British frontier. In the integrated design of Wall, projecting forts and Vallum, we have a vision of the ideally conceived end product that Hadrian and his advisers dreamt of. The Wall as actually built and used for three centuries did not quite live up to the dream, for it had to serve a practical purpose, and was built and maintained by an army facing acute difficulties. ✿

Chapter 3

HADRIAN'S WALL AND THE ANTONINE WALL: AD122–60

The two walls: piecing together the evidence for a narrative of events

Hadrian's Wall under Hadrian

THE BASIC 'PACKAGE' OF THE WALL AS described in the introduction and long known to archaeologists was all implemented and operated under Hadrian: the Wall curtain, the obstacles (where completed) and frontal ditch, milecastles, turrets, garrison forts and rearward Vallum. There is some uncertainty, as we shall see, about the nature of the communication road that linked the Wall installations together at this early stage – the visible 'Military Way' is seemingly later.

From inscriptions we know of just two or three of the military units stationed on the Wall in the 120s and 130s. These include the *ala Augusta*, recorded at Chesters, and (probably) *cohors I Tungrorum* at Housesteads. The presence of these units, along with the Hadrianic plans of forts where they can be reconstructed, does suggest that the idea was for each fort on the Wall to accommodate a single and complete auxiliary unit. These were originally some twelve in number. A military zone was formed by the Vallum to the south. Undug causeways with non-defensive, monumental arched gates closing to the south opposite each fort (and presumably where the main roads, such as Dere Street, reached the Wall) were intended to be the only means of crossing the Vallum. The limited excavation that has taken place on the Vallum suggests that there were no original causeways across the Vallum ditch at milecastles. There were apparently gaps in the north Vallum mound to allow access to the Vallum from milecastles, but the Vallum ditch and south mound were, as far as we know, continuous and uninterrupted.

In other words, in Hadrianic times arrivals from the south – whether reinforcing army units, expeditionary forces directed north of the Wall, civilian traders or individuals – would only have been able to enter the Wall zone at one or more of fifteen or so carefully controlled points. The Wall as thus 'ideally' arranged has the appearance of a sealed corridor within which the twelve auxiliary units were intended to conduct whatever surveillance or defensive operations as were envisaged necessary. Lateral movement from forts along the Wall corridor to the openings through the Wall provided by milecastle gates – in front of which there is some evidence for primary causeways across the Wall ditch – is implied.

We have no historical information whatsoever about events in Britain following the completion of the Wall while Hadrian still lived. By 134 the Governor Severus had been transferred to the East to deal with the Jewish revolt (132–5), a great crisis for the empire, which might have drained military resources from Britain, helping to explain why only a limited part of the Turf Wall had been replaced in stone by the time of Hadrian's death in 138. The replacement of the Turf Wall was started at the Irthing, working westwards, and for the first two miles (49 and 50) the stone replacement Wall (to narrow gauge, 2.3m (7ft 6in) wide) was built on an entirely different line, a short distance to the north, laid out from the north corners of Birdoswald Fort so that the fort no longer projected. West of Milecastle 51 the replacement stone curtain is on the same line

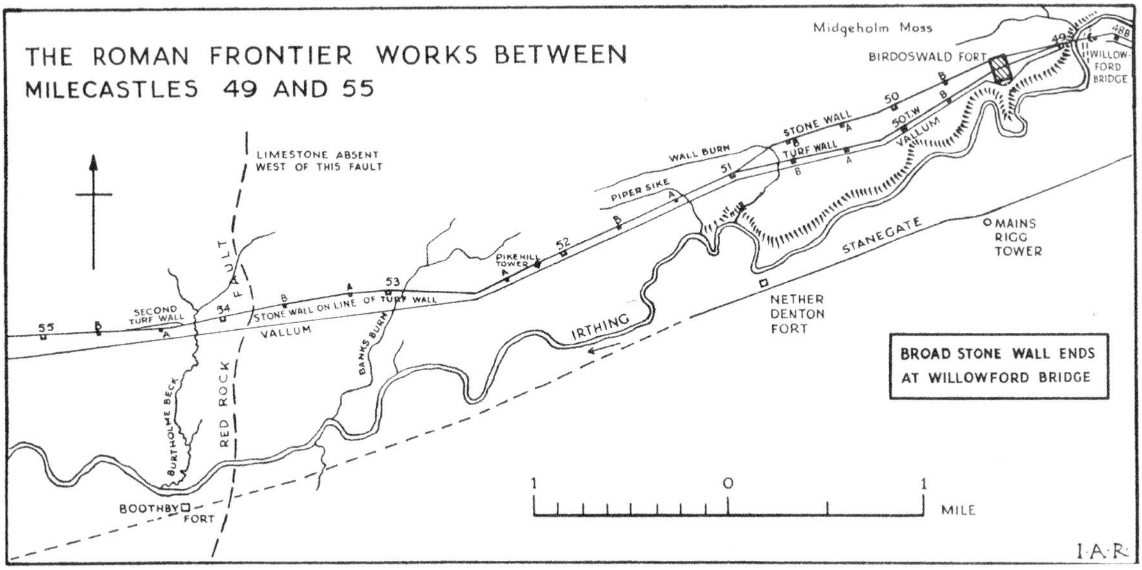
THE ROMAN FRONTIER WORKS BETWEEN MILECASTLES 49 AND 55
Midgeholm Moss
BIRDOSWALD FORT
WILLOWFORD BRIDGE
LIMESTONE ABSENT WEST OF THIS FAULT
STONE WALL
TURF WALL
WALL BURN
PIPER SIKE
VALLUM
STANEGATE
MAINS RIGG TOWER
PIKEHILL TOWER
FAULT
SECOND TURF WALL
STONE WALL ON LINE OF TURF WALL
BANKS BURN
IRTHING
NETHER DENTON FORT
BROAD STONE WALL ENDS AT WILLOWFORD BRIDGE
BURTHOLME BECK
RED ROCK
BOOTHBY FORT
MILE
I.A.R.

Fig. 3.1 The Turf Wall and the replacement stone Wall west of the Irthing. Between Milecastles 49 and 51 the turf and stone Walls run on different alignments. Excavations in the 1930s established that the replacement in stone went at least as far as Milecastle 53 in Hadrian's reign.

as the Turf Wall, though exactly how far it was carried before Hadrian's death is unclear – it may only have been as far as the Burtholme Beck (Mile 53).

The Antonine Occupation of Scotland

Hadrian's death in 138 was immediately followed by a change in frontier policy in Britain. Under his successor, Antoninus Pius (138–61), the army advanced once more into Scotland, planting a network of forts and roads in the Scottish lowlands and building a new frontier Wall on the 60km (37-mile) wide isthmus between the Forth and the Clyde, 120km (75 miles) north of Hadrian's Wall. The new northern barrier was built of turf, not stone. According to a reliable passage in the *Scriptores Historiae Augustae*: 'Antoninus waged many wars, using his legates. Lollius Urbicus, a legate, conquered the Britons for him, and when he had driven the barbarians off, built another wall, of turf.'

The eastern route of advance was Dere Street, leading north from Corbridge towards the great first-century military base at Newstead, on the Tweed, re-established as a nodal point in the reoccupation of southern Scotland. On the west side the two main advance routes via Annandale and Nithsdale were studded with forts and large numbers of fortlets for small detachments.

The explanation for this reversal of Hadrian's policy must lie in the opportunity provided by his death. Suddenly Antoninus and his military advisers were free to abandon Hadrian's scheme and try something new. But why should they do this? One school of thought suggests that the primary motive was to secure a quick, easy and spectacular military victory for Antoninus, an aged and unlikely successor to Hadrian, with none of the military background so valued in Roman emperors (Hadrian may well have selected him as a place holder for the future Emperor Marcus Aurelius, too young to succeed in 138). A triumph and territorial expansion in Britain would cement his political position in Rome and endear him to the army. Antoninus accepted the title *Imperator* for the second time in the summer of 142, and this can have done no harm to his position or reputation.

However, it seems inconceivable that this was the sole reason for the invasion of Scotland. The Greek writer Pausanias has a passage that suggests that a pro-Roman people north of Hadrian's Wall was attacked, late in Hadrian's reign or at the accession of Pius:

Antoninus Pius never willingly made war; but when the Moors took up arms against Rome he drove them from the whole of their territory. Also in Britain, he appropriated most of the territory of the Brigantes, because they too had begun a war, invading the *Genunian* region, the inhabitants of which were subjects of the Romans.'

Even if the tribal name *Genunia* has been, as seems likely, erroneously introduced from another part of the Roman Empire, the context of the passage – a list of the wars in the reign of non-belligerent Emperor Antoninus Pius – identifies the event firmly with the Antonine advance into Scotland. Making sense of the passage in this way depends on 'Brigantes' being used as a general term for upland northern Britons, rather than a specific reference to the tribe of the Brigantes who had been incorporated into the province (with their *civitas* capital at Aldbrough, North Yorkshire).

The people of south-east Scotland, although far north of Hadrian's Wall, may have been in a treaty relationship with Rome. At least some of their fertile coastal plain may have been enclosed within the Devil's Causeway part of the 'Stanegate frontier' as recently as the eve of the building of Hadrian's Wall. On the other hand, we have already discussed the various indications that Hadrian's Wall, as operated under Hadrian, was directed towards a perceived threat from south-west Scotland. Attacks on the Roman allies in the east from the south-west are likely to have provoked the Roman intervention. This interpretation is borne out by the map of Roman military bases in Antonine Scotland – there is a disproportionate density of military occupation in the valleys of the south-west, while the military occupation of

the south-east was much lighter, and at the site of Inveresk near Edinburgh inscriptions record the presence of the provincial procurator, a civil official perhaps charged with the organization of the settled south-east into a new part of the province.

Raids may also have come from peoples beyond the Forth–Clyde isthmus, emergent as a hostile grouping in response to Hadrian's Wall. Here, a group of stone towers ('brochs'), occupied in this period by warrior families who acquired Roman material in the late first and earlier second centuries, may indicate the emergence of a response to Hadrian's Wall. Several of these structures have evidence of violent destruction, possibly wrought during the Antonine invasion of Scotland around 140 (the broch at Leckie seems to have been assaulted by Roman artillery), and it is hard to believe that they would have remained in use where they are, immediately north of the new Antonine frontier wall. Were these the *barbaris summotis* – 'barbarians driven off' – of the literary source?

Julius Severus will have dealt with troubles north of the Wall during his tenure in the early 130s, and when he was moved to Judaea to deal with the rebellion there, which ended in 136, one of the officers serving under him was Lollius Urbicus, who as governor of Britain in 139–42 would lead the Antonine advance into Scotland. They would have had ample opportunity to discuss the situation in Britain, and probably agreed on the conclusion that Hadrian's Wall had been built too far south for effective control of lowland Scotland and the area beyond the Forth–Clyde line. Perhaps they calculated that a shorter wall further north would ultimately lead to a saving in troops required to man the frontier. While Hadrian lived they could not openly recommend that his Wall be abandoned and direct control be asserted in southern Scotland.

Hadrian's death changed everything: in a way commonly attested on the imperial frontiers, barbarians north of the Wall might have taken the opportunity of uncertainty and interregnum to attack both the province and their hated pro-Roman neighbours, while a Roman military policy that could only be whispered in secret under Hadrian could now be implemented. The prestige that would accrue to Antoninus Pius helped ensure the approval of the scheme.

Hadrian's Wall was not dismantled or completely deserted, which proved to have been a wise precaution when it was hurriedly recommissioned sixteen years later. At some stage much of the Vallum was slighted, with gaps in the mounds and crossings inserted at every 41m (45yd), and the Antonine advance seems the only plausible occasion for this to have happened. The milecastle gates are said to have been removed at this time – this is certainly true in some cases. It looks, therefore, as if the Vallum was symbolically breached and Hadrian's Wall thrown open to movement. The Wall forts may have been held on a care-and-maintenance basis: there are some legionary inscriptions that may date from this time. Archaeologically it is difficult to detect a break in occupation in the Wall forts, but occupation must have been on a vastly reduced scale. Certain units (the Hamians from Carvoran, the Tungrians from Housesteads) were definitely transferred to the Antonine Wall. The network of forts in the Pennines south of Hadrian's Wall was also largely abandoned.

The new Wall in Scotland was made of turf, and almost all forts in Antonine Scotland were of turf and timber construction. As with the Turf Wall of Hadrian, this probably signifies anxiety for rapid completion, rather than a feeling that occupation was to be short-lived. This is especially the case given that two of the earliest forts built on the Antonine Wall were of stone. One of these, Balmuildy, had stone wing walls, obviously in the expectation that the frontier Wall itself would be of stone. In all probability Lollius Urbicus fully intended the new conquest to be permanent, and that the Antonine Wall should one day wholly supersede Hadrian's Wall, and no doubt eventually be converted into stone.

Yet the intention was not the conquest of the whole island. No legionary fortress was advanced into Scotland, as we should expect if total conquest was the aim. The operation appears more an adjustment of the frontier line in Britain (like the advance in Germany carried out a few years later, around AD159). Two inscriptions from Scotland suggest that during the invasion the three British legions were reinforced with detachments from the legions of Upper Germany, but the British garrison was not permanently enlarged and was now spread dangerously thinly. This might account for the nervousness apparent in the concern to get the Antonine Wall built as rapidly as possible using the most economic materials, and in the retention of the basic structure of Hadrian's Wall while the success of the replacement was assessed. As it turned out, such caution was justified, for after the rapid and spectacular victory of 142 the conquest was soon to unravel.

The Antonine Wall

The great interest of the Antonine Wall is that its first design seems to have replicated the arrangements on Hadrian's Wall as completed. At first there were only six large forts, spaced at 12km (7.5-mile) intervals, like those on Hadrian's Wall. These 'primary' forts are structurally earlier than the curtain. The materials utilized were different from those on Hadrian's Wall, of course: although two of the primary forts, Balmuildy and Castlecary, were built in stone (and the former in expectation of a stone frontier wall), the others, like the Wall itself, were built of turves, with only their principal buildings of stone.

Between the primary forts, at intervals of roughly one Roman mile, there were fortlets allowing access through the Wall itself, the equivalent to the milecastles of Hadrian's Wall. Only a few have actually been found, and the regularity of the series is not yet proven. Where investigated, these fortlets have always proved to be earlier than, or contemporary with, the Wall curtain.

The structural evidence suggests that it must have been early in the building programme, even before much of the turf rampart itself had been completed, that a series of forts, mostly smaller than those

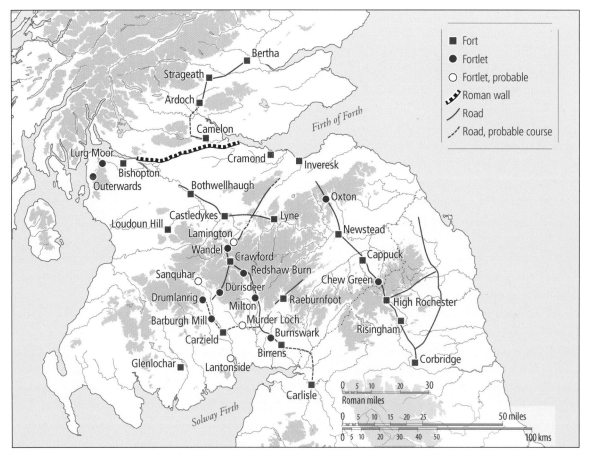

Fig. 3.2 Sites in Scotland occupied under Antoninus Pius (around 142–58), with the Antonine Wall on the Forth–Clyde isthmus. FRONTIERS OF THE ROMAN EMPIRE CULTURE 2000 PROJECT/D. J. BREEZE

classified as 'primary', was built on the line of the Wall, in two cases superseding or incorporating one of the fortlets. At the fort of Duntocher, first a free-standing fortlet was built with squared northern corners ready to receive the Antonine Wall; then a small fort was constructed, which incorporated the fortlet; and finally the Antonine Wall was brought up to incorporate the fort.

Forts considered to be 'secondary' were built so early in the construction sequence that there is a school of thought that maintains that all these struc-tures – both 'primary' and 'secondary' forts, and fortlets – were planned from the outset, although it is difficult to explain away the evidence for fortlets being superseded at Duntocher and at Croy Hill,

where a fort and fortlet lie closely adjacent to one another. Only the discovery of more fortlets (nine are known to date in the 60km (37-mile) length of the Wall) will resolve the question of whether they originally fell into a regularly spaced series, or were planned to be interspersed among the totality of forts, large and small.

Whatever the original intention, in its completed state the Antonine Wall had an appearance quite different from Hadrian's Wall: in its 60km (37-mile) length there were some nineteen forts, spaced at intervals of about 3km (2 miles), in contrast to the fifteen or so forts eventually built on Hadrian's Wall, spaced at 11km (7-mile) intervals along a barrier twice as long. No Vallum was built on the Antonine Wall:

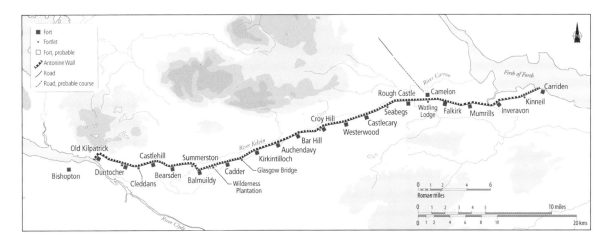

Fig. 3.3 The Antonine Wall in its completed state. FRONTIERS OF THE ROMAN EMPIRE CULTURE 2000 PROJECT/D. J. BREEZE

instead, a defended annexe, attached to most forts, however small, is a characteristic feature.

The building of the Antonine Wall itself is firmly dated archaeologically by two inscriptions from Balmuildy naming Lollius Urbicus. The curtain itself was built on a cobble foundation throughout, the width of the base varying between 4.30 and 4.90m (14 and 16ft), with the superstructure built of laid turves in the west, and more use of clay in the east. Beyond a berm of about 6–9m (20–30ft) it possessed a formidable ditch on its northern side, of varying dimensions but generally larger – about 12m (40ft) wide by 3.60m (12ft) deep – in the central sector of the Wall than east of Falkirk and west of Kirkintilloch, where it is 7–9m (23–30ft) wide. In the eastern sector additional defensive features in the form of obstacles on the berm between Wall and ditch, like those in the same position on Hadrian's Wall, have been discovered.

On the map, the Antonine Wall has a strikingly different appearance from Hadrian's Wall in being much more closely adapted to topography: the Scottish Wall weaves across the landscape, employing a number of re-entrants and sudden turns in areas where Hadrian's Wall might have cut an arbitrary straight line. The basic explanation for this is that the builders of the Antonine Wall chose the fort and fortlet sites first, and filled in the Wall in between, whereas on much of Hadrian's Wall the surveyed

line of the Wall came first (in lowland areas often dead straight), and the installations were fitted on to that line. This might show a keener appreciation by the builders of the Antonine Wall for the visual and topographic qualities of individual fort and fortlet sites, although much the same approach was taken in the hilly central sector of Hadrian's Wall.

A few auxiliary units are attested at the larger, primary forts, although one, Castlecary, is too small to accommodate the whole of either of the thousand-strong units attested there (one being *cohors I Tungrorum*, probably moved up from Housesteads on Hadrian's Wall). At Bar Hill, one of the larger forts, probably primary, we find the Syrian archers who had so recently been building at Carvoran.

Of the secondary forts, or at least those whose dimensions are known, only three out of eight can possibly have been large enough to hold an entire unit: Cadder (1.10ha/2.7 acres), Auchendavy (about 1.10ha/2.7 acres) and Castlehill (about 1ha/2.5 acres). At Castlehill the whole of what is known at other times to have been a part-cavalry unit, *cohors IV Gallorum*, attested at the site, could not have fitted into the fort. Was the cavalry elsewhere on the Antonine Wall? At 1.35ha (3.3 acres) Bearsden might have been intended for a complete unit, but before completion it was subdivided to form a small fort/annexe combination.

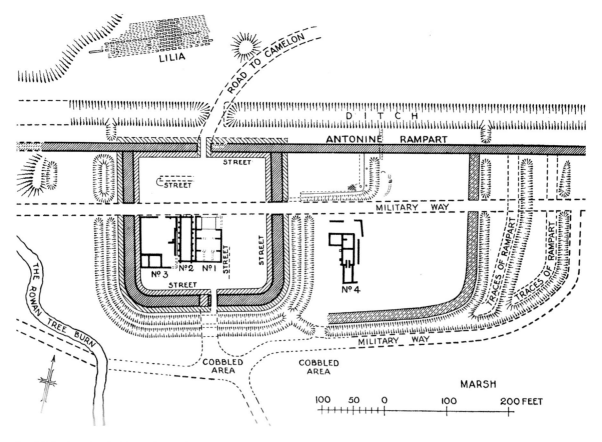

Fig. 3.4 The Antonine Wall fort of Rough Castle. This is a small fort held by a detachment of a whole unit. The prominent annexe is typical of the Antonine Wall forts.

The remaining forts can only have held detachments: at Rough Castle (0.50ha/1.2 acres) part of *cohors VI Nerviorum* was commanded by a legionary centurion. The presence of a legionary centurion at Westerwood (0.80ha/2 acres) implies a similar situation. Croy Hill was only 0.60ha (1.5 acres) in size, Duntocher only 0.50ha (1.2 acres). The forts at Croy Hill and Auchendavy have produced legionary altars and tombstones in sufficient quantity to suggest that they were garrisoned by legionary detachments. At other forts, such as Rough Castle and Westerwood, legionary centurions commanded detachments from auxiliary units.

Most of the nineteen forts of the Antonine Wall therefore contained incomplete units: units may have been split between several forts, or may have left parts behind in the hinterland, or even in the Hadrian's

Wall area. There were nineteen forts compared to twelve on Hadrian's Wall, but the number of troops was not greater by that ratio. A very close spacing of modestly sized troop concentrations was achieved by splitting auxiliary units and bringing in some small legionary detachments. One recent estimate gives 4,000–5,000 troops on the Antonine Wall forts, which compares to perhaps 7,000 for the original twelve forts of Hadrian's Wall.

At least some of the milefortlets went out of use after a time. They may simply have become defended watchtower enclosures, or points of access to the Wall top. No equivalents of the turrets of Hadrian's Wall have yet been discovered. Timber towers (turret equivalents) incorporated into the superstructure of the Antonine Wall could have escaped detection, but perhaps the 3km (2-mile) fort spacing, interspersed with fortlets, was such a close surveillance screen that towers in the rampart were not thought to be necessary when it was supplied to join up the installations. Certain smaller installations are known to have been attached to the rear of the Antonine Wall. These include three irregularly spaced enclosures known near Wilderness Plantation Fortlet, not part of any known regular series.

Known for longer are three pairs of 'expansions', or turf projections from the rear of the Wall, 5–6m sq (6–7yd sq), founded on a cobbled base. Pairs lie to either side of Rough Castle, and a further pair west of Croy Hill. Perhaps such occasional observation or beacon platforms compensated for the lack of a regular tower series, filling in gaps in the observation chain formed by the forts and fortlets.

A substantial road – the 'Military Way' – was built, from the beginning, to run from fort to fort behind the Wall. The final element in the Wall system was a series of outpost forts. The old first-century road, running north-east from near Falkirk to pass between the Highland fringe and the fertile Strathearn and the Fife peninsula, was held again in the Antonine occupation and led to outpost forts at Camelon, Ardoch, Strageath and Bertha, on the Tay.

The Abandonment of Antonine Scotland

The Antonine Wall was once thought to have been occupied down to the 180s or even later, but a breakthrough study of the samian pottery from Scotland in 1972 showed that the Antonine Wall and other forts in Scotland north of Newstead cannot have been occupied after the mid-160s, indicating a very short occupation indeed. Conversely, the post-160 samian types that were absent from northern Scotland occurred on both Hadrian's Wall and the forts to its south, showing that by the 160s the southern Wall, and the network of forts behind it, had been reoccupied.

Until recently archaeologists divided the occupation of the Antonine Wall into two periods ('Antonine I' and 'Antonine II'), separated by a brief abandonment.

'Antonine I' and 'Antonine II' periods were found in influential early twentieth-century excavations at two *southern* Scottish forts, Newstead and Birrens, and archaeologists looked for, and believed they had found, a similar sequence on the Antonine Wall. The army was thought to have returned south around 155 to put down a revolt among the Brigantes in the area of the Pennines, and then returned to reoccupy the Antonine Wall for a brief second period (158–63). But the 'Brigantian revolt' is a modern invention, concocted to explain an inscription found in the River Tyne in 1900, interpreted as recording the arrival of reinforcements from Germany for the three British legions under the Governor Julius Verus, around 155–8.

At the time, this was linked to the statement in Pausanias that Antoninus Pius had 'appropriated most of the territory of the Brigantes, because they too had begun a war...'. But as we have seen, Pausanias was almost certainly referring to the invasion of Scotland in AD139–42; the passage has no relevance for the 150s. A re-examination of the evidence has shown that the old arguments for two, or even three periods of occupation on the Antonine Wall do not stand up to scrutiny, and it is now generally accepted that the northern Wall was held for a brief single period. The legionary detachments recorded in 155–8 were in fact arriving (or leaving, we are not certain which) in connection with the decision to abandon Scotland and reoccupy Hadrian's Wall. The moment of that decision is dated by an inscription from mile 8 or 9 of Hadrian's Wall, which records that the Wall or one of its minor structures (but definitely not a fort) was being rebuilt in 158 (the date comes from the names of the consuls for that year).

It is possible that a revolt in Britain triggered the decision to start rebuilding Hadrian's Wall, but there is no evidence for a revolt in the Pennines. We do, however, find evidence for a revolt around 155–8 within the area *north* of Hadrian's Wall invaded by Lollius Urbicus, and in particular in that most intractable area of south-west Scotland. After having

Fig. 3.5
Detachments from
the three British
legions recorded
on an inscription
at Newcastle in
the period 155–8,
either leaving for,
or returning from
Germany. These
troop movements
are connected
with the decision
to abandon the
Antonine Wall and
recommission
Hadrian's Wall.
SOCIETY OF ANTIQUARIES
OF NEWCASTLE UPON
TYNE AND GREAT NORTH
MUSEUM: HANCOCK

been destroyed by fire, the fort of Birrens was rebuilt in the year 158. Other forts concentrated in south-west Scotland seem to have been enlarged or altered at this time. Of course, the upland peoples of Britain south of the Tyne–Solway isthmus may have joined in such an uprising.

The rebuilding of Hadrian's Wall, definitely taking place in 158, suggests that there had been a major reappraisal, and that it had been decided to end the Antonine adventure in Scotland. The reason was not simply revolt and resistance in southern Scotland, although this was a more significant factor in Roman thinking than has been credited in recent times, when the Roman army has been thought of as an invincible force whose movements were little affected by the actions of the natives. But trouble was brewing on the German frontier, and increasing calls for troop transfers from Britain in the 150s may have weakened the Roman hold on Scotland. The detachments from the British legions recorded at Newcastle in 155–8 were returning from, or leaving for Germany, where, in about 159, in a great precautionary and

preclusive move, the last unenclosed frontier areas of the provinces of Upper Germany and Raetia were provided with a new advanced frontier barrier and sealed within the empire. The first historically attested serious invasion there came in 161–2.

By then it had already been realized that the Scottish conquests could not be held with appreciably fewer troops than had originally been made available, and increasing numbers of those troops were now needed elsewhere. It seems likely that the withdrawal from Scotland and the completion of the Upper German–Raetian frontier were simultaneous and associated events, precipitated by a threat of invasion on the continent and against a background of persistent military difficulty in Scotland. The sudden need to build one frontier fortification line led to the abandonment of another.

The Antonine Wall was perhaps not immediately abandoned in 158 – facing an actual threat of invasion, the Romans took the sensible precaution of completing the recommissioning of Hadrian's Wall before evacuating the wall in Scotland. Units

Fig. 3.6 A visual impression of the second-century army: auxiliary cavalry crossing a river depicted on Trajan's Column. They have helmets, mailshirts and oval shields. The bridge is guarded by legionary soldiers.

returned from Scotland to Hadrian's Wall and its hinterland over a period between 158 and 161 (or slightly later), rather than all at the same instant. It seems likely that around 158 the units in two of the biggest Antonine Wall forts – the Hamian archers at Bar Hill and the First Tungrians at Castlecary – returned to their former bases on Hadrian's Wall (Carvoran and Housesteads respectively). Each was replaced, briefly (between 158 and 161), by another unit on the Antonine Wall. The rebuilding of Birrens in 158, and Newstead at the same time, heralded their new role as outposts of the reoccupied Wall of Hadrian. That is why those two sites displayed the two Antonine periods which were then sought, and found through wishful thinking, everywhere on the Antonine Wall.

The final abandonment of the Antonine Wall was probably left until Antoninus Pius died in 161; then the magnificent distance slabs erected by the legions who had built this wall of turf for the glory of that emperor were taken down and ceremonially buried.

The recommissioning of Hadrian's Wall then went on in earnest. The Wall on the Tyne–Solway isthmus was now to remain the northern fortification line of Britain until the end of the Roman period.

The Army of the Wall, AD122–60

The Auxiliaries of the Wall under Hadrian

We have already come across the citizen soldiers of the legions doing the work of building the Wall, and legionaries, as we shall see, continued to be involved in its manning. But the major forts on Hadrian's Wall were designed to accommodate not legionaries, but units of non-citizen auxiliaries. Trajan's Column offers our only sustained visual impression of soldiers of the Hadrianic period. Until recently archaeologists tended to treat the column as if it offered a series of photographs of the Roman army in action. Historians are now wary of taking it as an absolutely realistic depiction, and suspect that the images offer ideals and stereotypes to suit the story being told. The column depicts auxiliaries with mail-shirts, helmets with pronounced neckguards, and oval shields easily distinguishable from the bowed rectangular *scutum* of the legionary. The column also emphasizes the important part played by cavalry among the auxiliary forces.

The auxiliary soldiers on the Wall were certainly not Italians, and would mostly have had origins in various of the north-western frontier provinces, whatever the 'ethnic' name of their unit. Some units had been raised relatively recently: the cohort of Dacians that was attested to have built the Vallum in western Newcastle had presumably been raised during Trajan's Dacian wars of 101–2 and 105–6, less than twenty years earlier. In Hadrian's reign many of them would still have been Dacians. The members of such ethnic units were rapidly assimilated into Roman culture, and there is a notorious absence of anything in the archaeological record to betray their origins. This is shown by the Vindolanda tablets, where a unit of Batavians (an originally Germanic people from the Netherlands part of the Lower Rhine frontier) were commanded by a Batavian aristocrat (to judge from his name) at the beginning of the second century. The unit had been raised from defeated tribal warriors only thirty years earlier at the time of the Batavian revolt of AD69; by the time they were at Vindolanda, prefect and soldiers were thoroughly steeped in Latin language and culture.

Some auxiliary units maintained connections with their original homeland: unless it is a remarkable coincidence, the Wall fort at Chesters (*Cilurnum*) seems to have come to be named after a people (the *Cilurnigi*) from the part of northern Spain that gave birth to *ala II Asturum*, its garrison from about 160. This probably indicates the maintenance of a regimental tradition, rather than continued large-scale recruitment from the homeland. Such units proudly retained their original names, but came to draw their recruits from diverse areas, predominantly from Gaul and the frontier areas of northern Europe. We know from inscriptions that the second cohort of Tungrians (originally raised in Belgium), stationed in Antonine Scotland, contained drafts recently acquired from the Condrusi (quite near the original homeland of the Tungri) but also from the more distant Vellavi of southern Gaul and from Raetia (Switzerland/southern Germany). A diploma of 178 shows a Dacian cavalryman retiring to the Danube after completing his service in a cohort of Gauls in Britain.

By Hadrian's reign some auxiliary units contained a greater or lesser number of Roman citizens. How many recruits in the Wall units would have been drawn from Britain itself in the early second century is unknown, but the number is not likely to have been high: only two Britons are recorded in auxiliary units in Britain, but many more in auxiliary units on the continent. Many Britons were recruited into the Roman army, but they were sent to serve on other frontiers.

The Wall Forts under Hadrian

Only the fort at Wallsend has produced anything like the complete plan of a Wall fort as built under Hadrian: at this badly damaged site in an urban environment it has been possible to penetrate the accretions of later centuries and excavate the earliest levels extensively. Something of the original arrangements can be deduced at Housesteads, thanks to extensive excavations in 1959–60 and 1974–81. Both of these plans can be understood as model accommodation for a particular kind of auxiliary unit. Wallsend has barracks for the six centuries and four cavalry troops for the 480 infantry and 120 cavalry of a part-mounted cohort. Housesteads probably started life with the ten barracks necessary for an infantry cohort nominally 1,000 (actually 800) strong. Chesters has had no excavation of its early levels, but we can see that the fort is the right size for the sixteen barracks necessary for the *ala Augusta*, which an inscription attests was there under Hadrian. Each Wall fort, then, was designed for an individual and complete unit.

The fort plans offered a vision of urban and civic life, with the grid pattern of streets familiar from

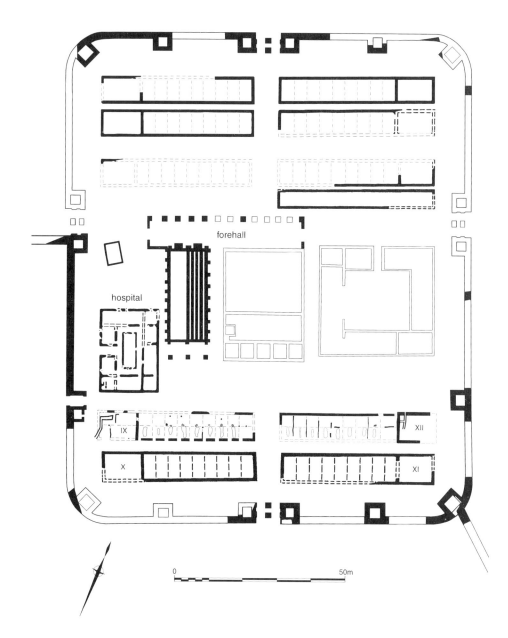

forehall

hospital

IX

X

XII

XI

0   50m

Mediterranean cities, and at the centre the *principia* or 'headquarters building' that in its plan recalled the forum basilica complex, the civic centre, of a Roman town. On entering the *principia*, a colonnaded court led to a great basilican hall, beyond which was a range of offices flanking a shrine (*aedes*). This was the administrative nerve centre of the fort, but also, for the ordinary soldier, a focus of religious devotion and demonstration of loyalty to Rome. Here in the shrine the standards of the unit were revered and – with the pay chests – constantly guarded. When the unit went out on campaign, the standards processed from the *principia* and along the vista of the main street to the ceremonial front gate (*porta praetoria*), and out, beyond the Wall.

More mundanely, it was in the offices to either side of the *aedes* that the soldier drew his pay or banked his savings, and where the record of his account and service with the unit was kept, in a voluminous archive of documents. To judge from the examples from Vindolanda and Carlisle, these would have been ink-written, wooden writing tablets; the standard bearers who traditionally undertook the book-keeping and other administrative officers are frequently depicted on tombstones with a bundle of writing tablets, as a symbol of their office.

The cavernous *basilica*, with a tall tribunal at one end from which the commanding officer could preside, was the scene of disciplinary hearings and communal religious gatherings. Nothing like the whole unit could have fitted into this space, but in several Hadrianic *principia* on the Wall the *basilica* had no less than five arched entrances from the court-yard, so that troops assembled outside could have some participation in the ceremonies.

The *principia* was the central unit of three blocks that made up a central range of stone buildings. Looking out from its front entrance, to its right was the *praetorium*, or commanding officer's house. This was a peristyle house (that is, with a colon-naded courtyard at its centre), built according to the typical plan of an urban mansion in which the commanding officer and his family would have lived in their home town: unlike his soldiers, he was likely to be from the Mediterranean area, possibly even Italy itself. Unlike the legions, auxiliary units were not commanded by men of the highest senatorial class, but by a prefect (or a tribune for the 1,000-strong ones), typically a young Roman aristocrat of the equestrian order, who took up the post, prob-ably for three years, as part of his progress through the ranks of the imperial service. The Vindolanda tablets establish without doubt that these officers were routinely accompanied by their wives and chil-dren during their posting. The *praetorium* therefore housed a complete Roman aristocratic family, and an extensive household, consisting mainly of slaves. On the other side of the *principia* were the granaries (*horrea*), great buttressed stone warehouses, prob-ably two storeys high, that stored grain and other perishable foodstuffs.

Fig. 3.8 The southern granary at Birdoswald, under excavation in 1987. Its outer wall stands 2.5m (8ft) high and displays the buttresses that identify these military storehouses.

Outside the central range most of the fort interior was taken up with tightly packed and neatly arranged barrack blocks. At Wallsend, and perhaps at all the Wall forts, these were of timber when first built under Hadrian. On the basis of a single ancient text – which refers to a campaign camp, not a permanent fort – it is assumed that infantrymen were accommodated in units of eight (a *contbernium*). A row of ten of these made up a barrack block, living quarters for the eighty men who constituted a century in the imperial period. Each *contubernium* was divided into a front room, thought to be for equipment storage, and a rear room, where the eight men had to sleep in a floor space of 13sq m (15.5sq yd), which also included a hearth for heating and cooking. There is absolutely no evidence to date for how the sleepers were arranged – all reconstructions showing bunk beds or other furnishings are entirely conjectural. At one end of the block was a spacious multi-roomed apartment for the centurion in charge, which may also have accommodated his junior officers, the *signifer* and *optio*, and slaves.

The cavalry were housed differently. One of the most commonly asked questions about Roman forts is: 'Where did they keep the horses?' Archaeologists have had great difficulty in recognizing a regular type of stable building in forts, and now we know why. In 1998–2000 the first modern complete excavation of cavalry barracks on Hadrian's Wall took place at Wallsend and South Shields. Each of the *contubernia*, or living rooms, contained, in its front compartment, a centrally placed, elongated pit. Corresponding to each front-room pit was a hearth in the rear room, where the soldiers had lived.

This arrangement was immediately recognized as exactly resembling that found in certain Roman fort buildings on the continent, where preserved hay and fodder showed that horses had been stabled in the front room. The pits, covered with boards or stone slabs, collected horse urine and kept the floor dry. Such buildings, only ever revealed fragmentarily, had up to then been interpreted as stables. However, the buildings at Wallsend and South Shields were clearly not stables, but, as the plans revealed in their entirety showed, barracks of conventional type, complete with end buildings for officers. They demonstrate that cavalry mounts were accommodated in the same buildings as their riders.

The elusive separate stables are now known to be a myth, and stable barracks have since been recognized at many other forts in the Roman Empire. Each of the front rooms (at least 3.60m sq, or 12RF sq) would have been able to accommodate three horses, close by their riders and available for instant deployment, a military advantage that would be completely lost if the cavalry

mounts were stabled or corralled elsewhere. In each rear room slept three troopers. So a barrack with ten *contubernia* would have neatly housed the thirty or so men and horses that are known to have made up the cavalry equivalent of a century – a *turma* or 'troop'.

The officer in charge of the troop was a decurion, and he and his junior officers (*duplicarius, sesquipli-carius, vexillarius*) occupied the extensive house at the end of the barrack. A fort such as Chesters would have contained sixteen such barracks, for the sixteen *turmae* making up the *ala*. At Wallsend, the six centuries of infantry were accommodated in the northern part of the fort, while the four *turmae* of cavalry were placed in the southern part, where a wide open space between the central range and the barracks was provided for the movement and exercise of horses and the assembly of mounted troops.

Many people are reluctant to accept that Roman cavalrymen would have lived in the same buildings as their horses. But this archaeological discovery shows that we should overcome our modern preconceptions, and remember that these soldiers were the descendants of the barbarian horsemen from whom the Roman auxiliary cavalry had originally been raised. There was a natural bond between these mounted warriors and their steeds, and the trooper and his mount rode and lived together in a tight-knit community. Cavalrymen owned slaves (*calones*) who attended to the horses and carried about equipment and horse tack; they must have been included in this set-up, sleeping on the floor somewhere, or under (or sometimes in) the soldiers' beds, or in the capacious roof space.

There were other kinds of building in the fort, notably workshops for the repair and manufacture of equipment. There also seem to have been hospitals at Wallsend and Housesteads in the original Hadrianic plans. Set into the earth rampart that backed the fort wall were large circular bread ovens (rather like a pizza oven on a very large scale). To judge from examples found at Housesteads and South Shields, and in the first-century fort of Fendoch in Scotland, in this early period there was an oven opposite the

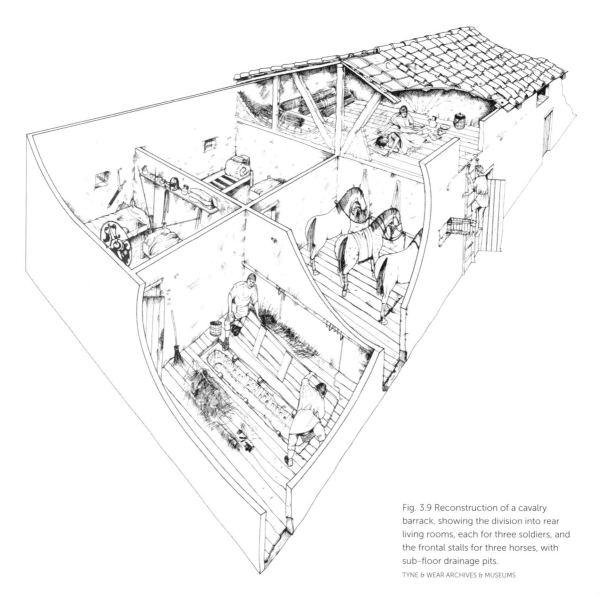

Fig. 3.9 Reconstruction of a cavalry barrack, showing the division into rear living rooms, each for three soldiers, and the frontal stalls for three horses, with sub-floor drainage pits.

end of each barrack block, suggesting communal use by the century or *turma*.

The communal ovens show that rations for baking bread must have been issued by the unit to each century and *turma*, with the individual *contubernia* perhaps taking turns to prepare the food. A writing tablet found at Carlisle, dating to around AD100, records the routine issue of a three-day ration of barley and wheat, *turma* by *turma*, to a cavalry *ala*. The barley was for the horses, the wheat for the men and their slaves. All this implies a high level of central organization and co-ordinated communal activity to avoid wasting time, and to maximize the efficiency of the unit. In the Hadrian's Wall forts it is unclear where the wheat was ground, but presumably this was also on a communal basis to avoid the waste of time that each solider doing it individually would entail. We can only assume that the soldiers cooked meat and consumed their food in their individual barrack rooms: there was no equivalent to a dining hall or central messing area in the Roman army.

The soldiers did not live on bread alone, for the study of animal bones from the Wall shows that they ate meat, predominantly cattle, though pig and sheep/

goat are also found in quantity. One excavation in the Antonine Wall, which probably holds good for the army in general in the second century, found human sewage containing wheat and barley, and the seeds of bean, fig, dill, coriander, opium poppy, hazelnut, raspberry, bramble, strawberry, bilberry and celery; it also showed that soldiers suffered from whipworm and roundworm. Finds of pottery containers, *amphorae*, show that the soldiers made lavish use of olive oil, in their diet and for other purposes. The Vindolanda tablets suggest that beer was a staple, and the Roman army was also famed for its consumption of wine – again the Vindolanda tablets confirm this. On Hadrian's Wall wine *amphorae* are scarce compared to those containing olive oil, but the likely explanation is that the main source of supply was the Rhineland, and wine from there was shipped in barrels.

The consumption of bread, along with olive oil and wine, shows that the auxiliary soldiers of Hadrian's time, although in some cases only recently drawn from conquered peoples, were consuming food and drink in a thoroughly Roman manner, with some regional distortions, such as a fondness for beer, reflecting their north-west European milieu. In their physical surroundings they lived in a microcosm of a Mediterranean town, and had grown thoroughly accustomed to rectilinear buildings, glazed windows, storm drains and baths. Of course this is the environment – the fort and the barracks – that we see archaeologically, and in reality the soldiers may have spent little of their time in the fort. So what did they actually do, and what was their lived experience like on the Wall?

Routine

The soldier's life revolved round a number of regular routines or cycles. Josephus, writing fifty years before the Wall was built, described how times for reveille, meals, changes of guard and bed-time were announced by trumpet calls. In this highly regulated camp routine there was little space for privacy or individual initiative. We have seen the communal way food was prepared, and even going to the latrine was a communal activity (as the preserved latrine at Housesteads shows, which was capable of seating up to forty), no doubt performed at a set time.

Surviving fragments of legionary duty rosters from the early empire found in Egypt hint at the likely daily work of Wall soldiers when in the fort. Assignments include cleaning the latrines and servicing the baths, patrolling or cleaning streets inside the fort, and guard duty at various points, including gates and the headquarters building. The Vindolanda documents describe groups of soldiers assigned building work and work in the lime kilns, or quarrying or obtaining building materials. In the Roman army a class of soldiers, *immunes*, were excused fatigues because they had specialist craft skills or carried out administrative duties, including clerical work and book-keeping. These soldiers presumably had a bit more time to themselves to reflect on their life, as did a legionary stationed in Egypt in 107, who wrote in a rather self-satisfied manner to his parents that his promotion to a clerical post meant that he could drift around doing nothing while others laboured for the whole day cutting building stones.

Military training and exercises must have been carried out on a regular basis, although less documentation for the organization of these has survived. For the auxiliary cavalry of Hadrian's time we have an account of the *Hippika Gymnasia*, a cavalry sports show consisting of complex manoeuvres, with the riders and horses bedecked in colourful gear and the men wearing gleaming, androgynous face masks representing gods and mythological figures. Hadrian's speech at Lambaesis records his inspection of such exercises there. But there must have been regular, less glamorous exercise for cavalry and infantry, ranging from weapons training to route marching. A training ground ('parade ground' in older archaeological parlance) will have lain outside every Wall fort, though few have been discovered (examples are reported at Stanwix and Maryport). A small, mid second-century example found at South Shields belongs to an undiscovered predecessor to the known fort.

The Roman writer Vegetius stressed that the army was careful to allow for constant training, even in bad weather, by building facilities for indoor exercises. Despite a long-standing belief, there is no evidence that the great covered forehalls sometimes attached to the front of headquarters buildings – of which two examples are known on Hadrian's Wall, at Wallsend and Halton Chesters – were riding schools used for cavalry drill. They probably functioned as imposing covered spaces where troops could assemble for announcements and ceremonies carried out in the headquarters building; at Wallsend the forehall, built around 160, also gave shelter to the movement of supplies and transactions conducted at the entrance to the granaries. A building more convincingly interpreted as a drill hall (though perhaps not for cavalry) has been excavated at Birdoswald, and is not connected to the *principia*. This was a stone *basilica*, 42 by 15m (46 by 16.5yd), part of the primary Hadrianic arrangement of the fort.

Bathing was another part of the Wall soldier's routine. Baths were usually built outside auxiliary forts, since the standard fort layout had evolved before auxiliaries had adopted the Roman custom of bathing by about AD80. The baths could be a considerable distance from the fort – some 300m (330yd) at Benwell, 120m (130yd) at Wallsend, 70m (77yd) at Chesters – the convenience of the water supply, usually by aqueduct, dictating the position. Four Wall forts and two of the western outposts have baths with plans drawn from the same blueprint – a block plan consisting of a series of heated rooms through which the bather could progress from tepid heat to the hottest steam room with hot plunge bath, and the bather would circulate through the rooms, returning to his starting point, rather than going from one room to the next in a simple row where the same route had to be retraced. The detail of this circular plan is unparalleled anywhere in the Roman Empire. Since no earlier fort baths are known on the Wall, this must

Fig. 3.10 Plan of the recently discovered fort baths at Wallsend, as built under Hadrian (left) to a standard plan used in several of the Wall forts, and (right) as rebuilt a century later. TYNE & WEAR ARCHIVES & MUSEUMS

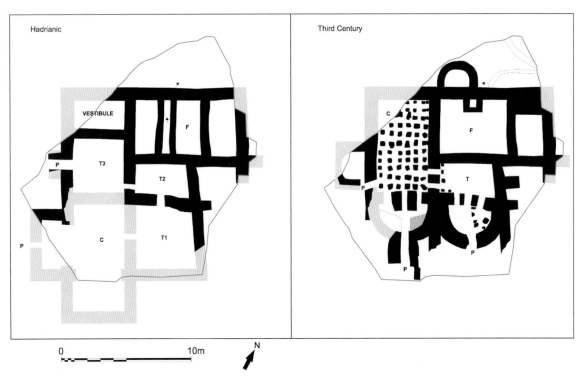

indicate a Hadrianic design specially created for the Wall forts. The baths were impressively built of stone with glazed windows.

The hot water was supplied from a boiler over a furnace from which gases were drawn beneath the raised cement and flagstone floors, up wall flues and even through the ceiling vaults, giving radiant heat from every surface. The bather began or finished with a cold plunge or douche in an unheated room. For the Romans, bathing was essentially a social activity, combined with games, exercises and conversation, preferably in the afternoon. Unfortunately we have no evidence for when or how often the soldiers bathed, whether it was an entirely off-duty activity, how much they paid, or the mechanism for sharing the baths with women or other civilians.

How was the Wall Manned under Hadrian?

Was patrolling and maintaining the Wall itself part of the routine of the auxiliaries on the Wall? Here we enter into a very difficult area, because as already stressed in the introduction, there is not one iota of documentary evidence for how the Wall was patrolled, or who manned the milecastles and turrets.

The milecastles and turrets correspond to two classes of installation, namely fortlets and watchtowers, familiar from the Upper German and Raetian frontier, although the regularity of their spacing is quite peculiar to Britain. Both milecastles and turrets were retained in use alongside the Wall forts for most of the second century (excepting the Antonine occupation of Scotland). Most turrets, where excavated, have produced Hadrianic and later pottery from their early occupation levels, and go on to have a history extending until at least the later second century; they formed an integral part of the Hadrianic 'Wall as built' scheme. Milecastles were occupied into the late fourth century. The milecastles contain buildings for long-stay accommodation, and milling stones commonly found in turrets suggest that soldiers were supplied with provisions for several days and prepared food in the turret; board games point to considerable 'down time' amongst members of the turret crew, such finds suggesting that groups of soldiers were outposted to turrets for substantial periods.

Without going into the question of what their purpose was and how they actually functioned, which we will come to later, we can make a crude guess at the number of soldiers necessary to man these structures. We can envisage a minimum of half a dozen men to keep watch at a turret (allowing for shifts and sleeping), which is a large enough group to put up resistance in the event of an attack and to organize a signal or dispatch a messenger.

The interiors of very few milecastles have been fully explored. There seems to have been a variation in the amount of internal accommodation offered. Either a pair of barracks faced each other across the internal road (in a way reminiscent of many German fortlets), or a small two-roomed building occupied one corner of the enclosure. This variation occurs as follows in the milecastles whose interiors are known. In certain of the 'small building' milecastles the accommodation would later be extended and longer blocks provided.

small building	barrack pair
9	
35	
37?	
	39?
	47
	48
50TW	
	51
79TW?	

The 'small building' milecastles look as if they should have accommodated about eight men, and the ones with full barrack accommodation more like thirty to forty (thirty-two is a figure offered in much of the modern literature). It is quite possible that the 'small building' variety contained other structures more difficult to detect. This was certainly the case at Milecastle 9, where a timber building was detected on the other side of the interior, while coastal Mile-fortlet 21, excavated in 1990–91, contained timber, or possibly turf, buildings resting directly on the surface, surviving merely as lines of compacted sand. These would almost certainly have escaped detection in the older excavations on which most of our understanding (or lack of it) of milecastle interiors is based.

The distinction between the two types of interior may therefore be illusory. If there is any reality in it, the explanation for this variation may lie in the fact that so many milecastles were provided – more than

on the German frontier, where fortlets were irregularly dispersed amongst a more regular cordon of watchtowers, the fortlets built only at danger points. On Hadrian's Wall every milecastle had to be manned because there was a watchtower over the north gate and a vulnerable opening through the Wall. However, especially after the decision to place forts on the Wall, the function of many milecastles may have been limited to manning the tower (as if it were merely another turret) and securing the gate.

Some milecastles, on the other hand, may always have retained their role as garrisoned fortlets, dispersed irregularly through the system, where required. It is notable that Milecastle 48, with its fortlet-type accommodation, controls the Poltross Burn, in the same way as many of the German frontier fortlets were situated by rivers or passes that crossed the frontier there. Those milecastles with limited internal accommodation may simply have been used by a small group of soldiers manning the tower and gate, and controlling an access point to the top of the Wall.

In short, not every milecastle was manned by a substantial detachment of thirty-two or more soldiers, but an unknown number probably were. In Ming China, towers on the Great Wall were normally manned by seven to ten men, and a figure in this range is appropriate for both turrets and those milecastles that did not accommodate a larger detachment.

The milecastles and turrets, then, were a way of accommodating troops in a dispersed manner, often in very small groups, so that an uninterrupted surveillance could be maintained along the Wall, and also of having more substantial forces on the ground at particularly dangerous points. The kind of surveillance necessary evidently could not be achieved by forces based in the auxiliary forts alone. But the great unknown is: did the auxiliary units in the Wall forts provide the detachments to man the milecastles and turrets, or were these men drawn from some other source entirely? It has been suggested in the past that a separate force of irregular troops (*numeri*) manned the milecastles and turrets.

However, this suggestion can be straightaway dismissed because there is absolutely no evidence for an irregular force, and there is nowhere that could have served as its administrative headquarters. Who would oversee them and inspect their activities? There is some second-century material evidence to suggest that the garrison of at least one milecastle was drawn from the same background as the soldiers of its nearest auxiliary fort: on the basis of decorated metal small finds, the soldiers manning Turret 35A, Milecastle 35 and Housesteads Fort seem to have shared a devotion to Taranis, the Celtic wheel god. The same milecastle has also produced a lead sealing inscribed 'CIT', almost certainly of *cohors I Tungrorum*, the Housesteads unit that lay less than 3km (2 miles) away.

There are a few inscriptions from in, or near, milecastles naming military units, legionaries and auxiliaries, and these have been scrupulously studied. Unfortunately there is almost no case where we can be certain that the inscription records an actual garrison of the structure, and that it is not brought from elsewhere and reused in building work; but such stones do not occur commonly in the fabric of the Wall curtain, so if they occur near milecastles, as they seem to do, that may have some significance. An altar from Milecastle 19, dedicated by a detachment of *cohors I Vardullorum* – not attested at any Wall fort, but which has connections with nearby Corbridge, on the Stanegate – is intriguing. The altar was deliberately buried under a roadway outside the milecastle south gate in the course of the second century. This could have been when the milecastle was decommissioned during the Antonine advance, which would suggest that the vexillation manned this milecastle under Hadrian. Then, at or near Milecastle 59 another auxiliary unit, *cohors I Batavorum*, dedicated an altar to Mars Cocidius. They were at Carrawburgh (many miles away) after *c.* 180, and their Hadrianic base is unknown.

Then there is a series of altars, all dedicated to Cocidius, which occur in association with Milecastles 52, 55, 60 and 65, and which are dedicated by

legionary detachments. Those from Milecastle 52 are certainly third century, and perhaps come from a nearby shrine, but the others could be second century and could denote detachments serving in the milecastles. Further stones might indicate a legionary presence at Milecastles 37 and 73. These inscriptions hint at the use of small legionary detachments in milecastles, particularly in the western area, in a way reminiscent of their use in small forts on the Antonine Wall.

We can perhaps envisage a very complicated picture where men detached from the legions, the auxiliary units stationed on the Wall, and auxiliary units from the Stanegate road and even the more distant hinterland of the Wall, took a share in manning the minor structures. An inscription at Corbridge dating to the time the Antonine Wall was abandoned (around 158) attests a detachment of the VI legion under a tribune. The Stanegate sites of Corbridge and Carlisle housed legionary detachments later, and along with Vindolanda, these would have been convenient places for legionaries manning the Wall to be based.

It is often said that the popular image of the legionary patrolling the Wall is a myth, but it may be that in the second century the burden of manning the minor wall structures did not fall entirely on the auxiliary units in the forts – and the fact, already noted, that the forts were designed to hold whole units may indeed suggest that the designers of the Wall did not envisage these units being heavily fragmented on a permanent basis. Trajan, in a letter to Pliny the Younger, voiced doubts about the practice of dispersing detachments from units. Yet in the first and second centuries strength reports and duty rosters from other parts of the empire, and from Vindolanda, show that it was standard practice to detach large parts of units. Hadrian himself addressed the Third Augustan legion with these words: *Quod multae, quod diversae stationes vos distent:* 'Many and far-flung outposts keep you scattered.'

Maybe in Britain it was the legions and other auxiliary units that suffered this kind of fragmentation in order to preserve the Wall-fort units, including the 1,000-strong *ala Petriana*, as near-whole entities that could respond when emergencies did occur. No doubt in practice at least some of the Wall-fort units did supply detachments for the milecastles and turrets also – and for the 800-strong infantry regiment at Housesteads this would hardly have reduced their military capability. Furthermore, if the Wall units were not bearing the burden alone, the numbers involved would have been far from debilitating for the army of the Wall taken overall, leaving units intact enough to be gathered together to respond to large incursions or to undertake raids or campaigns far north of the Wall.

Pay, Prospects and Relationships

Payday was not a weekly or monthly occurrence, but came three or four times a year. No surviving record of pay scales exists, and the amount of pay for different grades and at different times is heavily reconstructed from a very few snippets of literary and documentary evidence. The most popular reconstruction indicates that an auxiliary infantryman under Hadrian – and for the whole of the second century – earned 250 silver *denarii* (ten gold pieces) a year, a cavalryman in a part-mounted cohort 300 *denarii* (the same as a legionary), and a cavalryman in an *ala* 350. According to Matthew 20:2, a rural labourer earned a *denarius* a day (say, 260 a year if employed full time), which seems similar, but the soldier was paid all the year round, had no unemployment, and enjoyed free accommodation and heavily subsidized food and clothing.

What was the soldier's pay worth in real terms? According to the Vindolanda documents, a cloak might cost between 3 and 11½ *denarii*, a bowl 2 to 5 *denarii*, and a night's lodging ½ a *denarius*. If we think in today's terms of the infantryman earning £18,000 in today's money and the *ala* trooper £25,000, a multiple of about seventy should give a modern equivalent to the *denarius*. So: between £210 and £805 for a cloak is believable, if it was a high-quality

garment; £140–£350 for a bowl sounds too much; but £35 for a night's lodging sounds cheap. At 12 denarii a saddle cost £840, which you might pay today. There were various stoppages for equipment and clothing – and a cavalryman had to pay for his horse, which might have a value of 20 per cent of his annual salary (think in terms of £5,000 or more). Sometimes soldiers drew advances or deposited savings, their credit and debt with the unit being recorded by the clerks in the *principia*.

By Hadrian's time a term of service of twenty-five years had become standard, at the end of which the soldier would be honourably discharged and would become a Roman citizen, if he wasn't one of the increasing number of auxiliaries who already had citizenship. He was also awarded *conubium*: the right to marry a non-citizen, but for his offspring themselves to be Roman citizens. Many examples of bronze certificates of citizenship and *conubium* issued to veterans, known as diplomas, survive, and a few have been found on the Wall.

These documents gave one of our most precious insights into the everyday lives of auxiliary soldiers, by revealing the kind of relationships they had with women. Soldiers were banned from contracting legally recognized marriages, but the diplomas issued to some auxiliaries show that unofficial marriages were contracted and families raised, with the issue receiving citizenship on their father's discharge down to AD140. After that only children that were born after his discharge and grant of *conubium* (legal right to marry a non-citizen) became citizens. We do not know what proportion of soldiers contracted unofficial marriages while in service; the figure need not have been high, and many more will have had girlfriends. There was probably a higher rate of marriage among the better paid centurions and decurions.

Various strands of evidence show that there were considerable numbers of women in the military ambit. The military unit at every fort had a satellite community of civilians, including perhaps wives, daughters, grandmothers and aunts who had thrown in their lot with the military and helped supply the goods

Fig. 3.12 'The Malpas diploma' of AD103, granting citizenship and marriage rights to a soldier after twenty-five years' service. On the upper sheet the names of auxiliary units serving in Britain can be seen. The name of the recipient, Reburrus, is in the third last line of the second sheet; in the last line the words 'fixa est Romae' mean that this is a copy of a document displayed in Rome.

and perhaps living, within the fort walls as well as in the attached civilian settlement.

Besides the family members and slaves attached to the commanding officer's household, we can envisage female slaves, and free women, often including relatives, admitted into the fort to carry out various kinds of work. That said, the archaeological evidence from excavated barracks, on Hadrian's Wall and elsewhere in the empire, does not support the claim made by several recent writers that women routinely lived as concubines with soldiers in barrack rooms.

On discharge, in his early or mid forties, a veteran might start a family of citizen offspring, either with his formerly 'unofficial wife', or he might perhaps just as often abandon his 'unofficial' family for a new and younger partner: as an honourably discharged veteran, often with considerable savings and with the assurance that his children would be Roman citizens, he would be quite a catch. As many veterans settled near their old base, some of their citizen children will have followed them into their old unit, meaning that more and more of its members became Roman citizens over time. But even they could not have legitimate children during service, for the ban on legally recognized marriage for soldiers was maintained down to at least AD197, and possibly beyond.

Religion

Stone altars with inscribed dedications to the gods are probably the commonest sort of written evidence from the Wall, and give some insight into the beliefs and feelings of the soldiers, although most recovered examples tend to be dedicated by the officers rather than ordinary *milites*. Two kinds of deity were honoured in ceremonies and sacrifices conducted over such altars. First there were the 'official' gods of the Roman state, such as Jupiter, Juno, Minerva and Mars. Their statues and altars stood either in the fort headquarters building or at dedicated temples outside the fort. The 'feriale Duranum', a document found at Dura Europos in Syria, has been interpreted as a calendar, used by army units all over the empire, laying down

and services that made life possible for hundreds of men living in a concentrated, quasi-urban location. This is implied by the Vindolanda documents, and made explicit by writing tablets from continental military sites. Internal fort buildings at Vindolanda have produced quantities of women's and children's shoes, and the pattern of finds in general suggests that considerable numbers of women were working, the feast days on which these great deities of the state were to be honoured. The birthdays of long-dead emperors, deified after their death, were also celebrated at regular intervals in the calendar.

The most striking Hadrianic example of the conduct of 'official' religion comes from 300m (330yd) north-east of Maryport, one of the Cumbrian coast forts, where a series of altars dedicated by the commanding officer on behalf of the unit, *cohors I Hispanorum*, has been found buried in pits. The dedications were presumably made annually either on 3 January, when Roman army units are believed to have made vows for the welfare of the emperor and the eternity of the empire, or on the anniversary of the emperor's accession. It was once universally accepted that the old year's altar was buried next to the parade ground where the unit assembled for the ceremony, on the occasion of its replacement with the new year's dedication. However, recent re-excavation of the Maryport 'pits' has cast doubt on this interpretation, and it seems that the altars had been reused as packing in the postholes of a timber structure – but the basic point that they originally represented an annual dedication, somehow connected to a nearby temple of Jupiter, which has also been recently re-excavated, remains unaffected.

These altars preserve the full sequence of names of the commanding officers of the unit throughout Hadrian's reign, starting with M. Maenius Agrippa, a friend of Hadrian's from Camerinum in Italy who had participated in the *expeditio Britannica* (of 122?), and who founded the fort at Maryport as the base for *cohors I Hispanorum*. The altars are nearly all dedicated to the head of the Roman pantheon, *IUPPITER OPTIMO MAXIMO* (always abbreviated to IOM), 'to Jupiter the best and greatest', with some including the *numen Augusti*, the divinity of the emperor. The series of altars continues into the reign of Antoninus Pius, during which a different unit (*cohors I Delmatarum*) garrisoned the fort, but there are only four altars for the whole of that period (139–61). Finally a third unit, the First cohort of Baetasians, takes over the series, after the abandonment of the Antonine Wall.

After two commanding officers who dedicated altars twice and four times respectively, the series of altars ceases abruptly, seemingly around 167.

The other category consisted of the unofficial cults, often of local, presumably native gods such as Cocidius, or from other parts of the Celtic North West, such as Coventina, also known in Spain and Gaul. The sacred well of 'the Nymph' Coventina was found outside the west wall of the fort at Carrawburgh in 1876, filled with offerings, including twenty stone altars and reliefs and over 16,000 coins. The shrine was active in the second century and throughout the later history of the Wall. We can only guess as to what fortune or benefits individual soldiers of the Wall thought Coventina would bring them in return for their offerings.

The Romans often identified local gods with their own, resulting in hybrids, or interpretations, such as Mars Cocidius (a particularly respected war god confined to the western half of Hadrian's Wall), Apollo Maponus (from Britain, and perhaps Gaul) and the ubiquitous Jupiter Dolichenus (from Syria), who makes his earliest appearance in northern Britain at Croy Hill on the Antonine Wall. In the headquarters the commanding officer presided over the 'official' ceremonies, although there were other priests and sacrifice technicians on the staff of units. Outside the fort, the unofficial cults presumably had their own priests.

For most ordinary soldiers adherence to the 'official' religion showed loyalty to the emperor, and in practice there was no choice but to go along with it; but such festivals involved food, drink and merry-making, and were no doubt very popular and a way of cementing the relationship between soldier, unit, commanding officer and emperor. But almost everybody had a private religious life in which local Celtic gods and mystery cults originating in distant corners of the empire could loom large. Religion seems to have played a big part in their lives: they were seriously terrified, enchanted, moved and inspired by the gods. In this respect the incoming Romans, soldiers or civilians had very similar and related beliefs to the people of pre-Roman Iron Age Britain. There was no

Fig. 3.13 Objects found in the sacred spring of the goddess Coventina, at Carrawburgh in 1876, from a contemporary account in *The Illustrated London News*.

clash of religious cultures: everybody believed that as well as supreme or general gods, there were local gods or spirits (*genii*) in every person and place.

It made sense to honour and placate these spirits, and for most ordinary soldiers that would have been their most acute concern. An altar which may well be of second-century date was found in 1813 near Mileacastle 59. It had been dedicated by a centurion of *cohors I Batavorum*, and as we have seen, possibly indicates a detachment that had manned the milecastle. The dedication is to the much feared Mars Cocidius, but there is more: at the end of the inscription are the words *GENIO VALI*, in addition dedicating the altar to the *genius* or guardian spirit of 'the Wall'. In the past this interpretation has been rejected because the word should be spelt *Valli*, but the same misspelling occurs on the recently discovered Ilam Pan, which describes the Wall as *Vali Aeli* – Hadrian's Wall. We can sense something of the trepidation with which these soldiers made offerings to a local version of Mars and to the protective power of a spirit residing in the Wall itself.

Civilians in the Wall Zone in the Hadrianic Period

A conspicuous feature of the Wall forts is the extramural settlement, which by the third century had become an integral part of any military base of the period in north-western Europe, the inhabitants referring to themselves as *vicani* – the inhabitants of the *vicus* attached to a particular Roman fort. A discussion of the civilian settlements or *vici* of the Wall is held over until Chapter 4, because most of our information comes from a later period, between *c.* 160 and *c.* 250. The role of civilians, and the nature of their settlements on the Wall as first completed under Hadrian, is in fact a problem.

The earliest Roman forts in northern Britain were accompanied by extramural settlements. Where there have been excavations, as at Carlisle (Cumbria), Castleford (West Yorkshire) and Roecliffe (North Yorkshire) – all established in the conquest of the early AD70s – we see that rather than accreting gradually, the settlements were planned and established with the first foundation of the fort. These appear to be settlements of the civilian camp followers – traders, manufacturers and others essential for army supply – who worked hand-in-glove with the administrators of the unit in the fort: as in the west today, the market was the main instrument of military supply, and these 'civilian contractors' came not from the indigenous population in the locality, but were immigrants drawn from the same background as the soldiers. One civilian, probably a trader, in the Vindolanda documents describes himself as a *homo transmarinus* – a man from overseas.

In principle we would expect the Hadrianic garrisons on the Wall to have the same requirements and a need for the same kind of attached civilian community. This is especially so as *vicani* are explicitly attested on a near contemporary inscription from the fort at Carriden, on the Firth of Forth at the eastern end of the Antonine Wall.

At Vindolanda an annexe defended by a stone wall, containing baths, an inn for official travellers (*mansio*) and other buildings, was seemingly attached to the side of the second century, possibly Hadrianic stone fort – but Vindolanda is detached from the Wall, lying on the Stanegate, and not necessarily typical of those Wall forts in the envelope formed by the Wall and Vallum. There is no fort where excavation has unequivocally shown that civilian settlement started in the area north of the Vallum under Hadrian. One of the very few excavations of a civilian settlement, at Housesteads in the 1930s, found that the stone buildings clustering around the south gate of the fort were third century. Early timber structures for civilian occupation, which *possibly* go back to the Hadrianic period, were found in the 1960s *south* of the Vallum. On the basis of all this it became widely believed that in the second century the civilians were regarded as a 'nuisance', and were prohibited from settling in the area north of the Vallum, and that the focus of civilian settlements only shifted from the south to the north of the Vallum when the latter was eventually filled in.

It seems impossible to be sure that there was not an earlier phase of occupation, perhaps timber, that was simply not detected in the excavations north of the Vallum at Housesteads in the 1930s; and the timber buildings found south of the Vallum could have been outlying parts of a settlement whose nucleus was closer to the fort. There has been so little extensive excavation of the Wall fort *vici* that for all we know they could all harbour fugitive remains close to the fort extending back in time to its foundation. On the other hand, the Wall is so unusual in its architectural design, and in having the Vallum, that the exclusion of any civilian settlement under Hadrian is conceivable. It is striking that the fort of Carvoran, which existed as a Stanegate fort before the Wall was built and which may already have had a thriving *vicus*, was carefully excluded from the Wall corridor by the Vallum. If *vici* were banned in the initial Wall–Vallum corridor, we might look for the civilians who would be integral to the well-being of the Wall units at places such as South Shields, Corbridge, Vindolanda and Carlisle.

At present, then, we are unclear as to the whereabouts of the civilians in the Hadrianic scheme for the Wall. There is a similar problem on the Antonine Wall: despite the *vicani* inscription from Carriden, and despite our knowledge of some extensive civilian settlements at forts in Antonine Scotland in general, no civilian settlement at an Antonine Wall fort has been confidently recognized and planned.

Finds of diplomas do indicate one kind of civilian, the discharged, veteran soldier, settling in the Wall zone, but all three date to after Hadrian's death. A diploma of 146 issued to a veteran of *cohors I Tungrorum* suggests that he settled at Vindolanda, the findspot. This was an old base of the unit, which had moved on, probably to Housesteads under Hadrian, and in 146 was probably at Castlecary on the Antonine Wall. If he had a family, they would have lived at Vindolanda with him. Diplomas of 146 and 140–61 from Chesters may suggest second-century veteran settlement there (perhaps by soldiers of the *ala Augusta* attested under Hadrian), but in the period when Hadrian's Wall had been evacuated in favour of the Antonine Wall.

Civilians and Military Supply

How bulk supplies, such as grain, made their way into the fort granaries is not understood. We do not know whether it was requisitioned or purchased by some central authority (the procurator? A legionary officer?), and having been delivered by appointed contractors, whether it was distributed to the auxiliary forts, or if the individual units had to proactively acquire their foodstuffs. Second-century documents from elsewhere in the empire make it reasonably clear that the units stationed on the Wall would have sent out groups of soldiers to requisition supplies (paying civilians a price fixed by the state) or to procure them on the open market, but this might have been for relatively small-scale procurements. It is also possible that the cities of southern Britain were ordered to deliver grain to the army units, for a fixed requisition price.

In the second century the army on the Wall sucked in products from its hinterland, southern Britain and from the continent. As bulk-traded goods such as textiles and grain rarely survive, archaeologists tend to rely on pottery to understand patterns of trade and supply, and mostly we have to imagine the food-stuffs, livestock, textiles and other perishable goods that would have formed the bulk of consignments. Samian ware from Gaul, the lustrous red pottery used throughout the Roman Empire, was traded from the continent to supply the troops of the Wall. Imports arrived via the trading ports such as London, which grew rapidly into one of the largest Roman cities north of the Alps.

By the 120s the army in the north was using pottery produced by industries in southern and midland Britain, as well as Gallic imports. British landowners and their workers, as well as economic migrants and merchants from overseas, had joined in the military supply chain and developed industries to profit from the requirements of the army. At first, pottery industries were set up in close co-op-eration with the military in the frontier area itself, which produced grey wares and grit-studded mixing bowls (*mortaria*) for the military market. But with the building of the Wall, the northern frontier was increasingly supplied from industries in southern Britain (for example the so-called 'black burnished ware 1', and *mortaria* traded from southern centres such as Colchester, identifiable by the leaf-shaped maker's mark), and from Gaul.

It is not known to what extent the 'invisible hand' of the market – manufacturers and traders seeing opportunities and getting their wares to where the demand lay – made the supply system work, and to what extent the government or army placed orders and awarded 'official' contracts or encouraged individual suppliers. There is no evidence for the latter, but there is almost no surviving historical evidence for any large-scale supply transactions.

The Life of the Local Population

What impact did the Wall have on the locals? Until recently the settlement sites of the pre-Roman Iron

Age in the region were impossible to date closely because they produced very few artefacts – typically sherds of handmade pottery in the crude local Iron Age tradition, a very few Roman pottery sherds, glass bangles, stone tools and potboilers, and quernstones. The scatter of Roman objects from these sites have tended to be the only datable ones, and this led to a general belief that life went on in these Iron Age farmsteads much as it had done before the Romans came, with minimal adoption of Roman-style 'material culture'. In eastern England the story seemed very much the same for sites north of the Wall (in Northumberland) and to the south (in County Durham): the tradition of native roundhouse settlements seemed to continue unchanged to either side of the Wall.

On the south-east Northumberland coastal plain, immediately north of the Wall in the Newcastle area, the indigenous settlements showed up in air photographs in considerable numbers as early as the 1960s. The predominant settlement form in the north-east appeared to be a ditched and banked rectilinear enclosure, the sides typically 40–50m (44–55yd) long, containing a few roundhouses, and sometimes a large central house. The buildings were of timber on the coastal plain, sometimes of stone in the uplands.

When these sites were first examined in the 1960s, archaeologists believed that they had continued to flourish under a *pax Romana*, attaining their final and most developed form (sometimes with the use of stone construction) under Roman rule. Air-photographic survey has discovered many more sites of later Iron Age type very close to Hadrian's Wall, particularly in the central sector. These have also been assumed to be contemporary with it, the homes of people who lived with the Wall in their midst, who were little affected by Rome materially, but who benefited from the peace, communications and markets that the Roman military presence offered.

The last ten years have at last yielded new information about native settlement north of the Wall, thanks largely to large-scale developer-funded archaeology. Crucially, the financial resources made available through developer funding mean that it is now possible to date sites that are poor in artefacts, by means of extensive programmes of radiocarbon dating of organic materials such as carbonized wood, plant remains and bones.

The radiocarbon evidence shows that the earthwork enclosures were formed around 200BC as the latest phases on roundhouse settlements continuously occupied since the late Bronze Age. The late Iron Age settlements were not the isolated single enclosures we usually think of; rather, the substantial earthworks often occurred in concentric arrangements or even in pairs, indicating more than one leading family in a settlement. The settlements often had outworks and subsidiary enclosures attached. The radiocarbon dates make it clear that all these developments occurred before the Roman conquest of the region, and were not caused by economic development under Roman rule.

The new site types and their dates show that on the coastal plain of Tyne and Wear and Northumberland we are dealing with a late pre-Roman Iron Age society with more variation in wealth and status than was previously thought: it looks as if the substantial earthwork enclosures represent the social élite, while contemporary small unenclosed roundhouse settlements (not previously known in the region), and agglomerations of small-ditched enclosures, may have been dependent on the more substantial sites that up to now have monopolized the archaeological record. The biggest roundhouses of all occurred in the substantially enclosed settlements. There is evidence that these great houses were two-storeyed, with cattle accommodated on a low-ceilinged ground floor, and the human inhabitants (presumably members of a leading family) on an upper or mezzanine floor.

The radiocarbon dates now available indicate that, rather than flourishing contemporaneously with Hadrian's Wall, all these sites came to an abrupt end relatively early in the Roman period. Abandonment did not come with the first contact with the Roman military (in this region in the 70s AD). There is evidence that in the lower Tyne Valley the traditional agriculture of the region was still being practised on

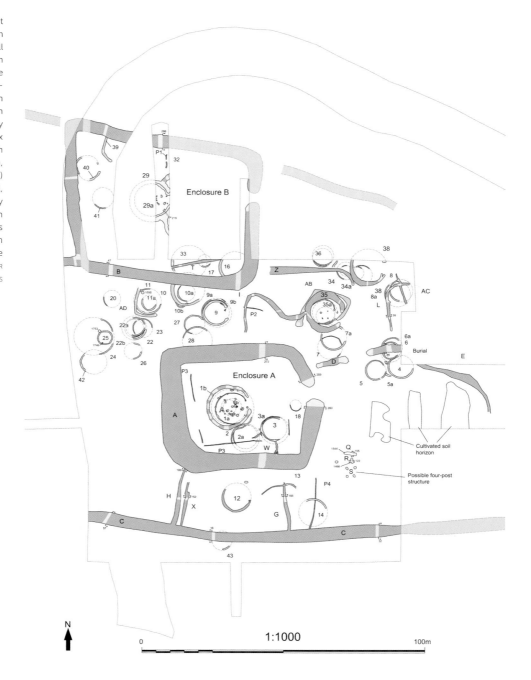

Fig. 3.14 Recent discoveries in the eastern Wall area have shown a much more sophisticated pre-Roman agrarian civilization than was previously thought. Complex enclosures such as West Brunton, just 6.5km (4 miles) north of the Wall, reached their fully developed form three centuries before the Roman conquest of the region. TYNE & WEAR ARCHIVES & MUSEUMS

Enclosure B

Enclosure A

Burial

Cultivated soil horizon

Possible four-post structure

N

0   1:1000   100m

the eve of the construction of Hadrian's Wall, around AD120, because active Iron Age cultivation regimes have been found and excavated beneath the construction levels of the Wall and its forts. This suggests that traditional life had gone on for the fifty years between the conquest of the 70s and the decision

to build Hadrian's Wall in the 120s. But occupation at all scientifically dated native sites north of the Wall ceased by some date in the second century AD, probably when the Wall was built or not long after.

It is also now clear that south of the Wall traditional life did not go on as before. A previously unsuspected settlement resembling what in southern Roman Britain would be termed a large village or a 'small town' has recently been found in the County Durham area at Hardwick Park, Sedgefield, and has been shown to have developed in the second century, not long after the Wall was built. This type of site has no Iron Age antecedents. A site at Faverdale, near Darlington, saw the rapid development in the Hadrianic period (around 120–40) of a roundhouse settlement into an enclosure complex, making conspicuous use of Roman pottery, metalwork and building technologies: it seems undeniable that either a member of the indigenous élite or some immigrant entrepreneur was profiting from their role in the supply infrastructure of the Wall and its garrisons. A distribution of Roman villas is now known in the County Durham area, again starting in the second century. That published in most detail, at Quarry Farm Ingleby Barwick, on the Tees, started life after the middle of the second century.

These discoveries suggest that Hadrian's Wall was no mere backcloth against which rural life went on much as before. They point to a major social dislocation occurring north of the Wall, and the creation

of a supply network and rudimentary Roman provincial society under the protection of the Wall to the south. At present this picture has been established for the east side of the country – we have no comparable new data from native sites in the central and western sectors of the Wall. In remote upland areas south of the Wall in Cumbria, there is a continuity of Iron Age settlement forms into the later Roman period, with sites with roundhouses such as Ewe Close producing late Roman finds. Here the immediate impact of Rome and the Wall was perhaps less than in the fertile lowland areas of the east, where the exploitation of economic resources led to rapid social change in the North Yorkshire–County Durham area.

Perhaps some settlements north of the Hadrian's Wall were abandoned as an act of Roman policy – the imposition of a cleared zone 16km (10 miles) wide, say, north of the frontier line, something paralleled beyond the Roman Rhine and Danube frontiers. This was once universally thought probable for the Wall, although it is no longer a fashionable idea (largely because of the discovery of settlements immediately north of the Wall, assumed to be contemporary with it – though the radiocarbon dates now suggest they

Fig. 3.15 Radiocarbon dates showing the lifespan of activity at three recently excavated pre-Roman enclosures north of the Wall. Activity ceases around the time that Hadrian's Wall is built. TYNE & WEAR ARCHIVES & MUSEUMS

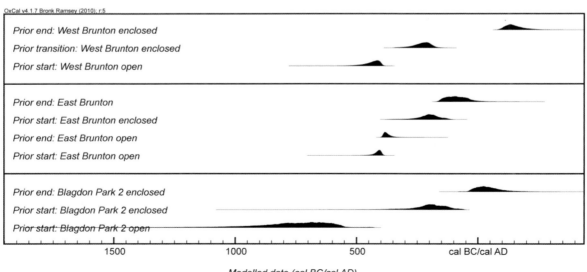

OxCal v4.1.7 Bronk Ramsey (2010); r:5

Prior end: West Brunton enclosed
Prior transition: West Brunton enclosed
Prior start: West Brunton open

Prior end: East Brunton
Prior start: East Brunton enclosed
Prior end: East Brunton open
Prior start: East Brunton open

Prior end: Blagdon Park 2 enclosed
Prior start: Blagdon Park 2 enclosed
Prior start: Blagdon Park 2 open

1500   1000   500   cal BC/cal AD

Modelled date (cal BC/cal AD)

are not). But site abandonment seems to extend further north than a 16km zone, and it seems likely that severed communications, disruption and warfare caused by the building of the Wall weakened the agricultural wealth and stability of social bonds that had allowed a complex society to express itself in earthwork enclosure and substantial roundhouse building. This must cast doubt on the view that the Wall regulated the economic movements of a native population that straddled the isthmus. On the contrary, Hadrian's barrier seems to have brought an agrarian civilization of long standing to an end, and replaced it with new social structures, different on either side of the Wall.

Peoples North of the Wall

What of the people to the north, beyond the immediate shadow of the Wall? Here a considerable population of agriculturalists (in the lowland areas) and pastoralists (in the remoter valleys), divided into a complex patchwork of peoples, faded into distant Scotland. Most had come into direct contact with the forces of Rome briefly in the period between 80 and 105. Although there was a multiplicity of peoples, they shared a common culture and could be united into larger groups co-ordinated under temporary leaders in time of war against an external threat, or for the purpose of making treaties with Rome.

No great reliance should be placed on the time-honoured tribal names that adorn maps of Roman Britain: the Novantae of Galloway, the Selgovae of the central Scottish Lowlands and upper Tweed basin, the Votadini of Northumberland and Lothian, and beyond, the Dumnonii of Strathclyde. The names are probably drastic simplifications that gloss over a multiplicity of smaller groups, which in any case will have changed by the second century AD – the two Roman written sources where these names occur are using source material that predates the building of the Wall by about half a century, reflecting the Roman interpretation of what was found when Scotland was invaded under Agricola. The Votadini

name may have had some enduring use to refer to the people centred on the hillfort of Traprain Law, near Edinburgh: the name is supposed to survive in the early Welsh poem the *Gododdin*, which describes the migration of some of this people from the mouth of the Forth to North Wales in the fifth century.

Archaeology does seem to reveal differing responses to Rome on the part of different regions of the Scottish Lowlands. In Lothian and the south-east, small numbers of Roman objects are widely found in the enclosed settlements that had been established in the later Iron Age and remained occupied in the early Roman period. There are also recognizable power centres, notably Traprain Law, indicating a society – loosely equated with the 'Votadini' – with some centralized political structure that could deal with Rome. Here, especially during the Antonine occupation of 140–60, imported Roman pottery and other materials made its way on to the native farmsteads.

In the area just north of the Forth–Clyde isthmus, the destruction layers in round stone towers ('brochs') such as Leckie and Fairy Knowe, perhaps destroyed during the Antonine invasion around 140, preserve evidence, which would not normally survive, of the trappings of life in these upper-echelon households: stone and lead lamps, stone spindle whorls, a bone weaving comb, sheep shears, fragments of shale and glass bangles, iron objects including a sickle and weapons (swords and spears), and Roman luxuries such as samian ware or a bronze mirror.

In the south-west Lowlands, and especially in Dumfriesshire, there was much less uptake of Roman material, and no clear power centres. A more diffuse social structure is indicated, more difficult to influence and control, and the upland landscape, indented with remote valleys, suggests separate and isolated communities. In south-east Scotland, in the Lothian area, there was a society that may have come to an accommodation with Rome following the first-century invasion, while in the south-west there were at least pockets of persistent hostility.

It is possible to understand, then, why Hadrian's Wall, as designed and operated under Hadrian, was directed towards a perceived threat from south-west Scotland and perhaps from other places across the Irish Sea. This is apparent from various facts. First, the elaborate system of surveillance along the Cumberland coast was not replicated on the east side of Britain. The only thousand-strong *ala* was at Stanwix, in the centre of the frontier line if the coastal defences are taken into account, but firmly in the west in terms of the Wall itself. The only three outpost forts beyond the Wall that we know to have been occupied under Hadrian were all in the west, with one of them, Birrens, guarding the gateway to Annandale.

The initial use of turf in the west was to prioritize completion in a sector where a barrier was needed most urgently. During the Antonine occupation of Scotland, Annandale and Nithsdale have a peculiar concentration of heavily fortified forts and fortlets, indicating a high security threat in an area which, as we have seen, was probably a seat of resistance and rebellion. But while Hadrian's Wall was originally directed towards this north-western threat, the Antonine Wall itself, and the military attention directed to the brochs beyond the Forth–Clyde, indicate how rapidly the social response to Hadrian's Wall shifted to the area out of reach beyond the isthmus, reducing the effectiveness of the Wall as conceived under Hadrian.

The presence of the Wall probably had the same baneful effect on native settlement on the northern shore of the Solway and in southern Dumfries and Galloway as on the north-east coastal plain of Northumberland: at any rate, it is difficult to find any sites in this zone immediately north of Hadrian's Wall that can be shown to have been still in occupation after the Antonine occupation. Presumably life went on as before in settlements and hillforts in the remoter valleys of the interior south-west, and this must have been a source of resistance for much of the second century.

There would have been an immense Roman appetite for economic products from far north of the Wall, especially cattle for meat and hides, and perhaps horses. Those groups prepared to deal with Rome, as in the Lothian area, would need a way of trading their products into the empire, especially if their leaders wanted to acquire high status Roman objects. If we are to envisage trade through the Wall, we should be thinking of long-distance trading delegations, perhaps of considerable size and arriving periodically, rather than routine passage through the milecastle gateways by a strictly local population. As we have seen, the Wall led to economic collapse in local society, rather than promoting the continuation of normal economic movement and exchange.

We would also expect trading parties from far away to come to the Wall at a limited number of arranged supervised crossing places – and recent metal detector discoveries have revealed the possible location of just such a one. Around the village of Great Whittington, just two and a half kilometres (a mile and a half) north of Milecastle 21, has been found an extraordinary concentration of Iron Age metal objects, Roman coins, brooches and military equipment. This was thought to indicate a settlement site, but the finds are not typical of settlements north of the Wall, and a geophysical survey found no trace of a built site.

A much more attractive suggestion is that this was a frontier trading place or market, or a waiting area where trading delegations camped under military supervision while waiting to be escorted to a market on the Roman side of the Wall. Significantly, Great Whittington lies close to the convergence of two Roman roads from the north – Dere Street and the Devil's Causeway – which approach the Wall here. The former passed through the Wall via a special gate, 'The Portgate', which stands outside the normal milecastle series, and just 3km (2 miles) further south was the Roman frontier town of Corbridge, which by the 160s had developed as a marketing and distribution centre for the eastern Wall zone. In medieval times the Roman roads remained important for droving cattle to the famous cattle fair at Stagshaw bank, held just south of the Portgate. The coins from Great Whittington suggest that the activity began in the earliest days of the Wall; such a special trading place was therefore a Hadrianic institution. There might be others: Carlisle and Newcastle are possibilities. ✿

Chapter 4

THE HEYDAY OF THE WALL: AD160–250

WITH THE FINAL ABANDONMENT OF Scotland we cross a threshold into the period on the Wall that is richest in archaeological information, especially inscriptions, but also all other classes of finds. After some final shuffling around, individual auxiliary units became permanently attached to the forts they would occupy for centuries to come. The individual forts became the foci of extensive settled communities of civilians, as well as soldiers. Now a once mobile army of conquest was irretrievably linked to a static frontier.

A narrative of events 160–250

One Roman literary source says that on the accession of the Emperor Marcus in 161 'war was threatening in Britain'. Marcus sent two formidable generals to govern Britain. The first was Statius Priscus, who was immediately recalled to deal with a sudden crisis that blew up on the eastern frontier. The second was Calpurnius Agricola, sent in 161 or 162, who probably oversaw the final and ceremonial abandonment of the Antonine Wall, when the magnificent distance slabs recording its construction were taken down and buried. He reconditioned Hadrian's Wall and much of the network of forts to its north and south, and we are told (we know nothing of the details) campaigned against the Britons.

Hadrian's Wall as Restored after the Withdrawal from Scotland

Hadrian's Wall was thoroughly restored, a process beginning in 158 and continuing into the early 160s. At Byker and Walbottle the berm obstacles had been reconstructed in a second phase, which could belong to this time. This is the most likely time for the rebuilding of the remainder of Hadrian's Turf Wall in stone, to a width of 2.4–2.9m (8–9.5RF), a gauge intermediate between the Broad and Narrow Walls of the original stone sector. The replacement incorporated the stone turrets of the Turf Wall, and the turf milecastles were replaced in stone. At Garthside (Turf Wall turret 54A), the first Turf Wall turret had collapsed into the ditch and been replaced by a second free-standing stone turret and a length of Turf Wall and ditch on a new alignment. Later, the stone Wall that replaced the Turf Wall was brought up to abut the turret. This arrangement lasted for some time before the turret went out of use and was overlain by a rebuild of the stone Wall.

The pottery from the final turret showed that the whole sequence occurred before the late second or early third century. Assuming that the final demolition of the turret and the rebuild of the stone Wall took place then, as it seems to have elsewhere, this would most comfortably place the original stone Wall around 160. At Turf Wall Milecastle 79 there was only pottery of the first half of the second century, and none of the period after 160, suggesting that the stone replacement had taken place by then.

The Forts

We know few of the units that reoccupied the Wall forts. There is an inscription of Calpurnius Agricola from Carvoran, where the Hamian archers had moved back into their old base as early as 158, and a few others of the 160s, but all these arrangements were transitory: the later 160s were a period of dire emergency on the Danube frontier, and many units in Britain might have been under strength at that time, having supplied detachments to the continent; it is only in the 170s or 180s that the single units we later associate with the Wall forts become permanently based there. There are exceptions: for example, at Housesteads there is evidence that its permanent unit in the third and fourth centuries, *cohors I Tungrorum*, was there as early as the 150s/60s.

Milecastles and Turrets

Judging from the limited sample of excavated sites, the milecastle gates that had been removed during the period *c.*140–60 were replaced, although the replacement pivot stones in which they swung show little wear in the period after *c.*160, suggesting that from now on the great 3m (10ft) wide gates did not see as much use by the army. Perhaps by this time most of the causeways across the ditch in front of milecastles were removed.

The turrets were reoccupied, as datable pottery found in them shows. However, none of the towers and only a small selection of the milefortlets along the Cumbrian coast were recommissioned, and those not for very long. Some, or all of the forts at Beckfoot, Maryport, Moresby and perhaps Burrow Walls were reoccupied, but the surveillance system in between had had its day. That might indicate that the campaigns of Calpurnius Agricola had done their work, and marks the shift in attention away from south-west Scotland towards new threats from the north-east.

The Vallum

The Vallum was reconditioned, and this is the likeliest time for the removal of causeways that had slighted the Vallum at the beginning of Pius' reign. Material from the removed crossings was used to form a second mound on the side of the Vallum, the 'marginal mound', which is still conspicuously visible in many places today and runs along the south lip of the Vallum ditch itself.

It has recently been claimed that the 'marginal mound' is a primary, Hadrianic element of the Vallum, because in places it has been found to consist of clean, freshly dug clay rather than dirty silt cleaned out of the ditch, and set on freshly striped subsoil. This is unlikely, however: the marginal mound is structurally later than the Antonine slighting of the Vallum – it is *never* cut by the crossings in the way that the north and south mounds are – and rather than being placed on the original lip of the Vallum ditch, it is placed on the edge of the ditch as widened by the effects of erosion. At some milecastles the crossings that had been inserted were not removed, but at Milecastle 23 the mounds were reinstated, so this was not a new regular series of entrances into the Wall–Vallum zone.

The Military Way and the Wall Bridges

The main service road running behind the Wall from fort to fort (and with branch roads or tracks going to milecastles and turrets) is often said to have been provided for the first time now, and was not part of the Hadrianic scheme. The road is known by an antiquarian term, the 'Military Way' – not to be confused with the Military Road, as the B6318, which overlies 50km (30 miles) of the Wall curtain, is known locally. The basic evidence for ascribing the Military Way to the reoccupation of the Wall is that in places it overlies the Vallum, sometimes riding along the top of the previously slighted north mound. Yet we have seen that the Hadrianic design of the Wall forts anticipated a Military Way, and it seems inconceivable that there was not some Hadrianic precursor to the known road, perhaps extensively re-engineered and re-routed when the Vallum was recommissioned, and possibly observed by antiquaries who claimed to have seen a 'lesser military way'.

The Military Way was only one of a number of east–west routes along the rear of the Wall: a service track immediately behind the curtain itself is known in various places, and there are intermittent examples of tracks on the Vallum berms; for anyone wanting to move swiftly through the central sector, from Corbridge to Carlisle, say, the Stanegate, which provided a direct arterial route behind the Wall, like a string to a bow, would be the best choice.

A grand architectural conception for the restored Wall and its associated works is implied by the bridge where the Wall crossed the River North Tyne at Chesters. This was a stone, arched structure from the beginning, but it has now been rebuilt as a road bridge, where formerly it had only carried the Wall walk itself over the river. Older reconstruction

drawings show the second bridge as a timber platform raised on stone piers, but a careful study of the many (still visible) massive stone blocks fallen from the bridge has shown that some are from a decorative cornice that ran above stone arches. There is thus no doubt that the road bridge at Chesters was also of stone, carrying the Military Way across the North Tyne on four graceful arches, each some 10m (33ft) wide. The other major rivers crossed by the Wall were the Irthing (at Willowford) and the Eden (at Stanwix), and here, too, road bridges succeeded earlier Wall walk crossings. The bridge at Willowford was less elaborate than the other two, and apparently did have a timber superstructure when reconstituted as a road bridge.

The New North-East Outpost System

The work of building stone bridges also extended to the main road (Dere Street), running from the

Fig. 4.1 The outpost fort system north of Hadrian's Wall at its most far-reaching extent, immediately after the abandonment of the Antonine Wall around 160. FRONTIERS OF THE ROMAN EMPIRE CULTURE 2000 PROJECT/D. J. BREEZE

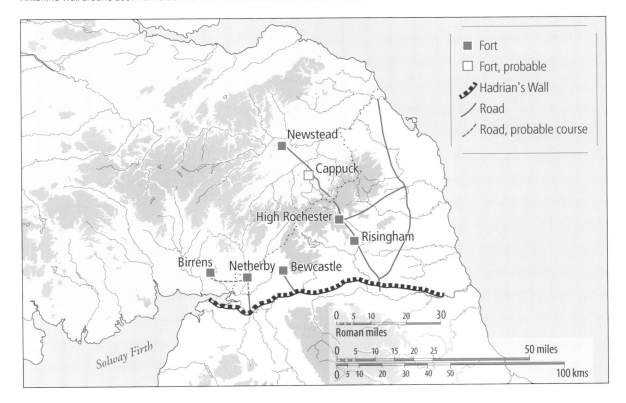

Fig. 4.2 Temple façade at Corbridge, restored from architectural fragments found at the site. Note the *Sol Invictus* inscription, which would have adorned a temple of this type.

0   6m

Portgate on the Wall up to Scotland; the bridge at Corbridge carrying Dere Street across the Tyne was rebuilt in stone, probably at the same time as that at Chesters, while at Risingham, 19km (12 miles) north of the Wall, the River Rede was crossed by a stone bridge. An ornate inscription from the outpost fort at Risingham shows that it was rebuilt in the period 161–9 (or less likely, 176–80). This was the first in a series of outposts extending north of the Wall along Dere Street for a distance of 80km (50 miles), all the way to the great fort at Newstead, which had been retained and rebuilt following the abandonment of all of Scotland further north, and which housed a cavalry *ala* and a detachment of the Twentieth legion.

Intermediate forts at High Rochester and Cappuck were also occupied at this time.

Calpurnius Agricola's restoration of the Wall therefore envisaged a projection of military strength from the eastern side of the Wall towards far distant south-east Scotland. Such a chain of outposts along a road projecting from the main military baseline was known as a *praetensio*, and that term, or an equivalent – *praetentura* – is fragmentarily preserved on an inscription from Corbridge, seemingly dedicated by the commander of one of the outposts, Risingham. The findspot at Corbridge is significant, because the former auxiliary fort there was transformed under Calpurnius Agricola to function as the rearward base

Fig. 4.3 The fine masonry of 'Site XI' at Corbridge: a great market building that lay at the centre of the town and legionary base, but which was mysteriously abandoned in an unfinished state sometime in the period 165–85.

for the far-extended chain of outposts. Detachments of legions VI and XX built a religious enclave there, graphically attested by a large collection of sculpture and architectural fragments from classical temples, found before World War I, reused in the later Roman town at Corbridge. Most striking is the dedication slab from a temple to *Sol Invictus* – the unconquered sun – carved by masons of the Sixth Legion and naming Calpurnius Agricola. Another massive slab of the Twentieth Legion, from an unknown building at Corbridge, names Agricola and dates to 163 or 164.

The legionary detachments at Corbridge had a dual role: they sent troops to man the outposts (and also the minor structures on the Wall?), and they oversaw Corbridge, which lay at an intersection of routes, as a place where military supplies were gathered and marketed or distributed, at least to the eastern half of the Wall. We might expect Carlisle, in the west, to have had a similar function; here, as at Corbridge, a legionary detachment base and urban development are very clearly attested later, in the third century

– but for the moment excavations in Carlisle have not revealed a clear picture of what was going on there in the 160s. The Hadrianic outpost forts on the west side were probably all retained in this period: Birrens, in Annandale (rebuilt in 158), Netherby on the Esk, and Bewcastle.

Calpurnius Agricola's campaigns must have been so effective that the focus of resistance in south-west Scotland was snuffed out or driven north of the Forth–Clyde isthmus, allowing him to decommission the Cumbrian coast system, while he evidently foresaw where the threats of the future would emerge in response to the presence of Rome – eastern Scotland, north of the Forth. The Newstead *praetensio* points in this direction, and was perhaps also intended to provide support to Rome's allies centred on Lothian. The success of his campaign is also implied by the fact that there was no catastrophic invasion during the difficult years between 166 and the mid-170s, when the Roman world was shaken by serious barbarian incursions on the Danube and many troops will inevitably have been withdrawn from Britain, while the empire was wracked by plague brought back by the army from the east.

The development of Corbridge may have been arrested by these events. An immense courtyard building there, 66m (216ft) square, probably intended for the storage and marketing of goods, was left unfinished, possibly in these years. The cohort of Tungrians at Housesteads erected a dedication to all the gods and goddesses on the advice of the oracle at Claros, in Asia Minor, possibly given to Marcus Aurelius who had sought guidance on how to counter the destructive force of the plague. There must have been many other disruptions. Unsurprisingly, we hear that in 169 'the Britons were on the verge of war', but the Wall and its outposts continued to be held and did not fall.

The Wall is Breached

By 180 the Romans had the upper hand on the Danube, and controlled territory to the north of the river, but Commodus, who became sole ruler on Marcus' death in 180, came to terms with the northern peoples, withdrawing Roman armies from enemy territory. Something similar was to happen in Britain; around this time most of the outpost forts beyond the Wall were abandoned: Newstead and Birrens, probably Cappuck, High Rochester and Risingham, and perhaps others. The historian Cassius Dio offers the only direct evidence we have from the whole of the Roman period of Hadrian's Wall being broken through by a major invasion. Dio claims this was the greatest war of Commodus' reign: in the early 180s 'The tribes in the island crossed the Wall that separated them from the Roman legions, did a great deal of damage, and cut down a general and his troops...'. This 'general' was probably a legionary commander.

This was, then, a serious invasion. On one interpretation of the evidence, Commodus sent a renowned general, Ulpius Marcellus, who had already governed Britain in the years 177–80, back to his old province to deal with the emergency. Troops were rushed to Britain from other provinces. Finds recovered since 1830 from the Herd Sand at the mouth of the River Tyne at South Shields, or dredged from its northern edge, include a shield boss of the *Legio VIII Augusta*, a helmet cheekpiece, sixty-seven coins, and other items. All are remarkably close in date: the latest coin is of 176–80. It is probable that the objects and coins, which still come to light from time to time, are being washed out of the wreck of a ship that came to grief entering the mouth of the Tyne in the later second century. The presence of a legionary of *VIII Augusta* (based at Strasbourg) suggests a troop ship bringing reinforcements into the northern frontier zone, perhaps in response to the invasion attested in the early 180s.

Corbridge was affected by a destructive fire in the second half of the second century, very possibly the result of enemy action. The so-called 'Corbridge destruction deposit' represents an event that could well coincide in date with the attested crossing of the Wall by barbarian invaders in the early 180s. Another possibly contemporary destruction deposit has been recorded at the nearby Wall fort at Halton Chesters. To connect these archaeological deposits with the attested invasion is highly speculative, but if there is a connection, it is interesting that these sites lie on or close to Dere Street, suggesting the route of an invasion with its source in eastern Scotland. Corbridge also has the remains of the Shorden Brae mausoleum, one of the largest and most elaborate tower tombs in the Roman world, constructed about this time, which might just be a memorial to the fallen commander and his troops, and a suggestion that the breaching of the Wall and the military catastrophe occurred near Corbridge.

Dio implies that extensive damage must have been done to the province south of Hadrian's Wall. Most towns in Britain, previously unenclosed, were provided with earthwork defences around this time, a much earlier trend than on the continent. Not all archaeologists believe that the town walls were constructed simultaneously, and some may pre-date the 180s, but the Commodan war exemplifies what was feared by the authorities who sought to build town defences in this period. We have no historical information about the war that Ulpius Marcellus fought against the invaders; Commodus took the title *Britannicus maximus* in 184, and the text of Cassius Dio implies that following a Roman victory, Ulpius Marcellus concluded peace treaties with the peoples of north-east Scotland. It is not clear whether Commodus gave up the outpost forts as a matter of policy at the beginning of his reign, unwittingly encouraging an invasion, or whether they were evacuated as part of the peace agreement with the northern peoples around 184.

Rebellion and Neglect: the Northern Frontier from 184 to 197

A handful of inscriptions show that by the 180s certain units had moved into the Wall and hinterland forts they would occupy for decades, in some cases centuries, to come: this seems possibly the case at Benwell (*ala I Asturum*); and at Chesters, *ala II Asturum* was in place by this time and would stay there until the end of the Roman period. The long-term units at Housesteads and Stanwix were already there, probably since the 160s. The third-century units at the hinterland forts of Old Penrith and Old Carlisle were there by 178 and 188 respectively. It seems possible that many other Wall-fort units well attested in the third century were settled into place in the 180s, perhaps in a reorganization conducted by Ulpius Marcellus, but we cannot be sure; a few – including *cohors IV Gallorum* at Vindolanda – might have been moved into their final positions later, in the early third century.

The scanty historical sources indicate that during Commodus' increasingly eccentric and tyrannical rule, the senators commanding the legions in Britain were potential usurpers, and the legions themselves were in a state of mutiny in the mid-180s. Perhaps Commodus restrained the British generals, jealous of any potential victory they might win; perhaps the army in Britain was kept short of reinforcements.

Finally, in 192, Commodus was assassinated. There were three generals with powerful armies ready to step into the vacuum: Clodius Albinus, governor of Britain 192–7, Pescennius Niger of Syria, and, cleverest and most ruthless of all, the African Septimius Severus, who had sprung to the purple from his military command in Pannonia on the Danube.

Although Albinus was given the title of Caesar (junior emperor) by Severus in 193, he must have known that one day soon he would have to fight Severus for his life. Unsurprisingly, given these distractions, we hear of no major campaigns or building programmes on the northern frontier of Britain in these years. Severus eliminated his only other rival, Niger, in 194. In 196 Albinus crossed to Gaul to face Severus, taking much of the British garrison with him, but probably leaving enough troops to man the Wall. With his death following defeat at Lugdunum (Lyon) in February 197, Britain fell to Septimius Severus, now master of the Roman world.

The Wall under Septimius Severus

Severus' first governor in Britain, Virius Lupus, had to pay the northern tribes to keep the peace after they had broken treaties made at the conclusion of Ulpius Marcellus' campaign in 184–5, or with Albinus before his departure, or both. While Severus campaigned in the east, in 197–202, the British army was deliberately left in its depleted state following Albinus' bid for power, so no usurper could make a bid for power from the island. There is evidence that some forts in north Britain were not fully occupied at this time. The northern tribes took advantage of this situation to raid the province, and there seems to have been continuing warfare in the period 197–205, though there is no evidence that the Wall was catastrophically overrun and extensively damaged after the removal of the army by Albinus, as was once universally believed.

When at last the imperial administration turned its attention to Britain, Alfenus Senecio, who probably governed Britain around 205–8, undertook an ambitious programme of refurbishment of the forts

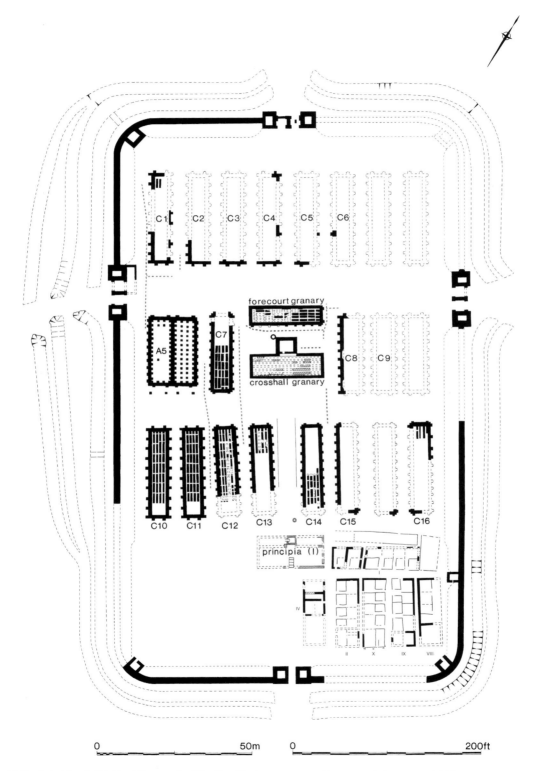

Fig. 4.4 The fort at South Shields, at the mouth of the River Tyne, was converted into a supply base around 208. In its fully developed form, seen here, it contained twenty-four granaries. TYNE & WEAR ARCHIVES & MUSEUMS

throughout the north – we know of this entirely from inscriptions. This probably included a programme of rebuilding work on Hadrian's Wall itself, on such a scale that later Roman historians credited Severus with having been the first to build the Wall. The coastal fort at South Shields was converted into a supply base at this time.

With the northern frontier of the province secured against counter attack, Severus, aged sixty-three but 'in his heart more enthusiastic than any youth', arrived in Britain in 208 and made preparations for a great campaign in the north – though this was not with the intention of extending the empire into Scotland. That ambition was now dead, and no network of roads and forts was built in Scotland, as had been during the Antonine occupation; also, only two permanent military bases were occupied (at Cramond, near Edinburgh, and Carpow, in Fife): these were held as outposts north of Hadrian's Wall for a few years. Rather, the intention was to exert Roman dominance, by means of a brutal and destructive raid, over the peoples in a zone 130–320km (80–200 miles) beyond the Wall.

With the emperor travelled the Empress Julia Domna, his elder son and Augustus (co-ruler), Caracalla, his younger son, the Caesar (junior emperor), Geta, and the whole of the imperial court. For three years the empire was ruled from Britain, while an army numbering perhaps 40,000, supplied by sea and road from rearward bases at South Shields and Corbridge, invaded and ravaged north-east Scotland. There is evidence that Severus toured the forts of the Wall area, inspecting the refurbishment of the frontier that he had ordered as a prelude to his great invasion of the north. Undoubtedly he will have inspected granaries at Corbridge, where an inscription records their use during the *expeditio felicissima Britannica* – 'the most fortunate British expedition'. But even the celebrated Roman army was unable to locate and destroy an elusive enemy, and there was to be no decisive victory in Scotland. A peace agreement was made.

Severus died in York in 211, and his sons returned with their father's ashes to Rome. Having murdered his brother at the end of 211, Caracalla was sole ruler until 217.

Hadrian's Wall in its Restored State

It was probably under Alfenus Senecio in 205–7 that a return was made to the policy of the 160s by reinstating a powerful and far-reaching system of outpost forts north of the Wall. These no longer reached as far north as the Tweed, but nominally 'milliary' – 'a thousand strong' – mixed units of infantry and cavalry were installed at Risingham and High Rochester on Dere Street, the last 35km (22 miles) north of the Portgate; a third outpost possibly lay near Jedburgh. In the west there were outposts at Netherby and Bewcastle, the former certainly with the same kind of part-mounted cohort. These formidable military concentrations were reinforced with various irregular units. We have inscriptions naming 'Raetian spearmen' at Risingham, and *exploratores* (spies and scouts) at both Risingham and High Rochester. The *exploratores* must have cut romantic figures, perhaps adopting the dress and language of native peoples, and engaged in spying and commando missions over great distances.

The whole outpost system, with its variety of units, reminds us that for nearly the whole period from 160 to the early fourth century the Wall was simply one layer in a forward-looking network of military intelligence, observation and defence.

The Wall itself saw major changes. These cannot be dated more closely than the late second or early third century: some may belong to Senecio's restoration of the Wall, others may have occurred more gradually. A new fort, of small size and innovative design, was added to the Wall at Newcastle, where previously the bridgehead had been guarded by a fort, putative and undiscovered, on the southern, Gateshead side. The Wall curtain itself was reconstructed in various places, as seen at Garthside turret. In the crags sector this rebuild is often to a very narrow gauge of 2m (6ft) or so, and the use of hard white

Fig. 4.5 Later rebuilding: the south side of the Wall in Peel Gap (Wall-mile 39) under excavation in the mid-1980s. Beneath the extra narrow Wall of the late second or early third century can be seen the original Hadrianic Narrow Wall, and below that, the Broad Wall foundation. Note the appearance of the unexcavated Wall behind the figure, merely a stony mound.

mortar is characteristic. The obstacles in front of the Wall were not renewed, and their emplacement pits were filled.

A series of building inscriptions recording work on the Wall curtain by corvées of civilian labour from the southern British *civitates* – and perhaps the Brigantes – are possibly from this general phase of refurbishment of the Wall, although an even earlier date, when the Wall was reoccupied around 160, has also been suggested. These stones were once dated to the end of the Roman period (around 370), but that now seems impossible: inscriptions of this kind do not occur at such a late date, and their character is

unmistakably second or third century. The first stone fort at Vindolanda was demolished under Septimius Severus, and for a brief period, before being rebuilt, was replaced by neat rows of at least 200 stone roundhouses, buildings of native British type but arranged under military supervision.

It has been suggested that this striking and utterly unparalleled phenomenon might be explained by the accommodation of the levies from southern Britain, engaged on rebuilding the Wall under Severus. If the inscriptions are of this period, they sit alongside the supply base at South Shields in indicating large-scale requisition from the civil part of Britain – both supplies and labour – for the maintenance of the northern Wall and the conduct of war in the north.

Milecastles generally remained in occupation, but their gates were frequently narrowed to mere foot passages, and in some cases there is evidence that the towers surmounting the gates were demolished. On the other hand, they still routinely contain accommodation for a full complement of troops, in the region of thirty to forty.

Around this time many turrets were dispensed with. The obliteration of turrets was almost total on the crags in the central sector, which is why there are so few to see there today, although even here there are exceptions, such as 44B. Turret interiors were recessed into the thickness of the great Wall, and following their obliteration the recess was usually walled up so that the Wall curtain was carried across the site at full width. We only have information for the later history of 38 out of 157 or so turrets (subtracting those that underlie forts), and, as the following figures suggest, many more may have been kept in the lowland zones than in the central sector where the precipitous crags rendered them superfluous:

	Abandoned at end of C2	Occupied in C3/4
East of North Tyne:	7	3
Central Sector:	15	4
West of Irthing:	4	5

The Vallum seemingly lost its former significance: while it remained (and remains) a conspicuous linear feature behind the Wall, in the vicinity of the forts it was filled in, forgotten about, and overlain by the buildings of the civil settlements that now clustered outside the fort walls.

The Lack of Literary Sources for Third-Century Britain

Probably in 213 or 214 Britain was divided into two provinces: Britannia Superior, with its capital at London, and Britannia Inferior, governed from York. This was a measure against feared revolt, preventing the whole British army being concentrated in the hands of a potential usurper. Provinces throughout the empire were divided in a similar way. Hadrian's Wall now lay in the single-legion province of Inferior. However, there was much co-operation and transfer of military detachments between the two provinces, and soldiers and officials from Britannia Superior are often encountered operating on the Wall.

At this point our historical sources for Britain fall abruptly silent. The already meagre accounts of Dio and Herodian have nothing more to say about Britain, and the island no longer features in imperial biographies. The conclusion usually drawn from the silence of the sources for this period is that Britain was at peace in the third century, Severus' campaigns having cowed the northern tribes for a generation or more. It is true that the forts and their attendant civilian settlements were at the peak of their development and artefactual richness for the first few decades of the century, and that there is none of the graphic archaeological evidence for widespread destruction and plunder by invaders, both at frontier forts and rural sites, that is found in the German provinces in the 230s.

But the relative stability of the British frontier was probably only maintained because of constant vigilance and action by the army, which has gone unrecorded in our written sources; this is because the latter concentrated on the momentous and, for the Romans, disastrous events that unfolded in the 220s and 230s on the Rhine, Danube and eastern frontiers. The rise of Sassanian Persia from 224 threatened the Roman Empire in the east, and a Roman campaign to retrieve Mesopotamia in 231–3, the first of a series of debilitating wars against the Persians, was immediately followed by a destructive breach of the German frontier in 233.

In this scale of things Britain was a backwater indeed, and we only have archaeology to shine a light into the darkness of the period 211–50 on the Wall: the utter lack of any historical framework of events is to some extent compensated for by the survival of stone inscriptions, which were erected in their greatest numbers in the earlier part of this period. This evidence shows that after 211 the army in Britain continued to receive reinforcement from the continent, itself increasingly short of troops to deal with the crises of the third century, and suggests that quite striking changes were made in military dispositions in Britain.

For example, a new fort was built, probably shortly before 217, at Piercebridge, 50km (31 miles) south of the Wall, well placed near a junction of roads to send a force either north up Dere Street, or west in the direction of Carlisle and south-west Scotland. Part of the Sixth Legion was stationed there, accompanied by detachments of legions from the provinces of Upper and Lower Germany. The concentration of strength represented by this large fort (4.58ha/11.32 acres), and the presence of legionaries from Germany, suggest that major incursions from the north were still anticipated. Piercebridge is part of a continuing shift of military orientation from the west to east, which we have already noted. We also see this in the foundation of new coastal forts on the Norfolk and Kent coasts, forerunners of the later 'Saxon Shore forts', at Brancaster, Caistor and Reculver; *cohors I Baetasiorum*, formerly at Maryport on the Cumbrian coast, built and occupied the fort at Reculver.

As we shall see, silver-coin subsidies continued to be paid to the peoples of northern Scotland down to the 230s, showing that Severus' campaigns had not harried them to destruction, and that there was still a perceived threat that had to be placated. The civilian settlements attached to forts in the hinterland of the Wall were routinely surrounded by defences, as were some on the Wall. The overall impression for the first half of the third century, then, is of a stable situation on the restored northern frontier, managed by units that were now permanently tied to long-standing bases, but one where, from the Roman perspective, there was a constant underlying threat of raids, violence and attacks on the provinces. Conversely, the Romans may have routinely and without provocation undertaken raids north of the Wall, of which we know nothing. We shall see more evidence that these were not wholly settled times as we turn to the life of the third-century army of the Wall.

The Army of the Wall: 160–250

The Enhanced Status of the Soldiery

The army of the Wall that Hadrian would have recognized seems to have lasted until the time of Septimius Severus in the early third century, but after that a number of changes in the life and appearance of the soldiers becomes apparent. The number of citizens in the auxiliary forces had gradually increased in the second century, as increasing numbers of the sons of discharged soldiers followed their fathers into the army, a process facilitated by the permanent settlement of veterans close to their former bases, now permanently fixed.

In 212, citizenship was granted to virtually all free inhabitants of the empire, recognition that Rome no longer meant merely a city, but rather a world empire – and a cynical means of gathering more tax. The regimental distinction between legionaries and auxiliaries continued, even though all were Roman citizens now. But even before the introduction of universal citizenship, the diplomas that are such a rich source for the origins of soldiers and the history of auxiliary units in the second century dry up. Now, the prospect of citizenship on discharge was no longer

Fig. 4.6 An authentic and well researched recreation by *Cohors Quinta Gallorum* of a third-century auxiliary infantryman of the Wall. ALEXANDRA CROOM

the lure that attracted recruits (as far as we know, army recruitment remained voluntary in principle).

There was no shortage of recruits because by the third century the army was increasingly well paid and prosperous. Severus and succeeding emperors knew that they were precariously dependent on the loyalty and support of the army, which might easily abandon them for a more generous benefactor; by the mid third century the army had become the appointer of emperors, often men of no social distinction drawn from its own ranks.

Severus had seen this coming, and from his deathbed had advised his sons to 'enrich the soldiers, scorn the rest'. Severus had doubled the pay of the soldiers, the first pay rise they had received since the reign of Domitian, a century earlier; under Caracalla there was a further 50 per cent rise. The unreliable Greek historian Herodian claims that pay was doubled again in 235–8.

The real value of these rises may have been eroded by the monetary inflation developing in this period, but the need to be seen to be enriching the army is obvious. Although we know little about it, there was probably increasing use of payment in kind – in foodstuffs, clothing and equipment – in addition to the soldier's cash payment.

The Appearance of the Wall Forts in the Third Century

Rather in the same way that monks in the middle ages abandoned their original austere and mendicant ideals to live and work in great and prosperous institutions, the army of the fixed frontiers of the early third century came to live in more comfortable conditions and more splendid surroundings than previously. The earlier third century is the absolute heyday of epigraphy in the empire, and a long series of inscriptions from the forts of northern Britain – itself doubtless only a fraction of the original total – records the construction or repair of buildings and facilities such as granaries, aqueducts, baths and temples. Buildings such as an armament store, a cavalry drill hall and artillery platforms are also mentioned at individual forts.

With the trend towards units becoming permanently associated with particular forts, the archaeology of the sites gradually changes. This period sees a shift from timber to stone construction in those lesser buildings, such as barracks, which had sometimes first been built in timber under Hadrian – although it is important to stress that timber post-hole construction continues to be found in all periods, and that stone buildings, including barracks, could often have had internal partitions of timber. Where excavated, all other buildings in forts, including the *principia*, commanding officer's house, granaries and workshops, show a series of complex modifications.

In the *principia* it was now common for a flight of steps to lead down from the shrine of the standards, an underfloor barrel-vaulted strongroom, where the unit funds were kept. The offices to either side were

Fig. 4.7 One of many inscriptions from north Britain in the early third century documenting construction or repair at forts. This example is from South Shields and records that an aqueduct was built in 222. The words *aquam usibus mil coh V Gall induxit* – 'water brought in for the use of the soldiers of the Fifth Cohort of Gauls' – can be seen in lines five and six.
TYNE & WEAR ARCHIVES & MUSEUMS

closed off from the basilica by counters and grilles like an old-fashioned bank or ticket office. Here the soldiers could bank their savings or withdraw their deposits. By the first half of the third century the *principia* in every fort was richly adorned with inscriptions, statues and wall paintings, a crowded and colourful affirmation of the unit's loyalty to the emperor and awareness of its own long history in the service of Rome. The basilica of the *principia* of the outpost fort at Risingham carried a stone inscribed panel 5.72m (almost 19ft) long, listing the titles and victories of the Emperor Caracalla, and affirming the 'joint duty and devotion' of *cohors I Vangionum* and the two units of irregulars who accompanied the cohort at this remote outpost (the 'Raetian spearmen' and 'the Scouts of *Habitancum*'). This is in fact one of a series of protestations of loyalty found throughout north Britain, dating to 213 under the Governor Julius Marcus: in vain, however, for the erasure of his name shows that, suspected of disloyalty, real or imagined, he was eliminated.

Some of the sculptural decoration from the headquarters of one of the legionary detachments stationed at Corbridge in the early third century has survived, evoking the brightly coloured shrine once packed with altars, statuary and standards: fragments of a statue base inscribed '*To the Emperors' Discipline*' found cast into the strongroom, and one panel of a dado depicting the labours of Hercules. Fragments of a stone panel that once adorned the walls of the shrine of the standards show the *vexillum*, or flag, of the detachment from the Second Legion. It is flanked by fluted pilasters, one of which is crowned with roses in a reference to the festival in May, *rosaliae signorum*, when the standards of Roman army units were worshipped and bedecked with roses. Other panels show standards with roundels attached to a pole, of the kind seen on Trajan's Column.

Changes in the Style of Barracks

Nothing so captures the orderliness of the Roman army as the regular barrack blocks of the first and second centuries, derived from the tent rows of marching camps, and replicated throughout the permanent fort for each century or *turma*. The single visible example of a barrack, such as this on the Wall is at Chesters, uncovered in the 1890s. Excavations at Housesteads between 1959–61 and 1974–8, and at Wallsend in 1975–84, expected to find something similar, but were confronted with a more complex reality.

At both sites, the barrack remains first encountered appeared informal and jumbled, a maze of walls that showed rebuilding on numerous occasions and great variation in plan from one barrack to another. They all shared the characteristic of a lesser number of accommodation units than the expected ten – often five or six. The accommodation units were detached from each other and separated by narrow alleys. Planning appeared highly irregular, but there was always a larger block where a centurion's or decurion's house would be expected. Underneath these complicated remains in each case there peeped out of the lower levels the remains of an earlier barrack with the more regular layout and the nine or ten *contubernia* that the text books had led excavators to expect. So at some stage there had clearly been a great change in the character of barracks – indeed, had they ceased to be barracks at all?

By the 1970s such buildings were not interpreted as barracks in the normally understood sense, but as rows of huts, given the term 'chalets', and also recognizable on older excavation plans at Great Chesters, High Rochester and elsewhere. They were thought to have originated in the late empire, with the reforms of Diocletian or Constantine (so late third or early fourth century), and to signify the movement of soldiers' families into the forts, with consequent reduction in unit strength (there being, it was suggested, only one soldier and family per chalet) and decline in military order.

It has been recognized in recent years that the key characteristic of the so-called chalets – five or six accommodation units, often detached from one another – began to appear in the barracks of

Fig. 4.8 A pair of barracks face each other across a street at Chesters Wall Fort. Each contained around ten *contubernia* or living rooms, plus projecting officers' houses, which can be seen at the far ends.

some Hadrian's Wall forts in the first half of the third century. At Vindolanda, a back-to-back pair of barracks built *c.* 235, excavated in 1980, have all the characteristics of the so-called chalets. But at the same time the living units are divided into front and rear rooms in the manner of regular *contubernia*, and the front rooms are bypassed by side passages. In barracks of *c.* 225–35 at South Shields, the salient feature is the presence of only five *contubernia*. As at Vindolanda, each *contubernium* is divided into two rooms and a side passage.

At Wallsend, barracks now understood to originate in the period *c.* 225–50 provide a further example, its closest parallel being found at Vindolanda. The width of the two barracks, placed back to back in each case, is identical at 18m (20yd). In the Wallsend building plots, once imbued with much significance

in the understanding of changed conditions in the early fourth century, it is now known that most of the fourth-century levels had been ploughed away even before the 1970s.

All these discoveries show that there is a type of building in the earlier third century that appears as a formally arranged barrack, but at the same time exhibits one or both of the principal features used to define a 'chalet'. Whether or not the *contubernia* are built as separate units seems to be a matter of local exigency, without any profound meaning about the level of military organization or discipline. The building style of these barracks does seem more irregular than that of previous times, perhaps because legionary technicians no longer came in from outside to build barracks wholesale: now each *contubernium* of soldiers built its own accommodation. The

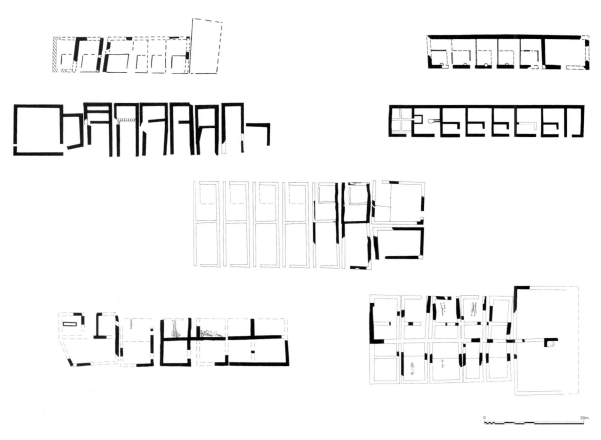

Fig. 4.9 Barracks of later type, with fewer *contubernia*, which begin to appear in the course of the third century. Top row: South Shields, *c.* 208 and *c.* 225–35. Second row: Housesteads, later third century; South Shields, *c.* 300. Third row: Vindolanda, *c.* 235. Bottom row: both Wallsend, *c.* 225–50.

detached *contubernia* could be roofed separately without the technical difficulty and organizational challenge of building a single roof for the entire length of a barrack. It was increasingly rare for the entire barrack accommodation of a fort to be rebuilt in one operation (although this did happen at South Shields in *c.* 225–35); much more often an individual barrack was replaced or renovated when the old building collapsed or wore out.

There is therefore no single point in the third century when a decisive shift to the new style of barrack building took place, and some are genuinely late in the third century, possibly Diocletianic: one of two excavated barracks in the new style at Housesteads overlies layers containing the extremely common 'radiate' coins of the 270s or a little later.

But its neighbour does not, and has a rather different plan, suggesting the possibility of an earlier origin, perhaps in the mid third century.

Reduced Centuries

The five *contubernium* barracks of *c.* 225–35 at South Shields and Vindolanda, all of which certainly housed infantrymen, imply centuries of half the notional second-century strength of eighty, now numbering forty or less. There may have been an even earlier reduction from the 'text-book' figure of eighty: infantry barracks of *c.* 208–11 at South Shields and *c.* 213 at Vindolanda have eight *contubernia*, suggestive of centuries of about sixty. There is no need to think that these are isolated instances of reduced centuries; in all probability barracks were not generally rebuilt to reflect the actual number of men using them until the old buildings decayed or there was a general replanning of a fort. Irrespective of when barracks were actually renovated to reflect the fact, and in many cases that might well not have been until around 300, infantry centuries of forty or so had probably become the norm by the 230s.

The reduction of centuries is thus deduced entirely from the archaeological evidence. There is no written evidence to support the hypothesis, but there is no written evidence for *any* developments in the army in this period. The proposed reduction of centuries may have been peculiar to the backwater province of Britain at this time. Although reduced unit sizes were later to be universal in the Roman army, in the third century British units may have been run down to allow those elsewhere to be bolstered up. The evidence of the one unit of this period whose structure we know of in some detail, *cohors XX Palmyrenorum* (from its archive found at Dura Europos in Syria), is at variance with that from Britain. In 219 at Dura – a strategically vital outpost on a frontier where war was threatening – some centuries were almost double, rather than half, the second-century norm. Unfortunately nothing is known of the accommodation of this unit.

The proposed reduction by half probably does not apply to cavalry *turmae*, where thirty may have been an operationally effective minimum. At Wallsend the cavalry barracks were reorganized by the mid-third century so that they had only five *contubernia*, but these were larger than formerly, and capable of accommodating six horses and men each – so a barrack still accommodated a *turma* of thirty, in reorganized fashion. The visible cavalry barracks at Chesters, entirely stone built and traditional in their layout, could be as late as 205–7, when major building work at the site is attested. By this stage, however, there may only have been twelve, rather than the expected sixteen *turmae*, and only 360 men in the *ala*, for it is only possible to fit twelve of the visible type of barrack into the available space at Chesters.

The same applies to the cavalry fort at Benwell, and the stone barracks uncovered there in the 1930s.

Why the overall size of *alae* on the Wall might have been reduced, and why infantry centuries in Britain were of such reduced size by the 220s or 230s, are questions that cannot be definitively answered. There was an increasing need for manpower on the continental and eastern frontiers in those years, and it is possible that troops were taken from Britain at various times, never to return. We have already noted the pay increases awarded the army from the time of Severus. Reducing the structural size of units may have been a way of controlling expenditure on military pay. Whatever the reasons, such reductions risked undermining the military effectiveness of units on what, as we have seen, was still a militarily active frontier – but there is one clear trend which both suggests that the mainstream units had indeed lost some of their strength, and shows that measures were taken to counteract that reduction.

Germanic War Bands in the Third-Century Wall Forts

In the third century, irregular (often Germanic) units were stationed alongside auxiliaries in northern Britain, and it is possible that this was a deliberate means of maintaining overall numbers in the face of a decreasing number of traditional cohort infantrymen. However, the irregular units were predominantly of cavalry rather than infantry. Often recruited from warrior peoples beyond the Rhine frontier, formed into small units and imported into the northern frontier zone of Britain, these irregulars are known to us from a series of inscriptions that begins in the reign of Severus Alexander (222–35), significantly at a time of major military upheaval on the German frontier when defeated or allied tribesmen may have been conscripted into Roman service, or supplied as drafts to fulfil treaty obligations.

Inscriptions from Housesteads indicate that in the period 222–35 several war bands (*cunei Frisiorum*) were based there, raised from Frankish tribes from

Frisia beyond the Rhine, and named after their warrior leaders: one was *numerus Hnaudifridi* (Notfried's unit). They rubbed shoulders with *Germani cives Tuihanti*, Germanic tribesmen recruited from the Twenthe area of the Netherlands, north of the Rhine; they were probably not an irregular unit, but a levy drafted in to replenish the ranks of the main unit at Housesteads, *cohors I Tungrorum*, showing that the main units had not switched to purely local recruitment, but still received recruits from other frontier areas in north-west Europe.

That the irregular units arrived with dependent civilian communities of women, children and slaves in train is indicated by the occurrence of a form of hand-made pottery, so-called 'Housesteads ware', at a number of sites along Hadrian's Wall. Analysis has shown that the pottery was made on Hadrian's Wall, but used Frisian forms and technology. At both Housesteads and Birdoswald most of the Housesteads ware was found in the settlement area outside the fort. This does not show that the irregulars were accommodated outside the forts, as has been suggested: these could be the areas where dependent civilian communities manufactured and used the pottery.

At Wallsend a rather haphazardly planned cavalry barrack of post-hole construction belonging to the period 220–50 was inserted into a space in the regular fort plan, possibly to house irregular cavalry of the kind so common in this period. The plan suggests more sizeable accommodation at one end for the warrior commanding the *cuneus*. It seems possible that the timber construction was determined by traditions of building with which the irregulars were familiar in their (possibly Germanic) homeland. Especially if numbers in the regular units were run down, there would have been space inside other Wall forts to accommodate irregulars. There is an 'available' extra-barrack block at Housesteads that is supernumerary to the ten required by the regular unit there; 'empty' spaces in other forts may one day turn out to contain 'additional' timber barracks, as at Wallsend. If the interpretation of the Wallsend barracks is correct, the irregular cavalry would have numbered around

thirty. Maybe the individual *cunei* attested at Housesteads were only around thirty strong.

We have no idea what such irregular levies were paid, or what their long-term prospects were; nor do we know for how long they were maintained. Housesteads ware is essentially a third-century phenomenon; we lose our means of knowing about these units' existence when the practice of cutting stone inscriptions tails off in about 250, although a recently discovered inscription at Chesters, dating to 286, may refer to *symmacharii* – a rare word for non-Roman allied troops. The additional Wallsend barracks, for what it is worth, seem to have been demolished by the late third century.

One thing is certain: in the 230s these warrior bands, marshalled and supervised by the cohorts and *alae*, but still of alien and exotic appearance, must have been a familiar sight for the regular soldiers of the Wall and the northern Britons who attempted raids on the province.

Life in the Third-Century Barracks

The additional Wallsend barracks, if correctly associated with irregular cavalry, suggest that the accommodation for such units was arranged on traditional lines: these buildings consist of five *contubernia* (detached, and individually built in the chalet style, but entirely of timber) divided into a front room with underfloor drain, showing that it was used as a stable, and a rear room for human accommodation, containing a hearth. Cavalry barracks for a mixed cohort and *ala* at Wallsend and Halton Chesters respectively were organized on the same principle, the only difference from the second century being the apparent increase in the *contubernium* from three to five or six riders.

It should be stressed that surprisingly few barracks have been excavated using modern techniques, but where they have, at Vindolanda, Wallsend and South Shields, the traditional internal arrangement of space in the *contubernia* was maintained through the third century. In infantry barracks, the front room was still bypassed by a corridor running along one side, which gave access either to that room or the rear sleeping room. The floor area remains roughly constant, enough for the theoretical eight men, although that must be regarded as a maximum. Rear rooms still have hearths. We still have no evidence for furnishing or sleeping arrangements.

Food preparation is also indicated by hand milling stones, present in the barracks at South Shields from the early third century (and absent from those of the period 160–200). This suggests a third-century augmentation of, or shift from, the communal bread baking of earlier times, to food preparation at the individual *contubernium* level – perhaps linked to the increase in army food rations under Severus reported by one source, possibly alluding to an increasing element of payment in kind. As in the time of Hadrian, the army remained omnivorous, and as well as the evidence for cereal consumption, the third-century layers on the Wall continue to show a high level of meat consumption, predominantly cattle.

Ordinary barrack rooms never have built latrines: the soldiers must have used portable vessels or gone out to the communal latrines. In the officer's end, in contrast, latrine pits and chutes leading out into the alleys between the barracks or into the fort's drainage system were usual. A further difference between officers and men lay in decoration: there is a very limited amount of excavated and published evidence, but it appears that the ordinary men's rooms would have been simply whitewashed, while there was more use of reds and other colours in the wall painting of the centurions' and decurions' houses.

Women in Barracks?

One (often unreliable) source, the Greek historian Herodian, reports that Severus allowed soldiers to live with women for the first time; this is usually taken to mean that from around 197 the marriage ban was lifted and soldiers' marriages were legally recognized. There is some doubt about this – there are diplomas running down to 237 that still award the veteran the right of *conubium*, suggesting that marriage during service was still not legally recognized. But Herodian's statement raises the question of whether there is any archaeological evidence for women in forts and in barracks in the period 160–250. Does Herodian's statement mean they were now living in barrack rooms, with the men?

There is an interesting development in the third century in the few barracks on Hadrian's Wall where detailed information is available. At Housesteads, in Barrack XIII, a scattering of female objects (a silver and a bronze earring, and a glass bead) occurs for the first time (there is a virtual absence of such objects in the barrack before 200), but these objects are confined to the centurion's house at the end of the block. In the barracks built at South Shields in the 220s or 230s, there is an occurrence of gold objects, including a female finger ring and a necklace, again all in centurions' or junior officers' quarters. The ordinary *contubernia* are entirely taken up with the standard arrangements for soldiers, with no sign to date of 'special' rooms that might have been married or family quarters.

This evidence suggests that there were wives and families now routinely living in barracks, but only those of the centurions and decurions, and perhaps junior officers. At South Shields in the third century, junior officers' houses become recognizable as entities distinct from the main centurion's house, usually at the other end of the block. This suggests more space and privacy for the centurion, and supports the idea that it was now more common for him to have a family resident with him. Infant burials are another indicator of the presence of women, and in general they become more common in the later Roman period at the only Hadrian's Wall site to have produced large numbers, South Shields. Here only two instances occur within the third century: one in an ordinary *contubernium*, and one, significantly, in a junior officer's house.

There is therefore still no strong evidence in this period for a general presence of women throughout barracks: rather than meaning that all soldiers had wives living with them in the barracks, Herodian may have alluded to a relaxation in discipline that led to more co-habitation for ordinary soldiers outside the fort, and which allowed centurions and decurions to have families living with them in the house formerly shared with junior officers. Now such officers may well have been allowed to marry 'legally' in service, as legionary centurions of a certain status (equestrians), and possibly of long service, had always been.

Military Routine and the Manning of the Wall

In Britain there is no equivalent of the Vindolanda tablets to shed light on this later period on the Wall, but rare surviving documents from elsewhere in the empire, particularly the archives of *cohors XX Palmyrenorum* from the eastern city of Dura Europos, dating to around 220, show that soldiers in the third century were rostered in the same way as in Hadrianic times to undertake routine duties in and away from base. At Dura a quarter of the men at any given time were on guard duty at the fort gates and at other key points within and outside the fort. Men were sent out to requisition or collect grain, foodstuffs, animals or fuel, while others were assigned to escort officials, or served on the provincial governor's bodyguard, or were on scouting duties, attending to religious ceremonies or the hospital.

In principle the third-century units on the Wall and elsewhere in northern Britain could easily have sent out detachments of varying sizes to man the milecastles and those turrets that continued in operation. Two rosters from Dura show that almost half the men with assignments, between a quarter and a third of the unit, were out-stationed in at least nine outposts, the largest of these detachments being ninety-three and sixty-four, the smallest mere handfuls – three, five or seven.

The Army in Action

As we have seen, a military clash between the army of the Wall and barbarian attackers is explicitly mentioned by Cassius Dio, early in Commodus' reign, but we have no detail of what this meant for soldiers on the ground. Such major confrontations were no doubt rare, and low-level encounters must have been more frequent. Although there are no surviving historical records of such day-to-day military action on the Wall, a few pieces of evidence – the fragments that just happen to have survived – give us an oblique insight into the occurrence and nature of conflict with raiders from the north in the mid-Roman period.

A commander of the Sixth Legion dedicated an altar, unfortunately not closely datable but probably of the years 160–214, at a shrine 3km (2 miles) south of the Wall at Kirksteads (Wall-mile 69), *ob res trans vallum prospere gestas* – 'on account of successful achievements beyond the Wall'. This gives little away, but two other inscriptions are more specific. At some time in the period 180–250 the *ala Augusta* erected a statue of Hercules at Carlisle, with an inscription stating their gratitude to the god for their successful defeat of a body of what are termed 'barbarians'.

At this time the unit was based in the fort of Old Carlisle, a fort lying only 19km (12 miles) away, behind the Wall. A late second- or third-century altar dedicated to Jupiter Dolichenus found in Hexham abbey in 1725 records that a cavalry unit, probably the *ala II Asturum* based at nearby Chesters, had 'wiped out a host of *Corionototae*' – an otherwise unknown people, but the name obviously had everyday significance as that of an enemy familiar to those erecting the inscription. The word '*manus*', referring to the numbers of *Corionotatae* involved, is usually translated as 'a band', but the Latin dictionary definition is 'an armed force...body, host, number, company, multitude', implying a raiding force of considerable size; this would explain why a crack Roman cavalry regiment several hundred strong should be so careful to commemorate the confrontation.

Both this and the Carlisle inscription are interesting in their implication that the auxiliary units were operating alone, suggesting encounters with raiders that they had shadowed or intercepted on a day-to-day level as individual units, rather than as part of a larger campaign.

It is also a fair assumption that both clashes were with mounted raiders. One of the most striking things about the reduction in the size of infantry centuries of the Roman auxiliary units, combined with the import of irregular Germanic cavalry, is that it had the effect of increasing the *proportion* of cavalry to infantry in the part-mounted cohorts on the Wall. Under Hadrian, the unit based at Wallsend, for example, would have had a theoretical strength of 600, of which 120 were cavalry – a ratio of infantry to cavalry of 4:1. In the third century, six reduced centuries of forty would give 240 men, but there were still 120 cavalry plus (say) 60 additional irregulars, so that the ratio was now 240:180, or 4:3.

There is no reason to think that restructuring of this kind was peculiar to Wallsend, and it is evidence for an increased importance of cavalry amongst the part-mounted units on the Wall in the course of the third century, a shift in emphasis that has been noted on other frontiers of the empire, and which anticipates the army reforms of the later Roman period. In turn this can be taken as indirect evidence that raiders from the north, who had always had a mounted capability, were now being encountered in larger mounted formations.

Military Religion

The religious beliefs and concerns discussed in the previous chapter continued to be to the fore for the Romans manning the Wall, and indeed, for the civilian communities that enveloped them. The increasing prevalence of stone construction and inscriptions following the restoration of the frontier in the 160s brings with it a growing amount of evidence for both official and unofficial religious cults, making the early third century an age of pagan splendour on the Wall.

The 'official' dedications to Jupiter at Maryport come to an abrupt end in the 160s, but there is one more similar series, probably emanating from an area 100m (109yd) east of the fort at Birdoswald (site

of another Jupiter temple?), third century in date, where the number of dedications to Jupiter exceeds that at Maryport. The calendar from Dura Europos, mentioned in the last chapter, if correctly interpreted as a military document, shows that the schedule of official religious observances, as old as the time of Augustus, was still current in the 220s.

Moving from the 'official' to the 'unofficial', what is most striking is the wide range of deities and combinations of deities attested in the diverse community of the Wall in its heyday. The cult of Jupiter Dolichenus merged the Roman god Jupiter with an all-powerful sky god originating in Asia Minor. It co-existed with the worship of Jupiter alone and of other merged versions of Jupiter, and by the third century was popular throughout the Roman army. The god appeared in cult effigy in his temples standing on the back of a bull brandishing an axe and thunderbolt; his consort, Juno Regina, was depicted next to him standing on the back of a heifer. A beautifully carved fragment of the Juno Regina statue survives at Chesters, where inscriptions confirm the existence of a Dolichene temple. An altar recently found at Vindolanda depicts the god standing on the back of his bull. The legionary detachments stationed at Corbridge left behind them rich sculptural evidence for the Dolichene cult, though little is known of its liturgy. Its temples were fitted out for dining, since participation in ritual meals was an important element of what went on.

The only Dolichene temple to be located with certainty on the Wall is at Vindolanda, where the building was found built into the rampart space *within* the walls of the fort, a remarkable discovery, as the normal expectation is that temples, especially of 'unofficial' cults, would be located outside. Although it remains uncertain whether the Vindolanda Dolichenum had been situated within the fort during the whole of the third century, or whether it was moved there following the abandonment of the *vicus* around 260, rampart areas are an under-explored part of fort anatomy, and there are hints that other temples might await discovery in similar positions:

Fig. 4.10 The temple of Mithras at Carrawburgh.

a row of three altar bases was found *in situ* in the rampart backing at Housesteads, while three altars to Minerva were found together 'in the ruins of a large building on the west side of the south gate' of the outpost fort at High Rochester.

Cults such as that of Jupiter Dolichenus were not just about good feelings and enjoying ritual meals – they were felt to imbue the army with tangible power, the ability to overcome foes, as we see from the dedications made by the commanders of *alae* that had overcome barbarian hosts. A concern with the power of good to overcome evil is evident in the celebrated cult of the god Mithras. Temples of this mystery religion have been found at Rudchester, Carrawburgh (the best known, found in 1949 and still visible) and Housesteads. The Mithraic temples on the Wall were small, semi-subterranean structures, evoking the legendary cave in which Mithras was supposed to have slain a bull, symbolic of primeval force and vitality, to release its concentrated power for the benefit of mankind. Inside, secret ceremonies would be followed by ritual feasts, the devotees reclining on benches running along the side walls. Fragments of a relief of the bull-slaying scene were found when the Housesteads Mithraeum was excavated in 1822, and are now displayed in the Great North Museum at Newcastle.

Also at Housesteads were found pieces of a sculpted stone slab, pierced so that it could be dramatically lit from behind, depicting the birth of Mithras. Mithras is seen emerging from an egg (rising naked from the lower part of an eggshell while the

Fig. 4.11 Mithras born from an egg: found in the Housesteads Mithraeum in 1822, now in the Great North Museum: Hancock, Newcastle.

upper half of the shell caps his head). Usually in birth scenes Mithras springs from a rock. The egg birth and the surrounding signs of the zodiac show that at Housesteads Mithras has been fused with other gods – the Orphic Phanes, born from an egg as first ruler and creator of all, and Aion, god of time, usually depicted as a youth standing in a wheel bearing the signs of the zodiac. The altars found in the temple were dedicated to 'Mithras Saecularis', 'Mithras, Lord of this Age'.

The combination of gods and concepts is not found anywhere else, and was probably conceived by a man named Litorius Pacatianus, who dedicated the earliest altar in the Housesteads Mithraeum, and was probably responsible for commissioning the sculptures. He was a *beneficiarius consularis*, an army officer detached for service on the staff of the provincial governor, evidently based at Housesteads for a time in the early third century AD on special duties. Clearly some officers on Hadrian's Wall found time to think deeply about religion and philosophy.

At Benwell we find very high-ranking Roman officers dedicating to an otherwise unknown deity, possibly of local origin. The little temple of the god Antenociticus, just outside the south-east corner of the fort, was found in 1862 and is still visible, and we have fragments of the cult statue, including the finely sculpted head, which shows the god as a youth with luxuriant hair. One of his adherents was the commanding officer of the *ala* stationed at Benwell in 177–80, Tineius Longus, who recorded his recent promotion to senatorial rank – truly a 'top drawer' Roman, and how interesting that he should express his gratitude to a deity otherwise unknown in the Roman world. This shows the real awe in which the Romans held indigenous Celtic deities, and underlines again that conqueror and conquered shared a basically common religious culture.

This is most graphically illustrated by the outpost fort at Bewcastle, whose Roman name was *Fanum Cocidii*, 'the shrine of Cocidius'; this evidently pre-Roman spot was sacred to the native war god interpreted by the Romans as Mars Cocidius. Here, in the most sacred shrine and focus of imperial loyalty at the heart of the fort, the walls were adorned with silver plaques bearing crude and menacing images of the god. We know this because the contents of the shrine were cast into the underground strongroom beneath when the fort was abandoned by the Romans in the early fourth century.

As well as a projection of military power north of the Wall, the fort at Bewcastle expressed control of a religious centre, which in the wrong hands might have been a focus of resistance or even a sinister

Fig. 4.12 Altar from the temple of Antenociticus, Benwell, in which Tineius Longus, commander of cavalry, records his elevation by the emperor to the senate of Rome.

eighth-century Bewcastle cross, an imposition of Christian power over the place.

The persistence and importance of the pre-Roman beliefs of 'Celtic' north-west Europe is seen in the significance placed in sculpture on horned gods, and in the occurrence of gods in groups of three, such as the *matres*, or mothers, and the three hooded deities (*genii cucullati*) so hauntingly carved in stone at Housesteads. It is also seen in the deliberate ritual deposition of groups of objects, which show an interest in wet places, heads and ritual wells and shafts. None of these images or practices need necessarily have any direct connection with local indigenous tradition, but might have been imported with soldiers and civilians coming from Gaul and other parts of the empire. Only a god with a specific focus confined to north Britain, such as Cocidius, can be assumed to be of local origin, and even he has probably been thoroughly re-imagined by the Romans.

Some deities were imported with the Germanic irregulars who were such a feature of the wall in the early third century. These include Mars Thincsus, whose temple has been found at Housesteads, but also the numerous very crude, cheap and portable altars found along the Wall dedicated to the 'Veteres'. The name of the deity or deities once seemed unique to the Wall, and it was once thought referred to 'the old gods', but more recently it has been suggested that the name, which has a variety of spellings, is a transliterated interpretation of a spoken Germanic form of the name of the god Loki. These altars are an indication of the numbers in which Germanic irregulars arrived on the Wall in the early third century, and show them adapting a deity, whose name was not previously written down, to Roman forms of worship and language.

Cemeteries

Roman law forbade burial within cities and towns, and this applied to the forts and *vici* of the Wall. As in any Roman town, the cemeteries are found beyond the outer fringes of the settlement, memorials

power. The memory of Bewcastle as power centre of a pagan war god probably remained strong in the locality for centuries: it is no coincidence that this remote site was chosen for the late seventh- or early lining the roads to be seen by travellers as they arrived or left. When soldiers or civilians died, disposal of their remains was a private matter for their relatives and heirs. In the second century the burial rite was predominantly cremation, but in the third century inhumation was gradually more prevalent.

The physical traces of burials vary according to the wealth and status of the deceased, from cremations placed in pots and covered with a modest earth barrow just 4 to 5m (13 to 16ft) across, to elaborate stone-built tombs, circular or rectangular in shape, assumed to be for officers and wealthier civilians. Inhumations might take the form of a simple coffin burial with no superstructure above ground, but instead a gravestone or other marker.

Cemeteries have great archaeological potential, because many pagan burials – whether cremations or inhumations – include well-preserved grave goods to serve the deceased in the next world, and if skeletons are preserved, analysis of the bones can reveal much about diet, health and (with the new science of isotope analysis) even the place of origin. On the Wall this harvest still has to be reaped: the exact whereabouts of few of the cemeteries are known, and where they are located, there has been little investigation. A cluster of over seventy small earthen barrows can still be seen by the side of Dere Street, 400m (440yd) south of the remote outpost fort of High Rochester. A classic excavation showed that several of them contained cremations that had been carried out on the spot, but found few grave goods beyond pottery, a few coins and hobnails – they dated predominantly to the third century. 200m (220yd) further out from the fort some stone tombs, excavated in the nineteenth century, can still be seen.

Recent excavation of part of a cemetery at South Shields found cremations and inhumations intermingled in the third and earlier fourth centuries, and included a grave containing a jet spindle and distaff, bone, copper and iron bracelets, a string of 100 glass beads, rings, and a knife and chain set (a kind of chatelaine), which undoubtedly belonged to a woman; however, here only ghostly traces of the skeletal remains survived. To judge by the magnificent tombstones of Regina and Victor, found close by in the 1880s, there must have been much more elaborate tombs in this area.

Other cemeteries have been examined on a small scale at Beckfoot, on the Cumbrian coast, and at Birdoswald, where pyre debris contained numerous fragments of intricately decorated bone veneer that had adorned the funeral biers on which bodies were borne to their cremation.

The Civilians of the Wall

The 'Military *Vici*'

Outside the walls of every full-sized auxiliary fort in the north-western empire was an adjoining settlement in which there lived and worked a community of civilian suppliers and traders, and others with a connection to the army. We have seen that there is some difficulty in understanding where such civilians fitted into the initial Hadrianic concept for the Wall. However, by the third century these settlements were unmistakably one of the most conspicuous features of the Wall, clustering around each fort on the south side of the Great Wall, and extending over the Vallum, now infilled and forgotten in the vicinity of forts.

The predominant building type is the timber or stone 'strip-house', the term referring to the long rectangular shape, typically some 5–7m (16–23ft) wide at the street frontage, and extending back from the street for a length of 10–15m (33–50ft) or more. The narrow shop frontages jostle closely along one or more roads leading to the fort gates, showing that commercial street frontage was at a premium, and that the buildings were intended to pick up trade along the busiest routes in and out of the military base.

The first modern excavation in such a settlement at a Wall fort took place at Housesteads in the 1930s. Despite the presence of some really substantial stone buildings, the resulting plan gave a rather misleading impression of quite a small and disorganized settlement. It is hard to shake off the old view, still to be found in archaeological literature, of essentially unplanned shanty towns, which grew over time as enterprising members of the local population – and traders from afar – arrived to exploit the market for goods and services required by the well-paid soldiers. The uncovering at Vindolanda in the 1970s of what is still the most extensive visible example anywhere did little to change this picture. Today, some still fondly believe that the extramural settlements might hold the key to knowledge of the indigenous population and its relations with the Roman army.

We now know that these settlements were much larger and more complex than previously thought. At several Wall forts their plans have been graphically revealed at a new level of detail by geophysical survey – a remote sensing technique that in the right conditions can produce a plan of otherwise invisible buried remains. The disadvantage is that it cannot disentangle different periods of activity, but it is infinitely less expensive than excavation, and can produce plans that could only be achieved by many seasons of intrusive work. Most of these surveys have been carried out by the same independent team of researchers, and they have been truly revolutionary – since the mid-1990s we have, through geophysical survey, a more detailed anatomy of some fort interiors, and also especially of their external settlements, than could have been dreamt of only thirty years ago.

At Maryport, for example, geophysics showed

Fig. 4.13 Geophysical survey of Maryport, on the Cumbrian coast. The square shape of the fort, with surrounding ditches, can be seen at bottom left. The strip buildings of the *vicus* line a road running from the fort, and cover a greater area than the fort itself. ALAN BIGGINS AND DAVID TAYLOR, TIMESCAPE SURVEYS

Maryport Vicus

100 metres

Fig. 4.14 Conjectural appearance of the extramural *vicus* at the Wall fort of Benwell as it had developed in the third century, overlying the Vallum, backfilled and forgotten in the vicinity of forts. Note the predominant building type, the so-called 'strip-house'. TYNE & WEAR ARCHIVES & MUSEUMS (DRAWING BY PETE URMSTON)

that strip buildings with enclosed backplots densely lined a road running out of the fort for a distance of almost 400m – something like a quarter of a mile. At Birdoswald, over a distance of 200m (220yd), strip buildings line a road running from the west gate, widening to form a marketplace, and more settlement clusters thickly around the east side of the fort. The newly available plans imply a considerable population for each settlement, certainly outnumbering the unit in the fort, and possibly in the low thousands.

Since the 1980s there have also been more excavations in fort civilian settlements, particularly on the continent (although relatively little on Hadrian's Wall). The excavated finds reveal a population that is highly Roman in character, with finds assemblages often indistinguishable from those from fort interiors; and detailed examination of the strip-house type suggests that it is based on Italian prototypes. In Britain, roundhouses of the indigenous Iron Age type are all but absent. Furthermore, it appears that in most cases forts were sited to leave room for a civilian

settlement, and that the planning and building of that settlement can be seen in some cases (but not yet on the Wall) to take place wholesale and simultaneously with the foundation of the fort, often having to be carefully integrated with extra-mural buildings that were provided by the army, such as the baths and the *mansio* (an inn for official travellers).

In short, there is no evidence for any significant involvement of the *local* indigenous population: everything points to a substantial immigrant population of merchants and traders who moved with, and co-operated closely with the army – camp followers – who established their settlement with official sanction. A good comparison in our time is found in the enclaves of civilian contractors who have supplied Western military bases in environments such as Afghanistan or Iraq, and who come close to outnumbering the military themselves.

The closeness of the link between fort and *vicus* is emphasized in those cases where the latter is defended, perhaps a commoner occurrence than was once generally realized. At fort sites throughout the Wall hinterland, defended annexes housed *vicus* buildings and activities. On the Wall itself at least parts of the *vicus* were enclosed by defences at Wallsend and Housesteads, and other examples probably await discovery. The presence of a civilian community is proven by an inscription at Carriden on the east flank of the Antonine Wall – but despite searches, no substantial *vicus* has ever been found on the Antonine Wall itself. Similarly no outpost fort – in the sense of one of the isolated forts north of Hadrian's Wall or the Antonine Wall – has yet produced good evidence for a *vicus* such as those on the Wall itself.

Inscriptions of the second and third centuries from Britain and Germany confirm that the inhabitants of these settlements referred to themselves as *vicani* – 'the inhabitants of the *vicus*'. The term *vicus* – which normally just means a small town or country village – was evidently applied to the civilian trading settlements outside Roman forts, and is now widely used in popular and archaeological literature to refer to the complex of extra-mural buildings and activities – although strictly speaking the term could apply only to the part of the settlement built and occupied by civilian traders, and we do not know whether military buildings (baths, *mansio*) or even civilian military dependents (such as veterans) were included in the concept of the *vicus*. An inscription from Housesteads shows that the *vicani* issued decrees, implying a governing body or council, which we also find making communal religious dedications. The *vicani Vindolandenses* – 'the townspeople at Vindolanda' – made a dedication to Vulcan, an appropriate deity for the metalworkers who made up a large part of the civilian population. Excavations on the German frontier have shown that *vicus* buildings were built respecting common boundary lines and utilizing party walls, suggesting that the constituted representatives of the *vicani* directed the work and maintained a land registry.

For direct evidence of what the *vicani* actually produced or did, excavation can detect industrial processes, and evidence for iron-working and the casting of bronze objects indicates the manufacture and repair of weapons, equipment and decorative items such as belt plates and buckles, but also agricultural tools, horse trappings and household items. There was also a market for fine jewellery, for men and women: a gold and silversmith's workshop has been found outside the walls of third-century South Shields, and a goldsmith is mentioned on an inscription from Malton (North Yorkshire). But many of the trades practised in the *vicus* will be archaeologically invisible: the premises of grocers, butchers, vets, textile and clothing traders and manufacturers, shoemakers, saddlers, wheelwrights, doctors and medicine men, astrologers, carriers, tavern keepers, carpenters, joiners and cabinet makers will, except in exceptional circumstances, prove, when excavated, to be just another anonymous strip house.

In this, the golden age of inscriptions, we do have the evidence of often touching funerary epitaphs for the names of some of the husbands and wives, brothers and sisters, and sons and daughters who lived beneath the fort walls. While the majority of inhabitants were traders and craftsmen and their families, there were other substantial constituents of the *vicus* population. There must have been priests of the many religious cults attested. An inscription from Halton Chesters mentions a society (*collegium*) of slaves. Inscriptions clearly attest veterans living at forts, presumably in the *vicus*, with their families. At Great Chesters, Vacia, the sister of the *cornicularius* (clerical adjutant) of the unit, set up his tombstone: presumably she lived in the *vicus* there. Soldiers might find wives among the sisters and daughters of the trading population already mentioned.

Increasingly, perhaps, the *vicus* accommodated army wives and provided new recruits for the unit, sons following fathers into the army, so that the military community of fort and civilian *vicus*, a Roman enclave on a distant frontier, perpetuated itself, although the *vicus* never became the exclusive source of new recruits for the unit. The homogeneity of background of the soldiers and *vicani*, and the fundamentally *Roman* character of the extra-mural settlements, is emphasized by the continuing importance throughout this period of the baths, a landmark building at every fort, showing evidence of extensive use, maintenance and repair, and resorted to by soldier and civilian alike.

Supply and Communication

The *vicani* – and often the soldiers themselves, in the fort workshops – manufactured items of metal, wood or leather that were most economically produced by craftsmen on the spot, assuming the necessary materials could be obtained or bought in. Pottery and bulk agricultural products were more economically produced where the land was more fertile and raw material available. We have already seen that on the fertile east side of the Pennines indigenous society was transformed with the building of the Wall, in a way that suggests that it became thoroughly geared to the production of foodstuffs and supplies for the army of the Wall and its supporting forts. Local pottery production for the military petered out during the second century, and the Wall came to rely on industries in southern Britain, where agricultural estates and pottery industries developed to supply the military market. The idea that the army of the Wall was supplied with grain primarily, or even to any significant extent, by the immediately local indigenous population, is almost certainly false.

The principal sources of pottery were in the West Midlands, the Severn Valley, the Nene Valley (near Cambridge), East Anglia, south-east Dorset and the South East, particularly Colchester, Verulamium and the Thames estuary. Pottery was usually a low-value supplementary cargo that rode on the back of bulkier and more valuable commodities such as grain (which does not survive archaeologically), so the distance of these industries from the Wall is an indicator of the distance over which foodstuffs, textiles and luxury goods travelled to the northern frontier zone.

Animal products – meat and leather – are more likely to have been sourced nearer the Wall itself, although there is still evidence for beasts being driven over considerable distances: isotope analysis of third-century animal bones from South Shields suggests that cattle were imported, presumably on the hoof, from distant Cumbria or even south-west Scotland beyond the Wall. For traders in livestock and agricultural products from Yorkshire, transport or cattle droving by road, along Dere Street, was a practical proposition, but long-distance bulk transport by road was uneconomic, and for this the principal means of transport was shipping, and the predominance of types of pottery made in the Thames estuary area on the eastern half of the Wall, and the dominance of south-east Dorset types on the west side, shows that these wares, and the cargoes they accompanied, were shipped to the Wall up the east and west coasts respectively.

One reason for the concentration of so many of the known industries in the south-east is that their products were sometimes redistributed through the great port of London. The fort full of granaries at South Shields, active throughout the third century as a coastal supply base for the Wall, attests the arrival of grain from southern Britain or the continent, shipped up the east coast, and stored ready for redistribution along the Wall and to other inland sites. The Thames estuary wares do not occur in quantity at coastal sites intervening between London and South Shields, and were not widely distributed locally in their area of manufacture, suggesting that these wares, and the invisible commodities that accompanied them, were produced primarily for the military market and shipped directly to the Wall.

This vital seaway was secured by the forts we have already mentioned that were established on the east coast at places such as Brancaster, Caistor (both Norfolk) and Reculver (Kent). It is possible that this military presence in the south was also directly involved in the procurement and dispatch of supplies from the hinterlands of these forts, in areas such as East Anglia and the Thames estuary. The lack of villas in the lands of the East Anglian *Iceni,* and the attenuated appearance of their tribal capital at Caistor-by-Norwich (*Venta Icenorum*), might suggest that much of the land may have been in imperial ownership, and that communities there were tasked with military supply: Brampton, a defended town in Norfolk that specialized in industrial and pottery production, has an unusual defensive circuit, suggesting the hand of the army or the state. It was at its peak of activity between 150 and 250.

London was also the transhipment point for many of the imports that reached the Wall from the continent or the Mediterranean. Amphorae, large ceramic shipping containers for liquids, brought olive oil and fish sauce from Spain, or wine from southern France or Italy. Their thick sherds are found in immense quantities in excavations on the Wall, though only the Spanish olive-oil containers are really common. The import of samian ware continues throughout this period, with the centre of production moving from central to eastern Gaul. Other Rhineland products, especially mortaria (grit-studded mixing bowls), are notable. We have already noted that the scarcity of wine amphorae on the Wall denotes the import of wine from this area in barrels.

Hadrian's Wall thus exerted a huge gravitational pull on the productive economy of the whole of the British provinces, and must have had an effect in much of north-west Europe and Spain. On the Wall in the first half of the third century, the complexity and sophistication of a trading system that extended all the way from the Mediterranean to the north-western frontiers was at its peak. Each fort/*vicus* community was supplied by arteries of trade that connected the population, economically and culturally, to supply centres in Britain south of the Wall and beyond: to the continental empire and to the Mediterranean. As in our world, for the inhabitants of the Wall forts and *vici* it was commonplace to buy commodities that had been transported over an entire continent for their use in remote Northumberland or Cumbria. As in the second century, the extent to which any of this was centrally organized is not understood: it is possible that from the time of Septimius Severus onwards there was a greater element of taxation in kind on provincial populations to enable the state to supply military units directly, foreshadowing the practices of the late empire; but clear evidence is lacking.

The Life of the Local Population

If there was any substantial native rural settlement of the mid-Roman period in the immediate vicinity of Wall forts on the south side of the frontier, it remains steadfastly invisible, archaeologically speaking. Had such sites been occupied in significant numbers, we might expect them to produce the kinds of pottery and metal objects that are at their most copious in the forts and *vici* of the third century, but on the whole this kind of material is encountered only at the known Roman sites and, to some extent, in remoter upland settlements in Cumbria. In County Durham, the eastern hinterland of the Wall, the economic developments discussed in the last chapter, exemplified by the small town at Sedgefield, continue to the end of this period – and the villas now known in the area still flourished, presumably part of the supply chain that served the units of the Wall and its hinterland. Inevitably the local population had a role in this activity, but whether this was as an exploited or enslaved peasantry, or whether indigenous entrepreneurs and their retinues owned and worked the villa estates, we simply do not know.

The two major towns of the Wall zone, Carlisle and Corbridge, became civil centres – or 'civitas capitals' – in the period 160–250. Although there was a continuing military presence in each case in the form of legionary detachments (based in a fort at Carlisle and in special compounds at Corbridge), considerable civil towns developed around the military nuclei. Carlisle acquired the rank of *civitas Carvetiorum*, taking its name from a local tribal group, the *Carvetii*; a milestone records this status in 223, though it could have had the name from the 160s. At Corbridge we only have corrupt versions – in such forms as *Corstopitum* and *Corie Lopocarium* – of whatever 'tribal' name was added to *Coria*, the basic place name.

The adoption of 'tribal' names like this does not necessarily mean that there was a significant

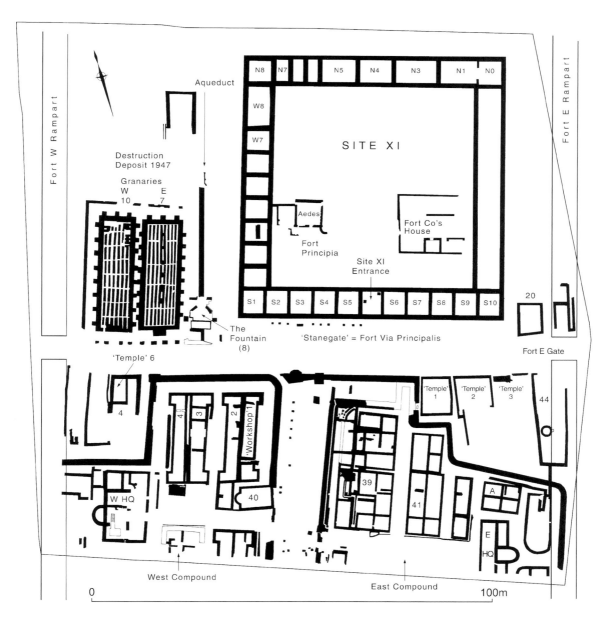

Fig. 4.15 The centre of Corbridge, dominated by military compounds, granaries, Site XI (probably a marketing complex) and some commercial strip buildings. These remains are the centre of a civil town that covered some 20ha (50 acres), now invisible beneath the surrounding fields.

participation, political or otherwise, of the indigenous population in the life of these frontier towns, which archaeologically, like the fort *vici*, have a distinctly immigrant and Roman character. On the other hand, it is difficult to imagine a complete absence of inter-action between the locals and emergent centres of administration and trade – again, the problem is there is no archaeological indication of local people, although it is not clear what form that would take, and it should be stressed that there has been relatively little modern excavation of the urban elements of Carlisle, and none at Corbridge.

Society North of the Wall

It is reasonable to expect that any cleared zone north of the Wall instituted under Hadrian would have been maintained in later times, after the final settlement of the frontier fortification line on the Tyne–Solway after *c.* 160. It is notable that the single known later Roman settlement of the immediate trans-frontier zone, Huckhoe, which has produced third-century material and possibly had an importance beyond the individual homestead level (as a place of central authority for a neighbourhood?), lay on the Devil's Causeway road, just beyond the 16km (10-mile) mark from the Wall. Could this site have been a native counterpart to the Portgate through Hadrian's Wall, the two places standing at either end of the passage of the Devil's Causeway through a 16km trans-frontier cleared zone? The Roman outpost forts of Risingham and Netherby lie approximately on the northern edge of such a putative 16km strip.

Whatever residual population or network of settlements persisted beyond the 16km line remains at present stubbornly invisible to the archaeologist. Apart from Huckhoe, it is hard to find a single indigenous site in Northumberland that can be illustrated with a clear plan and confidently be said to have prospered after the second century AD. This is not to say that the landscape in the 120km (74-mile) zone north of the Wall was utterly depopulated, but the lifestyle of whatever settled population there was had changed utterly from the late pre-Roman Iron Age and has left little permanent trace, former traditions of building and settlement having been abandoned. Pollen evidence does not suggest regeneration of woodland. Perhaps there was a shift from a settled agrarian to a less firmly rooted cattle-ranching society, led by those who could hold their own against raiders from the north and exert control over products valued by the Roman army and requisitioned or traded through the Wall; we can imagine herds of horses and cattle being driven to markets such as that envisaged at the Portgate, near Great Whittington.

More sites occupied after 160 can be recognized in Scotland, but still not many are known. The general picture throughout south-east Scotland – and in Dumfries and Galloway in the west – is that there were far fewer sites occupied by AD200, and that those that were, are harder to recognize archaeologically. In the few cases where there is relatively good dating evidence from excavated sites, it is rare to find occupation continuing uninterrupted beyond this time – as in the recently published hillfort at Broxmouth, East Lothian, where long-standing occupation came to an end in this period. Even this far from the Wall, some major restructuring of society was evidently taking place.

Throughout the zone stretching for 320km (200 miles) north of Hadrian's Wall, a striking change takes place around about 160 in the pattern of Roman finds found on native settlements. During the periods of Roman military activity in Scotland, in pre-Hadrianic times and again in 140–60, Roman objects, particularly samian pottery vessels, glass bangles (products of the invasion periods) and metalwork, found their way on to large numbers of sites. The absolute number of finds is very small, but the impression is that certain classes of Roman objects were distributed widely through the numerous nobility of late Iron Age Scotland. After 160, far fewer Roman finds are recorded from native sites: the examples could be listed on a single page, they are so few. Where they do occur, they have a more exotic quality than previously: samian ware still looms large, but now so do high-quality glass vessels and jewellery. The material has been selected for the purpose of prestige personal ornament and for drinking and feasting, and is concentrated at a few sites of presumably high status.

One such site is the hill fort at Traprain Law, 105km (65 miles) north of Hadrian's Wall via the Dere Street road. Several contemporary sites that cluster in the plain around Traprain have been investigated. Some show a new style of occupation, making greater use of stone and sunken rectangular buildings than in the pre-Roman and early Roman Iron Age, sometimes, though not always, reusing earlier settlement sites.

Some Northumberland sites may also show signs of these later buildings in a new tradition – Huckhoe contains some sub-rectangular stone buildings.

After 160 these sites in the shadow of Traprain produce hardly any Roman finds, yet material of the period 160–250, particularly fine glass, does occur on the summit of the hill itself. This suggests the emergence of a local central power holder – presumably a leader whom Roman diplomats and traders dealt with – to whom the new, poorer style of settlements

Fig. 4.16 The settlement at Huckhoe, on the Devil's Causeway road, 16km (10 miles) north of the Wall. This is one of very few indigenous sites in the area immediately north known to have been occupied after the building of the Wall. SOCIETY OF ANTIQUARIES OF NEWCASTLE UPON TYNE

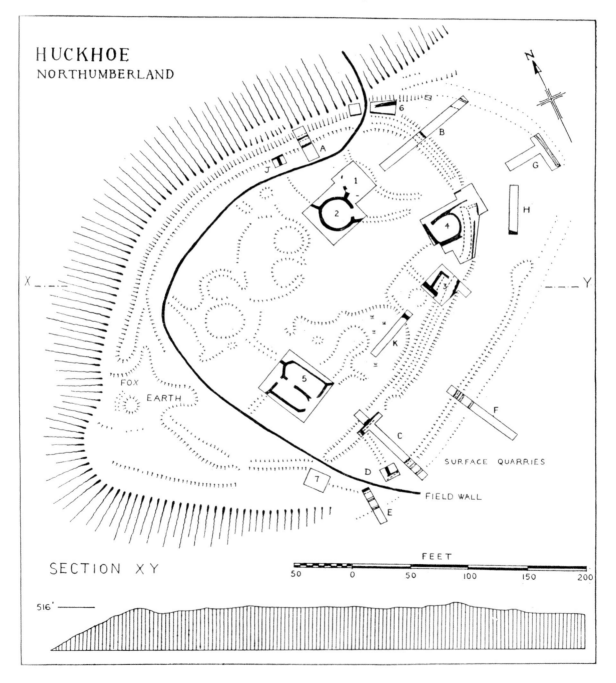

were subservient. What had probably been a centre for occasional gatherings in pre-Roman times was intensively inhabited during the Roman invasions, and after the Roman withdrawal of 160, Traprain became the seat of some group dominating the whole area, possibly in a friendly relationship with Rome (and conventionally labelled 'the Votadini' in much modern literature).

But there was no trickle-down of the Roman feasting gear and adornments enjoyed by this central authority into surrounding society. Roman objects were used to reinforce the position of a ruling élite, and the sharp division between élite and subservient; there was not a general 'Romanization' of rural society in southern Scotland. Perhaps Traprain, and other lesser centres of which we are aware, originated or controlled merchant delegations and parties sent to the Wall, where at markets such as that hypothesized near Great Whittington (active in this period), trade was conducted under strict military supervision.

But there are also clusters of Roman finds of the period 160–250 in the north-east Scotland area of Perth and Angus, with outliers reaching as far north as the Moray Firth and the Atlantic north-west. Souterrains, underground chambers for ritual or storage purposes, which characterize later Iron Age settlements in this area, are now abandoned or pass out of use. The implication is that after 160 new social élites or society leaders emerged in the wake of the social disruption wrought by proximity to the Roman Empire, particularly in an area out of the immediate reach of the Roman army, north of the Forth.

This area is also the focus of hoards of silver *denarius* coins distributed from the Roman Empire in the period 160–230 (on the continental frontiers as well as in Britain) as presents to manipulate and buy peace from trans-frontier peoples. It is in this area that we should place the Maeatae and Caledonii, the peoples whom Cassius Dio says were the targets of the Severan expedition of 209–11. The Maeatae probably occupied the northern Scottish lowlands, the Antonine Wall area and Fife, while the heartlands

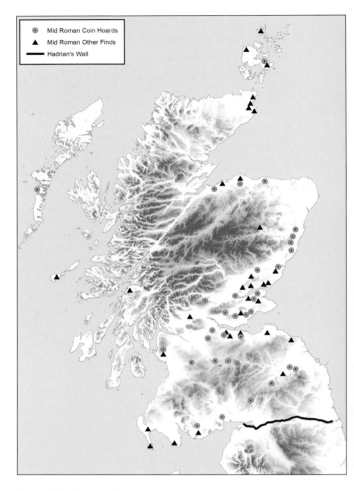

Fig. 4.17 Distribution of Roman coins, coin hoards and other finds in Scotland in the period 160–250. Adapted from F. Hunter's *Beyond the Edge of the Empire – Caledonians, Picts and Romans*, Rosemarkie (2007).

of the Caledonii lay in north-east Scotland, perhaps beyond the Tay.

Excavations at Birnie on the Moray Firth have given an insight into a specific (presumably 'Caledonian') settlement of this period. There is nothing about the architecture of the site, except perhaps the sheer size of its largest timber roundhouses, to reveal it as the base of an élite warrior, but its status is betrayed by two hoards of silver subsidy *denarii* ending in 193 and 196 – a remarkable archaeological illustration of Cassius Dio's statement that the Governor Virius Lupus was forced to buy peace from the northern peoples in 197. The same source mentions hostage exchanges. This is a reminder that between the raids and wars that occurred periodically, Rome had diplomatic relations with these distant peoples. The literary sources make it clear that formal treaties were agreed. The Romans employed a battery of techniques for dealing with societies beyond the imperial frontier: silver coin subsidies, present giving, hostage taking and exchange, treaties, and only from time to time outright warfare: these were standard techniques for managing trans-frontier peoples, as they have been on more recent imperial frontiers.

The names 'Maeatae' and 'Caledonii' are probably gross Roman oversimplifications, and there must have been many more names, local polities and subdivisions of which we are unaware. A collection of names in a late Roman geographical source, once regarded as a third-century list of Roman-sanctioned tribal meeting places ('loca') in the Scottish Lowlands, is now believed to be an assortment of first-century tribal, river and other names, without significance – but that is not to say that such trysting places, where Roman agents and soldiers might be seen, did not exist.

The name 'Maeatae' is heard of for the first time in the 190s. 'Caledonii', although not a new name, now apparently had a much wider application: Dio says that the names of all other peoples had become merged in these two. Again this suggests that new social structures, led by new warrior élites, had emerged from the ruins of a society first invaded by, and then walled out of, the Roman Empire. This was evidently a regional response to the Roman presence, much more north-east centred than the south-western Scotland area, which seems to have been the source of opposition in the days of Hadrian. Ability to play the Roman Empire for subsidies or to raid the Roman province might have rapidly overtaken traditional routes to status in the most fertile and populous areas of north-east Scotland. With the social upheaval and collapse of traditional society – at least in the most populous and fertile lowland areas – that followed the Roman withdrawal of 160, warrior groups among peoples occupying a zone between 160 and 320km (100 and 200 miles) distant from Hadrian's Wall evidently developed the ability to launch long-distance raids into the empire, less easily done from lowland Scotland immediately north of the Wall, an area controlled by the outpost forts and within reach of routine Roman retaliation.

Both north and south of the Wall we have seen that Roman material was being concentrated in the hands of the controlling élites and not distributed down the social scale, so that the lower status settlements become archaeologically less visible. There is the same problem recognizing a post-160 native rural settlement site type in the immediate vicinity of Wall forts, or just south of the Wall, as there is in north Northumberland or most of Scotland. There was no longer a widespread native nobility with the wealth and social power to construct splendid earthwork enclosures, but rather a peasantry subservient to those profiting from the Roman occupation (immigrant merchants and villa estate owners) south of the Wall, or to newly emerged warrior élites in Scotland. ✧

Chapter 5

THE WALL IN THE LATER EMPIRE: AD250–367

Crisis and transformation: a narrative of events

O F EVENTS IN BRITAIN IN THE MID-THIRD century there is hardly any written record. The histories that we have are more concerned with the continent, where the Roman Empire was now facing an existential crisis. The situation on the continental and eastern frontiers had degenerated disastrously for the Romans by mid-century. The lines of barriers and forts beyond the Rhine and Danube (in modern Germany) had fallen in the mid-250s, and the train of disasters culminated in defeat in the East and the capture of the Emperor Valerian by the Persian Sapor I in 259 or 260. Some troops – we do not know how many – had been transferred from Britain to the continent, where British units are attested in 255. In 260 Postumus, the military commander on the Rhine, revolted against the Emperor Gallienus and established his own 'Gallic Empire', which included Gaul, Britain and Spain. These lands were not recaptured by the central empire until 274. Without 'local' emperors to ensure its protection, the west succumbed in 276 to the greatest of all Germanic invasions across the Rhine, devastating Roman provincial society in Gaul.

From 286 to 296 Britain was once more separated from the central empire (with parts of Gaul), as the 'British Empire' proclaimed by Carausius, who had been given a command to suppress barbarian raiders in the English Channel. Under Carausius, construction work took place on the massively constructed Saxon Shore forts, which line the coast of Sussex, Kent and East Anglia, and have counterparts on the other side of the channel; he may have been continuing an initiative begun following the great invasions of 276 and before he seized power.

Throughout all these episodes of military crisis on the continent and usurpation in Britain, more and more troops may have been taken from the Wall forts to serve elsewhere. There is also patchy evidence for dereliction and poor maintenance in this period, notably at Birdoswald. Earlier claims of outright abandonment of forts on the Wall and in its hinterland have not been substantiated by more recent excavation, but it is probable that troop numbers were very low at a number of places.

Britain was finally recaptured from Carausius' successor, Allectus, in 296, when Constantius I Caesar entered London in triumph. Now or later Britain was reorganized as a 'diocese' of four provinces. Constantius returned to Britain in 305, now supreme emperor (Augustus) in the west, to campaign in the far north against the Picts. On his death at York in 306, his son Constantine I ('the Great') was proclaimed emperor there.

Literary and numismatic sources indicate various fourth-century campaigns against the northern barbarians in Britain. There is evidence that suggests that Constantine the Great might have returned to Britain twice, in around 310–12 and in 314, the first time to gather troops for his coming struggle with his rival Maxentius, whom he was to eliminate at the Battle of the Milvian Bridge in 312. It is widely believed that these troops included the big mixed infantry and cavalry units of the outpost forts north of the Wall at Risingham, High Rochester, Bewcastle and perhaps Netherby, and that the outposts were therefore abandoned

Fig. 5.1 Building inscription dating to 296–305, naming the Emperor Diocletian and his colleague Maximian, the western Tetrarchs. It provides important evidence for renovation on the Wall following the difficult years of the later third century: 'The commanding officer's house, which had become covered with earth and fallen into ruin, was restored along with the headquarters and baths.'

at this time. This is supported by the date of the latest excavated coin from the outpost forts: 309–10.

There were further campaigns in north Britain in 343 and 360. Britain was briefly part of another separatist western empire under Magnentius in 350–3. Then in 367, Ammianus Marcellinus records the infamous barbarian conspiracy, when co-ordinated invasions of Picts, Saxons, Franks, Scots and Attacotti (from Ireland) allegedly caused widespread death and destruction. The account may be exaggerated, but leaves little doubt that Hadrian's Wall had either been penetrated or bypassed by northern invaders.

Hardly any of the events in this skeletal record have left any detectable trace on Hadrian's Wall. The same units continued to man the Wall during and after the separatist 'Gallic Empire', as is made clear by a series of Jupiter altars dedicated by the Dacian cohort at Birdoswald, of which the last is dated 276–82, and an inscription of *cohors IV Gallorum*, of the same date, at Vindolanda. It was once believed that the Wall fell to the northern barbarians, having been drained

of its garrison by Allectus in 296 in order to combat Constantius' invasion, but there is no evidence of destruction at this time. In fact there is no archaeological evidence on the Wall for any of the recorded campaigns in the north. The 'barbarian conspiracy' of 367 has left no coherent and consistent evidence of destruction on Hadrian's Wall, or indeed anywhere else in the island. That is not to say there was no such destruction: the chain of 'signal stations' built in the following years down the east coast south of the Wall is clearly a response to raids (from the sea) that had bypassed the land frontier line.

On the other hand, there was rebuilding on the Wall in the years following Constantius I Caesar's capture of the British provinces from Allectus. The evidence is an inscription from Birdoswald, describing the restoration of the *praetorium* (commanding officer's house) which had 'collapsed into ruin and become covered with earth', along with the *principia* (headquarters building) and (probably) some baths, in the period 296–305. A more fragmentary but originally very elaborate inscription of the same period from Housesteads is probably connected with a substantial new stores building there.

These could be isolated instances, but they are possibly the sole surviving attestations of a Wall-wide programme, which might have extended to the minor structures, because an unusual incidence of coinage of the Emperor Diocletian has been noted at milecastles. Around this time the coastal fort at South Shields, 6km (4 miles) from the eastern end of the Wall, was completely rebuilt to a new plan, and for a new unit.

By the time Constantius I reclaimed Britain and restored the Wall, a sea change had overcome the Roman Empire. Half a century of barbarian invasion and civil war had ended the stable prosperity on which the culture of the high empire had been based, at least in western Europe. The destruction and horror wrought by incursions into provinces such as the Gauls, Germany, Raetia and Pannonia resulted in the reconstruction of society on wholly new lines. Artistic skills were lost within a generation, civic institutions and values collapsed, and temples, tombs and other sacred monuments were broken up to be reused in the defence of settlements that were dramatically shrunken or moved to hilltops.

Military and civil institutions were brutally reformed to be able to respond to the troubles of the times. The 'Tetrarchy' – a college of four emperors – was introduced to counter the tendency for regional breakaways such as the Gallic Empire. From the 260s onwards, the highest military commands were removed from the senatorial aristocracy. The 'light touch' government of the high empire, and the system by which military command had been undertaken as an aristocratic duty, were replaced by a sprawling bureaucracy of direct imperial appointments. The military was now supplied through the direct requisitioning of food, clothing and other vital materials (in the form of taxation in kind) from the provincial population, rather than through the free market and the myriad of civilian contractors that had flourished in more prosperous times.

The effects of the crisis on the towns of Britain were less dramatic than on the continent, but a profound transformation of society is still evident. The networks of trade that linked Britain to the Mediterranean via Gaul were devastated, and from the mid-third century the supply of Gaulish samian ware and Spanish olive-oil amphorae to Britain abruptly ceases. With a few exceptions, the practice of erecting inscriptions and of sculpture in stone faded out completely, even in the military zones where this culture had always been most prevalent. Anyone returning to Hadrian's Wall in the early 300s after a forty-year absence would be shocked at the change. They would find the once thriving *vici* outside the fort walls in ruins or replaced by fields, and the temples where colourful altars had been dedicated and sacrifices made in the name of the imperial and a myriad other religious cults, neglected or abandoned. The forts were still busy places, packed with buildings and thronging with soldiers, but soldiers of a materially poorer and less impressive-looking kind, for whose general appearance we have very little surviving evidence.

The Fourth-Century Army of the Wall

The *Notitia Dignitatum*

We have to navigate the fourth century on the Wall without the help of inscriptions. With the exception of some milestones, the two dedications of 296–305 from Birdoswald and Housesteads already mentioned are the last datable inscriptions from the Wall. Neither of them names the unit in the garrison. There is in fact no explicit archaeological evidence for the garrison of any Wall fort after the inscriptions of 276–82 at Vindolanda (*cohors IV Gallorum*) and Birdoswald (*cohors I Dacorum*). How, then, can we know what kind of units manned the Wall forts in the fourth century?

We rely on a document compiled around about the time that Britain was lost to the Roman Empire, known as the *Notitia Dignitatum*. This translates as 'Register of offices', and it is a list of high-ranking civil service posts and military commands throughout the Roman Empire, east and west. Although full of difficulties and clearly not representing the overall situation at any one time, the *Notitia* is a key source for the administrative and military structure of the later Roman Empire. The western half was compiled perhaps as late as 420, but it still contains a chapter on Britain. First are listed the forts under the command of 'the Count of the Saxon Shore'; then comes the command of the *Dux Britanniarium* – 'The Duke of the Britains' – meaning the five provinces of Britain. This list starts with the Sixth Legion at York and various units in the area south of the Wall. Then, introduced by the famous phrase *item per lineam valli* – 'Also, along the line of the Wall...', comes the list of Wall fort commands, running from east to west, each entry giving the place name and the name of the unit stationed there.

In the eighteenth century it was realized that the name of (nearly) every unit on the Wall listed in the *Notitia* also occurred on inscriptions found at a given Wall fort. Thus it was possible to work out the Roman names of the forts with confidence. The remarkable thing is that the regiments named are the ones that had been on the Wall two centuries or more earlier. The inscriptions themselves, as we have seen, date to the years before 300, but the *Notitia* lists the same units in place at the end of Roman Britain. Many historians over the years have refused to believe that this could be true, and have regarded the list *per lineam valli* as a fossil, preserving a record of regiments that had long gone by the end of the fourth century. This was because, according to the 'Wall periods' chronology current from 1930 onwards, the Wall had been abandoned by its garrisons and violently overthrown in 296 and 367 – surely the same order of regiments could not have been restored after these disasters? But it is now generally accepted that, whatever troubles the Wall faced, there is no evidence that the Wall forts were evacuated and destroyed at those times. Also, there are several other army lists in the *Notitia Dignitatum*, in Raetia (Bavaria and Austria), Armenia and Egypt, for example, where it is clear that cohorts and *alae* dating back to the second century survived in their stations at the end of the fourth century.

Although it is the only evidence that we have, the *Notitia Dignitatum* is best taken at face value as a record of the distribution of units in Britain at some time about the close of the fourth century. Around 400, *ala I Asturum* had been stationed at Chesters for at least 220 years; *cohors I Tungrorum*, probably the Hadrianic unit at Housesteads, had garrisoned that remote spot for nearly three centuries.

For the first part of the Duke's list, which names forts to the south of Hadrian's Wall, the situation is entirely different. In the *Notitia* the old cohorts and *alae* that are named on third-century inscriptions from the forts in the hinterland of the Wall have largely vanished, and are replaced with newer-style units, both mounted (*equites*) and infantry (*numeri*). These have the fancy names characteristic of newly founded units in the late Roman army: the unit of *vigiles* ('watchful ones') at Chester-le-Street, for example, or the *supervenientes* ('surprise attackers') at Malton. This indicates that the third-century *alae* and cohorts from behind the Wall had been removed wholesale at some time.

There is no way of knowing exactly when, but one strong possibility is that they were removed by an emperor needing to gather an army, or by a usurper defending, or launching a bid for the empire from Britain. In these circumstances the natural thing to do would be to leave the Wall units in place, in order to safeguard the province from invasion, but to remove the mobile reserve behind the Wall. This might have happened in 296, when Allectus prepared to repel the assault of Constantius I, but a more attractive possibility is the time in 310–12 when it is thought that Constantine the Great gathered troops from Britain for his confrontation with Maxentius. It is suspected that the cohorts of the outpost forts were removed then, and if they truly were, units may have been taken from the hinterland forts as well. But why did these units never return?

The Reformed Late Roman Army

The answer is that Constantine reformed the army. The Roman Empire had been ineffective in its response to the invasions of the mid-third century because the army had become too thinly spread out along the frontiers, in now absolutely permanent bases; moving troops to meet an emergency immediately created holes in the ring of frontier defences, which could be exploited by further invaders. The idea gradually evolved of separating frontier troops (*limitanei*) with permanent bases from a central mobile field army (*comitatenses*) which accompanied emperors and could be moved rapidly to any theatre of war without leaving frontier lines undefended. Recent research points to the reign of Constantine (306–37), rather than that of his predecessor Diocletian, as being the time when the restructuring of the army was completed.

Troops removed from Britain in 312 are likely to have been formed into field army units, which could have been posted anywhere in the empire, and it was limitanean units of a new type that were used to refill the forts behind the Wall, quite possibly on the occasion of a second visit to the island by Constantine in 314. The change in the garrison of Britain is therefore better dated to this time, than to 296–305. It is possible that the two commands we see in the *Notitia* – that of the Duke of the Britains, and that of the Count of the Saxon Shore – were instigated at the same time.

As we shall see, at least five of the units listed south of the Wall in the *Notitia* are actually much later arrivals, not being imported until after 367. But there is archaeological evidence that shows that the old third-century *alae* and cohorts there had been replaced by new-style units early in the fourth century. The clearest case is South Shields, where at some time between 286 and 318 – the dating, based on coins and pottery, is very imprecise – the former fort of *cohors V Gallorum* was completely replanned for a new unit with ten subdivisions, numbering an estimated 300–400 men. South Shields is probably the *Arbeia*

of the *Notitia Dignitatum*, said there to have been garrisoned by a unit of boatmen from the Tigris in Mesopotamia – the *barcarii Tigrisienses*. It is possible that the fort was replanned for this aquatic unit.

At Binchester, an impressive internal bath building was constructed in the first half of the fourth century, incorporating tiles stamped 'N CON', indicating that there already existed either a *numerus Constantinianorum* ('Constantine's own'), or perhaps a *numerus Concangensium* from the neighbouring hinterland fort of Chester-le-Street (*Concangis*). For the most part, however, there has been very limited excavation in the hinterland forts, and the internal plans and histories of most are obscure.

South Shields was not redesigned on the traditional principles of fort planning, with that familiar central range of granaries, HQ and *praetorium*, with barracks to front and rear. The plan is an entirely new concept, where all accommodation is divided into

Fig. 5.2 The late Roman plan of South Shields, showing how a cruciform arrangement of streets divided the accommodation into four quadrants, overlooked by the HQ to the north. The northern part of the fort enclosure was not used for military accommodation.

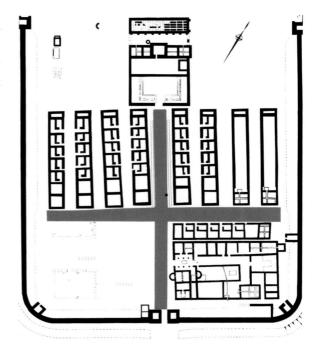

four quadrants separated by a cruciform arrangement of streets, one of which leads up to the HQ. The arrangement is seen in well-known sites such as the Diocletianic legionary fortress at Palmyra, Syria, and the retirement palace of Diocletian at Split, Croatia.

In the Wall forts no such change in overall internal arrangements took place, as we would expect if long-standing units remained in residence. Rebuilding took place along old lines. The *numeri* and *equites* of the hinterland forts may have been of a nominally higher status than the old cohorts and *alae* of the Wall – that is why they take precedence in the list of units under the *Dux Britanniarum* – but there does not appear to have been any great difference in material well-being or standard of building between Wall and hinterland forts in the fourth century. One change from the past, at the Wall forts and elsewhere, was that the external bath buildings of the high empire were abandoned. The soldiers still bathed, but internal baths inserted in the late third or early fourth century are known at Chesters, Housesteads and Binchester, and will probably be discovered at more forts in the future.

Numbers of Troops on the Fourth-Century Wall

The discovery in the 1970s of late Roman types of barrack led at first to the belief that under Diocletian and Constantine, soldiers' dependants moved into the fort, with each individual building unit or 'chalet' occupied by a single soldier and his family. This would imply an extremely small number of effective soldiers – fifty in the case of a formerly 500 strong unit. But, as explained in the last chapter, the irregular-looking barracks with five *contubernia* are now known to have originated during the heyday of the Wall, before 250. They denote a reduction in infantry centuries, not from eighty to five, but by about half, and the numbers were made up by the presence of irregular Germanic units.

Fig. 5.3 One of the fourth-century barracks at South Shields under excavation, showing that regular and traditional barrack planning was maintained in this period.

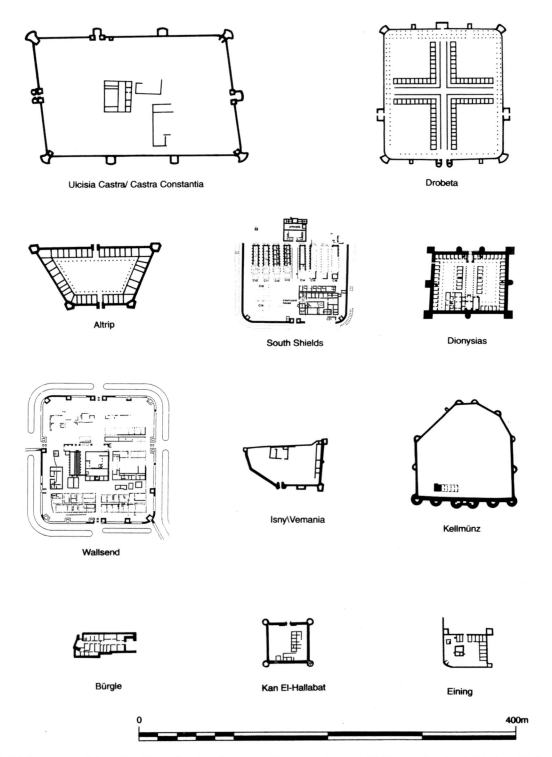

Ulcisia Castra/ Castra Constantia

Drobeta

Altrip

South Shields

Dionysias

Wallsend

Isny\Vemania

Kellmünz

Bürgle

Kan El-Hallabat

Eining

0   400m

Fig. 5.4 Comparison of sizes of late Roman forts in various parts of the empire. Hadrian's Wall forts such as South Shields and Wallsend are clearly larger than the smallest forts shown here, and suggest accommodation for units of considerable size (300–400) in the first half of the fourth century.

	Second century	Third century	Fourth century: 30 men per century	Fourth century: 40 men per century
	Quingenary mixed cohort	Quingenary mixed cohort	Quingenary mixed cohort	Quingenary mixed cohort
Infantry	480	240	180	240
Cavalry	120	120	120	120
Irregulars	-	60?	?	?
TOTAL	**600**	**420?**	**300?**	**360?**
	1,000-strong infantry cohort (Housesteads)	1,000-strong infantry cohort (Housesteads)	1,000-strong infantry cohort (Housesteads)	1,000-strong infantry cohort (Housesteads)
Infantry	800	400		
Irregulars	—	120?	?	?
TOTAL	**800**	**520?**	**300?**	**400?**
	Second-century **ala** (16 **turmae**)	Third-century **ala** (12 barracks)	Fourth-century **ala** (12 barracks)	Fourth-century **ala** (12 barracks)
TOTAL	**480**	**360**	**360**	**360**

There have now been several excavations that have examined the phases of these late Roman barracks which date to the first half of the fourth century. Examples at South Shields and Vindolanda show that the traditional arrangement of the infantry *contubernium*, with front storage and utility room bypassed by a corridor leading to the accommodation unit at the rear, was maintained throughout this period, suggesting a continued traditional formality of living arrangements for large numbers of men living together according to a carefully regulated lifestyle. At South Shields, the fourth-century barracks do not even have the division into separate 'chalet' units, but only internal stone partitions, so they follow exactly the classic arrangement of earlier times. The fourth-century barracks always feature substantial end blocks for the officers in charge of individual centuries or troops of cavalry, but it is not clear how these figures (formerly centurions and decurions) were designated.

We do not know whether each *contubernium* still accommodated the traditional sub-unit of eight men. It is possible that this was reduced to six (a late Roman rank of *hexarchus*, a commander of six men, is attested). Cavalry barracks, as explained in Chapter 4, probably continued to hold around thirty men and their horses.

On the basis of its plan with ten new barracks, fourth-century South Shields housed a unit of 300–400 men; according to our general knowledge of their barracks, the Wall forts in the first half of the fourth century, as seen from the table, would have been *capable* of housing units of between 300 and 400 men. That does not mean that the units were kept up to this strength at all times: there is no way the archaeology can demonstrate that. On the other hand, there is no evidence for large areas of barrack accommodation being abandoned, and there is no reduction in the used area of the Wall forts. The maintained area of the fourth-century Wall forts is larger than that of small late Roman forts on the Danubian and eastern frontiers thought to have held around 120 men, and compares well with, say, the fort of Dionysias in Egypt with its space for some 240 horsemen. The idea that fourth-century frontier units were *all* of extremely small size is a myth:

on the Wall they were between 50 and 25 per cent smaller than in Hadrian's day, but only between 38 and 0 per cent smaller than in the third century, and still constituted substantial forces.

The restoration of the Wall units to reasonable size after the difficult times of the later third century might well have involved absorbing the irregular *cunei*, *numeri* and *symmacharii* attested in the first half of the third century into the regular units. These numbers should also include a special sort of personnel we hear about from the generally reliable Ammianus Marcellinus: the *areani*. These he describes as scouts or spies who moved rapidly over great distances beyond the Wall 'to give information to our generals of the clashes of rebellion among neighbouring peoples'. These seem to be the fourth-century equivalent of the *exploratores* once stationed in the outpost forts, but since these had probably been abandoned around 312, the *areani* were presumably based on the Wall. Ammianus makes it clear that they were a long-standing institution. We can imagine small groups of specialists in the geography of the lands to the north, adept in disguise and in the enemy language.

Similar frontier spies and scouts are described in detailed documents from the Ming period on the Chinese Great Wall. Here their role was to spy on enemy movements and settlements, but also to act as commandos and saboteurs, raiding enemy camps and settlements or penetrating them to assassinate individuals. They could be away from base for years, and lived in constant danger of recognition, apprehension, torture and execution. They were seen as an essential arm of intelligence, but were prone to 'going native', as such frontier spies must always be, becoming too like the enemy whose appearance they adopted, and becoming unreliable, and liable when captured or bribed to betray military secrets to the enemy. This brings us full circle to Ammianus, who describes how the *areani* were bribed in 367 to betray secrets to the northern barbarians and so helped bring about the 'barbarian conspiracy' that devastated the island in that year.

Operation and Maintenance of the Wall in the Late Roman Period

A possible phase of intense activity at milecastles around 300, indicated by coinage of the Emperor Diocletian, has already been mentioned, and the milecastles whose interiors have been extensively excavated were certainly used until late in the fourth century, as both coins and pottery make clear. The original small buildings inside Milecastles 9 and 35 (if correctly so interpreted) were superseded by more extensive building arrangements of barracks on either side of the central road. Extensive modern excavations inside Milecastles 35 and 39 have produced plans of their internal buildings, but these are badly preserved, showing many phases of alteration, and make little overall sense: like the barracks in forts, they had evidently become more irregular in plan, featuring detached building units separated by alleys, probably during the course of the third century.

Milecastle 35 was used for intensive metalworking in the fourth century, but it is not clear what was being made, repaired or recycled. The intensive activity later in this period at these milecastles in the remote crags sector is interesting, suggesting that surveillance along the whole Wall line was maintained, and that there was a continued need to concentrate troop detachments at points between the forts. While most turrets in the central sector had long been suppressed, some at least were still occupied in the fourth century, particularly in lowland areas, as we saw in Chapter 4. There is little reason to believe that the basic operation of the Wall changed much from the third to the fourth century.

Given the intensive manning of forts and milecastles in the fourth century, it would be a natural assumption that the Wall curtain itself was maintained in good condition and in an uninterrupted state. Unfortunately the later structural history of the Wall curtain is very poorly understood. We have already seen that parts of the Wall were reconstituted with a hard white mortar core in the later second or earlier third century, but what about later? The Wall was clearly still there at the end of the Roman period, but did it still stand to full height? Or was it a ruin?

Recently more evidence for the state of the Wall in the late Roman period has come to light. Excavation at Wallsend has shown that the Wall collapsed on successive occasions because of landslip at a point where it crossed a stream valley. On each occasion – although we have no way of knowing after what interval – it was built up again, with the associated pottery showing that this sequence of repairs continued up to at least the mid- to late third century, when there was a final repair with massive blocks reused from the nearby fort. Occupation material running up to the back of the Wall suggests that it was still standing in the late fourth century, and did not finally collapse until after the end of the Roman period.

West of Newcastle, the south face of the Broad Wall at West Denton collapsed at some date in the third century or later. Here, too, the fallen stones from the collapse were used to repair the Wall. At both Wallsend and Denton rebuilt sections resulted in a greater Wall width, which projected from the original face, set back at either end of the rebuilt length. These conspicuous outsets and insets are exactly similar to a well-known series that can be seen in the exposed Wall on the Whin Sill, west of Housesteads. Once explained as the joins between the work of different building gangs, these are more likely to have been caused by the rebuilding of lengths of the Wall. These awkward joins never occur on the north face: if that required rebuilding from ground level it was evidently done carefully so that the north face remained flush. All this amounts to important evidence for the continued maintenance of the Wall in something like its original form.

At Birdoswald, the Wall west of the fort may have been in a ruinous state by the later third century, for by then the fort was separated from the Wall line to the west by a ditch, the curtain that had once attached to the north-west angle of the fort having been removed, presumably after decay, so that the fort was free standing. This is an interesting pointer to the possibility that the condition of much more

of the Wall might have deteriorated in the crisis years after 250 when, as we have seen, there is some evidence for undermanning, dereliction and poor maintenance at fort sites. The continued importance of the Wall barrier is shown by the fact that the fort ditch was later filled in and the Wall reinstated over it to rejoin the fort at its full original (Narrow Wall) width.

The Life of the Soldiers: Origins and Appearance

In the later third and fourth centuries there is a complete absence of inscriptions or other documents to tell us anything about the ethnic or geographical origins of the soldiers of the Wall. From around 300 onwards it was compulsory for soldiers' sons to follow their fathers into service. Hereditary service had already become widespread (on a voluntary basis) in the third and even the second centuries, so this might not have made a vast difference. Also from this period there was an annual regular conscription of the provincial populations. The only other clues come from the character of frontier units as revealed elsewhere in the empire, notably Egypt, by surviving documents. These suggest that the soldiers were predominantly local, with business and family ties to the people in the towns and villages of the province (not necessarily very close to the fort), while still forming a distinct military caste. We can only assume that static frontier units like the cohorts and *alae* of the Wall were predominantly sprung from the civilian population of Britain, with a broadly Celtic background if they came from the southern *civitates*, but with more Latinity and a memory of the military past if their ancestors came from the military north.

Because there is so little surviving material from soldiers' equipment, and because there is a complete absence (from Britain) of sculptural representations, we do not have such a strong visual impression of the fourth-century Wall soldiers and their clothing, armour or weapons. The military or paramilitary figures on the fourth-century mosaics at Piazza

Armerina, Sicily, give us a rare glimpse of the likely appearance of what remain fairly ghostly figures. The overall impression is of well fed and supplied frontier soldiers, effective but essentially static, lacking the wealth and spending power, and much of the Mediterranean-inspired culture of their ancestors.

We have no idea how literate the army of the Wall remained; subjectively, there seems to be less use of what is termed 'graffiti' – names and ownership marks inscribed on pots and other personal possessions, characteristic of the essentially literate army of the high empire – but there was doubtless copious documentation that has not survived in the archaeological record. The fact remains that we do not know the name of a single soldier who served on the Wall after 306.

Pay and Status

To judge from the numbers and types of artefact found in excavations, the army of the Wall in the fourth century was much poorer than before. Bronze coins are more common in this period (from about 320) but this is because they had a much lower intrinsic value than in the high empire, so less effort was made to retrieve them if dropped. But military equipment, brooches and belt fittings, and objects

of bone and glass, are all much scarcer in excavated fourth-century levels than earlier. This must tell us something of the level of pay, otherwise almost a complete mystery. The frontier troops – *limitanei* – were still a paid professional force, but by the early fourth century their regular pay was largely in kind – food and clothing, levied by the government as taxation in kind from the provincial populations and directed to the army through a system known as the *annona militaris*.

The Wall soldiers continued to receive cash payments, a regular *stipendium* and annual 'donatives' on imperial anniversaries, but the value of these had been eroded by inflation so as to become nominal. This meant less buying power for the items of luxury and ornamentation that would be so much more common in second- or early third-century contexts. The late Roman army is also known to have received periodic 'donatives' in gold on the accession of emperors and their subsequent quinquennial celebrations, and it has been argued that the effect of these payments would have given fourth-century *limitanei* a spending power not far short of their second-century predecessors. The argument assumes that this most important element of late Roman military pay was paid to the low-grade *alae* and cohorts at the same rate as to the élite units of the field army, but this is not stated in any source and appears unlikely, especially as we know that around AD300 the humblest frontier troops were receiving the other sort of donatives, the annual ones, at 20 per cent of the rate received by higher grade troops. The evident material simplicity in which the fourth-century troops of the Wall lived tells its own tale.

The Commanding Élite

The system of appointing frontier unit commanders from Mediterranean city aristocracies had disintegrated in the crisis of the mid-third century, and in the fourth century the tribunes of the Wall were either promoted non-commissioned officers or directly appointed and well-connected individuals. Especially in the former case this would imply someone possibly local and from a much humbler social background than in former times. The view that commanding officers were now risen from the ranks has been influenced by the career of Flavius Abinnaeus, prefect of an *ala V Praelectorum,* stationed in Egypt under

Constantius II in the years 342–51. Abinnaeus was no aristocrat, but had been appointed to his command after distinguishing himself in the emperor's service and serving in the ranks of the *protectores,* a kind of late Roman staff college. His archive of correspondence happens to have survived, and gives us a rare insight into the life of a low-grade frontier unit and its commander in the first half of the fourth century. Remarkably, the fort of his *ala* at Dionysias has been excavated, and we have its plan, including the accommodation in which Abinnaeus and his family lived, on rather a modest scale by the standards of second- and third-century *praetoria.*

However, some fourth-century military commanders in north Britain were still of high social status in the fourth century. This was revealed in the 1980s and 1990s by the complete and detailed excavation of the *praetorium* – commanding officer's house – built as part of the early fourth-century replanning of South Shields already discussed. This residence, covering an area in excess of 1,000sq m (measuring 42 by 24m) contained an entrance court, porter's

Fig. 5.6 Plan of the late Roman commanding officer's house (*praetorium*), built around 300, at South Shields, which has remarkable affinities with late Roman peristyle houses in the Mediterranean area. TYNE & WEAR ARCHIVES & MUSEUMS

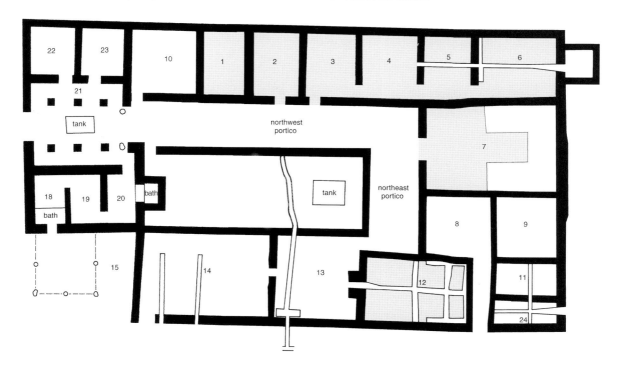

lodge, a suite of bedrooms and reception rooms, two dining rooms (for summer and winter), a kitchen, stable and bath suite.

What was most remarkable was the close affinity of the plan with late Roman peristyle houses in North Africa, Ostia (the port of Rome) and Syria. No models can have been found in the north-western provinces, and this indicates an architect and owner from such a Mediterranean milieu, the latter a city dweller of high social rank. The house was maintained in grand style and reconditioned for a good half century, suggesting successive commanders of like stamp.

In the *Notitia*, South Shields is not one of the forts *per lineam valli*, and as we have seen, its new plan was a product of the latest ideas in military architecture at the heart of the empire. Not all the Wall forts might have been commanded by such a substantial figure, but at both Housesteads and Vindolanda the *praetorium* was apparently maintained as a sizeable peristyle house for the whole of the first half of the

Fig. 5.8 Part of the South Shields *praetorium* under excavation in 1987. Just left of centre a large room shows the cuts for three flagged couch emplacements at its near end, identifying it as a dining room (*triclinium*). To the right are mortar floors with hypocaust (heating) channels.

fourth century, evidently for a commander of some social consequence; it is significant that the *praetorium* at Birdoswald was marked out for reconstruction in 296–305.

Wives and Relationships

Soldiers were free to marry (as they had been in the third century), but there is still no strong archaeological evidence to suggest that their wives lived inside the forts, still less in the barracks. At Housesteads barrack block XIII in the fourth century, artefacts that may be associated with women occur in the centurion's quarters more than in the rest of the barrack block by a factor of 2:1 – the figures are eight finds in the centurion's house and four scattered in *contubernia*; the sample is therefore too small to draw firm conclusions, but suggests that, as in the previous century, officers might be accompanied by wives and families but not usually the ordinary soldiers in the *contubernia*. Structurally, the conservatism of *contubernium* plans is maintained for at least the first half of the fourth century – no examples have yet been found of special rooms or areas that might have been for family accommodation.

As we will see, the civilian settlements outside the fort walls no longer existed in this period, and this has caused a great deal of modern consternation: where were the soldiers' wives, girlfriends and children, if not in the fort? But there were substantial towns never too far away (Corbridge, Carlisle, Catterick), and other civilian settlements in the hinterland of the Wall. Soldiers' wives and children are mentioned in the correspondence of Abinnaeus, but always apparently located in towns or villages at a considerable distance from the fort: for example, a report on a missing soldier, Gerontius, says: 'I found him gone from Plekeesis to the village of his wife...'. Infant burials occur on some fourth-century military sites, but have not been found in quantity at any of the Wall forts except South Shields; it is not clear how many belong to the first half of the fourth century.

The Religion of the Fourth-Century Soldiers

In the crisis of the later third century, the practice of setting up inscribed stone altars ceased, and our primary source for military religion fades away completely. This phenomenon is not confined to Hadrian's Wall but was common to the western empire. This does not mean that religious beliefs were not still held and that cults were not still followed. What was different everywhere was that there was no longer a prosperous class of town councillors anxious to compete in the erection of statues and temples. In the reformed empire of the fourth century, such building inscriptions as there were tended to be erected by emperors and imperial officials, rather than private individuals. On military frontiers, the practical application of this was that there were no longer commanding officers of equestrian aristocratic status to lead the way in paying for and erecting shrines and their inscribed altars.

Religious behaviour therefore becomes practically invisible at every social level on the Wall. In a way, this is not quite the decisive change it seems: if we set aside the substantial shrines and altars of earlier times, often paid for and used by higher ranks, even then we had little solid evidence for the day-to-day spiritual beliefs of the humblest soldier or his family. But even inexpensive portable stone altars, ritual depositions of objects in foundations and wet places, and the ubiquitous practice of carving a *phallus* on stone buildings, including the Wall itself, to ward off malign powers – testaments to everyday superstition and fear at the lowest social level – even these seem to fade away in the fourth century.

The Emperor Constantine famously favoured the Christian religion from 312 onwards, as did subsequent emperors, with the exception of Julian in 360–3. Constantine is said to have outlawed sacrifices in the 330s. This must have become a factor in the lack of outward adherence to the old religion by the higher ranks on the Wall, but it comes too late to explain the cut-off in inscribed religious dedications, which occurs before the end of the third century and was, as we have seen, more of a social than a religious change. For pagan commanding officers and soldiers alike, religion became a more private and less ceremonial matter, now that devotion to the old gods no longer equated to loyalty to the emperor. The temple of Mithras at Carrawburgh was destroyed in the early fourth century, and it is *possible* that this was carried out in deference to the emperor's support for Christianity.

We do not know how long other shrines surviving from the third century might have been used, regularly or occasionally, or continued to stand as respected monuments in the landscape. A series of temples at Corbridge does not appear to have been torn down until some time after 370, when their stones were used to resurface the main Stanegate road running through the town.

Pagan belief and practice probably continued to predominate among the army; at this stage emperors did not have the power or the will to suppress deeply entrenched local traditions. There are few explicitly Christian objects from the Wall, but there were Christians around in the forts of the north, perhaps in some numbers from the third century onwards, as we see from a scattering of finger rings with symbols that would have identified them to fellow devotees. There are a very few tombstones with formulae that are possibly or likely to be Christian: the chi-rho symbol of Christ appears on a silver bowl found at Corbridge, probably part of a buried hoard that also contained the famous 'Corbridge lanx', a dish embellished with a thoroughly pagan scene showing the worship of Apollo on the island of Delos in the Aegean.

Abinnaeus' letters of the 340s describe a world where Christians and pagans tolerantly co-existed with each other. There is no indication that he himself was Christian. His fort still had statues of Fortune and Victory standing in the headquarters building when it was abandoned in the late fourth century. On Hadrian's Wall the sacred spring of the goddess Coventina at Carrawburgh is important evidence for the continuation of pagan practice. Offerings of coins continued to be thrown into the well as late as the 380s, but at a reduced rate as the fourth century wore on. Cremation also continued into the late fourth century in the military cemetery at Beckfoot, on the Cumbrian coast, and was not supplanted by inhumation, as favoured by Christians.

There is no evidence for any sort of organized Christian services for the soldiers of the fourth-century army, and the buildings on the Wall that have been tentatively identified as churches are better placed in the period after the end of Roman rule in Britain, as explained in Chapter 7. Ceremonial devotion when it was organized probably focused on the emperors, who saw no contradiction between their support for the Christian religion and being revered as god-like figures themselves, and whose images may have assumed a more prominent role in the shrine of the headquarters building, where they no longer had to compete with the old gods.

Disposal of the dead continued to be outside the walls of the forts and towns of the Wall, perhaps moving closer as outlying areas were abandoned, though we have no specific examples of this. In the western empire as a whole the trend away from cremation in favour of inhumation continued. If there are extensive late Roman cemeteries on the Wall, containing burials with grave goods and human remains that might shed light on the lives and origins of the people, these have yet to be discovered.

The Civilians of the Wall in the Later Empire

The Abandonment of the Military *Vici*

Fifty years ago it was still believed that the civilian extramural settlements reached their apogee of development in the fourth century, as the economic development of the province came to its fruition under the protection of Hadrian's Wall. It is now known that these sprawling developments, which so characterized the landscape of the Wall in its heyday, had in fact drastically contracted, or been almost wholly abandoned by the end of the third century.

The coin list from the only really extensively excavated example, at Vindolanda, suggests that it was abandoned by about 270, while excavated samples of other military *vici* on the Wall – South Shields, Wallsend, Halton Chesters, Housesteads, Burgh-by-Sands, Maryport – have shown that the buildings of the *vicus* have only stray fourth-century finds.

The story is much the same at the few excavated *vici* of the forts to the south, in the hinterland of the Wall. There are a few exceptions: civilian settlements attached to military bases at Catterick, Malton and possibly Binchester have continued activity in the fourth century, suggesting that they survived and prospered as regional market centres in an area where there were few civilian towns. The *vicus* at Greta Bridge, situated on an important trans-Pennine route, was in use until the 330s. In the fourth century these areas were not utterly without human activity. At South Shields a system of fields interspersed with wells has been found overlying the remains of the third-century *vicus*. There are various cases where fourth-century buildings have been found, usually immediately outside fort walls (for example Old Penrith, South Shields). But the general picture is clear: by the earlier fourth century, the once extensive development of strip-buildings, vibrant with enterprise, that lined the roads running to forts, often over a distance of many hundreds of metres, had vanished.

We are still a long way from understanding exactly when the process of abandonment began and how gradual the process was, or, indeed, whether *vicus* buildings (the majority of which may have been half timbered) were deliberately cleared away or left to fall into ruin. As for the cause: it seems indisputable that the abandonment of the *vici* was linked to the military and economic difficulties in the mid-third century, which eventually led to a reconstruction of so many aspects of society along new lines. There are a number of factors that probably had an effect, but it must be remembered that this is historical speculation: we have no written evidence about the fate of these settlements.

The simple threat posed by warfare and insecurity to lightly defended or undefended extramural settlements may have been a factor. This is not directly attested in Britain before 284, but unrest in Britain related to the continental invasions of the mid-270s seems likely. Some *vicus* businesses may have been owned or supplied by traders or merchants from Gaul, whose activities were disrupted or terminated by the invasions there of the late 250s and 275.

That it was a direct result of the structural reduction in unit sizes on the Wall as time went on – meaning there was a reduced market for the goods and services provided by the *vicus* – seems doubtful. As already discussed in the table in the foregoing section 'Numbers of Troops on the Fourth-Century Wall' on p.143, the most decisive fall-off in numbers came in the *early* third century, when in fact the *vici* on the Wall reached their peak of development.

What is more likely to have had an immediate effect is a decline in the numbers of soldiers due to drafts from units during times of crisis on the continent, from the time of Valerian (253), under Gallienus (before 259), and under the Gallic Empire (260–74). The impact of third-century inflation on the spending power of the remaining soldiers' salaries would reduce their buying power and compound the difficulties of the *vicus* traders. The Wall units were probably brought back up to strength in the early fourth century, but this was too late to revive the *vici*, for the whole system of military supply had changed. Now, the majority of the soldiers' pay was in kind, and its distribution centrally organized by the state through the *annona militaris*, where previously their cash salaries had been used to buy goods and services on the open market in the *vici*. Economically, the traders of the *vicus* had been bypassed. In any case, the spending power of the fourth-century soldiers was, as we have seen, far less in real terms than before.

All these factors might account for a drawn-out decline between *c.* 250 and *c.* 270, with the *vici* on Hadrian's Wall largely deserted after that date, though a few in the hinterland developed roles as regional centres. Insecurity and reduced numbers of soldiers at individual bases may have led veterans and soldiers' families to take up residence in urban centres (Corbridge, Carlisle), which by then were probably defended by walls and are thought to have been in full occupation in the 270s/280s (as shown by the level of 'radiate' coinage of that period at Corbridge). Thus we see a *consolidation* of the civilian population engaged in services and supply in fewer centres with an urban character, presumably the centres through which collection of the *annona* and its distribution to individual forts was organized by the state.

Unlike the *vici*, these frontier towns – Corbridge, Carlisle, Catterick, Malton – continued as busy places in the fourth century, and acquired importance as regional market and distribution centres. When thinking of supplies and services, of the homes of their wives, brothers, sisters, sons, daughters and parents, and indeed of new recruits, the commanding officers and soldiers of the individual Wall forts now looked out to the region and to their nearest urban centre – which is very much the picture offered by the letters of Abinnaeus, in which the far-flung villages and towns of the Egyptian Fayum play such a prominent part in soldiers' lives. Unlike the distantly supplied enclaves of military and civilian immigrants of the second century, which obtained their fullest expression in the fort/*vicus* combination, forts in north Britain were now manned and supplied by local society at large. This is illustrated by fourth-century pottery, predominantly coming to forts now from East Yorkshire and Midland Britain, rather than more distantly traded as before.

Markets at Forts

At four separate sites on the Wall, evidence has recently been found that markets were held *inside* forts in the fourth century. This is the most convincing explanation of concentrations of low-value fourth-century coins found on internal street surfaces at Wallsend (just inside the minor west gate), Newcastle (in front of the *principia*), at Vindolanda (just inside the west gate, in front of the granaries) and at Carlisle (again in front of the headquarters building).

The coin loss suggests activity from the later third through to the later fourth century, with a peak in the period 330–50 and fading out by 380. At Wallsend and Vindolanda, and presumably at the other Wall forts, it looks as if local people, or sellers from the nearest town, or from further afield, were travelling to the Wall forts to market goods or foodstuffs. Carlisle and Newcastle are situated at possible north–south routes across the Wall, and may have been market centres for people to the north. This intriguing evidence suggests that although the extra-mural settlements had disappeared, the forts were now tied in to a complicated network of economic relationships with people in the region, including those far to the north of the Wall.

The Towns

In contrast to the military *vici*, the urban centres at Corbridge and Carlisle flourished in the fourth century. As we have seen, as early as AD223 Carlisle was designated a regional capital, notionally the tribal capital of the Carvetii (*civitas Carvetiorum*), and in the east Corbridge almost certainly had a similar status. These local government units continued to exist in the fourth century. Each would have had well-defined boundaries, both with each other and with the *territoria* of individual forts, and no doubt the Wall itself. A group of seven milestones all found together at Crindledykes, just east of Vindolanda on the Stanegate, the latest dating to the period 306–37, may possibly mark the boundary of the *civitates* centred on Carlisle and Corbridge.

There is no firm evidence for walls surrounding either town, but old excavation reports and anti-quarian accounts suggest their existence at Corbridge. At Carlisle the overlying medieval city has prevented resolution of the problem. In terms of Roman Britain as a whole, it would have been grossly untypical for these towns not to have been defended by the fourth century. Both were extensive, Corbridge covering perhaps 20ha (50 acres), but materially rather poor – there are none of the fine mosaics that graced town houses further south in the province, and these were essentially remote and rather bleak frontier towns. Without inscriptions, and without much in the way of modern excavation, it is difficult to get much insight into the identities and daily lives of their inhabitants, but we can surmise that many will have had close relationships with the soldiers of the Wall.

The Life of the Local Population

The relationship between the people of the towns and forts, and the indigenous population of the countryside in the lea of the Wall is just as difficult to fathom in the late Roman period as before. On the western side of the Pennines small farming communities continued to exist in the third and fourth centuries, with settlements and lifestyle little different from that of the pre-Roman Iron Age, to judge from finds of later Roman pottery on some sites that were investigated long ago. On the east side, too, there are low-status rural sites that produced later Roman material, but there is no sense of a typical settlement plan or house type.

Thus the general late Roman character of rural settlement is still obscure. The small town at Sedgefield and the Faverdale site did not continue strongly into late Roman times. The villa at Ingleby Barwick was still in use, but we have no type example of a fourth-century, non-villa rural settlement in County Durham. However, traces (mostly unpublished) have been found of sites with mid to late Roman field systems at Newton Bewley; sunken floored sub-rectilinear buildings of third to fourth-century date at Newton Bewley again, and Street House; a settlement consisting of roundhouses and extensive field systems with second- to third-century Roman pottery at Dixon's Bank; late Roman finds and rectangular buildings at Catcote; late Roman finds and a cist burial at Green Lane, Levington and Yarm; and late Roman finds and a possible rectilinear building on an abandoned Iron Age site at Apperley Dene.

One gets the feeling that it is only a matter of time before one of these late Roman peasant settlements is revealed and published in an extensive area excavation, as recently happened so unexpectedly and spectacularly at Wattle Syke (near Wetherby) in West Yorkshire, where excavation in advance of road widening revealed the dramatic abandonment of the enclosure/roundhouse traditions of the Iron Age and earlier Roman times, and the emergence of a new, completely different sort of settlement with rectilinear, sunken-floored buildings interspersed with human burials. The site, previously invisible and unsuspected archaeologically, dated to the fourth century and surely heralds a late Roman site type that developer archaeology will reveal in greater numbers in the area south of the Wall in the years to come. The excavators of the Wattle Syke settlement saw it as a low-status agricultural site, possibly subservient to a nearby villa, whose foodstuffs and products were destined for the military supply chain.

Any settlement in the Wall area that was functioning beyond subsistence level and receiving pottery from the regional industries that mainly supplied the military, must have had contacts with Roman authorities or the markets of the northern frontier towns – but the evidence for that contact and the nature of the relationship eludes us. However, the passing of Iron Age building traditions, and the assumption of archaeologically less visible forms of settlement, might suggest that peasant villages subservient to some higher authority had replaced the numerous independent households of the pre-Roman and earlier Roman periods.

Society North of the Wall

By the 230s the silver *denarius* subsidies that the Romans had used to manipulate the peoples of north-east Scotland came to an end. The empire was too cash strapped, and had too many distractions elsewhere, to continue this policy of diplomatic control. It has been argued that this will have undermined the authority of the élites who had redistributed these subsidies to their followers, and a drastic restructuring of society does seem to have followed, seeing the emergence of new and powerful leaders, and the disappearance of much traditional settlement – very few earlier Roman period settlements with radiocarbon dating evidence have produced dates that show their history to extend beyond 250. The newly emerged and successful leaders were those who could obtain gold, silver, slaves and other valuable commodities by organizing raids on the distant Roman Empire, which meant crossing or bypassing Hadrian's Wall.

In the Roman historical sources that we have, one term for the people of Scotland north of the Forth who conducted such raids dominates: the Picts, although raiders from Ireland (the Attacotti and the Scotti), as well as the Saxons, are often mentioned in association with them. The name of the Picts is first found in writings dating to around 300, and continues to be used for the inhabitants of the far north of Britain until the end of the Roman period. Like all similar Roman versions of 'tribal' names, it is probably a gross simplification of various different groupings, and is not necessarily what the people originally called themselves – although the term did survive to give the early medieval kingdom of the Picts its name. The name probably does mean 'painted' or 'tattooed' people. In the 360s Ammianus Marcellinus divulges the detail that the Picts were contained in two sub-groups: the Dicalydones (obviously related in some way to the earlier Caledonii); and the Verturiones. Perhaps these were descendants of the Caledonii and Maeatae respectively.

The idea that Hadrian's Wall was built to keep out the Picts is therefore anachronistic – the name did not arise until the Wall had been in operation for nearly two centuries. Rather, with the Picts we are seeing a response to the very long-term presence of Hadrian's Wall. The first- and second-century Roman occupations of Scotland were brief interludes, lasting only seven and twenty years respectively, but it would be wrong to think that this allowed traditional Iron Age society to survive essentially unchanged into the late Roman period and beyond.

In fact it was not the Roman invasions, but the brooding permanence of the imperial frontier that changed society in Scotland, the tipping point coming in the third century. The hierarchies and social bonds of traditional Iron Age society having been weakened by the manipulations of Roman diplomacy and trade, and the northern peoples having been walled out of the empire and denied access to its wealth, it is not surprising that new political structures emerged, and that raids on the Roman Empire became a permanent and integral part of the economy and culture of the societies of north-east Scotland. Gold, silver, slaves and other precious items, such as glass drinking vessels, obtainable from the empire, were the essential means by which warrior élites maintained their position of authority by impressing and rewarding their followers – an example of the archaeological so-called 'prestige goods systems' theory.

Archaeologists tend to debate whether it was trade or plunder that brought valued Roman items into this society, but it need not have been exclusively either of these simple categories. On more recent imperial frontiers, such as the Russian steppe, goods from the empire were traded or offered as diplomatic gifts to maintain the peace, and nomadic societies conducted raids not just for plunder, but to enable them to bargain for further presents.

It was against land raids from north-east Scotland that Hadrian's Wall was maintained in the fourth century, and against sea-borne raids from the same quarter that new defences (the 'Yorkshire coast signal stations') were extended down the eastern coast south of the Wall. In one sense the Wall faced merely a banal succession of raids from this source, rather than an existential threat of invasion or destruction – hence the rather old-fashioned appearance of the Wall forts, never rebuilt along new lines as happened on the Rhine and Danube frontiers, where there were large-scale military pressures on the empire. In Scotland there was no such impetus as the west–east domino-fall of population movements driving in from on the Eurasian plain: native society in Scotland could exist in stable fashion by raiding, and did not have a direct interest in invasion for the sake of settlement within the empire.

Although this explains why the same units that had manned the Wall for over two centuries could remain in place, and why in continental terms the Wall was a relative backwater, there is no doubt that the threat from the north was taken seriously and was highly destructive. A fourth-century dice tower (for throwing dice without the possibility of cheating) found on the continent carried the inscription PICTOS VICTOS HOSTIS DELETA LUDITE SECURI – 'The Picts are defeated, the enemy destroyed, play in safety'. This is direct evidence for a fearsome reputation. The far north continued to be the objective of Roman punitive campaigns until the final years of Roman Britain. It is also interesting that to the medieval inhabitants of Northumberland and Cumberland, Hadrian's Wall was always known as 'The Picts' Wall'.

For all the resonance of the name, it is extraordinarily difficult to identify settlements in Scotland, which could confidently be associated with the 'Picts' of the Roman period (as opposed to the Picts of early medieval times). Without excavation and radiocarbon dating, settlements of this period are impossible to distinguish from those of the pre-Roman (or post-Roman) Scottish Iron Age, and the limited repertoire of metal objects that might identify them (knob-shaped butt ends of spear shafts, for example, particular types of ring-headed pins, or massive terret rings from horse gear) continue to be used up until the seventh century.

The settlements themselves would generally produce little more than the same unprepossessing assemblage of crudely worked stone objects and milling stones as an earlier Iron Age site – traces of the items sought from the empire, precious metals and slaves, would naturally not survive amongst the finds on such sites. The possible sites known to archaeologists come in a range of forms, such as hill forts, ring forts, enclosures, open roundhouse clusters and single stone buildings, but in the lowlands of Perth and Angus, which one would suspect was the Pictish heartland, none has been closely dated or comprehensively excavated, although work in progress might change this picture.

In the uplands along the south-east fringe of the highlands, near Pitlochry, a settlement of fortified stone roundhouses or 'homesteads' has been excavated at Aldclune. This may have been in use through the later Roman Iron Age in Scotland, and beyond, and may allow a glimpse of the fortified homestead of one of the farmer–warrior families who lie behind the blanket term 'the Picts'. A similar homestead site has recently been excavated at the Black Spout, Pitlochry. Elsewhere it is probable that Pictish sites presently dated to the early medieval period will turn out to have had hitherto unrecognized Roman period origins.

One reason for the difficulty in pinning down the Picts archaeologically is that, in contrast to the period before 250, fewer Roman – and therefore recognizable and closely datable – objects found their way into the Pictish heartland. Whereas the second- to third-century Roman policy had been to manipulate élite groups in Perth, Angus and Moray by means of targeted trade and subsidies, now it is almost as if these peoples have been sealed off and prevented from acquiring goods from the Roman Empire. However, such items do, in fact, get as far as the northern isles and coastal regions, suggesting that their absence from the north-east lowlands is significant and the result of a deliberate policy.

Nevertheless, the 'Picts' of the north-east lowlands did enjoy contacts with other areas: some of the identifier items also occur in Ireland, giving an archaeological expression to the contact and collaboration implied by the literary account of the 'barbarian conspiracy'. Some of these objects occur on Hadrian's Wall and further south in the British provinces. One possible explanation for this is that these notorious enemies of Rome were sometimes conscripted into Roman military service, or supplied recruits as their part of some diplomatic bargain.

In contrast there are some notable coin hoards and concentrations of late Roman finds such as tablewares, glass drinking vessels and brooches in *southern* Scotland, south of the Forth (though again it is important to note that late Roman coin

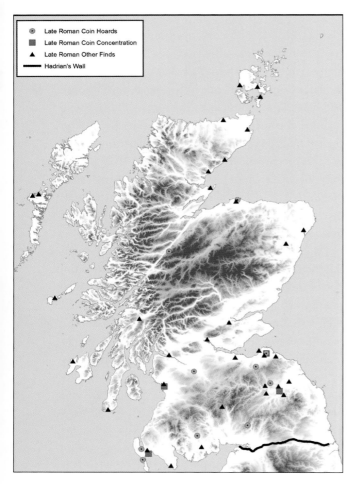

Fig. 5.9 Distribution of Roman coins, coin hoards and other finds in Scotland in the late Roman period, 250–410. Adapted from F. Hunter's *Beyond the Edge of the Empire – Caledonians, Picts and Romans*, Rosemarkie (2007).

of the Emperor Diocletian (306). Was this looted from some campaigning Roman army (the traditional explanation), or a present to some southern Scottish potentate?

The general nature of these late Roman finds suggests concern with personal adornment, feasting and drinking, and they were not widely distributed through subservient settlements, some of which have now been identified and dated in the vicinity of Traprain. The distribution suggests that late Roman policy may have been to subsidise and support the élite leaders of a number of 'buffer states' in southern Scotland that intervened between Hadrian's Wall and the Pictish areas. Support of such allies was a high priority following the emergence of the Picts in south-east Scotland, north of the Forth, and the probable abandonment of all outpost forts north of the Wall around 312.

It has been suggested that the genealogies of the kings of Galloway, Strathclyde (centred on Dumbarton?) and Manau Gododdin (Edinburgh, replacing Traprain?) show that these dynasties were founded by the Romans as early as the 370s; however, this is no longer generally accepted. But it seems plausible that these power centres were crucial to the Roman management of the frontier in the fourth century, and that by some process they emerged as kingdoms in the early post-Roman period.

Closer to Hadrian's Wall there are indications that the remnant population of the Northumberland coastal plain had direct dealings with the empire. This is indicated by the internal market at Newcastle Fort, active in the fourth century: here, sherds of native pottery suggest the possibility that people from north of the Wall were being admitted to a super-vised market. It is possible that the proposed market site at Great Whittington still operated: there is less evidence for coin-based transactions in the fourth century, but predominantly non-monetary trade with people from north of the Wall might have continued, and significantly a purse of eight copper alloy coins, lost no earlier than 406 and including the latest known coin from Hadrian's Wall, has been found there. ☼

hoards and high-status objects are found in the *far* north of Scotland, apparently the result of some kind of coastal contact or trade). In the south they occur at hillforts and other sites that were centres of social authority, such as Traprain Law, with its famous hoard of late Roman silver treasure, hacked into pieces and probably representing a diplomatic payment from the empire. From Erickstanebrae in Dumfries and Galloway comes a remarkable gold 'crossbow' brooch with an inscription that says it was given as an imperial gift on the twentieth anniversary

Chapter 6

WHAT WAS THE PURPOSE OF HADRIAN'S WALL?

The General Idea behind the Wall – the security of the provincial population

WE HAVE LITTLE SURVIVING ANCIENT Roman explanation of the purpose of the Wall. Hadrian's biographer commented that it was 'to separate the Romans from the barbarians', and although this statement was written long after Hadrian's time, it has interesting overtones. It does not stress military defence *per se*, rather cultural division or separation, and the protection of a way of life.

On one level, Hadrian and his advisers and succeeding Roman administrators probably did conceive of the purpose of the Wall in such a general, theoretical way. Hadrian, as we have seen, came to believe that the empire had to be contained within manageable limits – there is a hint of this in the fragmentary Jarrow inscription – and provincial society protected and nurtured behind the military protection of fortification lines. Hadrian's Wall, it has been argued, was part of a self-conscious policy of provincial economic development, allowing those within and right up to the border, whether settlers or indigenes, the peace and security to develop into Roman provincials. There is some truth in this, and the same policy can be seen at work in other provinces of the empire. Equally, the Wall had obvious political potential, at least in its early days, to prevent interaction and collusion between hostile groups north and south of the isthmus.

In the first century, Tacitus spoke of the empire having both land and river boundaries, using the word *limes* (pronounced '*lee*-mays'), a term for a demarcated land boundary of the empire, for the former. The Jarrow fragments suggest that in Hadrian's time the Wall in Britain was regarded as a land boundary of the Roman Empire. In the book of road routes known as the *Antonine Itinerary* (late second or early third century in date), one of the routes in Britain is said to lead to 'the *limes*, that is, the Wall'. This source shows that in Britain this notion was synonymous with Hadrian's Wall itself.

This does not mean that the Wall functioned as a legal border to the province of Britannia, or indeed the Roman Empire. It was not a limit to Roman authority or a line beyond which the empire would not collect taxes or plunder the landscape for resources – the outpost forts show that military authority did not end at the Wall. Peoples beyond the Wall with whom the Romans had diplomatic or trade relations would have been regarded as part of the Roman Empire, and within the sphere of responsibility of the governor of Britain. But the tidy-minded Romans always thought in terms of boundaries, legal and religious, and it is no surprise to find them delineating the ordered, inner part of their world with a Wall. An ordered inner space was separated from an area of external control, just as the markers of the ploughed ritual boundary of a Roman city – the *pomerium* – defined its area of internal order, but did not limit the territory it controlled and exploited.

Most would agree on this general idea behind Hadrian's Wall, and there is some evidence for it to be gleaned from ancient writings. But none of this helps us to understand how the Wall was intended to function, and did function, in detail. The problem is that we lack any ancient Roman records or explanation, and any modern vision of its purpose is therefore a reconstruction, based on archaeological and circumstantial evidence, and incapable of proof. The view of the function of the Wall put forward in this chapter can only be an interpretation of the evidence, and other interpretations are possible, and will be found in other books about the Wall.

The Non-Military Interpretation

For the antiquaries of the eighteenth and nineteenth centuries the purpose of Hadrian's Wall was self-evident: it marked the extent of Roman power in the island of Britain, and secured the province against those Britons who remained unconquered. The Wall was seen as a fence against a northern foe, who might on occasion pour across the barrier to overwhelm defending Roman forces – as depicted in Robert Spence's painting *The Night Attack* (1912–14).

Although this image has continued to haunt the popular imagination, for those involved in the study of the Wall the twentieth century saw the dawning and gradual fruition of the idea of the Wall as a line of observation and control, rather than as a defensible fortification. In 1921 an influential essay suggested that the Wall top was too narrow to fight from, that there were insufficient men to defend the whole Wall line, that Roman soldiers would not have had the right weapons for defence of the Wall top, and that there were insufficient places where steps could have led to a Wall walk for such fighting to be possible. Any actual military threat would be dealt with by the Roman army in the open: the Wall itself was an unmistakeable warning and hindrance to 'smugglers, robbers and other undesirables'.

It ought to be stressed that this referred only to the Wall itself as a running barrier, with its milecastles and turrets. It was maintained then, and it is still generally held, that the units in the main auxiliary forts on the Wall were intended to defend the province, and for aggressive campaigns or in response to emergencies would march out to meet the enemy in the field.

The same applies to the forts and legionary bases in the hinterland of the Wall: they were there to defend the province in the event of a real military emergency. The argument runs that the Wall forts were situated on the Wall purely for convenience, and that the Wall as a barrier had the unrelated function of observing and controlling illegal movement by individuals. In this way of looking at it, the addition of the forts to the Wall, recognized in the 1930s, is critical: the lack of forts in the original scheme is held to demonstrate that the Wall was conceived of as controlling small-scale movement.

This 'non-military' interpretation of the Wall was developed in various ways after World War II. The Wall was portrayed as a customs and passport barrier, regulating the movement of native farmers and traders in and out of the province, and allowing the peaceful economic development of the area to the south. By 1970 it had been suggested for the first time that there might not have been a walkway on top of the Wall – not only was there no proof for the existence of a Wall walk, it was also demonstrably absent from Roman frontier barriers on the continent, such as the palisade and wall in Germany and Raetia. Milecastles came to be regarded as having functioned, at least in part, as checkpoints where civilians could be monitored as they passed through the Wall.

This view of the Wall as a non-defensive barrier with carefully controlled crossing points is held by many ancient historians and archaeologists, and has gained such momentum that it is now common currency among educated lay visitors to the Wall – so much so that in a light newspaper piece of 2010 about the Wall we can read that 'Since I was first taught about Hadrian's Wall there has been a groundswell of opinion that it was less a fortification than a means of monitoring the flow of people between the two regions and taxing them accordingly'. Surely this is one of the most striking examples in archaeological thought of the success of a counter-intuitive idea.

Fig. 6.1 Once provided, the Vallum hermetically sealed the Wall line. This rare complete section across the Vallum ditch, taken at Denton (Wall-mile 7) in 1987, shows what a formidable barrier to movement it was. Note that beneath the level of the figure's head the Vallum ditch has been cut through solid rock.

A Barrier for Economic Regulation?

The idea of the milecastle gates as checkpoints for civilians moving through the Wall always had a fundamental difficulty: as soon as the forts were added to the Wall, which was before the curtain and minor structures were completed, the Vallum hermetically sealed the line, preventing any direct north–south movement via milecastles. This necessitated suggestions that civilians were moved along the north berm of the Vallum under military supervision until they reached a fort Vallum causeway – an over-elaborate and rather implausible vision.

More decisive against the 'customs barrier' version of the Wall is what we now know of the effect that the Wall had on indigenous farming settlements to the north: as explained in Chapter 3, the advent of large-scale radiocarbon dating has shown that the pre-Roman settlement pattern did not continue unchanged, but that there was widespread social disruption and settlement abandonment north of the Wall in the wake of its construction. The belief in a continuity of indigenous agricultural life to either side of the Wall, which went hand-in-hand with that of milecastles as checkpoints, is false. Remarkably

few objects from the Roman Empire found their way north of the Wall, far fewer than we would expect if there were widespread day-to-day civilian movement across the barrier.

This picture is borne out on parts of the continental frontiers where studies have shown that exported Roman material occurs very unevenly in time and space, suggesting no routine access to Roman goods for people beyond the empire, the movement of goods occurring only in certain circumstances when it suited the Romans.

This is not to say, of course, that there was no trade across the Wall – we have noted a possible frontier market at Great Whittington, but its occurrence at Portgate, where a great route passes through the barrier, suggests that there may have been just a very few such recognized places, where 'trade' relations were mediated between the Roman authorities and élites beyond the Wall, and goods and presents exchanged. This kind of exchange point would explain the rarity and the élite character of Roman objects that do occur in Scotland, better than free-for-all movement through many points on the Wall.

For those with a first-hand knowledge of this and other archaeological evidence, this idea of the Wall as an economic filter has become less attractive in recent years, and even those archaeologists who maintain a non-military function for the Wall curtain now tend to stress the hindrance and prevention of raiding rather than economic regulation, although carefully speaking in terms of 'control' rather than 'defence'. However, while there can be no doubt that the Wall had a political role in the separation of peoples, and a role in preventing illegal or unwanted movement by individuals, this in itself is not incompatible with there being other military functions for the barrier itself in distinction to the forts.

The Context in which the Wall was Built

The contrarian view that the Wall itself (as distinct from the forts) 'had neither strategic nor tactical value' has, over the last half-century, been accompanied by other suggestions: that it was merely a statement of Roman power, a magnificent but militarily useless piece of Roman rhetoric, or that it was 'displacement activity' to employ an army that was no longer engaged in conquest and imperial expansion. The idea that the building of the Wall was to keep busy an army that otherwise had little to do and might pose a threat to central authority has wide appeal.

In Chapter 2 we examined the build-up to the Wall. There is little in the evidence to suggest that the army in Britain was underemployed. Rather it was thinly stretched, with reinforcements needed from the continent (why bring across the Sixth Legion if the army was underemployed?), and engaged in bitter warfare, and it was perhaps in the context of a war (the *expeditio Britannica*), either recently concluded or imminent, that Hadrian made his visit and the Wall was raised. This is often ignored in discussions about its purpose, as is one vital source that alludes to circumstances in which the Wall was built: the Jarrow inscription (Chapter 2), probably from a monument at the eastern terminus of the Wall and perhaps embodying a speech by Hadrian himself, sums up a Roman understanding of what the Wall was originally for.

Reasonably reconstructed as stating that 'the barbarians were scattered and the province of Britain recovered… he added a Wall between either shore of the Ocean… built by the army of the province…'. The text places the building of the Wall against a background of serious revolt or invasion, and the repulse of the enemy: that is the context in which the Wall is built, and which is the basic motivation for its building. Solving the problem by further conquest had proved impossible; the Gods had decreed it was necessary to limit the Roman Empire. Here the Wall as a concept is intimately linked to the army, and seen as the defence and divinely sanctioned boundary of the empire.

The Potential Size of Raiding War Bands

In judging the function of the Wall and its forts we have to assess the numbers and capabilities of those who might have attacked or tried to cross the Wall. We have already dismissed the economic movements of agriculturalists and herdsmen as significant considerations in the design of the Wall. While the Wall prevented illegal crossings by individuals, this could have been achieved by a much smaller and less elaborate barrier. The Jarrow inscription (which may or may not have commemorated the completion of the Wall in its final form, forts and all) implies a response to the activities of war bands in northern Britain, who had inflicted severe casualties on the Roman army (remember Fronto: 'How many soldiers were killed by the Jews, how many by the Britons!'), and on the province.

This implies a highly fluid force of opponents, fragmented (and perhaps with no strong central organization), whom the Romans had been unable to pin down and defeat in battle. One Vindolanda tablet explicitly attests the very many cavalry used by the Britons. In its completed form the Wall excluded these opponents and would have been virtually impassable to small-mounted groups if properly manned. Presumably any raids from the north that followed would be

Fig. 6.2 A Pictish stone from Aberlemno (near Forfar, Angus) in Scotland. This possibly depicts the defeat of the English (helmeted, right) at the battle of Nechtansmere in 685. Although carved up to four centuries after the Roman period, the bare-headed Pictish warriors (left side), mounted and unmounted, give an idea of the capabilities of Rome's opponents.

mean that these were individuals or mere handfuls of thieves: Caesar speaks of *latrones* in Gaul gathering together in a great host to vent their zeal for war.

Medieval parallels are instructive: on the Anglo-Scottish border in the reign of Edward II, mounted Scottish raiders campaigned with a force several thousand strong and could not be brought to battle; earlier medieval war bands seem to have numbered in the low hundreds, but could be accumulated to make a larger force. In short, our few fragments of oblique evidence do not necessarily support the common image of mere handfuls or raiders trying to cross the Wall undetected, and allow for the possibility that from time to time larger numbers were involved.

The Form of the Wall as Evidence for its Function

Archaeology can help determine whether the Wall curtain itself was defensible. The existence of a patrollable walkway and crenellations along the top of the Wall cannot be proven, since we have no part of the Wall surviving to full height, but it is incorrect to say that the absence of a Wall walk is an equally likely possibility: archaeology is most often not about proving things, but establishing the most reasonable reading of the evidence, and the evidence is most reasonably taken as implying a patrolled Wall walk.

The Wall is built on an extraordinary scale, dwarfing that of other Roman frontier walls, which themselves constituted formidable barriers to movement. The sheer width of the Wall, even after the decision to narrow its gauge, is only satisfactorily explained by the presence of a Wall walk. A large number of chamfered (bevelled) decorative stones from a string course have been found fallen from the front face of the Wall; they were a standard means of marking the transition to the crenellated parapet on a defensive wall, and can have had no other conceivable purpose.

There are other indications: when some turrets were demolished around the turn of the second and

conducted by similar forces, trying to take advantage of parts of the Wall that were weakly manned or even undefended.

The only specific references to conflict that we have are post-Hadrianic. We have seen that the inscriptions recording the destruction of a *manus* of barbarians could denote a 'force', 'host' or 'multitude'; the great raid described by Dio for the 180s, which cut down all the troops accompanying (probably) a legionary legate, while hardly a day-to-day event, suggests attackers numbering thousands rather than hundreds. Direct descriptions of intruders on other Roman frontier lines are rare. In the 180s a series of towers and garrisons was established on the Danube 'Against the secret crossings of *latrunculi*'. The word *latro*, of which *latrunculus* is a contemptuous diminutive, means a robber, bandit or brigand, but does not

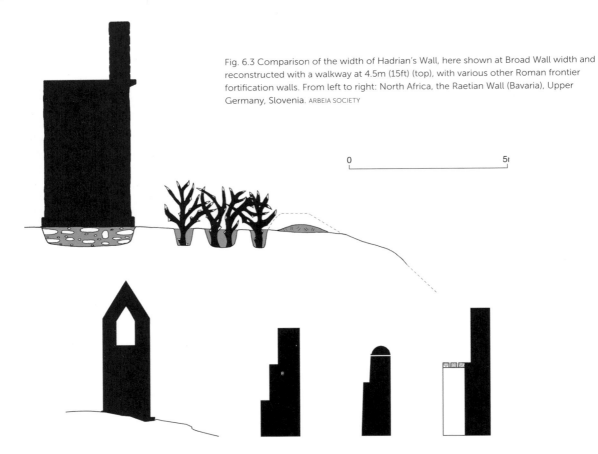

Fig. 6.3 Comparison of the width of Hadrian's Wall, here shown at Broad Wall width and reconstructed with a walkway at 4.5m (15ft) (top), with various other Roman frontier fortification walls. From left to right: North Africa, the Raetian Wall (Bavaria), Upper Germany, Slovenia. ARBEIA SOCIETY

0   5ı

third centuries, their recesses were carefully walled up, which would have allowed the Wall walk to be carried over the recess. The Hadrianic Wall was carried over the rivers Tyne and Irthing by bridges, which would have been pointless unless there was a walkway; this *could* have been for a patrol track rather than a Wall walk, but it is remarkable that the width of the bridge piers at Chesters suggest that the bridge top continued the same 3m (10RF) gauge of the Broad Wall. The continental palisades and walls that could not be walked upon merely came to an end at river banks and resumed on the other side.

The frontal ditch makes no sense unless it could be viewed and controlled from the Wall top; without supervision it would have served no purpose, and

Fig. 6.4 A collection of chamfered (bevelled) stones found by F. G. Simpson in 1909, fallen from the north face of the Wall on Peel Crag (Wall-mile 39). These would have been the other way up (chamfer downwards), and almost certainly marked the transition from Wall face to parapet at wall-walk level.

Fig. 6.5 The frontal ditch, and the obstacles found on the berm between Wall and ditch, support the view that there was a walk and parapet along the top of the Wall from which defenders could engage attackers. TYNE & WEAR ARCHIVES & MUSEUMS (DRAWING BY PETE URMSTON)

would be an easily negotiated obstacle. The German palisade and Raetian Wall, lacking a walk-walk, do not have a frontal ditch. The very presence of the ditch implies a wall top from which those trying to cross the ditch could be engaged.

The last ten years has yielded a remarkable addition to the archaeological evidence available: the recognition of the obstacles on the berm between Wall and frontal ditch, planned from the outset as part of the Wall anatomy. The impenetrable entanglement of forked branches most probably accommodated in the berm emplacements is close in appearance and function to what Caesar described as *cippi*. The purpose of the *cippi* or obstacles closest to the defences at Alesia was, on Caesar's explicit authority, to render attackers vulnerable to projectiles directed from a small number of troops on a defensive rampart, and

thus impede their progress for long enough for reinforcements to arrive.

Records of the width of the berm west of the Irthing, and observations in the Newcastle area, have been taken to suggest that it narrowed in front of turrets, and that the obstacles were discontinued there, effectively channelling attackers towards the turrets. Obstacles should be expected on the north side of the ditch; these might take the form of man traps (*lilia*), whose purpose was to break up a charge before it reached the defences; and indeed it is *lilia* in the true man-trap sense that are found north of the Antonine Wall ditch at Rough Castle.

It follows from this reading of the function of the obstacles that they would only have been effective if the ditch and berm of Hadrian's Wall could be commanded from both the turrets and the Wall

Fig. 6.6 The reconstruction of the Narrow Wall at Wallsend shows that even when reduced in width, the Wall top was wide enough for safe movement, and to function as a fighting platform.

been shown that there are plenty of Roman and medieval parallels for fort and town walls with functioning fighting platforms no wider that Hadrian's Wall. Town and fort walls may have had more frequent points of ascent to their wall tops than on Hadrian's Wall, but with turrets and milecastles providing this at every 500m (550yd), originally no point on the Wall was further than 250m (275yd) from an access point.

The Military Functions of the Wall Curtain

The archaeological evidence therefore suggests that the Wall curtain, in combination with its milecastles and turrets, was designed along conventional lines as a defensible structure. Yet today there is a deeply embedded reluctance to accept that the Wall might have been designed to function, and sometimes did function, as a fighting platform from which an attacking enemy might be engaged. The suggestion that soldiers actually fought from the Wall top, or hurled missiles from turrets on to forces trying to rush the Wall, is still guaranteed to provoke disbelief. This is because in most minds an image is instantly conjured of the might of the Roman army lining the top of a continuously defended barrier, or queuing up behind the Wall to await their turn to counter the assault of an organized barbarian army or horde – a static situation where the Roman army allows the enemy to take the initiative and counters them from a fixed defensive position. This is indeed a wholly implausible picture. But it is possible to see how a defensible wall top could have played a role as merely one device in a repertoire of responses to incursions.

Ideally, by means of intelligence, patrols or the outpost forts, groups of any size approaching the Wall would be detected long before they got there, and units sent north from the Wall forts would defeat and pursue them in the open area to the north. There must, however, have been times when attackers, including larger raiding parties several hundred or more strong, approached the Wall undetected. Occasionally, perhaps often, units in forts, milecastles and

top. The discovery of the obstacles can be seen to lend support to the view that there was a walk and parapet along the top of Wall from which defenders could engage attackers. One objection to the defensive use of the Wall top is that the Roman army did not possess, and was not trained to use, defensive weapons. This is untrue, however: sling shots, javelins, spears, bows and arrows and mechanically fired arrows were all available, but most commonly found on the Wall are small spherical throwing stones, abundant at the forts and recorded as finds at three of the turrets.

The second claim is that the Wall top was too narrow to have served as a fighting platform, but it has turrets facing these unexpected arrivals would have been under-strength because of active operations elsewhere. We have the explicit evidence of Ammianus Marcellinus that the northern peoples were able to find out about this sort of under-manning through spying, bribery, extraction of information from captives, indeed every possible means of counter surveillance.

In these circumstances small numbers of troops on the Wall would be vulnerable, and the priority would be to alert the nearest forces of any size. The Wall curtain would allow quite limited numbers of troops to delay an invading force – whether a raiding band or a more substantial gathering – for long enough for a response to be organized. Rather than reinforcing an attempted crossing point, the alerted forces would tackle the enemy north of the Wall, or to the south if the attackers had been let through, or had succeeded in penetrating the barrier. So the Wall curtain (or a turret or a milecastle) could function as a fighting platform for a small delaying force while at the same time the Roman army as a whole still operated against its enemy in the open.

The actual defenders on milecastle walls, in turrets, and on the Wall top would have played a small but critical part in the whole process. Hand-to-hand fighting with attackers trying to climb over the Wall was a means of delaying them, but might also be a matter of personal survival: defence of a milecastle and its gate by a very few soldiers might be critical in preventing a mounted war band from getting through the Wall. In larger incursions, if attempts were made in concert to cross the Wall in a number of places, or if the units in nearby forts were depleted in numbers because of operations outside the Wall area, then the ability of the small numbers immediately available to hold off the intruders from the Wall top for as long as possible would become even more critical. When intelligence failed, numbers were low, and weak points threatened, the capability was there to repel assailants and gain precious time.

The ability to fight from the Wall top was therefore planned in the design of the Wall, and no doubt on occasions exploited. The Wall cannot possibly have functioned as a *continuous* fighting platform, held by one army against another army, but could have been fought from for a limited time at particular points; it can be envisaged as defensible if we think of it being defended by Roman *soldiers* rather than the whole Roman *army* at once.

The idea that the Roman military just didn't operate like that, and didn't allow itself to be pinned down in defensive positions, is disproved by actual recorded instances, not from Hadrian's Wall, of course, where we have no records, but from other areas. An early Hadrianic potsherd (contemporary with the building of the Wall) from Egypt is inscribed with a report on a raid on a *praesidium* (military station), one of several along an important desert trade route. The attackers numbered sixty; unfortunately we don't have a figure for the defending Romans, but road stations in this area were manned by small numbers, often less than ten, as we might imagine with a turret or milecastle. The raiders ('*barbaroi*') attacked in mid-afternoon, and fighting went on until darkness, and they continued to lay siege to the post through the night. The fighting resumed the next day. The raiders eventually withdrew, with civilian captives, one of whom (a child) was executed and found by a later patrol. One or two Roman soldiers were killed in the fighting.

Most instructive here is the sustained period of the attack and the vulnerability of the defenders, who must have been grateful for the wall and fighting platform that surrounded their station. In this situation the defenders were unable to signal or send out a messenger for help, but their report, written by a cavalryman of a part-mounted cohort, was sent out to all neighbouring stations at the first opportunity. The close spacing of installations on Hadrian's Wall would make it easier to issue an alert and get help – but this could not always be guaranteed, and the Egyptian document illustrates the potential, in times when the Wall was under-manned, for raiders to penetrate the fortification line by seizing a milecastle.

This interpretation does assume that there were

larger forces stationed sufficiently close to be brought up in an emergency, and it might be objected that in the first plan for Hadrian's Wall the forts were too far away for it to have functioned in this way. But the introduction of forts to the Wall was almost instantaneous, being decided on before the Wall, milecastles and turrets were completed, and surely the simplest explanation is that this did not denote a major change in the principle of how the Wall should work, but simply an acknowledgement – perhaps triggered by some military setback – that there had been a miscalculation in the distance left between the forts and the barrier in the original scheme, and in the inconvenience caused by the Wall itself as an obstacle to units stationed to its rear.

The Wall curtain itself can therefore be seen to have had a potential military function which facilitated and complemented that of the units based in the Wall forts, rather than having a non-military 'control' function unrelated to that of the forts. As well as allowing direct delaying intervention at a local tactical level, the ditch, obstacles and Wall immediately frustrated the rapid movement that hostile forces of any size relied upon. The moment that the progress of raiders was hindered and larger Roman forces were alerted to their presence, the raid had gone wrong – like the *latrunculi* on the Danube, who needed to get across the border undetected in order to succeed. Every minute of delay counted against them, and so the actions of men in the minor installations or on the Wall top could be decisive.

Sometimes it is pointed out that the Wall does not always have a very extensive outlook to the north, as if that means that it cannot have been defensive, but this is a red herring: a good outlook and ground falling away from your position are the desirables of static siege warfare. The overriding consideration in siting the Wall was that it should take the shortest route possible across the narrow Tyne–Solway isthmus. Subject to that, the surveyors took advantage of hilltops and elevated land where they could, and of course utilized the Whin Sill ridge in the central sector – but in general the Wall did not try to achieve

an advantageous position for static and sustained defence, and for this reason it is better seen as an observation and stop line, meant to detect and hold up raiders for a limited time.

It seems possible, then, that the Wall curtain, defended in time of need, functioned *integrally* with the Wall fort units, giving them extra time to organize a response. This explains its physical character as a defensible fortification line, rather than the fence that would have sufficed if illicit movement by individuals was the main concern. Arguments for an isolated 'control' function for the Wall curtain explicitly include raiding among the illicit movements that were to be 'controlled'. If, as seems indisputable, the Wall was there to impede raiding war bands that were routinely scores or several hundred strong (let alone the larger concentrations that must have been raised for incursions like the one that succeeded in the 180s) and deliver them into the hands of the Wall fort units, is the distinction between control (Wall) and defence (forts) not a semantic one?

Threats to the Wall were probably always 'low intensity' in modern military jargon, but the structure and garrison of the Wall suggests that raiders were anticipated in numbers that defied a clear categorization into 'threats from individuals and small-scale raids' (to be dealt with by the Wall) and 'invasions by armies' (to be dealt with from the forts). Is an incursion by 500 warriors a small-scale raid or a military attack, and in such a case did the Wall itself really play no part in helping the soldiers in the forts to deal with the threat? It seems likely that the Wall and the forts were integrated facets of a single military system with both defensive and offensive functions.

Changes in the Function of the Wall over Time

The number and scale of milecastle gates and the multiple portals of the projecting forts indicate that the Hadrianic Wall was intended as an aggressive as much as a defensive device. The provision of gates seems to indicate that the army of the Wall was meant to pour out rapidly – the cover of the Wall allowing them to emerge at any point in surprise fashion – to destroy attackers in the open. On the other hand, the Wall as designed *looks* reactive. Three outpost forts in the west, Birrens, Netherby and Bewcastle, which formed a screen 10–13km (6–8 miles) north of the Wall, each looking into a valley or approach route from south-west Scotland, are the only forward outposts known for certain to have been occupied under Hadrian.

Limited range patrols and whatever spying could be done by scouts and secret agents provided the only close or extensive surveillance of the abandoned lands to the north, and as a system of early warning this was rudimentary. This would change in later times, but under Hadrian the Wall has the appearance of a device for tactical response to gatherings close to the Wall, or incursions, as they appeared. The newly discovered berm obstacles reinforce this impression. This would be quite compatible with the Romans mounting periodic military expeditions deep into the area north of the Wall, so to say that the Wall was designed for tactical response is not to state that the Romans were adopting a wholly defensive posture. The problem is that we have no knowledge of Roman campaigns or raids that could well have been conducted on a regular basis in the early second century.

From the defensible nature of the works as designed under Hadrian, and especially the hypothesis mentioned in Chapter 3 that the system of obstacles on the berm funnelled would-be attackers or infiltrators towards the turrets, it looks as if the turret detachments were there to detect and make a first response, hurling down missiles on an enemy, and moving out on to the Wall top to do so if necessary. The addition early in the life of the Wall of an extra tower, halfway between the regular Turrets 39A and 39B in the vulnerable access corridor of Peel Gap, and the actual discovery there of a *ballista* bolt, reinforces this. Surveillance was intended to be tight and intensive, and the tiny detachments of soldiers were to be capable of instant response, as well as able to

summon help from milecastles or from the forts. Should a crossing be attempted between turrets, a Wall-top patrol detecting it would have a maximum of 250m (275yd) – five minutes maximum? – to get to the nearest turret to raise the alarm.

The completed Hadrianic design implies that larger forces, once alerted, would move laterally along the Wall–Vallum corridor, with the wide portals and ditch causeways at the milecastle gates giving them more or less complete freedom to choose where to emerge on the north side of the Wall. This is consistent with the climate of active warfare in north Britain in which the Wall was conceived. Nothing can be proved in the absence of *any* evidence for the detail of events, but the unrest that is attested can plausibly be read as a war of resistance by the Britons of south-west Scotland and other groups further north, intent on preventing Roman conquest (or re-conquest), and potentially having allies south of the Wall. Having seen the Roman army withdraw from Scotland in stages between AD85 and AD105, it is likely that they were determined to resist any possibility of the reassertion of Roman rule by attacking the province. The extra tower at Peel Gap seems to anticipate attempts to cross the curtain itself, which implies at least some small, non-mounted bands of raiders attacking the Wall and bent on doing damage in the province for its own sake.

After the return from the Antonine Wall around 160, Hadrian's Wall had a much more extensive outpost screen, but all the essentials of the Hadrianic scheme on the Wall itself were recommissioned – obstacles (perhaps), milecastle gates, all turrets, and the Vallum. But not for long, because by the late second or early third century, several turrets were demolished in the lowland sectors, and nearly all in the upland central sector were eliminated, including the Peel Gap tower. Around the same time, most milecastle gates were reduced to posterns, the causeways across the ditch removed, and a number of north-gate towers demolished. Most milecastles and the surviving turrets show continued occupation in the third and fourth centuries. The Vallum

Fig. 6.7 Turret 39A, exposed by F. G. Simpson in 1911. Like most in the central sector, this turret was demolished in the Roman period and its recess into the Wall filled in, in this case with large blocks, so that the Wall walk could be carried over the site of the former turret.

became neglected and forgotten as the upland part of Britain south of the Wall was consolidated as a part of the province.

To some extent, these changes may be related to changes that had overtaken the societies north of the Wall from which threats to the province emanated. The Antonine occupation and the campaigns of Calpurnius Agricola (160s) may have suppressed the original focus of resistance in south-west Scotland and the central lowlands, and a more extensive outpost-fort system was put in place. Now a new response to the Roman Empire was emerging, further north-east in Perth and Angus. The numerous warrior élite of this area, well out of easy reach of the army on Hadrian's Wall, were no longer resistance fighters, but neighbours of an empire with an apparently fixed frontier. They received subsidies and gifts from the

empire, entered into treaties, and periodically raided the province, not for reasons of fanatical resistance, but to carry off gold, silver and slaves, and to manipulate the Romans into increasing the subsidies and presents that bought peace.

In other words, raiding the Roman Empire became a regular part of the culture and economy of north-east Scotland. It is likely that on the west side, too, the situation had consolidated, with distant warrior élites taking advantage of the now permanently present empire to enhance their status in their own society.

The social impetus behind this raiding means that it was perhaps more episodic, the rhythm of warfare managed and moderated by Roman diplomacy and gifts to a greater extent than in Hadrian's day. Rather than the often suicidal attacks that the Wall might have faced in the Hadrianic period, the raids of later times were perhaps more intent on obtaining captives and valuables, and on getting back safely. This might imply greater numbers, less frequent attempts, and more careful planning and organization, and the greater distances involved suggest a higher proportion of mounted raiding parties.

Such raiders must have known about, or hoped to find, sections of the Wall unmanned or undermanned, where they could attempt a crossing by seizing a milecastle or bribing its garrison. By the third century, the emphasis of the Wall seems to have shifted from one of direct action against a multiplicity of direct attacks, to one of detection of raiding parties that had slipped past the outpost screen, with the soldiers in the milecastles and remaining turrets essentially having a role of observation and alert (probably still using the Wall walk for patrolling), seeking assistance from larger forces when necessary, and intercepting smaller groups of infiltrators directly themselves. With the probable increase in the incidence of mounted raids there would be correspondingly less fighting directly from the Wall in the way envisaged in the Hadrianic scheme. Accordingly the obstacles on the berm were not maintained after the second century.

It is not difficult to imagine the upper part of the Wall curtain in a decayed state in later Roman times, and at various times and places such lack of maintenance may have prevented the use of the Wall top for surveillance or defence. Presumably, rather than emerging from the most tactically appropriate milecastle, the auxiliary units, when alerted, now went out from their forts to shadow and intercept raiders on the north side of the Wall. The character of the milecastles themselves had changed: their role was less of that of gateways for the issuing of troops on to the north side of the Wall, and more one of accommodating static garrisons for the surveillance and defence of the Wall line. This might explain the general increase in the amount of troop accommodation, if that is correctly understood.

The suggestion made here, that the changes in the way the Wall worked after the later second century reflect changes discernible in society far north of the Wall, themselves caused by the neighbouring Roman presence, is incapable of proof, but is consistent with the archaeological evidence emerging from Scotland. Whatever the reasons for the change in the way the Wall operated, there is no doubt that the Wall and its structures were renovated in major building programmes on a number of occasions. Under Marcus Aurelius much of the Wall was recommissioned, and the stone intermediate-gauge Wall, wider than the Hadrianic Narrow Wall, superseded the Turf Wall in the western sector. Extensive restoration work occurred around the turn of the second and third centuries, whether or not correctly attributed to Septimius Severus.

It is clear from the archaeological evidence that milecastles and a proportion of the turrets were occupied into the late fourth century, and the Wall curtain seems to have been maintained in the late Roman period. In other words, the Wall was continually reconstituted and maintained under later emperors, with the curtain substantially in its original form. This suggests that it retained a practical function, and makes it hard to accept periodical claims that the monument was merely a statement of Roman power, an empty piece of rhetoric, or to keep under-employed troops busy, or that in its original design it was a caprice of the amateur architect Hadrian, a vision of an ideal defensive wall, excessive in scale for its actual mundane purpose of controlling illicit border crossings.

If this were the case, we would expect the Wall to have fallen into ruin, its turrets and milecastles to have stood empty for long periods, or to have had its specifications drastically reduced over the course of the Roman period, rather than being periodically repaired and used into the last days of Roman Britain, so that it was still to be recalled in the sixth century by Gildas, and described as still standing a century later by Bede. The last classical reference to the Wall, in the sixth century, is by Procopius, who was well aware that the Roman part of the remote and mysterious island of Britain had been defended by a 'long wall'. By using this phrase, he indicates that he is seeing

Hadrian's Wall in the context of a series of other 'long walls' built for defensive purposes at various times and places in the ancient Greek and Roman worlds.

The Purpose of the Wall in the Light of other Long Walls in Antiquity

The curtain and minor installations of Hadrian's Wall are sometimes compared to modern border fences, especially the Berlin Wall and the Israeli West Bank barrier wall, in the belief that, like these security systems, it was not intended or able to function in the event of a large-scale invasion by an army. But are these the best comparators to choose? When Hadrian decided to address the problem of war in Britain by building a Wall, he was following in a long tradition in the military history of the ancient world.

There were precedents available to the Romans as wall builders in north Britain. Defensive long walls were a feature of ancient Greek civilization, the most famous being those connecting Athens to its port at the Piraeus, constructed in the early fifth century BC. The isthmus of Corinth, a neck of land 6km (4 miles) wide joining the Peloponnese to the Greek mainland, was fortified with long walls against 'Dorian' invaders in 1200BC, Persians in 480BC, Gauls in 279BC, against the Goths in AD250–60 and again in the late fourth or early fifth century AD. The Chersonese Wall on the Gallipoli peninsula was built by Miltiades in 550BC to protect the cities of the Hellespont from Thracian attacks, and it still functioned in the early first century AD.

Although they fell out of use during the peaceful times of the early empire, this and other long walls in the region were recommissioned in late Roman times. In the late Roman period the most celebrated of these long walls was a new construction, the Anastasian Wall, built 65km (40 miles) west of Constantinople, probably at the beginning of the sixth century AD, in response to the threat from the Bulgars. The wall stretches 46km (29 miles) from the coast of the Black Sea in the north to the Sea of Marmara. The curtain wall is 3.20m (10.5ft) wide, and the highest sections

survive to a height of 4.5m (14.75ft). There is evidence for a parapet, and hence a Wall walk on the curtain. A massive frontal ditch lay 23m (25yd) in front of the wall. There were small forts at 3.5km (2-mile) intervals. An approximate estimate suggests that there would have been at least 340 towers along the total length.

A series of valuable publications by one archaeologist who has excavated on both Hadrian's Wall and its relatives, the late antique long walls of the Balkans, has shown that in the cases of the Balkan long walls we have historical accounts (largely lacking from Hadrian's Wall), which make clear their purpose in deterring and repelling barbarian invasions. These describe how the Anastasian Wall was breached in 559 because it had been left unmanned, showing the importance of adequate maintenance and manning for such long walls to be effective: between 577 and 600 the Anastasian Wall repelled raids by Avars and Slavs six times. It has also been pointed out that the Greek tradition of defensive long walls would have been familiar both to Hadrian and his friend and Governor Platorius Nepos, who had governed Thrace, where the Chersonese long wall was still to be seen.

The construction of Hadrian's Wall was on a more economic scale than these other long walls of antiquity: compared to the Corinthian wall, with 153 towers spaced 40m (44yd) apart, or the Anastasian Wall, where a number of great towers carried torsion artillery and smaller towers were located at roughly 100m (109yd) intervals, with perhaps 340 towers in 46km (28 miles), the number of turrets and milecastle towers (240 along the whole 130km (80-mile) length of Hadrian's Wall) is less generous, which meant fewer points of access to the Wall top. This suggests that it was an economic response to serious but militarily less effective assaults than those anticipated by Greek city states, or the late Roman Empire facing invaders from the Balkans and the Eurasian steppe.

Yet Hadrian's Wall does seem to be conceived entirely in the spirit of the long walls of the eastern Mediterranean world, where there was no distinction between 'control' and 'defence', and the barrier was essentially part of a military package to repel incursions, and designed to function as a fighting platform in times of need. It has been argued that by stopping them in their tracks, barriers such as the Anastasian long Wall will have weakened barbarian armies that had no formal chain of supply, and were thus forced to keep moving rapidly in order to live off the land. We have seen how by holding up war bands who relied on rapid, surprise movement, Hadrian's Wall may have had a similarly debilitating effect.

Other Fortification Lines Resembling Hadrian's Wall

There are numerous examples of fortification lines belonging to ancient empires other than the Roman, and indeed to more recent empires. Contemporary with the late Roman long walls, the 195km (120-mile) long Gorgan Wall (traditionally known as the 'Alexander Wall' or 'Red Snake') protected the fertile Gorgan plain and the Sasanian Persian Empire, just to the east of the south-east corner of the Caspian Sea, from raids by nomadic huns (Hephthalites). It was in excess of 7m (23ft) in height, and has been dated to the fifth or sixth centuries AD by radiocarbon dates from its brick kilns. Along its length were thirty forts (typically around 5ha (12 acres) in area), holding an estimated total of 30,000 troops. There were much larger forts in the hinterland, typically 42ha (105 acres) in area.

In the case of China, the idea of a 'Great Wall' built all at one time may be a myth, but there are abundant documentary materials which show that walls were built and manned by dynasties extending over two millennia, not to 'control' movement, but as a defence against large-scale destructive raids by steppe nomads. Like the Roman walls, they were not statically defended as in a siege, and were used to launch aggressive campaigns, as well as to alert reserve forces to the arrival of raiders. But modern military commentators on Hadrian's Wall who claim that no mobile army would ever forego control of forward territory and operate from a defensive wall,

and that a wall could only ever be a fence against petty bandits, would do well to read the words of Gao Lü, a high-ranking official of the Northern Wei dynasty in the late fifth century AD:

> The northern barbarians are fierce and stupid, like wild birds or beasts. Their strength is fighting in the open fields; their weakness is in attacking walls. If we take advantage of the weakness of the northern barbarians, and thereby overcome their strength, even if they are very numerous, they will not bring disaster to our door, and even if they approach, they will not be able to penetrate our territory... we can look for the enemy on top of a wall, and no longer have to wait for an attack... at this present moment our best plan would be to follow the ancients in building a long wall north of the [frontier] garrisons, to protect us against the northern barbarians... when the barbarians come, there will be fortifications to defend and soldiers posted there will be able to defend them...

The Roman assessment of the situation in north Britain in the 120s and in subsequent centuries might not have been so very different.

On the Chinese walls of the Han dynasty, contemporary with the Roman period, watchtowers signalled to alert neighbouring forces to the approach of raiders, but the crews also defended themselves against direct attack. Over a thousand years later, copious documents of the Ming dynasty describe the same functions of alert and hand-to-hand defence. A 1553 description shows towers in action:

> [Weapons] and piles of rocks are stored up there, and in case of enemy attack upon the observation tower, people and animals in the tower yard move into the tower. From the lower and the middle level they hit the intruders with rocks and guns, so that the enemy can hardly come near. If the enemy approach the border, a

bright signal is given from the top, passed on to the interior [of the country] so as to prepare for battle. Smoke signals effectively given are the best means of defence.

A scale of warning signals reported different numbers of attackers, ranging from 1 to 100 up to 10,000.

There was an element of 'control' on the Chinese walls: trading parties were supervised and individuals approaching the border inspected, but such border crossings were supposed to take place at a limited number of special places, as we have suggested for Hadrian's Wall. The Chinese documents leave no doubt that the generality of walls and towers were there to detect and impede invaders. This is not to say that the working of the Chinese wall was always efficient, or that it was well maintained (it was clearly not), or that a modern state would wish to respond to the threat in a similar way – but the purpose of the wall and its towers (as distinct from forts or strong-holds) in the minds of the Chinese was unambiguously defensive, and the point is that it demonstrates that there is nothing inconceivable about Hadrian's Wall having been intended to function in a similar way. It should also be noted that the walls were also at times used aggressively: their construction could go hand-in-hand with wars of Chinese expansion.

Contemporary with the later Ming walls of China were depredations of the Russian Empire by raids from steppe nomads. In 1571 Moscow was burnt and sacked by Crimean Tatars. In raids in 1632, 1633 and 1637 alone, Crimeans and Nogays carried more than 10,000 Russians into captivity. In response, in 1635 the Russian Empire began the construction of fortification lines (consisting of moats, palisades, watchtowers and forts) along its southern steppe frontier. They provided cover for peasant colonization (recalling the Hadrianic policy of nurturing provincial economic development behind the shield of frontier walls) and thus defended Moscow against predations while serving as a tool of territorial expansion. The fortification lines were maintained and advanced well into the eighteenth century.

In all these cases there is a stronger resemblance to the Roman fortification lines of Britain and Germany than there is with modern security fences. In particular, they all share with Hadrian's Wall the physical or spatial integration of military units – a main army – into the systems of walls and watchtowers (not apparent in the Berlin or Israeli walls). In all cases the concern is with an enemy that cannot be located and destroyed in conventional warfare, which is raiding and threatening the rural and urban populations of an empire, and therefore undermining its tax base. In all cases aspects of the tactical function cannot be described as anything other than defensive, although this may be in the context of long-term policies of imperial expansion, colonization, or aggressive campaigning beyond the fortification line.

You will often read that the Wall curtain cannot have had a military purpose because the Roman army preferred to fight and defeat its enemies in the open – in the event of a military threat to the province the army would have marched out of the fort gates and dealt with it in the field. But throughout its history the Roman army built and manned defences when necessary. Siege works (as decribed, for example, by Caesar), long fortifications with a combination of ramparts or walls, towers, frontal obstacles and ditches, had their origins in the Greek world, many centuries earlier, and have been seen as the precursors of Roman frontier fortification lines, including Hadrian's Wall. During the Roman military heyday of the first century, we hear in the pages of Tacitus of the response in 69 of the army of Otho to the Vitellian advance through Italy: 'The city walls were reinforced, parapets added, towers increased in height, and provision and preparation made in respect of both arms and military obedience.'

Even the fighting of pitched battles in the open involved the construction of defensive devices designed to hinder and pin down an enemy under fire, like the systems of concealed trenches and pits into which Albinus lured part of Severus' army at the battle of Lugdunum in 197. Over a century later, the

Arch of Constantine depicts the army of Maxentius hurling down missiles on its assailants from the walls of Verona, including throwing stones of exactly the type known from the forts and turrets of Hadrian's Wall. The Roman army was always prepared to fight from walls if the situation called for it.

A Final Mystery: The Purpose of the Vallum

Ultimately the function of the Vallum remains unknowable, and scores of pet theories have been put forward over the last century and a half – some outlandish, many containing elements of truth and valuable insights, but none achieving general acceptance and recognition as a single 'theory of everything' explaining the Vallum. All theories about the purpose of the Vallum conform to one of six basic types. These are: the Vallum as a defence against the south; as a second line of defence against the north; as a protection or demarcation of a military zone to the rear of the Wall; as a route or roadway; as a temporary measure, either during the building of the Wall or a delay in that building; and the Vallum as the legal, administrative or symbolic boundary of the province.

In isolation most of these ideas fail: it is often pointed out that, overlooked by higher ground, the Vallum would be useless for static defence facing either north or south. It does not work as a communications route in its own right; there is insufficient evidence for a road on either of its berms; and there are too many obstacles to movement for either Vallum berm to have functioned this way. The Vallum cannot have been a temporary measure as it does not seem to have been decided on until the Turf Wall and the Broad Wall in Wall-miles 7–22 were substantially complete, yet it was provided throughout these areas as well as in the still incomplete crags area. By drawing upon several of the basic structural explanations in combination, however, it is possible to suggest how the Vallum *might* have been intended to work, symbolically and practically, in conjunction with the Wall as interpreted earlier in this chapter.

Given the hint in the fragments of the Jarrow inscription that Hadrian saw the Wall as being to do with keeping the empire within its bounds, we have to ask if the Vallum (as distinct from the Wall itself) was in some way meant to symbolize the boundary of the empire. There is no evidence for the idea of the Vallum as a civil customs barrier as distinct from the military line of the Wall, and this would be unparalleled on any other border of the Roman Empire. That it had significance as a boundary is suggested by the monumental arch of the (south-facing) Vallum causeway gate at Benwell, which surely carried an inscription.

Fig. 6.8 Artist's impression by Graham Sumner (for Hadrian's Wall Trust) of the Vallum gateway at Benwell, emphatically a south-facing opening in the style of a monumental arch. NIGEL MILLS

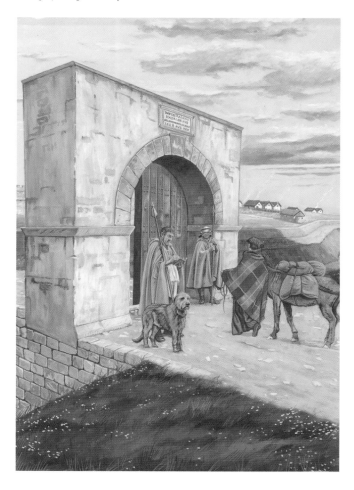

Fig. 6.9 The remains of the Vallum gateway at Benwell, under excavation in 1934, looking south. SOCIETY OF ANTIQUARIES OF NEWCASTLE UPON TYNE

Arches in the Roman world often have a liminal significance, being erected at the threshold of bridges across rivers, or at the notional east and west extremities of the empire, or at Richborough, at the gateway to the island of Britain itself. Did the Vallum declare the limit of Roman conquest in Britain and that the empire should remain within these bounds? This might at first sight also be suggested by the systematic way that the Vallum was slighted (and most of its building inscriptions removed?), seemingly when Antonius Pius overturned Hadrian's divinely ordained policy and determined to advance once more into Scotland.

However, the Vallum is paralleled on no other imperial border, which we would expect it to be,

if such a monument were required on its own to symbolize the boundary of empire. If Hadrian conceived of the Wall system as symbolizing a limit to Roman expansion, he must therefore have seen the whole package of the Wall and its associated works as doing this – a more elaborate and multi-layered version of the cordons of watchtowers, barriers, forts and roads that marked the land border of the empire on the continent. If, as well as forming a practical obstacle, the Vallum itself *did* announce the boundary between the Roman province and another sphere, it was perhaps to mark the transition from the ordered civil zone to a zone controlled by and reserved for the military, and not to be entered by any individuals or groups from the provincial population: 'You are now entering the zone of the soldiers.' The Vallum, after all, went hand in hand with the decision to place an army on the Wall. The army are seen to inhabit their own special space at the furthest boundary of the Roman world in the Roman oration of Aelius Aristides, describing the fortification walls of the mid-second-century frontiers:

> This circuit, which is much greater and grander than those [frontier fortification] walls, is on every side in every way unbreakable and indissoluble, shining far beyond all circuits... men, who hold out their shields in protection of those walls... In such harmony then have been enclosed the circle of their tactical revolutions and the circle on the borders of the whole world.

Such a philosophical conception of the army manning the Wall, and the need to mark a sacred boundary to the corridor within which it moved in its 'tactical revolutions', may have been in the mind of the Vallum's designer. But there were, of course, more immediately practical considerations. In Hadrian's Britain there was a recently conquered population south of the Wall, and the remoter hills and wooded valleys of the northern Pennines and Cumbria could well have harboured pockets of violent resistance

– this explains the upland emphasis of the continuing network of military occupation behind the Wall.

The most obvious explanation of the Vallum is as an impassable obstacle to prevent infiltration into the Wall zone from the rear, and assistance being given to raiders from the north trying to penetrate the Wall. The Vallum acknowledged that a policy of 'divide and conquer' had to address rebels to the south who might collude with enemies to the north. The size of the Vallum ditch and its vertical sides were designed to make it virtually impassable to men, especially mounted warriors, or animals in general; the flat bottom acts as a trap, and is consonant with the fact that the Vallum ditch was not observed and controlled from a rampart or Wall top, as was the Wall ditch.

Although the Vallum causeway gateways, facing south and with gate leaves closing to the south, make the Vallum an emphatically south-facing obstacle, its symmetrically arranged mounds give it the appearance of facing both ways: it would also serve as an obstacle to raiders who had successfully crossed the Wall, slowing their progress and allowing more time for interception to be organized. The raiders would be trapped in the Wall–Vallum corridor while Roman forces converged from east and west. The mounds served to accentuate the obstacle, and anyone trying to climb over them would be rendered highly visible (in daylight anyway). For mounted raiders, whether approaching from north or south, and for those returning with stolen herds of cattle, it would be an impossibility.

As well as looking both north and south, the Vallum also seems to be connected to a sense of east–west movement. The Vallum itself fails as a road or any other kind of communication route, though significantly tracks and roads did follow it in parts, and in places its north mound was overlain by the Military Way. However, it is possible to see, as already argued, that it defined and secured an east–west corridor of movement for the units in the Wall forts, forming the southern side of an envelope containing, or intended to contain (as the minor east and west gates of the primary Wall forts imply), a road or military way for troops to move rapidly to the appropriate gateway through the Wall or threatened point.

The lateral protection of a route in this way finds no close archaeological parallels, but something like it is referred to in a description by a surveyor, Balbus, who was called into service during wars in Dacia, under Domitian or Trajan. He describes how '*certo itineris spatio duo rigores ordinati, quibus in tutelam commeandi ingens vallorum adsurgeret molis*' – 'Along a certain sector of a road we needed to draw two straight regular lines, with the help of which we built the huge constructions necessary for the protection of routes.'

In short, the Vallum was not a defensible line that could be manned or defended by soldiers, whether facing south or north. It was rather an obstacle that worked without being directly manned, preventing surprise attacks on traffic moving laterally along the Wall–Vallum corridor: attackers would be slowed down, if not stopped outright and made visible so that the intended victims would become aware of them. Similarly it hopelessly impeded any attempted rapid surprise movement from the south aimed at reaching the Wall, and halted any force that had succeeded in breaching the Wall from the north. At the same time it unmistakably demarcated the sacred preserve of the army of the Wall.

Reinstated after the withdrawal from Scotland *c.* 160, by the third century the Vallum had lost its significance. As the separation of the populations north and south of the Wall was consolidated, and the two halves of the island went off on their different trajectories of development, there was less of an internal threat to the Wall; the military exclusion zone was forgotten, and the civilian settlements blossomed around the Wall forts and expanded over the filled-in Vallum ditch. The Wall, and the Vallum with it, had to some extent fulfilled their task of allowing the economic development and social change to the south that Hadrian had envisaged. But the developed province offered ever richer pickings for warriors from the far north, so the tactical interception of raiders remained the essential function of the Wall curtain and forts until the end of Roman Britain. ✧

Chapter 7

THE LAST DAYS OF THE ROMAN WALL: AD367−?

The passing of Roman north Britain: a narrative of events

AMMIANUS MARCELLINUS DESCRIBES HOW, following the barbarian conspiracy of 367, the *comes* ('Count') Theodosius came to the rescue of Britain. Since this Theodosius was the father of the emperor of the same name under whom Ammianus was writing, the glowing account of his achievements is hardly an objective one, but there are signs of major programmes of building and repair in the Wall area dating to this time. Behind the Wall, some of the units listed in the *Notitia Dignitatum* are apparently drafts from continental field army units made after the crisis of 367, showing the level of reinforcement that was thought necessary in Britain.

In the early 380s Magnus Maximus, probably *dux Britanniarum*, won a victory over the Picts and Scotti, but led an army from Britain when he was proclaimed emperor in 383. Usurpations launched from Britain were nothing new, but this was to be the first of a final series that would lead to the end of Roman rule. They were a reaction to the failure of the western empire to maintain security in Britain; withdrawals of troops from the island may have been in train since the disastrous Roman defeat at the hands of the Goths at Adrianople in 378. Security in the British and Gallic provinces could only be achieved, it was felt, if they put forward their own candidate to control the west. Magnus Maximus ruled in Britain, Gaul and Spain for five years until eliminated by Theodosius in 388; it is not clear if the army he took from Britain returned.

We get a vague picture of subsequent events from snippets in literary sources: the Picts and Scots were still a source of serious trouble, necessitating a campaign organized by the greatest general the western empire could offer, Stilicho, in 398–9, though he may not have come to Britain in person. After 401, troops were drained from Britain once more to meet the threat of Alaric and the Goths to Italy itself.

In 406–7 three more 'emperors' were proclaimed in Britain. The last, Constantine III, led an army to Gaul, and on to Italy, but he was defeated and killed by the Emperor Honorius in 411. The troops that Constantine had extracted from Britain never returned. In 410 Rome itself was sacked. It is probably a myth that Honorius wrote in that year to the cities of Britain telling them to look after their own defence: the source more likely refers to cities in southern Italy. More reliably, another literary source tells us that the Britons revolted against Roman rule, expelling the imperial administrators and looking to their own defence. Britain was no longer a Roman province.

Roman rule, and Roman responsibility for security, was at an end. 'Roman-ness' lived on, in the form of a provincial population with Roman cultural values, but there was complete economic collapse: when military and civil service pay ceased abruptly there was no money to pay producers of goods; specialist skills in craft, building and production rapidly disappeared; and the features of Roman civilization that had been sustained by the circulation of Roman money through the province (arriving as military and civil service pay, and departing as tax to the imperial treasury, but in between supporting a complex market-based productive economy in the island) were quickly and utterly forgotten. Within a generation or two Britain was made up of kingdoms bearing little relation to the governmental structure of Roman times, and despite the survival of some Roman administrative terms and, of course, the imperial religion of Christianity, even for the élite of society the material basis of life had reverted to a kind that was little different from that of the pre-Roman Iron Age.

On one level, the revolt against the Roman authorities was a simple matter of refusing to pay tax to an authority incapable of maintaining order and security. But when the British realized the powerlessness of Honorius to help them, they will have appointed their own emperor. In the Wall area it is probable that to begin with the civil authorities attempted to continue administration – and a co-ordinated response to barbarian attacks – along Roman lines. We might imagine that these authorities would be based at places such as Carlisle, Corbridge, Catterick and York. At some stage in the period between 420 and 500 these authorities seem to have vanished – perhaps quite suddenly – and to have been replaced by British kingdoms.

Unfortunately there is no reliable written record of the earliest form of the British kingdoms to emerge in the post-Roman vacuum in the fifth-century northern frontier zone. If, as seems likely, Carlisle and Corbridge were wholly or mostly abandoned in this period, we do not know of obvious successor sites. We have to work back from the situation that had emerged by the sixth century. North of the Wall were the tribal groups used by the Romans as 'buffer' states against the Picts and Scotti, and these formed the basis of later kingdoms: Strathclyde (centred on Dumbarton), Rheged (including probably north-west England as well as Dumfries and Galloway), and the Gododdin/Votadini (centred on Edinburgh). At the eastern end of the Wall it is assumed that Brittonic kingdoms lie behind the Celtic names of later Anglian kingdoms of Bernicia (centred on Bamburgh) and Deira (York). The western half of the Wall was probably in 'Rheged'. A further kingdom may have centred on Catterick (Catraeth).

The Wall Forts after *c.* 370

There are signs of continued, perhaps even renewed, central organization in the last decades of the fourth century. Coins from the great granaries at Corbridge show that they functioned as official storehouses (presumably for tax collections and the distribution of food to the population) down to at least 380. There was also rebuilding of the Stanegate, including bridge building, west of Corbridge in the late 360s or 370s, suggesting a concern among central authorities for maintenance of the road system.

Probably in the period 364–75 (although a later date in the 380s has been argued for) the Yorkshire coast of north-eastern Britain, south of the Wall, was fortified with a series of small forts each containing a lofty and massively constructed central tower, probably at least 20m (22yd) high. These are the so-called 'Yorkshire Coast signal stations'. Although only five examples are known, the chain could have extended all the way north to Hadrian's Wall, and south to the Humber, the others being lost to coastal erosion. These fort/tower combinations, identical to certain contemporary fortifications on the Rhine and Danube frontiers, gave early warning of seaborne attacks, and housed forces to intercept them. Along with the contemporary transfer of detachments from the continental field army into the hinterland forts, the 'signal stations' are direct evidence for the threat of raids carried out by peoples from north of the Wall, presumably from eastern Scotland, deep into the province, and for a bold imperial initiative, under Valentinian I ('the Great') to bolster the diocese of Britain. This would not have been effective if official attention was not paid to the Wall and its forts in the same period.

Whatever the truth of Ammianus' account of the restoration of towns and forts in Britain by Count Theodosius, any archaeologist who has dug extensively in Wall forts knows that, despite the fact it is no longer called 'Theodosian' rebuilding, there is a palpable change in the character of the forts that occurs some time after *c.* 370 (but possibly as late as

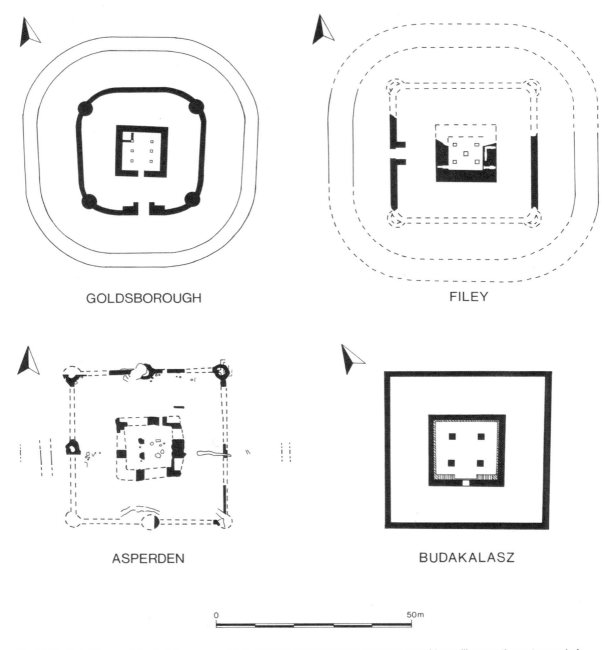

GOLDSBOROUGH

FILEY

ASPERDEN

BUDAKALASZ

0   50m

Fig. 7.1 The Yorkshire coast signal stations, erected around 370 or slightly later, to intercept sea raiders sailing past the eastern end of Hadrian's Wall. The lower two plans are of contemporary towers of almost identical type on the Rhine and Danube frontiers, showing that at this late date there were still strong links between the army in north Britain and the empire's central command.

the 380s/390s). At South Shields the commanding officer's house underwent alteration and was partly demolished, and while still occupied and used for manufacturing decorated bone inlays for furniture, no longer had the character of a Mediterranean peristyle house. Its hypocausts and bathing facilities may already have ceased to function and been filled before 370. At some sites the function of granaries changed:

Fig. 7.2 Stages of alteration in the *praetorium* at South Shields during the course of the fourth century; by the late fourth century (lower right) parts of the building had been demolished, dividing it into separate ranges. TYNE & WEAR ARCHIVES & MUSEUMS

granaries at Birdoswald and South Shields were either entirely demolished, or had their sub-floor spaces filled in and a sold floor laid above.

Barracks, as at South Shields, Housesteads and Vindolanda, now depart from the archetypal arrangements of the principate, losing the regularity of internal portioning, and the occurrence of infant burials (at South Shields) and the incidence of 'female' finds in the uppermost layers at Housesteads might suggest that the buildings were occupied by less regularly organized groups, with more indication than formerly of the presence of women and children.

Most strikingly, internal streets are crudely and heavily paved, often incorporating broken-up sculptures and inscriptions, in striking visual contrast to the cobbled and gravelled surfaces of earlier times. There is a good post-370 example of this at the town

of Corbridge. Crude paved surfaces of reused facing stones also occur in building interiors: there are clear examples at South Shields, Newcastle and Carlisle. This suggests that abandoned stone buildings were being dismantled in large numbers to provide the stone for these crude late surfaces. Such material may have been used in attempts to shore up and repair the now very old and in some cases leaning defensive walls of forts. There is evidence from Housesteads and Vindolanda that this was done by encasing the collapsing fort wall in a massive earthen rampart; at Housesteads, a late tower in this rampart was of timber.

Where excavation has taken place at a fort south of Hadrian's Wall, at Binchester, many of the same trends are evident: here a large internal baths went out of use and became a dumping ground for rubbish for the last two or three decades of the fourth century. Here

and at South Shields the internal pavings of facing stones (and possibly those on the streets) were not laid until sometime after 380 at the earliest.

What does all this signify? One possibility is that it reflects a reduction in the size of units brought about by the various withdrawals of troops from Britain. This can only be a possibility, as the various armies withdrawn from Britain did not necessarily include troops from the Wall: they may have come from forts further south, or from the mobile field army known to have operated in Britain at some time in this period. Yet as late as 407 Britain had an army substantial and effective enough to launch a usurper's bid for the western empire, and it is hard to believe that the *limitanei* on the Wall had no interaction with these troops and had become entirely unofficial in character over the preceding generation.

There was, then, perhaps no longer the time, manpower or skill to maintain the formerly orderly appearance of forts. Buildings such as granaries,

Fig. 7.4 View from the top of the Norman castle keep of Newcastle upon Tyne of excavations in the *principia* area of the Wall fort in the 1970s. This gives a good impression of the appearance of later Roman levels when Wall forts are excavated, with much dark soil and surfaces of crude paving in evidence. The strong-room of the *principia* can be seen at lower left. TYNE & WEAR ARCHIVES & MUSEUMS

designed to accommodate provisions procured through a far-reaching network for large bodies of troops, became redundant and were either demolished or turned over to other uses. Areas of large forts might have fallen out of use. Possibly there was a greater civilian presence by now: people from the local town (Carlisle or Corbridge), or rural population, might, in times of danger, have found refuge with the remaining soldiers in the Wall forts. Soldiers' dependants might already have lived in the forts for some time. As we hear from the life of St Severinus (*see* below: Eugippius' *Life of St Severinus*, a remarkable fifth-century literary source), this is similar to what happened on the contemporary Danube frontier in Noricum, where during the fifth century the units in the frontier forts withered away until only very small numbers were left, although there were clearly still sizeable communities at these places.

The turning point, where coins become scarcer and central administrative supply and support of the Wall forts evidently wanes, appears to be after 378, probably related to a reduction in numbers. But the remaining soldiers on the Wall were apparently still receiving pay (though as for the preceding century, much of it in kind) and continued to do so at least up to the turn of the fifth century. The latest coins to reach the Wall forts (and indeed Britain as a whole) are issues of the House of Theodosius, dating to 388–402, showing that official issues of small change were still being sent to the island. Coins from Milecastles 9 and 35 (interestingly in the remote crags sector) show that they were manned after 375. The maintenance of a major monetary-based trade to supply the Wall forts (and the towns) is illustrated by distinctive post-370 pottery types from East Yorkshire (Crambeck painted parchment ware and 'Huntcliff-type' cooking pots with internally grooved rims), which reached nearly all sites in considerable quantities until the early fifth century.

The analysis of animal bones recovered from the Yorkshire coastal signal station at Filey has shown that supplies were arriving from a distance via an organized network; its continued maintenance suggests

survival of a central command structure at the end of the fourth century. The Wall units of the period 370–400 co-existed and presumably co-operated with detachments from the highest quality continental field army units, based in the hinterland forts for at least some of this period. All this makes it unlikely that the years immediately after 370 saw a transition of the army of the Wall into militias or war bands evolving independently of the Roman state.

The Wall Forts after *c.* 410

Until recently there was no evidence for any activity in the Wall forts later than the latest coins of 388–402, and it was believed that the Wall was abandoned shortly after. It can no longer be assumed that the Wall forts were utterly deserted ruins after the fall of Roman administration in Britain; in recent years a number of archaeological indications of occupation in the fifth century have been recognized.

The fort at South Shields was apparently refortified, with a new ditch superseding one that had been in use in the years around 400. A late refurbishment of the south-west gate, partly in timber, could fit here. Later in the fifth century the new ditch was superseded by an inhumation cemetery outside the south-west gate. In the area of the *principia* forecourt what appears to have been an altar contained in a stone niche, which might have formed part of a Christian church, was found in 1875. There is no dating evidence for this, but the level of the remains suggests that they were not long post-Roman, while a pre-410 church in a headquarters building would be utterly unparalleled.

A particularly interesting sequence has been excavated on the site of the commanding officer's house in the eastern quadrant of the late Roman fort. As already stated, block paving was laid in parts of the building interior after about 380, and seems to have been the surface currently in use in the period around 400, when unworn coins of 388–402 were dropped. Part of the formerly grand commander's residence was being used at this time for the manufacture of

decorative inlays (worked from deer antler), apparently for fine furniture. Radiocarbon dates establish that it was in the early fifth century when the remains of two young adults (probably male) were buried in a pit deliberately placed in the centre of the central courtyard of the house. They had been killed, probably with swords, and their bodies had lain about to partly decompose and be gnawed by animals before being gathered up (presumably after some weeks or months, but not after years) and buried.

Those areas of the house which had not received the characteristic block paving were now covered by a paving in an even cruder style, which is structurally later than the block paving. Similar crude paving in another part of the fort was used by someone working deer antler into objects. In other areas pits were dug and filled with butchered animal bone and in places overlain by the crude paving.

Since there are hardly any reliably dated objects in

Fig. 7.6 Successive phases of very late paving in the *praetorium* at South Shields. The paving of reused facing stones (left) was laid sometime after 380; the even cruder paving abutting this (right) is of fifth-century date, representing the final surfacing before abandonment and ruin. TYNE & WEAR ARCHIVES & MUSEUMS

the fifth century – Roman coins and any kind of recognizable pottery, Roman or native, having completely ceased to appear in the archaeological record – it is difficult to say how late these activities occurred. Two radiocarbon dates show that the antler working over the latest crude paving was taking place later than about 430 (unfortunately in this period radiocarbon dating cannot tell us *how much* later, although it was before the mid-sixth century). The latest horizon of crude paving, the butchery and antler-working activities, and the possible church, are all immediately followed in the archaeological sequence by material from collapsed and ruined buildings, sometimes over an intervening accumulation of dark earth.

At Housesteads another possible church, a small stone apsidal building that overlay dark earth and ignores the Roman building plots, if correctly recognized – there is no proof that it is ancient – is probably fifth century. The identification is supported by a nearby cist burial. Another cist burial is situated by the Wall curtain itself at nearby Sewingshields Crag. Inside the fort, the remains of crude subcircular buildings have been found to overlie levelled Roman buildings in the north-east quadrant.

Vindolanda has late structural sequences that *could* run on after the early fifth century, and some crude structures overlying barracks in the manner of the sub-circular buildings at Housesteads. There is also another possible church, an apsidal stone-footed building constructed over the remains of the *praetorium*. Most telling is a 'Class I' inscribed tombstone of a Christian-British type usually dated to around AD500, commemorating some important person called *Brigomaglos*. The Christian significance of a symbol recently found on a stone slate is disputed. At both Housesteads and Vindolanda there is evidence for refurbishment of the defences which *could* be later than the early fifth century, although in the former case the process certainly started in the late fourth century. A second possible 'Class I' inscribed stone is claimed by some authorities, rejected by others, at the Wall fort of Castlesteads, naming one *Bedaltoedbos*.

Birdoswald has produced the most celebrated evidence for post-Roman activity. Excavations in the 1980s showed that the northern granary, having been partly demolished, perhaps as late as the 380s or even later, was eventually reconstituted as a timber structure. This in turn was superseded by a timber hall-like building offset to the north, ignoring the previous building plot but built in relation to the road in from the main west gate. A paved surface inside the first of the timber structures bears a striking resemblance to the second and latest phase of crude paving at South Shields, probably in use after 430. As well as this, Birdoswald also has a cist burial (by the Wall curtain east of the fort), and evidence for encasement of the collapsing fort wall in earth. A church tentatively suggested in a barrack building is not so convincing.

Turning to Binchester, a fort south of the Wall, in the area of the abandoned internal baths people were walking over and carrying out butchery and animal processing activities on the distinctive 'block' paving like that dated to the 380s or later at South Shields. An impressive group of radiocarbon dates suggest that this activity was going on in the late fourth and early fifth centuries, but not for very long in the fifth century – certainly no later than 430. However, in another area of the fort, pit digging, crude paving, bone deposition and antler working is radiocarbon dated, like the similar-looking activity at South Shields, to later than about 420, although again it is impossible to say how much later.

The evidence, then, is extremely thin, but points to the possibility, and in a few cases the actuality, of some kind of life in the Wall forts after 410. The sites above producing the evidence are, of course, the few that have seen the most intensive excavation and study, both in the past and in more recent times, and one can only suspect that more evidence would come to light at other Wall forts if they were to be excavated.

Explaining the Fifth-Century Archaeology – with Help from a Saint

If the forts were not deserted in the fifth century, who was living there? The evidence is so slight that it is impossible for us to have a clear understanding from archaeology alone of who these people were, and what they were doing. For what it is worth, there is some literary evidence for what happened to forgotten and unpaid units of *limitanei* elsewhere as other parts of the empire slipped out of Roman control.

In the case of the Danube frontier province Noricum Ripense, there is a remarkable literary source, Eugippius' *Life of St Severinus*, which describes how in the period 454–82 this holy man preached and both negotiated with, and organized protective measures against, barbarians, in the surviving forts and towns along the Danube frontier. He describes a situation in which the Roman military frontier defence no longer existed and barbarians crossed the Danube into the former Roman Empire at will. There was no provincial governor, no overall command. Archaeologically, coins cease to arrive at these Norican sites in any quantity at the beginning of the fifth century, as in Britain. From Severinus' life we learn that by the time of his arrival, there were hardly any effective Roman soldiers left in the forts. A unit lingered on at Batavis (Passau). We hear how they dispatched a detachment to Ravenna to collect their 'final pay' – not an option for any residual units in Britain.

The Passau unit never received their pay, for the detachment was slaughtered by barbarians before it had got very far. Passau was soon overrun anyway. A few ineffective soldiers were commanded by a tribune called Mamertinus at Favianis (Mautern). These are the only constituted Roman units we hear of, and the text makes it clear that they operated (or failed to operate) in complete isolation, confined to their walled enclosures without any hope of calling on reinforcements.

The inhabitants of other 'castella', which had formerly been occupied by military units and appealed to Severinus for help, are described in terms that make it clear that they were civilians. Severinus himself founded a monastery at Favianis, and there were others along the former frontier. The danger of barbarian attacks was ever present, although they were not daily occurrences: this meant that the inhabitants of a particular fort could farm the surrounding land and graze their cattle, but would bring everything inside the walls when there was news of an impending attack. This did not always work, however. Ioviaco, 30km (20 miles) from Batavis, was sacked by the Heruli, and most of the people, who had ignored a warning from Severinus, were led off into slavery. The attackers hanged a priest, Maximianus, on a cross. This was not a major town, but the site of a small fort (like those on Hadrian's Wall) that had originally been built in the second century.

The text reveals how places were progressively abandoned. The inhabitants of Quintanis (Künzing) went as refugees to Batavis, then most of the combined population moved on to Lauriacum, finally to be forcibly resettled by a barbarian king. All these places along the Norican frontier were finally abandoned in 488, and the remaining inhabitants marched as a body to Italy where they were resettled in various places.

A disintegration along these lines may well have occurred on Hadrian's Wall after *c.* 400: the account of Severinus' life shows at least that this is possible, but also shows how remnant communities could cling on tenaciously, practising agriculture, trade and monasticism, and maintaining Roman customs. It may very well be the archaeological traces of such relict survivals from the Roman world that we are beginning to glimpse in the archaeology of the Wall forts.

The cycle of military pay, taxation and trade only ended when Roman rule in Britain ceased around 410, and must have come as a sudden and debilitating shock to the inhabitants of the Wall forts, however neglected or reduced in numbers they had become since around 380. Theoretically the troops on the Wall could have been withdrawn to the continent, but the most effective had probably already been taken, and if, as is clearly stated, the civil authorities had taken over and rejected Roman rule, they would hang on to the remaining soldiers for their own protection. Inevitably some of the soldiers will have drifted away or become refugees with elements of the civilian population. There were therefore probably very few men left on the Wall, and those that were probably had dependants with them.

The area may have quickly become very dangerous, as we see the dramatic evidence of human remains from two of the Yorkshire signal stations, which shows that they were overwhelmed in the early fifth century and that the Wall was effectively bypassed. The human remains at South Shields are conceivably associated. Raiders and invaders – whether Picts, Scots or Irish, or even the Britons of southern Scotland – now raided or roamed the countryside at will. In this situation of reduced and ineffective garrisons and ever-present danger, it is easy to envisage remnant military units dispersing and the rural population concentrating in towns or forts for safety, with whatever soldiers had stayed at their posts. It seems likely that the maintenence and manning of the Wall itself, and the milecastles and surviving turrets, had ceased at the beginning of the fifth century – although that does not mean that structures could not still have been used as watchtowers and the Wall defended tactically against raiders on a local basis.

The fates of individual fort sites no doubt varied, with some, as in Noricum, holding out longer than others, with refugees from abandoned forts or towns moving into others that were managing to hang on. The availability of local resources would be important, with longer survival and cohesiveness in more agriculturally productive areas. It is notable that the fort with perhaps the strongest evidence for fifth-century refortification and occupation, South Shields, occupies a defensible hill top commanding the fertile area around the mouth of the Tyne. Monasteries were founded at some of the Norican sites, and this is a possibility for some Hadrian's Wall forts, given the evidence for churches; it has been tentatively suggested that the crude buildings at Housesteads would not be out of place as fifth-century monastic cells. In the same way as in Noricum, these communities were completely isolated; the frontier, in the sense of a co-ordinated response to invasion, had melted away around them.

As in parts of present-day (2016) Iraq following the end of Western occupation, it was a world where civil authority had collapsed, invaders enslaved and terrorized local populations, army units were ineffective, corrupt or had simply evaporated, and refugees were everywhere.

Collapse or Transition?

One persuasive school of thought has emerged over the last generation, which suggests a different interpretation. It is held that the end of Roman rule in 410 was not a decisive turning point in the life of Hadrian's Wall. Rather, it is supposed, in the last few decades of the fourth century the units in the Wall forts began to transform into a series of regional militias, which survived in place after the collapse of the Roman provincial administration as war bands supplied by the local population in return for the security and overlordship they provided. The fort of Birdoswald has supplied the archaeological paradigm. Here, towards the end of the fourth century, the southern granary was given a solid floor with a hearth at one end surrounded by a few high-status finds. It has been suggested that even before 410 this served as a hall for what had effectively become a warrior chieftan and his retinue. The two successive timber buildings over the site of the north granary, already described, are taken to be warlords' feasting halls, replacing and performing the same function as the 'hall' in the southern granary in the fifth century and beyond. It is a romantic and, for many, a compelling vision: a dark-age warrior aristocracy directly descended from the soldiers of *cohors I Dacorum* at Birdoswald, or the Tungrians at Housesteads.

Ultimately it is impossible to prove or disprove such a theory: the timber buildings at Birdoswald could theoretically represent a *reoccupation* of the site, and in any case are mute about the power or character of their inhabitants. None of the archaeological evidence from the sites, including Birdoswald, is incompatible with a sharp discontinuity occurring when the Roman state abandoned Britain. As set out

Fig. 7.7 Birdoswald: the site of the excavated late Roman sequence over the granaries. The north granary, seen here, was reconstituted as a timber building in the early fifth century. The timber uprights mark the position of a subsequent timber building or 'hall', which was offset to the north.

above, the evidence suggests a reduction in numbers, and a relatively late and sudden change in the appearance of forts and units occurring from the 380s, and even then they were still paid and supplied by the Roman state and the provincial economy – there is no coherent or compelling pattern of evidence for a gradual transition to local war bands in the period 370–410. The sequence of changes in the granaries at Birdoswald that has been so central to that claim is now thought to have started much later than the period 350–70; the activity centred on the hearth in the southern granary conversion could have taken place in the early fifth century.

We cannot be certain that there was any continuity of personnel at all at some places – some fort sites might have been completely abandoned by the military, and reoccupied by some unrelated community after an interval. This might be suggested by the evidence from South Shields, where the brutal execution of victims in a final overwhelming of the place in the early fifth century is followed by clearing up of the remains and later habitation. Note also the apparent interval between the abandonment of Roman buildings and the erection of possible fifth-century structures over their ruins at Housesteads.

Elsewhere, no doubt, some soldiers lingered on, but the archaeological evidence is surely as consistent with the dissolution of military units and some version of the fading and embattled communities of St Severinus as it is with a multiplicity of powerful war bands. The suspicion that some evidence for fifth-century life will come to be found at more forts on the Wall and in its hinterland sits uneasily with the war-band idea: it seems inconceivable that *every* fort *territorium* supported such a group. Surely in that case there would have been competition, conflict and consolidation, with the most successful warriors coming to dominate from a small number of high-status centres – which, even in the fifth century, might be expected to yield some high-status finds.

In general the widespread, if slight, nature of the evidence, sometimes coming from closely adjacent forts (Housesteads and Vindolanda), is much more suggestive of the continued occupation of *parts* of forts, or their *re*-occupation, as safe settlements and refuges for elements of the remaining Christian Roman-British population, following the catastrophic disjuncture with life as it had been lived before 410. The fort sites would be attractive to such people because of their Roman resonance, defensibility and even their suitability, as remote places, for monastic settlement. A few remaining soldiers, or descendants of soldiers, might trace a direct line back to the units *per lineam valli* in the *Notitia Dignitatum*, but they were isolated relics of the past, and the units were no more.

When were the Wall Forts Finally Abandoned?

The critical question is: for how long did this after-life of the Wall go on? As the last paragraph implies, different forts might have had different fates in the fifth century – there can be no single model that applies to all places. At South Shields, Newcastle and Binchester – forts on or near Hadrian's Wall where modern excavations have taken place – the sequence of structural changes and the laying of paved surfaces comes to an end at some point, and the next detectable event is the accumulation of material from collapsed and ruined Roman buildings, sometimes over an intervening accumulation of dark earth.

At these sites there is no way of dating how long

Fig. 7.8 The crypt at Hexham, dating to around 675, containing many distinctively tooled Roman blocks from bridges and other buildings at Corbridge and Chesters.

occupation continued – and radiocarbon dates will not help in this period. The only clue is the fact that there is no *extended* structural sequence of resurfacings. There is no continuing sequence beyond what has already been described, suggesting that it ends within the fifth century rather than extending later. It cannot be argued that later layers have been ploughed away or disturbed, because at these places the sequence ends with the collapse of Roman buildings, still intact. The bath house at Binchester had collapsed long before an Anglian burial was cut through the remains in the mid-sixth century. The ruins of the *praetorium* at South Shields seem to have collapsed straight on to the surfaces in use in the fifth century.

This area has produced numerous Anglian finds of the seventh to ninth centuries, which must have been deposited over the heaps of ruins as they only occur above the ruination levels. This suggests that the building was completely down by 600 or so, meaning that occupation must have ceased long before that. At Newcastle the Roman buildings were completely levelled before a succeeding phase of Anglian activity starting in the period 600–700. By arbitrarily allotting fifty years to each of the timber phases at Birdoswald, the excavator suggested a terminal date of 520 for that sequence, but of course such dead reckoning is unreliable and the sequence could be compacted into a shorter timeframe – or the second building could be of much later, medieval date.

Central to the question is the fate of the two frontier towns of the Wall, Carlisle and Corbridge. At Corbridge the pre-World War I excavations of the Roman town will have missed any evidence of post-410 occupation. Carlisle has seen much more modern excavation. Here, one high-status house was, it seems, maintained for a period into the fifth century, but it cannot be said how far. At Blackfriars, a timber building overlying the latest stone Roman buildings may be of fifth-century date – but unfortunately the sequence lacks dating evidence. If it is fifth century, it is interesting in being on an outlying site, far from the fort at the nucleus of the town: this might suggest an extensive surviving occupation. But even this timber building had utterly vanished when the site was overlain by a seventh-century Anglian building on a different alignment. There is no trace at Carlisle of the imported Mediterranean amphorae and glass vessels which after c. 450–75 are traded to a few sites in western Britain, including Whithorn and others in south-west Scotland.

At present, then, we cannot say how widely and for how long any use of forts and towns of the Wall area by groups with Roman and Christian affinities went on. In several cases it seems likely that the forts were long deserted and ruined by the time of the Anglian penetration of the eastern Wall area from around 550 onwards. On the other hand, an unknown number of other sites, particularly towards the west side of the country, might possibly have still had some form of occupation at that date. At Vindolanda, the Brigomaglos stone, if correctly dated, suggests some kind of occupation running beyond 500. The impression, for what it is worth, is that there might be widespread immediate post-410 occupation by communities of some size at several sites – signalled by the possible churches – but that in the majority of cases this did not last long into the fifth century.

That is not to say that there was not still some tenuous occupation after that, but significantly it has left no extended sequences or examples of the finds, whether metal and bone objects, rare inscriptions, or imported pottery and glass, which do occur at some fifth-century sites elsewhere. On any site, later fifth-century occupation on a much reduced scale hidden away in one part of a field of ruins, in timber buildings and with hardly any finds (as may yet turn out to be the case at Corbridge and Carlisle) will naturally be difficult to find. It is perhaps an academic question, for such fugitive evidence of occupation indicates a decisive break with the way of living in the past – rather than a transition, a rupture that had come in the early years of the fifth century.

Pollen analysis sheds little light on the problem. On the face of it, radiocarbon-dated pollen cores, by showing when a formerly cleared agricultural landscape was subsumed in regenerated woodland, might show when a farming population catastrophically declined. But radiocarbon dating of the samples is not precise, and commentators differ in their interpretation of the available cores. While some commentators have claimed to recognize woodland regeneration in the region specific to the early fifth century, the majority view is that it is impossible to be so precise, and the most we can say is that woodland regenerated, with much local variation, between 400 and 800. The *Life of St Severinus* makes it clear that in fifth-century Noricum, even in the most difficult circumstances, and even when barbarians were in control, people continued to farm the land and graze their cattle.

With the Saxon revolt in southern Britain in the 440s, and potential invasions by Picts, Scotti and the British kingdoms of southern Scotland, the Wall area was chaotic and dangerous. It seems probable, on present evidence, that by the mid-fifth century the Wall forts on the eastern side had been abandoned, while Corbridge and Carlisle and the forts on the west side may have followed after some unknown interval. The remaining inhabitants of all these places did not have the option of marching into Italy, as did those of Noricum Ripense in 488, but perhaps became refugees in the various British kingdoms that had emerged by now to supplant any ghostly remnant of the civil authorities surviving from the Roman province.

The Roman name of one of the Wall forts, Castlesteads, was *Camboglanna* (for long, but incorrectly, attributed to Birdoswald). This bears a remarkable resemblance to the name of Arthur's last battle, *Camlann*, as given in the manuscript copy (dating to shortly after 1100) of a set of Easter Annals compiled in the tenth century. Is this the place where in the early sixth century a British war leader fatally miscalculated in a struggle against pagan northerners or a rival British kingdom, around the time that the Wall was finally being abandoned by its remaining inhabitants? Unfortunately historians are not convinced, and most think that the Annals, constructed nearly 400 years after the supposed event, were embellished with references to an already legendary figure.

Anglo-Saxon Activity on the Wall

The Anglian invaders took a great interest in the Roman sites of the Wall area. In some cases they may have become early royal centres: this has been suggested for South Shields and Corbridge. South Shields has produced high-status objects of seventh-to ninth-century date, and the monks of Tynemouth recorded a tradition that Oswin, King of Deira, was born in the fort there, which would have been in the early 600s. Whether the Anglian royal site was inside the walls of the fort is unclear: the initial settlement could have lain just outside the heap of ruins, and the fort might then have been explored, colonized and robbed of precious materials. The Anglian site did not outlast the ninth century (the tradition is that it was destroyed by the Danes), and after that the site was finally abandoned to desolation and eventually agriculture.

Corbridge has produced evidence of early Anglian burials (550–600?), and an early royal centre may have lain here, again either inside or outside the ruins, but moved to the fording-place site of the modern town, half a mile away, perhaps when the Roman bridge carrying Dere Street across the Tyne collapsed. Carlisle was occupied by the Anglians with the Northumbrian expansion westward (by 600), and here also a monastery was founded. Newcastle is the only site on the Wall to have a clear overlying Anglo-Saxon phase: here the ruined and collapsed Roman buildings were cut through by a stone drain or aqueduct, itself succeeded by a cemetery, beginning in the late seventh or early eighth century, and presumably indicating the foundation of a monastery, yet to be discovered.

South Shields, Newcastle and Carlisle are the only places on the Wall to have produced substantial numbers of Anglo-Saxon finds. Early Anglian finds at Wallsend and Benwell are best explained by use of the abandoned sites for burial. An early sixth-century brooch at Vindolanda could indicate some interaction between the incoming Anglians and a remnant Britonnic community there, while stone robbing is enough to explain a later brooch from Chesters and two eighth-century strap ends from Vindolanda.

In the mid-670s the Northumbrian churchman Wilfrid, Bishop of York, ordered a new church to be built at Hexham. Wilfrid had visited Rome, and it was said that no other building north of the Alps could compare with his church at Hexham. The crypt, to display relics he had brought back from the continent, was rediscovered in 1725 and survives, built entirely out of Roman blocks brought from the nearby sites of Corbridge and Chesters. Because of the size of their blocks the two Roman stone-arched bridges at those places were particularly plundered, along with the Shorden Brae mausoleum at Corbridge. This shows that the bridges must have long ceased to function by the 670s: presumably they had collapsed following the removal in the fifth or sixth centuries of the highly recyclable metal clamps that bound the masonry together.

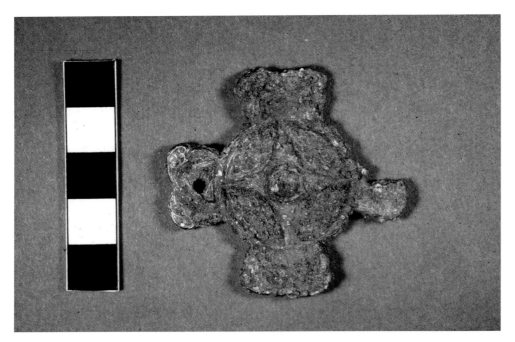

Fig. 7.9 Anglo-Saxon cross: one of a number of finds of seventh-to ninth-century date from above the Roman ruination levels at South Shields. TYNE & WEAR ARCHIVES & MUSEUMS

Fig. 7.10 Final desolation: fallen columns lie among the ruins of Housesteads in winter afternoon sun, 1988.

For Wilfrid and his contemporaries the landscape of Roman ruins which provided their materials held great resonance. Within a few years of this St Cuthbert visited Carlisle and was shown, and evidently admired, the fort or town wall and a fountain of what seemed wonderful Roman workmanship – although the source does not say it was still working, as often said. Around the same time the Hadrianic monument, probably at Wallsend, commemorating the building of the Wall, was being dismantled. Fragments of the inscription found their way, no doubt with other material, to the monastery at Jarrow.

The Wall in Later Times

It is notable that only at Corbridge and Carlisle, the two Roman administrative centres, has the Roman place name been transmitted into the medieval period: the modern names of Corbridge and Carlisle are derived from *Coria* and *Caer Luel/Luguvalium*; it has also been suggested that the name of South Shields preserved by the monks of Tynemouth – *Urfa* – derives from *Arbeia*. These are the only places that attracted Anglian settlement, and the former two the only places (except Newcastle) that were important in later times. The Roman names of the Wall forts were soon forgotten.

Newcastle went on to become the site of a royal castle and the present city; Carlisle, too, developed into monastery, cathedral and city. At Corbridge, as we have seen, the medieval town grew up a short distance from the Roman site. In all other cases the fort sites were completely abandoned to nature, or in later centuries, pasture and agriculture, so that now 'the wayfarer may pass through them without knowing it'. At Birdoswald a local notable was resident in a tower in the fort in the middle ages, and the west gate was apparently still standing in the fourteenth century. Villages developed inside the forts at the west end of the Wall at Burgh-by-Sands and Bowness-on-Solway – something not seen in the east.

The Wall itself, while remaining an unmistakeable feature, often an enduring boundary, passed from history into legend and embarked on its long journey of ruin and despoliation. ✿

A BASIC QUANTITY SURVEY FOR HADRIAN'S WALL

THIS BRIEF, BROAD-BRUSH SURVEY HAS BEEN undertaken in the belief that some quantifiable estimate of the material and man days required to build Hadrian's Wall is necessary if we are to understand the scale of the task for the Roman army and to arrive at a plausible timetable for the building programme.

There are many unknowns and obvious difficulties, which is perhaps why such quantity surveys have rarely been attempted: any such survey takes us into the realms of speculation. The resulting requirements in man days to build all the elements of the Wall are not claimed as accurate figures. But even with all the uncertainties, the figures establish an order of magnitude for the different elements and indicate in a very broad way the call that they would have made on the manpower of the legions. They suggest, for example, that the completion of the stone curtain was a proportionately much greater task than anything else, and would have taken many more man days than the milecastles or turrets or even the full-sized forts in a given section of the Wall.

The reader will be able to point to many elements of work that are missing from this survey, for example, provision and transport of food supply, for men and animals. The standing army in Britain would have required food and supplies in any case. Much of the preparatory work of road building and the procurement of scaffolding and other timbers might have been put in train before the main building programme started. In a sense the Wall had no monetary cost, as the army was being paid anyway and did all the work. What this survey attempts to isolate is the *extra* work necessary to build the Wall, in other words the cost to the army itself: the time and numbers of men taken up with Wall building, which might otherwise have been used for other military and administrative functions.

As suggested in the main text, the survey seems to confirm that the Wall could have been erected well within the usual timetable, but also suggests that certain elements, like the Turf Wall, could have been completed rapidly, within a single building season. With turf structures, overestimation has been preferred to underestimation, to avoid an over-optimistic picture of what could be achieved in a given season. This has interesting implications, leading on to the suggestion that the approach might have been to complete whole sectors rapidly, rather than working slowly and piecemeal on all parts of the Wall at once.

The survey is ultimately based on modern preconceptions and practice, and may well for that reason exaggerate the time it would take the Roman army, with its usual fanatical pace of construction, to quarry and build, but no doubt this is counterbalanced by the omission of many elements of the process.

The survey is partly based on the work of others, and has gratefully borrowed information, observation and time estimates from Peter Hill's book *The Construction of Hadrian's Wall* (Stroud, 2006). Some of the methodology derives from the one previously published attempt at a formal quantity survey for a Wall structure, Paul Bidwell's quantity survey of Chesters Bridge 2 in P. Bidwell and N. Holbrook, *Hadrian's Wall Bridges* (London, 1989), 47–9.

A 'quantitative survey' for the Wall has recently been attempted in a PhD thesis (Hartiss, R. G. (2010) *Beyond Functionalism: A Quantitative Survey and*

Semiotic Reading of Hadrian's Wall, Durham theses, Durham University. Available at Durham E-Theses Online: http://etheses.dur.ac.uk/332/). This is based on complex calculations and follows a rather different and more detailed approach to that taken here. However, out of interest, some of its person-day figures for various elements are included in the table giving the results of the present survey, for the sake of comparison. There is remarkable agreement in some areas. The present survey however arrives at much more economic programmes for the Turf Wall, which could surely have been built much more rapidly than the stone wall, and for the stone forts, where all but the central range buildings may have originally been of timber and perhaps supplied over an extended time period.

METHODOLOGY

The Stone Curtain Wall

The approach taken has been to quantify the materials and time needed to build a 100m stretch of the Broad Wall, the result being multiplied by 15 to give a rough estimate of what it would take to build one Wall-mile of approximately 1,500m, or by 75 to give a 5-mile block.

For quarrying the survey follows P. Bidwell, *Hadrian's Wall Bridges* (London, 1989), 47–9, in his quantity survey for Chesters bridge, which used figures from I. A. Baker's *Treatise on Masonry Construction* (10th ed., 1909) for man days to quarry a cubic metre of stone (3.37 man days), and also figures for cutting the stones to size, and laying by hand with no modern machinery used in heights under 6m.

The figure for the weight of sandstone of 2,320kg per cubic metre is taken from P. Hill, *The Construction of Hadrian's Wall* (Stroud, 2006). Hill has also been followed for the average size and weight of Wall facing stones, and numbers of facing stones per square metre of Wall surface. Hill's work has also been used as the basis of the estimate of how many men it would take to build a given length and

height of Wall in a given time, but the estimate has been converted here into man-days, and the result has been checked against Baker's figures for laying blocks, showing some agreement.

Throughout I have assumed a height for the Wall of 4.5m and added 20 per cent to allow for scaffolding and building the top surface, parapet and other details. This allowance also includes procurement of material for, and preparation of, mortar, but it ought to be remembered that the Broad Wall curtain made minimal or no use of mortar.

For foundation and core materials the source is http://www.simetric.co.uk/si_materials.htm, which gives weights for wet clay lumps of 1,602kg per cubic metre and broken sandstone 1,370–1,450kg; I have assumed an average weight of 1,600kg per cubic metre on the basis of this.

Milecastles and Turrets

Similarly Hill is the source for the height of a milecastle gateway or turret that could be built by a gang of a given size in a given time. The non-gate elements of the milecastles have been estimated as a fraction of the figure for 100m of Broad Wall. The internal buildings of milecastles have not been included here; there is little certainty as to their form in the Hadrianic period, their materials were relatively slight, and they could have been supplied by incoming garrisons.

Ditch and Vallum

Hill's figures for the size of gangs and the time needed to construct a given length of ditch and Vallum also form the basis for the overall man-day requirement calculated here.

The Obstacles on the Berm

No attempt has been made to quantify the labour needed to supply the obstacles on the berm – it is not yet known how extensively they were actually provided, but this underlines that the figures are unlikely to be a gross underestimate.

Turf Wall and Turf Milecastles

Figures for building in turf are based on B. Hobley 'An experimental reconstruction of a Roman military turf rampart', in *Roman Frontier Studies 1967* (Tel Aviv, 1971), 21–33. The Turf Wall turrets have been given the same figures as their stone Wall equivalents.

Transport

Estimates for transporting materials are based on the assumption that journeys were short, from nearby quarries or stockpiles, and that a cart carried about 1 tonne (1,000kg). A quantity survey of transport by R. Kendall 'Transport logistics associated with the building of Hadrian's Wall', *Britannia* 27, (1996), 129–52, arrived at a more pessimistic view of the time it would have taken to complete the building; it assumed carts and wagons to carry lesser loads than suggested in the present survey.

TURF WALL (TW)

Assuming that the Roman army could build a little faster than those doing the Lunt experiment, this showed that 300 men could cut, carry and stack 190,000 turf blocks to construct a rampart length of 282m in around ten days (sixty-three blocks cut and placed per man per day) = 190,000 blocks and 282m in **3,000 man days.**

Hobley also calculated that TW and milecastles would require 20 million turf blocks, but he was assuming the TW was not built of turf throughout; 30 million turf blocks (roughly 1 million per mile) would seem a safer estimate.

Therefore 30,000,000 blocks in **473,670 man days.**

Multiplying the 282m to arrive at the 46.50km length of the TW (31 × 1,500m) gives a higher figure of **494,680 man days.**

Ditch (*see* below): 390 man days per linear 100m = **181,350 man days**.

Turrets (*see* below): 1,407 man days per turret × 62 = **87,234 man days**.

TW TOTAL: 742,254–763,264 man days.

This figure ought to be a gross exaggeration, as it assumes construction throughout to an ideal specification with perfect turf blocks, whereas much upcast from the ditch and other earth was probably used in forming the core.

100m OF BROAD WALL

QUARRYING 100m OF FOUNDATION

3 × 0.20 × 100m = 60cu m sandstone slabs and general rubble and clay = 96 tonnes 3.37 man days to quarry 1cu m of stone.
This is for fine blocks so can be reduced to take account of non-quarried material (boulders etc.) – say, 2 man days per cubic metre

60 × 2 = **120 man days**

QUARRYING CURTAIN FACING STONES FOR 100m OF CURTAIN

Sandstone 2,320kg per cubic metre (Hill)
Stones on average 0.27 × 0.38 × 0.18m (Hill) = 0.018cu m before tapering
Each stone 0.018 × 2,320kg = 41.76kg
Tapering means stones as used in Wall average 30kg (Hill)
Number of facing stones based on Willowford elevation, and Hill, 20 per sq m: 4.5m high × 100m long × 20 = 9,000 per side × 2 = 18,000
18,000 × 0.018 = 324cu m [BUT 18,000 × 0.0129 = 232cu m after tapering]
Add 20 per cent for parapet, paving stones on top etc.

388cu m

3.37 man days to quarry 1cu m of stone

This is for fine blocks so includes rough squaring of Wall facing rubble at quarry

$388 \times 3.37 = $ **1,307 man days**

QUARRYING CORE FOR 100m OF CURTAIN CORE

Core material density = 1,600kg per cubic metre

Core = $100 \times 4.5 \times 3m - 232$cu m facing stones = 1,118cu m

$1,118 \times 1,600 = 1,788$ tonnes

Quarrying: Say 0.5 man days per cubic metre? (Much will be waste from quarrying for foundation and faces, or opportunistically picked up)

$1,118 \times 0.5 = $ **559 man days**

LAYING 100m OF FOUNDATION

Trench: Twenty men lay 32 linear metres per day (Hill's estimate, not including his allowance for quarrying).

Therefore 100m takes **60 man days**.

BUILDING 100m OF WALL FACES AND CORE TO FULL HEIGHT

Hill estimates that a gang of thirty men (not including the quarry workers, whom we have quantified separately above) could build 20 linear metres to a height of 735m/min one eight-hour day.

20 linear m @ height of 735mm = $20 \times 3 \times 0.735 = 44.10$cu m of Wall

100m of BW = $100 \times 3 \times 4.5 = 1,350$cu m of Wall

100m of Wall would therefore take a gang of 30

1,350/44.10 = 30 days to complete

Add 20 per cent for scaffolding, parapet, walkway, etc. = 36 days for 30 OR **1,080 man days**.

Double check, based on man-day rate for laying blocks in Baker 1909:

Laying wall stones:

1.793 man days per cubic metre

18,000 wall stones @ 30kg = 540 tonnes

540 tonnes/2.320 = 232cu m

1.793×232cu m = 415.97 man days

Add 20 per cent for scaffolding, parapet, walkway, etc. = 499.16 man days

Laying/building 100m of core:

Building: Say 0.5 man day per cubic metre?

$1,118 \times 0.5 = 559$ man days. Total: 1,059 man days.

Therefore the 1,080 figure can be accepted.

TRANSPORT PER 100m

Foundation 96 tonnes

Wall stones 900 tonnes

Core 1,788 tonnes

TOTAL 2,784 tonnes

Capacity of cart: 1,000kg (1 tonne)

Number of journeys from quarry(s) to buildings site: 2,784

Say, seven journeys in a day

Man days = 2,784 divided by 7 = **397**

Total for 100m of BW = 3,523 man days

STONE MILECASTLES

For milecastle walls, some 70m in total length, say 75 per cent of figures for 100m of curtain:

Quarrying foundations	90 man days
Quarrying facing stones	980 man days
Quarrying core	419 man days
Laying founds	45 man days
Building Walls and internal structures	750 man days
Add 20% for mortar, scaffolding, parapet, etc.	150 man days
Transport	297 man days

Quarrying gate blocks: each pier = 9cu m; $4 \times 9 = 36$

Voussoirs $0.6 \times 0.5 \times 0.4m = 0.12$cu m

60 voussoirs in all × 0.12 = 7.2cu m + 36cu m + 20 per cent for quarry wastage and cutting = 51.84cu m × 3.37 man days = 174 man days

Building gate piers and arches, Hill's estimate = 70 man days

For each tower above the gate arches, an arbitrary 700 man days is allowed, based on 50 per cent of the calculation for a turret, below; milecastle towers were smaller, and part of the elevation accounted for by the gate portal, already included. If there was a tower above each gate this would mean 1,400 man days.

TOTAL: 4,375 man days per milecastle

TURRETS

Foundations are not considered as this would have been counterbalanced by a saving in the construction of the curtain foundation.

Hill's estimate has twenty-two men building 1,470mm height in five days; at that rate it would take the twenty-two men forty days to build the turret to full height of 11–12m.

OR, a turret takes 880 man days; add 20 per cent for mortar, scaffolding, carpentry and roofing = 1,056 man days.

Turret quarrying: Number of facing stones in a turret = 6 × 11m = 66sq m = 1,320 facers (@ 20 per sq m) × 4 = 5,280 = 95cu m (@ = 0.018cu m) = 220 tonnes

3.37 man days to quarry 1cu m of stone. This is for fine blocks so includes rough squaring of Wall facing rubble at the quarry.

95 × 3.37 = 320 man days per turret

Turret transport: 220 journeys @ 7 journeys a day = 31 man days per turret

TOTAL: 1,407 man days per turret

SCAFFOLDING AND MORTAR

Amounts are impossible to quantify, as scaffolding materials could have been procured from the civil part of the province and would have been reused repeatedly in different places. However, the erection and moving of scaffolding must have added to the man days needed for the erection of each 100m length of wall and individual structures. Very little use was made of mortar in the Wall curtain, meaning that this could have been constructed in the winter months, but presumably more was used in the structures. An arbitrary allowance of 20 per cent has been added to the figures for superstructural building work to cover mortar, scaffolding, parapet, walkway and so on.

DITCH

Hill gives the ditch a length of 95km (59 miles) – allowing for discontinuity in the crags sector? – and a figure of 370,904 man days to excavate/construct, OR 6,266 man days per Roman mile, OR **390 man days per linear 100m.**

VALLUM

Hill's estimate (based on modern military manuals, not the probable fanatical Roman pace) is 949,667 man days, OR 12,495 man days per Roman mile, OR **833 man days per linear 100m.**

100m of NARROW WALL

QUARRYING 100m OF FOUNDATION

This is generally not necessary as the Wall is laid on Broad foundation, except between Newcastle and Wallsend and parts of the crags.

LAYING 100m OF FOUNDATION

Allowing for preparation of the existing Broad foundation, this would take, say, **50 man days.**

QUARRYING CORE FOR 100m OF 8ft CURTAIN CORE

Core material density = 1,600kg per cubic metre
Core = 100 × 4.5 × 2.4m − 232cu m facing stones = 848cu m
848 × 1,600kg = 1,356 tonnes
Quarrying: Say, 0.5 man days per cubic metre (much will be waste from quarrying for foundation and faces, or opportunistically picked up)
848 × 0.5 = **424 man days**

QUARRYING FACING STONES

As for the BW, this would take **1,307 man days**.

BUILDING 100m OF WALL FACES AND CORE TO FULL HEIGHT

Based on Hill's estimate: Hill estimates that a gang of thirty men (not including the quarry workers, whom we have quantified separately above) could build 20 linear metres to a height of 735mm in one eight-hour day.

20 linear m @ height of 735mm = 20 × 3 × 0.735 = 44.10cu m of Wall
100m of NW = 100 × 2.4 × 4.5 = 1,080cu m of Wall
100m of Wall would therefore take a gang of thirty men 1,080/44.10 = 24.5 days to complete
Add 20 per cent for scaffolding, parapet, walkway, etc. = 29.4 days for 30 men, OR **882 man days**

TRANSPORT PER 100m

Foundation 0 tonnes
Wall stones 900 tonnes
Core 1,356 tonnes
TOTAL 2,256 tonnes
Capacity of cart: 1,000kg (1 tonne)
Number of journeys from quarry(ies) to buildings site: 2,256 journeys
Say, seven journeys in a day
Man days = 2,256 divided by 7 = **322**

TOTAL for 100m of NW, where Broad foundation is already laid = 2,985 man days

THE WALL BRIDGES

I have followed P. Bidwell, *Hadrian's Wall Bridges* (London, 1989), 47–9, in his quantity survey for Chesters bridge, which arrived at a figure of **29,081 man days** for the construction of Bridge 2 at Chesters. The Hadrianic bridge was narrower but also of stone arched construction. The figures for Newcastle and Carlisle **(40,000)** and Willowford **(25,000)** are simple estimates based on this figure; Newcastle and Carlisle were larger bridges, Willowford smaller.

A STONE FORT

Using the same figures as for Broad Wall construction, but assuming a typical fort-wall width of 5RF = 1.5m (as at Benwell and Chesters), 100m of fort wall would take the man days described below.

QUARRYING 100m OF FOUNDATION

2m (foundations are typically wider than the fort walls) × 0.3m (foundations are deeper than the Broad Wall) × 100m = 60cu m sandstone fragments/boulders and general rubble and clay = 96 tonnes
Say, 2 man days to quarry 1cu m: per cubic metre = **120 man days**

QUARRYING CURTAIN FACING STONES FOR 100m OF CURTAIN

As Broad Wall: **1,307 man days**.

QUARRYING CORE FOR 100m OF CURTAIN CORE

Core material density = 1,600kg per cubic metre
Core = 100m x 4.5m x 1.5m − 232cu m facing stones = 443cu m
443 × 1,600 = 708 tonnes

Quarrying at 0.5 man days per cubic metre: 443 × 0.5 = **221 man days**

LAYING 100m OF FOUNDATION

As the Broad Wall (fort foundations are deeper but much less wide): **60 man days**.

BUILDING 100m OF FORT WALL

As discussed under the Broad Wall, a gang of thirty men could build 44.10cu m of Wall in one day.

100m of fort wall: 100 × 4.5 × 1.5 = 675cu m of Wall
100m of Wall would therefore take a gang of thirty
675/44.10 = 15.31 days to complete
Add 20 per cent for mortar, scaffolding, parapet, walkway etc. = 18.37 days for thirty men, OR **551 man days**

TRANSPORT PER 100m

Foundation 96 tonnes
Wall stones 900 tonnes
Core 708 tonnes
TOTAL 1,704 tonnes
Capacity of cart: 1,000kg (1 tonne)
Number of journeys from quarry(ies) to building site: = 1,704 journeys
Say, seven journeys in a day

Man days = 1,704 divided by 7 = **243**

Total for 100m of fort wall = **2,502 man days**

Total for a typical 600m fort circuit therefore = **15,012 man days**

Ten gate portals and ten gate towers: these might be seen to be equivalent to ten milecastle gates (10 × 244 man days) and ten turrets (10 × 1,407 man days) = **16,510 man days**.

Ditch system: say, broadly equivalent to the Wall ditch, so 600 linear metres would take **2,340 man days**.

Total = 33,862. Add a notional 100 per cent for internal buildings (some of which were architecturally ambitious), streets, rampart etc.

TOTAL FOR A STONE FORT = 67,724 man days

A TURF WALL FORT

No detailed calculations have been attempted here, but based on the Lunt experiment (*see* Hobley's 1971 paper, p. 31) the defences of a turf fort of 1.5ha area would take around eleven days for 600 men – around 6,600 man days. Adding 50 per cent for the internal structures arrives at around 10,000 man days. For a larger, 2.6ha fort, Hobley's figures suggest around 16,500 man days for the defences, which would suggest around 25,000 man days for the whole fort.

TOTAL FOR A 1.5ha TURF WALL W FORT = 10,000 man days
TOTAL FOR A 2.6ha TURF WALL W FORT = 25,000 man days

CUMBERLAND COAST

Forty-four turrets @ 1,407 man days = **61,908 man days**

Twenty-two timber fortlets: using the Lunt experiment rate of 300 men to cut, carry and stack 190,000 turf blocks to construct a rampart length of 282m in around ten days (3,000 man days), an average coastal fortlet perimeter of 100m would take some 67,375 turves, to be laid in 1,063 man days. Add 20 per cent for internal structures, timber gates etc. = 1,275 × 22 = **28,050** man days. This figure ought to be a gross exaggeration, as it assumes construction throughout to an ideal specification with perfect turf blocks, whereas much upcast from the ditch and other earth was probably used in forming the core.

TOTAL FOR CUMBERLAND COAST STRUCTURES = 89,958 man days

RESULTS: MAN DAYS TO BUILD VARIOUS ELEMENTS OF HADRIAN'S WALL

The results of this brief survey are given in the following table. Where it has been possible to make a direct comparison, the right-hand column gives comparable figures from the survey by Hartiss 2010.

	Man days	Hartiss 2010	
Turf Wall	473,670		
All TW turrets	87,234		
TW ditch	181,350		
Turf Wall total	742,254	1,559,798	Table A5.3
100m of Broad Wall	3,523	3,905	Calculated from Table A5.2
5 miles of Broad Wall	264,225	292,945	Table A5.2
Over equiv. distance of TW	1,638,195		
Each stone milecastle	4,375	6,137	Average – Table A2.29
Each turret	1,407	534	Average – Table A2.18
100m of Wall ditch	390		
5-mile block with 5 MCs, 10 turrets and curtain and ditch	329,420		
100m of Vallum	833		
Entire Vallum	949,620	1,000, 603	Table 6.23
Newcastle Bridge	40,000		
Chesters Bridge	29,081		
Willowford Bridge	25,000		
100m of Narrow Wall	2,985	3,305	Calculated from Table A5.3
5 miles of Narrow Wall	223,875	247,894	Table A5.3
Stone fort	67,724	32,821	Defences only – Table A2.45
		112,431	Scaled up for internal buildings Table A2.46
Turf Wall fort	10,000–25,000		
Cumberland coast (not forts)	89,958		

SUGGESTED BUILDING SEQUENCE AND MANPOWER REQUIREMENTS

YEAR 1			YEAR 2		
	Legionary man days	Auxiliary man days		Legionary man days	Auxiliary man days
NEWCASTLE BRIDGE	20,000		NEWCASTLE BRIDGE	20,000	
4–7 (Four MCs + BW + ditch)	197,652				
			7–12 (Five MCs + BW + ditch)	329,420	
			12–17 (Five MCs + BW + ditch)	329,420	
			17–23 (Five MCs + BW + ditch)	329,420	
			23–27 (Five MCs + BW foundation + ditch). BW begun here – gaps filled with 6ft Wall now or after an interval?	64,625	
CHESTERS BRIDGE	14,540		CHESTERS BRIDGE	14,540	

YEAR 3			YEAR 4		
	Legionary man days	Auxiliary man days			
Wallsend fort and extension	175,000		**Wallsend** fort and extension	175,000	
4–7 Vallum		37,485			
Benwell	33,862		**Benwell**	33,862	
7–12 Vallum	62,475	62,475			
Rudchester	33,862		**Rudchester**	33,862	
12–17 Vallum		62,475			
17–23 Vallum		62,475			
Halton Chesters begins	33,862		**Halton Chesters completed**	33,862	
23–27 Vallum		62,475			
28–34 Vallum		74,970			
Chesters begins	33,862		**Chesters completed**	33,862	

(continued)

YEAR 1				YEAR 2		
				28–34 (Seven MCs + BW foundation + ditch)	90,475	
				Crags 34–46 BW founds laid, structures begun	100,000	
46–48 (Three MCs + BW foundation +ditch)	38,775					
WILLOWFORD BRIDGE	12,500			WILLOWFORD BRIDGE	12,500	
CARLISLE BRIDGE	20,000			CARLISLE BRIDGE	20,000	
32 TW MCs, 60 stone turrets, TW curtain	742,254					
TOTAL	1,045,721	0			1,310,400	0
Men for 200 days	5,229	0		Men for 200 days	6,552	0

YEAR 3			YEAR 4		
28–34 Narrow Wall super-structure and structures here completed APPROX	313,425				
Crags 34–46: structures continued, NW gauge intro-duced	50,000		Crags 34–46: structures completed, NW largely built except on high crags	450,000	
Housesteads begins	33,862		**Housesteads completed**	33,862	
crags 34–46 Vallum		149,940			
46–48 NW	134,325				
46–48 Vallum		37,485			
Birdoswald begins	33,862		**Birdoswald completed**	33,862	
TW FORTS: Castlesteads, Stanwix, Bowness?	73,611				
TW VALLUM		387,345			
Cumbrian Coast	95,019				
Cumbrian Coast Forts	36,805		Cumbrian Coast Forts	36,805	
	1,143,832	**937,125**		**864,977**	**0**
Men for 200 days	5,719	4,686	**Men for 200 days**	4,325	0

The standard history, first published in 1976: Breeze, D. J. and Dobson, B. *Hadrian's Wall* (4th revised ed.), London 2000.

The most authoritative but accessible description of the visible and buried remains, with site-by-site bibliography: Breeze, D. J. *Collingwood Bruce's Handbook to the Roman Wall* (14th ed.), Newcastle upon Tyne 2006.

The best archaeological map: English Heritage *An Archaeological Map of Hadrian's Wall* (revised ed.), London 2014.

Other useful and informative introductory surveys: Johnson, S. *Hadrian's Wall*, English Heritage, London 1989 and 2004; Jones, G. D. B. and Woolliscroft, D. *Hadrian's Wall from the Air*, Stroud 2001.

Roman army: Goldsworthy, A. *The Complete Roman Army*, London 2003; Breeze, D. J. *The Roman Army*, London 2016.

Roman forts: Bidwell, P. *Roman Forts in Britain*, Stroud 2007; Johnson, A. *Roman Forts*, London 1983.

The Wall set in the context of Roman Britain: Frere, S. S. *Britannia: a history of Roman Britain* (4th revised ed.), London 1999; Mattingly, D. *An Imperial Possession: Britain in the Roman Empire 54BC–AD409*, London 2006.

The Wall set in the context of the other frontiers of the Roman empire: Breeze, D. J. *The Frontiers of Imperial Rome*, Barnsley 2011.

OTHER SOURCES OF INFORMATION

Reviews of previous research, essential for anybody making a serious study of Hadrian's Wall: Birley, E. 1961 *Research on Hadrian's Wall*, Kendal; Symonds, M.F.A and Mason, D.A. (eds) 2009 *Frontiers of Knowledge: a research framework for Hadrian's Wall*, Durham, vol. 1 – available online at: https://www.dur.ac.uk/resources/archaeology/pdfs/research/Vol_1_Resource_Assessment.pdf

The three most recent summaries of discoveries made in the previous decade of Wall research, issued for the decennial 'Pilgrimage' of Hadrian's Wall: Bidwell, P. T. (ed.) 1999 *Hadrian's Wall 1989–1999: A Summary of Recent Excavations and Research*, Kendal; Hodgson, N. (ed.) 2009 *Hadrian's Wall 1999–2009: A Summary of Recent Excavation and Research*, Kendal; Collins, R. And Symonds, M. 2019 *Hadrian's Wall 2009–2019: A Summary of Excavation and Research*, Kendal.

See also: Breeze, D. J. 2014 *Hadrian's Wall: A History of Archaeological Thought*, Kendal; Breeze, D. J. 2019 *Hadrian's Wall: A study in archaeological exploration and interpretation*, Oxford.

Hadrian's Wall after the Romans: Hingley, R. 2012 *Hadrian's Wall: a Life*, Oxford; Leach, S. and Whitworth, A. 2011 *Saving the Wall: the conservation of Hadrian's Wall 1746–1987*, Stroud.

The notes allow the reader to see on what the statements in the text are based. They are meant to answer questions such as 'How do we know that?' or 'Why does he think that?', but they also lead to primary source material (for example, inscriptions or excavation reports). The notes are *not* meant to form a comprehensive bibliography, although they do give a representative flavour of the available literature. Several of the works cited in the notes are very hard to obtain outside the immediate region of the Wall or outside certain specialist libraries, and only a minority are freely available on the internet – a specialist archaeological area is a small world, and archaeologists tend to rely on personal contacts to keep up to date with the literature.

Inscriptions are collected and individually numbered in 'RIB' = 'The Roman Inscriptions of Britain'. Vol. I is available online at: http://romaninscriptionsofbritain. org/. The printed volumes are: Collingwood, R. G. and Wright, R. P. 1965 *The Roman Inscriptions of Britain*, I; *Inscriptions on Stone*, Oxford; Tomlin, R. S. O. 1995 *Addenda and Corrigenda* to *RIB* I, in Collingwood and Wright 1965 (new edition 1995), Stroud; Collingwood, R. G. and Wright, R. P. (1990–95). *The Roman Inscriptions of Britain*, II: *Instrumentum Domesticum* (in eight fascicules), Frere, S. S. and Tomlin, R. S. O. (eds) Oxford; Tomlin, R. S. O., Wright, R. P., and Hassall, M. W. C. 2009 *The Roman Inscriptions of Britain*, III: *Inscriptions on Stone*, found or notified between 1 January 1955 and 31 December 2006, Oxford.

Sculpture is collected in 'CSIR': Phillips, E. J. (ed.) 1977 *Corpus Signorum Imperii Romani: Corpus of Sculpture of the Roman World – Great Britain*, vol. 1, fascicule 1: *Corbridge, Hadrian's Wall East of the North Tyne*, Oxford; Coulston, J. C. and Phillips, E. J. (eds) 1988 *Corpus Signorum Imperii Romani: Corpus of Sculpture of the Roman World – Great Britain*, vol. 1, fascicule 6: *Hadrian's Wall West of the North Tyne and Carlisle*, Oxford.

Abbreviations BAR = British Archaeological Reports CIL = *Corpus Inscriptionum Latinarum* CSIR = *Corpus Signorum Imperii Romani*, *see above* under 'Sculpture'

ILS = Dessau, H. (ed.) 1892–1916 *Inscriptiones Latinae Selectae*, Berlin RIB = *Roman Inscription of Britain*, *see above* under 'Inscriptions' SHA = *Scriptores Historiae Augustae*

INTRODUCTION: WHAT IS HADRIAN'S WALL?

Roman lists of forts along the Wall: Notitia Dignitatum and Ravenna Cosmography: *see* Rivet, A. L. F. and Smith, C. 1979 *The Place-names of Roman Britain*, London, 209 and 220.

1920s system of numbering structures: Collingwood, R. G. 1930 Hadrian's Wall: a system of numerical references, *Proceedings of the Society of Antiquaries of Newcastle upon Tyne* ser. 4, 4, 179–87.

The obstacles on the berm: Bidwell, P. T. 2005 The systems of obstacles on Hadrian's Wall: their extent, date and purpose, *Arbeia Journal* 8, 53–76.

Antiquarian research: The fundamental study is Birley, E. 1961 *Research on Hadrian's Wall* Kendal. *See also* Hingley, R. 2012 *Hadrian's Wall: a life*, Oxford; Breeze, D. J. 2014 *Hadrian's Wall: a History of Archaeological thought*, Kendal.

Percentage of Wall excavated etc.: Bidwell, P. (ed.) 2009 The Wall, in M. F. A. Symonds and D. J. P. Mason (eds) *Frontiers of Knowledge: a research framework for Hadrian's Wall*, Durham, 34–62, Table at p.40.

Plaster/whitewash on the Wall: Crow, J. G. 1991 A review of current research on the turrets and curtain of Hadrian's Wall, *Britannia* 22, 51–63, esp. 58–9; Bidwell, P. T. and Watson, M. 1996 Excavations on Hadrian's Wall at Denton, Newcastle upon Tyne, 1986–9, *Archaeologia Aeliana* ser. 5, 24, 1–56; Bidwell, P. T. 1996 The exterior decoration of Roman buildings in Britain, in Johnson, P. (ed.), *Roman Architecture in Britain* (CBA Research Report 94), York, 19–29.

Ilam or Staffordshire Moorlands Pan ('Vallum Aelium'): Tomlin, R. S. O. and Hassall, M. W. C. 2004 Roman Britain in 2003 III. Inscriptions, *Britannia* 35,

335–49, esp. 344–5; Breeze, D. J. (ed.) 2012 *The First Souvenirs: enamelled vessels from Hadrian's Wall*, Kendal.

1 HOW THE ROMANS CAME TO BUILD A WALL IN BRITAIN

The Limits to Roman Power

Roman expansion: Mann, J. C. 1974 The frontiers of the Principate, in Temporini, H. and Haas, W. (eds) *Aufstieg und Niedergang der römischen Welt* 2.1, 508–33, Berlin and New York. **Belief in empire without end, Varian disaster, bases on the Rhine:** Wells, C. M. 1972 *The German policy of Augustus*, Oxford. **Frontier on the Danube:** Mackensen, M. 1987 *Frühkaiserzeitliche Kleinkastelle bei Nersingen und Burladingen an der oberen Donau*, Munich.

An Introduction to the Roman Army

Augustus organizes *auxilia* into standing units: Keppie, L. J. F. 1984 *The Making of the Roman Army*, London, 150–2. **Unit structures:** Hassall, M. 1983 The internal planning of Roman auxiliary forts, in B. Hartley and J. Wacher (eds) *Rome and her Northern Provinces*, London, 96–113. **Trajan's Column:** Frere, S. S. and Lepper, F. 1988 *Trajan's Column*, Gloucester, Plate LI, Scene lxxii, Casts, 183–4. **Legionary first cohort:** Frere, S. S. 1980 Hyginus and the First Cohort, *Britannia* 11, 51–60; Pitts, L. F. and St Joseph, J. K. 1985 *Inchtuthil: The Roman Legionary Fortress*, London, 164–9. **Turmae of 42 in ala milliaria:** Scholz, M. 2009 *Das Reiterkastell Aquileia/Heidenheim*, Stuttgart, 55. **Origin of fort plan and forts in general:** Johnson, A. 1983 *Roman Forts of the 1st and 2nd centuries AD in Britain and the German provinces*, London; Reddé, M. et al. 2006 *L'architecture de la Gaule romaine: Les fortifications militaries*, Paris-Bordeaux.

The Pre-Roman Inhabitants of Britain

Haselgrove, C. and Moore, T. (eds) 2007 *The Later Iron Age in Britain and beyond*, Oxford; Mattingly, D. 2006 *An Imperial Possession: Britain in the Roman empire*, London, 47–84; Hodgson, N., McKelvey, J. and Muncaster, W. 2012 *The Iron Age on the Northumberland Coastal Plain*, Newcastle upon Tyne. **46 tribes in the Alpine region:** Pliny, *Hist. Nat.* 3.24. **South Cave weapons cache:** Halkon, P. 2013 *The Parisi*, Stroud, 118.

How Iron Age People were Absorbed into the Empire

Millett, M. 1990 *The Romanization of Britain*, Cambridge; Woolf, G. 1998 *Becoming Roman*, Cambridge.

The Invasion of Britain

Mattingly, D. 2006 *An Imperial Possession: Britain in the Roman Empire*, London, 87–154; Hanson, W. S. 1987 *Agricola and the conquest of the North*, London. **Impact of Danubian invasions:** Cassius Dio 54.24.3; Mócsy, A. 1974 *Pannonia and Upper Moesia*, London, 82–5.

Retreat from Conquest in Northern Britain

Hartley, B. R. 1972 The Roman Occupations of Scotland: The Evidence of the Samian Ware, *Britannia* 3, 1–55; Hobley, A. S. 1989 The numismatic evidence for the post-Agricolan abandonment of the Roman frontier in northern Scotland, *Britannia* 20, 69–74. **Vindolanda documents:** Bowman, A. K. and Thomas, J. D. 1994 *The Vindolanda Writing Tablets (Tabulae Vindolandenses II)*, British Museum, London; *Brittunculi* tablet: no. 164.

The Stanegate Frontier

Troop withdrawals from Britain and *vexillatio Britannica* in Nijmegen: Bogaers, J.E. 1967 'Die Besatzungstruppen des legionslagers von Nijmegen im 2. Jahrh', in *Studien zu den Militärgrenzen Roms*, Cologne, 54–76. **Synchronized fort rebuilding c. 105:** Bidwell, P. T., 1999 *Hadrian's Wall 1989–1999*, Carlisle, 12–13. **General:** Hodgson, N. (ed.) 2009 The pre-Hadrianic frontier on the Tyne-Solway Isthmus, and the Stanegate, in M. F. A. Symonds and D. J. P. Mason (eds) 2009 *Frontiers of Knowledge: a research framework for Hadrian's Wall*, Durham, 10–33, esp. 10–19. **Detailed analysis and doubts:** Dobson, B. 1986 The Function of Hadrian's Wall *Archaeologia Aeliana* ser. 5, 14, 1–30. **Rehabilitation:** Hodgson, N. 2000 The Stanegate: a frontier rehabilitated, *Britannia* 31, 11–22. **Western Stanegate:** Woolliscroft, D. J. and Jones, G. D. B. 2004 Excavations on the Cumberland Coast at Silloth and Finland Rigg, 1994, in R. J. A. Wilson and I. D. Caruana (eds) 2004 *Romans on the Solway*, Kendal, 186–94; Breeze, D. J. and Woolliscroft, D. J. (eds) 2009 *Excavation and Survey at Roman Burgh-by-Sands* (no place of publication, Cumberland and Westmorland Antiquarian and Archaeological Society Monograph). **East of Corbridge/Devil's Causeway:** Hodgson, N., McKelvey, J. and Muncaster, W. 2012 *The Iron Age on the Northumberland Coastal Plain*, Newcastle upon Tyne, 211–13.

The Unravelling of Trajan's Conquests

Bennett, J. 1997 *Trajan: Optimus Princeps,* London, esp. Caps. 13–14. **York IX Legion inscription:** RIB 665.

Hadrian

General: Birley, A. R. 1997 *Hadrian: the Restless Emperor,* London. **Hadrian pays for building out of his own purse:** ibid., 147; 157; 170; 177; 186; 196; 305. **Development of other frontiers of the Roman empire:** Breeze, D. J. 2011 *The Frontiers of Imperial Rome,* Barnsley. **Date of Upper German palisade:** Schallmayer, E. 2003 Der Limes, Marköbel und Kaiser Hadrian, *Denkmalpflege und Kulturgeschichte 2003,* 2, 12–21.

Events in Britain Early in Hadrian's Reign

Britons could not be kept under control: SHA Hadrian 5.2. **Fronto on casualties in Britain:** Fronto, Loeb translation ii.22. **Vindolanda inscription:** RIB 3364. **Carlisle armour:** Howard-Davis, C. 2009 *The Carlisle Millennium Project: Excavations in Carlisle 1998–2001, Volume 2: Finds,* Lancaster, 704–5. **'Augustan History':** SHA Hadrian 11.2 Hadrian first to build a Wall in Britain. **Timing of Hadrianic war in Britain:** Birley, A. R. 2005 *The Roman Government of Britain,* Oxford, 114–24; Birley, A. R. 2013 Two Governors of Dacia Superior and Britain, in Vl. Iliescu, D. Nedu, and A. R. Barboş (eds), *Graecia, Roma, Barbaricum. In memoriam Vasile Lica,* Galati, Romania, 241–260; Breeze, D. J., Dobson, B. and Maxfield, V. 2012 Maenius Agrippa, a chronological conundrum, *Acta Classica* 55, 17–30. *Expeditio Britannica* **meaning Emperor present:** Rosenberger, V. 1992 *Bella et expeditiones. Die antike Terminologie der Kriege Roms,* Stuttgart. **War in Britain placed in 124–6:** Breeze, D. J. 2003 Warfare in Britain and the Building of Hadrian's Wall, *Archaeologia Aeliana* ser. 5, 32, 13–16. **War in Britain placed in 130:** Frere, S. S. 2000 M. Maenius Agrippa, the *expeditio Britannica* and Maryport, *Britannia* 31, 23–28. **Ninth Legion:** Keppie, L. 2000 Legio VIIII in Britain: the beginning and the end, in R. J. Brewer (ed.) *Roman Fortresses and their legions,* London, 83–100; Haalebos, J. K. 2000 Römische Truppen in Nijmegen, in Y. Le Bohec, *Les légions de Rome sous le Haut-Empire,* Lyon, 465–89. Diploma of July 122: CIL xvi.68.

2 THE WALL IS BUILT

The Scale of the Task

Specifications of the Wall: There is no comprehensive study. **Nature of the Broad and Narrow Wall cores:** Bidwell, P. and Holbrook, N. 1989 *Hadrian's Wall Bridges,* London, 54–61. **Area of turf stripped for the Turf Wall:** Wilmott, T. (ed.), 2009 *Hadrian's Wall: Archaeological Research by English Heritage 1976–2001,* London, 127.

Where were the Troops Accommodated while they were Building the Wall?

Groups of temporary camps: Bennett, J. 1980 'Temporary' camps along Hadrian's Wall, in Hanson, W. S. and Keppie, L. J. F. (eds) *Roman Frontier Studies 1979* (BAR Int. Ser. 71), Oxford, 151–72; Welfare, H. and Swan, V. 1995 *Roman Camps in England,* London. **Shield-on-the-Wall:** Welfare, H. 2013 A Roman camp, quarries and the Vallum at Shield-on-the-Wall, *Archaeologia Aeliana* ser. 5, 42, 81–99.

The Sequence of Construction

Reduction in thickness of milecastle walls: Symonds, M. 2005 The construction order of the milecastles on Hadrian's Wall, *Archaeologia Aeliana* ser. 5, 34, 67–78. **Vallum surveyed out from fort sites:** Bowden, M. C. B. and Blood, K. 1991 The Roman fort at Rudchester: an analytical field survey, *Archaeologia Aeliana* ser. 5, 19, 25–31; Poulter, J. 2010 *The Planning of Roman Roads and Walls in northern Britain,* Stroud, 82, 99–110. **Wall originally planned to run to Wallsend:** Hill, P. R. 2001 Hadrian's Wall from MC0 to MC9, *Archaeologia Aeliana* ser. 5, 29, 3–18.

The Organization of the Building

Differing building styles and 'legionary blocks': Breeze, D. J. and Dobson, B. 2000 *Hadrian's Wall* (4th ed.), London, esp. Chapter 2; cf. Hooley, J. and Breeze, D. 1968 The building of Hadrian's Wall: a reconsideration, *Archaeologia Aeliana* ser. 4, 97–114. **Doubts about identification of *II Augusta* with the building plans of Milecastles 37, 38 and 42:** Hill, P. R. 1991 Hadrian's Wall: some aspects of its execution, *Archaeologia Aeliana* ser. 5, 19, 33–9. **Scepticism about the idea of five-mile legionary 'blocks':** Bennett, J. 2002 A revised programme and chronology for the building of Hadrian's Wall, in Freeman et al. *Limes XVIII* (BAR Int. Ser. 1084), Oxford, 825–34. **Legionary lengths on the Antonine Wall:** Hanson, W. S. and Maxwell, G. S. 1983 *Rome's North-West Frontier: the Antonine Wall,* Edinburgh, esp. Cap. 6 and Table 6.2.

The Change to Narrow Wall

Structural instability of Broad Wall: Richmond, I. A. 1957 *Handbook to the Roman Wall*, 11th ed., Newcastle upon Tyne, 16; cf. Hill, P. R. 2006 *The Construction of Hadrian's Wall*, Stroud, 24. **Narrow Wall as economy measure:** Richmond, I. A. 1966 *Handbook to the Roman Wall*, 12th ed., Newcastle upon Tyne, 15. **Central sector centurions from XX Legion:** RIB 1762 (Julius Florentinus), 3378 (Flavius Noricus); centurions attested at Chester: RIB 473–4 and 3386–7 (Maximus Terentius); RIB 468 and 1769; 1867 (Ferronius Vegetus). Rufius Sabinius: RIB 1659; 441. Claudius Augustanus: RIB 1770; 1811; 1855; 2409.4; 3297. Lousius Suavis building records listed at RIB 3401. *See also* Birley, E. 1939 Building records from Hadrian's Wall, *Archaeologia Aeliana* ser. 4, 16, 219–36, esp. 235. **Milecastle 37 completed to Narrow gauge, Milecastle 38 completed entirely to the Broad gauge:** Plan of 37 in Crow, J. 2004 *Housesteads*, Stroud, 17; Simpson, F. G. et al. 1936 Milecastles on Hadrian's Wall explored in 1935–36, *Archaeologia Aeliana* ser. 4, 13, 258–73, esp. 263–4. *II Augusta* stone in Wall-mile 34: RIB 1569.

The Forts on the Wall

Haltonchesters inscription: RIB 1427. **Original plan for forts:** Swinbank, B. and Spaul, J. E. H. 1951 The spacing of the forts on Hadrian's Wall, *Archaeologia Aeliana* ser. 4, 29, 221–38.

The Direction and Method of Building: Centuries at Work

Problematic study of 'legionary lengths' and building timetable based on centurial stones: Stevens, C. E. 1966 *The Building of Hadrian's Wall*, Kendal. **Sketch plan of 1807:** Bosanquet, R. C. 1929 Dr John Lingard's Notes on the Roman Wall, *Archaeologia Aeliana* ser. 4, 6, 130–62, p.146. **Lengths of 22ft:** RIB 1575, 1653. **Horizontal building school of thought:** Hill, P. R. 2006 *The Construction of Hadrian's Wall*, Stroud. **Alternating Broad and Narrow superstructure in mile 26:** References cited in Stevens, C. E. 1966 *The Building of Hadrian's Wall*, Kendal, 26–8. **Centurial stones between Milecastle 49 and Birdoswald:** RIB 3415–3437. **Libo:** RIB 1649, 1857, 3382, 3411. **Socellius:** RIB 1675, 1768, 3413. **Flavius Noricus:** RIB 1664, 1812, 3378.

The Timetable of Building

Platorius Nepos inscriptions: Milecastles 37: RIB 1634; 38: RIB 1637–8; 42: RIB 1666. Benwell: RIB 1340. Halton Chesters: RIB 1427. TW Milecastle 50: RIB 1935. **Estimate of 2,400 builders from each legion:** Hill, P. R. 2006 *The Construction of Hadrian's Wall*, Stroud, 114–16; **Criticism:** Graafstal, E. P. 2012 Hadrian's Haste: a priority programme for the Wall, *Archaeologia Aeliana* ser. 5, 41, 132. **Widely cited timetable:** Breeze, D. J. and Dobson, B. 2000 *Hadrian's Wall* (4th ed.), London, 86–7 (Table 7). **Josephus:** *Jewish War* 5.508–509; 3. 141–2. **Hadrian's speech:** Speidel, M. P. 2006 *Emperor Hadrian's speeches to the African Army – a new text*, Mainz, 10. Cf. Richmond, I. A. 1982 *Trajan's Army on Trajan's Column*, London, 25. **Evidence that Broad Wall completed to full height in miles 7–22:** Brewis, P. 1927 Notes on the Roman Wall at Denton Bank, Great Hill and Heddon-on-the-Wall – Northumberland, *Archaeologia Aeliana* ser. 4, 4, 109–121, esp. 120–21 (Broad Wall upstanding at Great Hill); Bidwell, P. T. and Watson, M. 1996 Excavations on Hadrian's Wall at Denton, Newcastle upon Tyne, 1986–89, *Archaeologia Aeliana* ser. 5, 24, 1–56 (Broad Wall still standing, to collapse a century or more later). **Speed of building aimed at as a spectacle in itself:** DeLaine, J. 2002 The Temple of Hadrian at Cyzicus and Roman attitudes to exceptional construction, *Papers of the British School at Rome* 70, 205–30.

The Building of the Wall in Perspective

Jarrow Inscription: RIB 1051. **Recent study introducing idea of priority programme in face of threat and Turf Wall as a 'quick fix':** Graafstal, E. P. 2012 Hadrian's Haste: a priority programme for the Wall, *Archaeologia Aeliana* ser. 5, 41, 123–84. **Temporary *principia* at Inchtuthil:** Pitts, L. F. and St Joseph, J. K. 1985 *Inchtuthil: The Roman Legionary Fortress*, London, 85–7. **Doubts about 'fort decision':** Crow, J. G. 2004 The Northern Frontier of Britain from Trajan to Antoninus Pius: Roman Builders and Native Britons, in M. Todd (ed.) *A Companion to Roman Britain*, Oxford, 114–35 esp. at 126–9. **Visual communication between Wall and Stanegate in central sector:** Woolliscroft, D. J. 1989 Signalling and the design of Hadrian's Wall, *Archaeologia Aeliana* ser. 5, 17, 5–19. **Squat portals in Wall fort gates:** Bidwell, P. 2013 The elevations of Roman fort gates, in C. Flügel and J. Obmann (eds) *Römische Wehrbauten: Befund und Rekonstruktion*, Munich, 82–7. **Dropping off in quality of work at fort and milecastle gates:** Hill, P. R. 2006 *The Construction of Hadrian's Wall*, Stroud, 140–4; Hill, P. R. 1991 Hadrian's Wall: some aspects of its execution, *Archaeologia Aeliana* ser. 5, 19, 33–9.

3 HADRIAN'S WALL AND THE ANTONINE WALL (AD122–60)

Events

Birley, A. R. 2005 *The Roman Government of Britain*, Oxford.

Hadrian's Wall under Hadrian

No original causeways across the Vallum ditch at milecastles; original gaps in the north mound: Heywood, B. and Breeze, D. J. 2008 Excavations at Vallum Causeways on Hadrian's Wall in the 1950s, *Archaeologia Aeliana* ser. 5, 37, 47–92; Swinbank, B. 1966 The Vallum: its problems restated, in M. G. Jarrett and B. Dobson 1965 *Britain and Rome, Essays Presented to Eric Birley*, Kendal, 85–94, esp. 86–8; Breeze, D. J. 2015 The Vallum of Hadrian's Wall, *Archaeologia Aeliana* ser. 5, 44, 1–29, esp. 5, 10. **Extent of replacement of Turf Wall under Hadrian:** Hodgson, N. and McKelvey, J. 2006 An excavation on Hadrian's Wall at Hare Hill, Wall-mile 53, Cumbria, *Transactions of the Cumberland and Westmorland Antiquarian and Archaeological Society* ser. 3, 6, 45–60; Breeze, D. J. 2014 *Hadrian's Wall: A History of Archaeological Thought*, Kendal, 85–90.

The Antonine Occupation of Scotland

Pius' personal need for victory: Breeze, D. J. 2006 *The Antonine Wall*, Edinburgh, 12–14. **Other factors:** Hanson, W. S. and Maxwell, G. S. 1983 *Rome's North-West Frontier: the Antonine Wall*, Edinburgh, 59–63. **Pausanias:** *Description of Greece* 8, 43. **Context of passage links it to beginning of reign:** Birley, E. 1961 *Roman Britain and the Roman Army*, 31–2. **Genounia erroneously introduced:** Hind, J. G. F. 1977 The 'Genounian' part of Britain, *Britannia* 8, 229–48. **Differences in response to Rome in NE and SW Scotland:** Hunter, F. 2009 Traprain Law in the Roman World, in W. S. Hanson (ed.) *The Army and Frontiers of Rome,* Portsmouth RI, 225–40; cf. Wilson, A. 2003 Roman and native in Dumfriesshire, *Transactions of the Dumfries and Galloway Natural History and Antiquarian Society* 77, 103–60, esp. 113–14. **Procurator at Inveresk:** RIB 2132, 3499. **Brochs:** MacKie, E. W. 1982 The Leckie broch, Stirlingshire: an interim report, *Glasgow Archaeological Journal* 9, 60–72; Main, L. 1998 Excavation of a timber round-house and broch at the Fairy Knowe, Buchlyvie, Stirlingshire, 1975–8, *Proceedings of the Society of Antiquaries of Scotland*, 128, 293–417. **Julius Severus and Lollius Urbicus:** Birley, A. R. 2005 *The Roman Government of Britain*, Oxford, 138–9. **Slighting of Vallum and removal of milecastle gates:** Birley, E. 1961 *Research on Hadrian's Wall*, Kendal, 124; Symonds, M. 2013 Gateways or garrisons? Designing, building and manning the milecastles, in R. Collins and M. Symonds, *Breaking down boundaries: Hadrian's Wall in the 21st century*, Portsmouth RI, 53–70, esp. 63. **Forts in Pennines abandoned:** Bidwell, P. and Hodgson, N. 2009 *The Roman Army in Northern England*, Newcastle upon Tyne, 17–19. **Reinforcements from Upper Germany:** RIB 2216, 3486.

The Antonine Wall

General account: Hanson, W. S. and Maxwell, G. S. 1983 *Rome's North-West Frontier: the Antonine Wall*, Edinburgh. **Archaeological description:** Robertson, A. S. 2015 *The Antonine Wall: a Handbook to Scotland's Roman frontier*, revised ed. L. Keppie, Glasgow. **Secondary forts supersede Hadrian's Wall-type scheme:** Gillam, J. P. 1975 Possible changes in plan in the course of the construction of the Antonine Wall *Scottish Archaeological Forum* 7, 51–56. **Antonine Wall planned as completed from outset:** Graafstal, E., Breeze, D. J., Jones, R. H., and Symonds M. F. A. (eds) 2015 Sacred cows in the landscape: rethinking the planning of the Antonine Wall, in D. J. Breeze, R. F. Jones and I. Oltean (eds), *Understanding Roman Frontiers*, Edinburgh, 54–69. **Discussion of troop numbers:** Keppie, L. 2009 The garrison of the Antonine Wall: endangered species or disappearing asset?, in A. Morillo, N. Hanel and E. Martin (eds), *Limes XX* (Anejos de Gladius 13), Madrid, 1135–45.

The Abandonment of Antonine Scotland

Breakthrough pottery study: Hartley, B. R. 1972 The Roman occupations of Scotland: the evidence of the Samian ware, *Britannia* 3, 1–55. **Single period of Antonine occupation:** Hodgson, N., 1995 Were there two Antonine occupations of Scotland? *Britannia* 26, 29–49. **Hadrian's Wall rebuilt in 158:** Hodgson, N. 2011 The provenance of RIB 1389 and the Rebuilding of Hadrian's Wall in AD158, *Antiquaries Journal* 91, 59–71. **Date of final abandonment of Antonine Wall:** Hodgson, N. 2009 The abandonment of Antonine Scotland: its date and causes, in W. S. Hanson (ed.) *The Army and Frontiers of Rome*, Portsmouth RI, 185–93.

The Army of the Wall, AD122–60

The Auxiliaries of the Wall under Hadrian

Trajan's column: Lepper, F. and Frere, S.S. 1988 *Trajan's Column*, Gloucester. **Batavians at Vindolanda:** Birley,

A. R. 2002 *Garrison Life at Vindolanda: a Band of Brothers*, Stroud. **Cilurnigi:** Fernández Ochoa, C. and Morillo Cerdán, A. 1997 Cilurnum and Ala II Asturum. A new epigraphic document relating to the Spanish origin of a military toponym in Britannia, in W. Groenman-van Waateringe, et al. *Roman Frontier Studies 1995*, Oxford, 339–41. **Condrusi and Vellavi:** RIB 2107–8. **Diploma of 178:** RMD IV, no. 293. **Auxiliary recruitment in general:** Haynes, I. 2013 *The Blood of the Provinces: the Roman auxilia and the making of Provincial Society from Augustus to the Severans*, Oxford, 121–42.

The Wall Forts under Hadrian
General: Bidwell, P. 2007 *Roman Forts in Britain* (2nd ed.), Stroud; Johnson, A. 1983 *Roman Forts*, London. **Barracks:** Hodgson, N. and Bidwell, P. T. 2004 Auxiliary barracks in a new light: recent discoveries on Hadrian's Wall, *Britannia* 35, 121–158. **'Single ancient text':** Hyginus, *de munitionibus castrorum*, 1. **Horses in cavalry barracks:** Hodgson, N. 2003 *The Roman Fort at Wallsend: excavations in 1997–8*, Newcastle upon Tyne, 37–90. **Carlisle writing tablet on wheat and barley:** Tomlin, R. S. O. 1998 Roman manuscripts from Carlisle: the ink-written tablets, *Britannia* 29, 31–84, no. 1. **Antonine Wall evidence for military diet:** Breeze, D. J. 2016 *Bearsden*, Edinburgh. **Wine in barrels from Rhineland:** Bidwell, P. and Speak, S. 1994 *Excavations at South Shields Roman Fort vol. 1*, Newcastle upon Tyne, 214–16.

Routine
Josephus: Jewish War 3.86. **Legionary duty roster:** Fink, R. O. 1971 *Roman Military Records on Papyrus*, Cleveland, Ohio, no. 9. **Vindolanda duties:** Bowman, A. K. and Thomas, J. D. 1994 *The Vindolanda Writing Tablets (Tabulae Vindolandenses II)*, British Museum, London, no. 155. **Egyptian clerk:** P. Mich. 8.465–466. *Hippika Gymnasia:* Arrian, *Ars Tactica* 34. **South Shields training ground:** Bidwell, P. and Speak, S. 1994 *Excavations at South Shields Roman Fort vol. 1*, Newcastle upon Tyne, 14–15. **The function of *principia* forehalls:** Hodgson, N. 2003 *The Roman Fort at Wallsend: excavations in 1997–8*, Newcastle upon Tyne, 181–2. **Birdoswald exercise hall:** Wilmott, T. 1997 *Birdoswald*, London, 95–98. **The standard Hadrian's Wall baths plan:** Gillam, J. P., Jobey, I. M. and Welsby, D. A. 1993 *The Roman Bath-house at Bewcastle, Cumbria* (Cumberland and Westmorland Antiquarian and Archaeological Society Research Series No. 7), Kendal.

How was the Wall Manned under Hadrian?
Finds from turrets: Allason-Jones, L. 1988 "Small finds" from Turrets on Hadrian's Wall, in J. C. Coulston (ed.) *Roman military equipment and the identity of Roman soldiers* (BAR Int. Ser. 394), Oxford, 197–233. **Relationship of MC35 to Housesteads:** ibid., 217; RIB 2411.146. **Studies of inscriptions at milecastles naming units:** Breeze, D. J. 2002 A Pannonian soldier on Hadrian's Wall and the manning of milecastles, *Zwischen Rom und dem Barbaricum* (Archaeologica Slovaca Monographiae 5), 59–63; Breeze, D. J. 2003 Auxiliaries, Legionaries, and the operation of Hadrian's Wall, in J. J. Wilkes (ed.) *Documenting the Roman Army: essays in honour of Margaret Roxan* (BICS Supplement 81), London, 147–51.

Pay, Prospects, Relationships
Military pay scales: Speidel, M. A. 1992 Roman army pay scales, *Journal of Roman Studies* 82, 87–106; cf. Alston, R. 1994 Roman military pay from Caesar to Diocletian, *Journal of Roman Studies* 84, 113–23; Breeze, D. J. and Dobson, B. 2000 *Hadrian's Wall* (4th ed.), London, 183–5. **Vindolanda prices:** Bowman, A. K. and Thomas, J. D. 2003 *The Vindolanda Writing Tablets (Tabulae Vindolandenses III)*, British Museum, London, 15–16. **Charge for cavalryman's horse:** Hodgson, N. 2003 *The Roman Fort at Wallsend: excavations in 1997–8*, Newcastle upon Tyne, 86. **Soldiers' marriages:** Phang, S. E. 2001 *The marriage of Roman soldiers (13BC–AD235)*, Leiden. **Diplomas:** RIB 2410.1-.401.13, esp. introduction pp 1–2; Eck, W. and Wolff, H. (eds) 1986 *Heer und Integrationspolitik: Die römischen Militärdiplome als historiche Quelle*, Cologne; Haynes, I. 2013 *The Blood of the Provinces: the Roman auxilia and the Making of Provincial Society from Augustus to the Severans*, Oxford. **Women in military life:** Allason-Jones, L. 1999 Women and the Roman army in Britain, in A. Goldsworthy and I. Haynes (eds) *The Roman army as a community*, Portsmouth RI, 41–51. **Wives in barracks?:** Hodgson, N. 2014 The accommodation of soldiers' wives in Roman fort barracks – on Hadrian's Wall and beyond, in R. Collins and F. McIntosh (eds) *Life in the Limes: studies in the people and objects of the Roman frontiers*, Oxford, 18–28.

Religion
Feriale Duranum: Fink, R. O., Hoey, A. S. and Snyder, W. F. 1940 The Feriale Duranum, *Yale Classical Studies* 7, 1–222; Fink, R. O. 1971 *Roman Military Records on Papyrus*, Cleveland, Ohio, no. 117; Haynes, I. 2013 *The Blood of the Provinces: the Roman auxilia*, Oxford, 198–206. **Maryport:** Breeze, D. J. 1997 The regiments stationed at Maryport and their commanders, in R. J. A. Wilson *Roman Maryport and its setting*, Senhouse Museum Trust, 67–89. **Coventina's Well:** Allason-Jones, L. and McKay, B. 1985 *Coventina's Well*, Chester. **Genio Vali altar:** RIB 2015.

Civilians in the Wall Zone in the Hadrianic Period

Vici laid out at the time of fort foundation:
Bidwell, P. and Hodgson, N. 2009 *The Roman Army in Northern England*, Newcastle upon Tyne, 30.
Homo transmarinus: Bowman, A. K. and Thomas, J. D. 1994 *The Vindolanda Writing Tablets (Tabulae Vindolandenses II)*, British Museum, London, 344.
Vicani at Carriden: RIB 3503. **Hadrianic settlement south of Vallum at Housesteads:** Birley, R. E. 1961 Housesteads Civil Settlement, 1960, *Archaeologia Aeliana* ser. 4, 39, 301–19; Birley, R. E. 1962 Housesteads Vicus, 1961, *Archaeologia Aeliana* ser. 4, 40, 117–33.
Idea that Hadrianic civil settlement kept south of Vallum: Salway, P. 1965 *The Frontier People of Roman Britain*, Cambridge, 13–14. **Possibility of undetected early settlement north of Vallum:** Sommer, C. S. 1984 *The Military Vici in Roman Britain* (BAR Brit. Ser. 129), Oxford, 15–17; Snape, M. E. 1991 Roman and native: *vici* on the north British frontier, in V. A. Maxfield and M. J. Dobson (eds) *Roman Frontier Studies 1989*, Exeter, 468–71, esp. 469. **Vindolanda diploma:** RIB 2401.9.
Chesters diplomas: RIB 2401.10; 2401.13.

Civilians and Military Supply

Bidwell, P. 2007 *Roman Forts in Britain* (2nd ed.) Stroud, 100–17 (Cap. 6); Breeze, D. J. 1973 Demand and supply on the northern frontier, in R. Miket and C. Burgess (eds) *Between and Beyond the Walls*, Edinburgh, 264–86.

The Life of the Local Population

General picture and new evidence from north of Wall: Hodgson, N., McKelvey, J. and Muncaster, W. 2012 *The Iron Age on the Northumberland Coastal Plain*, Newcastle upon Tyne. **South of Wall:** Proctor, J. 2012 *Faverdale, Darlington: excavations at a major settlement in the northern frontier zone of Roman Britain*, London; Willis, S. and Carne, P. (eds) 2013 *A Roman Villa at the edge of empire: excavations at Ingleby Barwick, Stockton-on-Tees, 2003–04*, York. **Cleared zone north of Wall:** Hodgson, N., McKelvey, J. and Muncaster, W. 2012 *The Iron Age on the Northumberland Coastal Plain*, Newcastle upon Tyne, esp. 217–18.

Peoples North of the Wall

Tribal names: Rivet, A. L. F. and Smith, C. 1979 *The Place Names of Roman Britain*, London. **Second-century Roman objects in Scotland and their distribution:** Hunter, F. 2007 *Beyond the Edge of the Empire – Caledonians, Picts and Romans*, Rosemarkie, esp. 19–22; 36. **Differences in Roman finds on native sites in SE and SW Scotland:** Wilson, A. 2001 The Novantae and Romanization in Galloway, *Transactions of the Dumfries and Galloway Natural History and Antiquarian Society* 75, 73–131; Wilson, A. 2003 Roman and native in Dumfriesshire, *Transactions of the Dumfries and Galloway Natural History and Antiquarian Society* 77, 103–60; Hodgson, N., 2009 The abandonment of Antonine Scotland: its date and causes, in W. S. Hanson (ed.) *The Army and Frontiers of Rome*, Portsmouth RI, 185–93, esp. 189. **Traprain Law:** Hunter, F. 2009 Traprain Law and the Roman World, in W. S. Hanson (ed.) *The Army and Frontiers of Rome*, Portsmouth, RI, 225–40. **Brochs:** MacKie, E. W. 1982 The Leckie broch, Stirlingshire: an interim report, *Glasgow Archaeolical Journal* 9, 60–72; Main, L. 1998 Excavation of a timber round-house and broch at the Fairy Knowe, Buchlyvie, Stirlingshire, 1975–8, *Proceedings of the Society of Antiquaries of Scotland*, 128, 293–417. **Great Whittington site:** Collins, R. and Biggins, J. A. 2013 Metal-detecting and geophysical survey at Great Whittington, Northumberland, *Archaeologia Aeliana* ser. 5, 42, 235–67. **Great Whittington as a frontier market/camp site:** suggestion by Brian Roberts, unpub.

4 THE HEYDAY OF THE WALL: AD160–AD250

Events

Birley, A. R. 2005 *The Roman Government of Britain*, Oxford.

Hadrian's Wall as Restored after the Withdrawal from Scotland

Second phase in berm obstacles: McKelvey, J. and Bidwell, P. T. 2005 The excavation of prehistoric features and Hadrian's Wall at Nos 224–228, Shields Road, Byker, Newcastle upon Tyne, *Arbeia Journal* 8, 5–28, esp. 15–17; Frain, T., McKelvey, J. and Bidwell, P. T. 2005 Excavation and watching briefs along the berm of Hadrian's wall at Throckley, Newcastle upon Tyne, in 2001–2002, *Arbeia Journal* 8, 29–2, esp. 49. **Date of replacement of Turf Wall in stone at Garthside turret:** Welsby, D. 1985 The pottery from the two turrets at Garthside on Hadrian's Wall, *Transactions of the Cumberland and Westmorland Antiquarian and Archaeological Society* ser. 2, 85, 71–6; **at TW MC79:** Richmond, I. A. and Simpson, F. G. 1952 Milecastle 79 (Solway), *Cumberland and Westmorland Antiquarian and Archaeological Society* ser. 2, 52, 17–40. **Units restored to Wall forts:** Hodgson, N. 2008 After the Wall periods: what is our historical framework for Hadrian's Wall in the twenty-first century?, in P. Bidwell (ed.) *Understanding Hadrian's Wall*, Kendal, 11–23, esp. 15 and n. 11–14. **Ravenglass diploma:** Holder, P. A. 1997 A Roman military diploma from Ravenglass, Cumbria, *Bulletin of the John Rylands Library* 79, 3–41. **Replacement of milecastle gates but less use after 160:** Symonds, M. 2013 Gateways or garrisons? Designing, building, and manning the milecastles, in R. Collins and M. Symonds (eds) *Breaking down boundaries: Hadrian's Wall in the 21st century*, Portsmouth RI, 53–70, esp. 62–4. **Vallum marginal mound seen as primary:** Wilmott, T. (ed.) 2009 *Hadrian's Wall: Archaeological Research by English Heritage 1976–2001*, London, 134–6. **Marginal mound post-dates Vallum ditch widened by the effects of erosion:** ibid. 92, Fig. 202. **Mounds reinstated at milecastle 23:** Heywood, B. and Breeze, D. J. 2008 Excavations at Vallum Causeways on Hadrian's Wall in the 1950s, *Archaeologia Aeliana* ser. 5, 37, 93–126, esp. 105–6. **Military Way and 'Lesser Military Way':** Birley, E. 1961 *Research on Hadrian's Wall*, Kendal, 111–16. **Lesser tracks behind Wall:** Bidwell, P. T. and Watson, M. 1996 Excavations on Hadrian's Wall at Denton, Newcastle upon Tyne, 1986–89, *Archaeologia Aeliana* ser. 5, 24, 1–56, esp. 33–4; Breeze, D. J. 2015 'The Vallum of Hadrian's Wall', *Archaeologia Aeliana* ser. 5, 44, 1–29, esp. 6–8. **Bridges, on Wall and on Dere Street:** Bidwell, P. and Holbrook, N. 1989 *Hadrian's Wall Bridges*, London. **Subsequent re-interpretation of Chesters bridge:** Bidwell, P. 1999 *Hadrian's Wall 1989–99*, 118–20.

The New North-East Outpost System

Risingham inscription: RIB 1227. **Newstead garrisons:** Manning, W. H. 2006 The Roman Fort at Newstead: the weapons and the garrisons, in R. J. A. Wilson (ed.) *Romanitas: essays on Roman archaeology in honour of Sheppard Frere*, Oxford, 74–94. **Praetensio/ praetentura:** Speidel, M. P. 1998 The Risingham Praetensio, *Britannia* 29, 356–59. **Corbridge:** Hodgson, N. 2008 The development of the Roman site at Corbridge from the first to third centuries AD, *Archaeologia Aeliana* ser. 5, 37, 93–126. **Birrens rebuilt in 158:** RIB 2110. **Oracle at Claros and Housesteads:** RIB 1579; Jones, C. P. 2005 Ten dedications To the gods and goddesses and the Antonine Plague, *Journal of Roman Archaeology* 18, 293–301. **Britons were on the verge of war in 169:** SHA Marcus 22.1.

The Wall is Breached

Abandonment of outposts around 180: Hartley, B. R. 1972 The Roman Occupations of Scotland: The evidence of the Samian Ware *Britannia* 3, 1–55, esp. 39–41; Roberston, A. S. 1975 *Birrens (Blatobulgium)*, Edinburgh, esp. 285–6. **Invasion:** Cassius Dio 72.8.1. **Ulpius Marcellus:** Birley, A. R. 2005 *The Roman Government of Britain*, Oxford, 162–70. **South Shields shipwreck:** Bidwell, P. T. 2001 A probable Roman shipwreck on the Herd Sands at South Shields, *Arbeia Journal* 6–7 (for 1997–98), 1–23. **Corbridge destruction deposit:** Hodgson, N. 2008 The development of the Roman site at Corbridge from the first to third centuries AD, *Archaeologia Aeliana* ser. 5, 37, 93–126, esp. 57–63. **Halton Chesters destruction deposit:** Dore, J. N. 2009 *Excavations directed by J. P. Gillam at the Roman fort of Haltonchesters, 1960–61*, Oxford. **Link with Shorden Brae mausoleum:** Bidwell, P. 2010, A survey of the Anglo-Saxon crypt at Hexham and its re-used Roman stonework, *Archaeologia Aeliana* ser. 5, 39, 53–145, esp. 73–4.

Rebellion and Neglect: the Northern Frontier from 184 to 197

Events: Birley, *Roman Government of Britain*. **Permanent units finally settled in Wall forts by 180s:** Hodgson, N. 2008 After the Wall periods: what is our historical framework for Hadrian's Wall in the twenty-first century?, in P. Bidwell (ed.) *Understanding Hadrian's Wall*, Kendal, 11–23, esp. 15 and n. 11–14.

The Wall under Septimius Severus

Events: Birley, *Roman Government of Britain*. **Forts not fully occupied 197–202:** Bidwell, P. 2012: The Roman fort at Bainbridge, Wensleydale: excavations by B. R. Hartley on the *Principia* and a summary account of other excavations and surveys, *Britannia* 43, 45–113, esp. 66–70. **Severan expedition:** Hodgson, N. 2014 The British Expedition of Septimius Severus, *Britannia* 45, 31–51.

Hadrian's Wall in its Restored State

'Severan' Extra-Narrow Wall rebuild in central sector: Crow, J. G. 1991 A review of current research on the turrets and curtain of Hadrian's Wall, *Britannia* 22, 51–63, esp. 55–7. **Milecastles and turrets:** Symonds, M. 2013 Gateways or garrisons? Designing, building and manning the milecastles, in R. Collins and M. Symonds (eds) *Breaking down boundaries: Hadrian's Wall in the 21st century*, Portsmouth RI, 53–70, esp. 64–5. **Numbers of turrets demolished and retained:** Charlesworth, D. 1977 The turrets on Hadrian's Wall, in M. R. Apted, R. Gilyard-Beer and A. D. Saunders (eds) *Ancient Monuments and their interpretation*, London, 13–26, esp. 24. **Civilian labour on the Wall and Vindolanda roundhouses:** RIB 1672–3, 1843–4, 1962, 2022; Fulford, M. 2006 Corvées and *civitates*, in R. J. A. Wilson (ed.) *Romanitas: essays on Roman archaeology in* honour of Sheppard Frere, Oxford, 65–71; Bidwell, P. T. 1999 Hadrian's Wall 1989–1999, Carlisle, 25; Birley, R. E. 2009 Vindolanda: a Roman frontier fort on Hadrian's Wall, Stroud, 138–40.

The Lack of Literary Sources for Third-Century Britain

Piercebridge: RIB 1022, 1026, 3253, 3258; Bidwell, P. and Hodgson, N. 2009 *The Roman Army in Northern England*, Newcastle upon Tyne, 145–50. **Brancaster:** Johnson, S. 1989 *The Roman Forts of the Saxon Shore*, London, 34–7. **Caistor:** Darling, M. J. and Gurney, D. 1993 *Caistor-on-Sea: excavations by Charles Green, 1951–55* (E. Anglian Archaeological Reports 60), Norfolk. **Reculver:** Philp, B. 2005 *The Excavation of the Roman Fort at Reculver, Kent* (Monograph 10, Kent Archaeological Rescue Unit), Dover.

The Army of the Wall

The Enhanced Status of the Soldiery
'Enrich the soldiers, scorn the rest': Cassius Dio 77.15. **Pay rises and third-century payment in kind:** Speidel, M. A. 1992 Roman army pay scales, *Journal of Roman Studies* 82, 87–106; Develin, R. 1971 The army pay rises under Severus and Caracalla and the question of Annona Militaris, *Latomus* 30, 687–95. **Building inscriptions from forts collected:** Jarrett, M. G. and Mann, J. C. 1970 Britain from Agricola to Gallienus, *Bonner Jahrbücher* 170, 178–210, Appendix. **Risingham inscription:** RIB 1235. **Corbridge:** Richmond, I. A. 1943 Roman legionaries at Corbridge, their supply base, temples and religious cults, *Archaeologia Aeliana* ser. 4, 21, 127–224; Hodgson, N. 2015 *Roman Corbridge* (English Heritage Guide), London.

Changes in the Style of Barracks and Reduced Centuries
Plans with references: Hodgson, N. and Bidwell, P. 2004 Auxiliary barracks in a new light: recent discoveries on Hadrian's Wall, *Britannia* 35, 121–157. **Radiate coins beneath one Housesteads 'chalet' barrack, not the other:** Rushworth, A. 2009 *Housesteads Roman Fort – the Grandest Station*, Swindon, 134. **Eight contubernium barracks at South Shields:** Hodgson, N. and Bidwell, P. 2004 Auxiliary barracks, 125–7; **at Vindolanda:** *Britannia* 43 (2012), 291, Fig. 10. **Century sizes at Dura Europos:** Fink, R. O. 1971 *Roman Military Records on Papyrus*, Cleveland, Ohio, 16–17. **Building work at Chesters in c. 205–7:** RIB 1462.

Germanic War Bands in the Third-Century Wall Forts
General discussion and possible irregulars' barrack at Wallsend: Hodgson, N. 2003 *The Roman Fort at Wallsend: excavations in 1997–8*, Newcastle upon Tyne, 148–52. **German units at Housesteads and 'Housesteads ware':** Rushworth, A. 2009 *Housesteads Roman Fort – the Grandest Station*, Swindon, 285–8; 293–6. **Symmacharii at Chesters?:** RIB 3299.

Life in the Third-Century Barracks
Hodgson, N. and Bidwell, P. 2004 Auxiliary barracks in a new light: recent discoveries on Hadrian's Wall, *Britannia* 35, 121–57.

Women in Barracks?
Hodgson, N. 2014 The accommodation of soldiers' wives in Roman fort barracks – on Hadrian's Wall and beyond, in R. Collins and F. McIntosh (eds) *Life in the Limes: studies in the people and objects of the Roman frontiers*, Oxford, 18–28.

Military Routine and the Manning of the Wall
Guard duties in Dura documents: Fink, R. O. 1971 *Roman Military Records on Papyrus*, Cleveland, Ohio, nos 12–19; Davies, R. 1989 The Daily Life of the Roman soldier under the Principate, in D. J. Breeze and V. Maxfield (eds) *Service in the Roman Army*, Edinburgh, 32–68, esp. 54–5. **Other duties at Dura:** Fink nos 1–2; Davies Table C; Fink no. 47 and Davies, Table E. **Outposting in Dura documents:** Fink nos 1–2 and Davies, 56 and 44, Table C.

The Army in Action
Kirksteads altar: RIB 2034; **Carlisle:** RIB 946; **Corionotatae:** RIB 1142 with Bidwell, P. 2010 A survey of the Anglo-Saxon crypt at Hexham and its re-used Roman stonework, *Archaeologia Aeliana* ser. 5, 39, 53–145, esp. 77–8. **Shift to emphasis on cavalry:** Hodgson, N. 2003 *The Roman Fort at Wallsend: excavations in 1997–8*, Newcastle upon Tyne, 120–21; cf. Breeze, D. J. 1992 Cavalry on frontiers: Hadrian to Honorius, *University of London Institute of Archaeology Bulletin* 29, 19–35.

Military Religion
Jupiter Dolichenus: Speidel, M. P. 1978 *The Religion of Jupiter Dolichenus in the Roman Army*, Leiden; Hörig, M. and Schwertheim, E. 1987 *Corpus Cultus Iovis Dolicheni*, Leiden; Richmond, I. A. 1943 Roman legionaries at Corbridge, their supply base, temples and religious cults, *Archaeologia Aeliana* ser. 4, 21, 127–224. **Vindolanda Dolichenum:** Birley, A. and Birley, A. 2010 A Dolichenum at Vindolanda, *Archaeologia Aeliana* ser. 5, 39, 25–51. **Altars in rampart at Housesteads:**

Rushworth, A. 2009 *Housesteads Roman Fort – the Grandest Station*, Swindon, 224; **at High Rochester:** RIB 1266–8. **Mithras cult at Housesteads:** Daniels, C. M. 1962 Mithras *Saecularis*, the Housesteads mithraeum and a fragment from Carrawburgh, *Archaeologia Aeliana* ser. 4, 40, 105–15. **Antenociticus and Tineius Longus:** RIB 1329. **Cocidius at Bewcastle:** Richmond, I. A., Hodgson, K. D. and St Joseph, K. 1938 The Roman Fort at Bewcastle, *Transactions of the Cumberland and Westmorland Antiquarian and Archaeological Society* ser. 2, 38, 195–237. *Genii cucullati* **at Housesteads:** CSIR Great Britain I.6, no. 152. **'Veteres' a Germanic form of the name of the god Loki:** Birley, A. R. 2008 Some Germanic deities and their worshippers in the British frontier zone, in H. Börm, N. Ehrhardt and J. Wiesehöfer (eds) *Monumentum et instrumentum inscriptum: beschriftete Objekte aus Kaiserzeit und Spätantike als historische Zeugnisse* (Festschrift für Peter Weiss zum 65. Geburtstag), Stuttgart, 31–46.

Cemeteries

High Rochester: Charlton, D. B. and Mitcheson, M. 1984 The Roman cemetery at Petty Knowes, Rochester, Northumberland, *Archaeologia Aeliana* ser. 5, 12, 1–31. **South Shields:** Snape, M. E. 1994 An excavation in the Roman cemetery at South Shields, *Archaeologia Aeliana* ser. 5, 22, 43–66. **Beckfoot:** Caruana, I. 2004 The cemetery at Beckfoot Roman fort, in R. J. A. Wilson and I. D. Caruana (eds) 2004 *Romans on the Solway*, Kendal, 134–73. **Birdoswald:** Wilmott, T. (ed.), 2009 *Hadrian's Wall: Archaeological Research by English Heritage 1976– 2001*, London, 275–91.

The Civilians of the Wall

'The Military Vici'

Extent revealed by geophysical surveys: Biggins, J. A. and Taylor, D. J. A., 1999 A survey of the Roman fort and settlement at Birdoswald, Cumbria, *Britannia* 30, 91–110; Biggins, J. A. and Taylor, D. J. A. 2004 The Roman fort and *vicus* at Maryport: geophysical survey, 2000–2004, in R. J. A. Wilson and I. D. Caruana (eds) 2004 *Romans on the Solway*, Kendal, 102–33; Biggins, J. A. and Taylor, D. J. A. 2004 A Geophysical Survey at Housesteads Roman Fort, April 2003, *Archaeologia Aeliana* ser. 5, 33, 51–60; *Britannia* 32 (2001), 330–32 (Carvoran); Biggins, J. A. and Taylor, D. J. A. 2004 Geophysical survey of the *vicus* at Birdoswald Roman fort, Cumbria, *Britannia* 35, 159–78; Biggins, J. A., and Taylor, D. J. A. 2007 The Roman Fort at Castlesteads, Cumbria: A Geophysical Survey of the Vicus, *Transactions of the Cumberland and Westmorland Antiquarian and Archaeological Society* ser. 3, 15–30. **Interpretation of surveys:** Sommer, C. S., 2006 Military

vici in Roman Britain revisited, in R. J. A. Wilson (ed.) *Romanitas: essays on Roman archaeology in honour of Sheppard Frere*, Oxford, 95–145. **Strip-house based on Italian prototypes,** *vici* **planned at fort foundation, respecting common boundary lines and utilizing party walls:** Sommer, C. S. 1988 Kastellvicus und Kastell, *Fundberichte aus Baden-Württemberg* 13, 457–707, esp. 569–80; Sommer, C. S. 1999 The Roman army in SW Germany as an instrument of colonization, in A. Goldsworthy and I. Haynes (eds) *The Roman Army as a community*, Portsmouth RI, 81–93, esp. 86–9. **Excavated finds:** Snape, M. E., Bidwell, P. T. and Stobbs, G. C. 2010 Excavations in the military *vicus* south-west of the Roman Fort at South Shields in 1973, 1988 and 2002, *Arbeia Journal* 9, 43–132. **Vicus defences:** Bidwell, P. and Hodgson, N. 2009 *The Roman Army in Northern England*, Newcastle upon Tyne, 31–33; Hodgson, N. 2003 *The Roman Fort at Wallsend: excavations in 1997–8*, Newcastle upon Tyne, 14–21; Biggins, J. A. and Taylor, D. J. A. 2004 A Geophysical Survey at Housesteads Roman Fort, April 2003, *Archaeologia Aeliana* ser. 5, 33, 51–60. *Vicani* **inscriptions:** RIB 3503 (Carriden); RIB 1616 (Housesteads); RIB 1700 (Vindolanda). **Malton goldsmith:** RIB 712. **Funerary epitaphs:** Salway, P. 1965 *The Frontier people of Roman Britain*, Cambridge. *Collegium* **of slaves at Halton:** RIB 1436. **Veteran:** RIB 1459. **Adjutant's sister:** RIB 1742.

Supply and Communication

General: Bidwell, P. 2007 *Roman Forts in Britain* (2nd ed.) Stroud, 100–17 (Cap. 6); Bidwell, P. and Speak, S. 1994 *Excavations at South Shields Roman Fort vol. 1*, Newcastle upon Tyne, 214–24. **Brampton:** Burnham, B. C. and Wacher, J. 1990 *The 'small towns' of Roman Britain*, London, 203–208.

The Life of the Local Population

Local government: Breeze, D. J. 2008 Civil government in the North: the Carvetii, Brigantes and Rome, *Transactions of the Cumberland and Westmorland Antiquarian and Archaeological Society* ser. 3, 8, 63–72. **Civitas Carvetiorum:** Edwards, B. J. N. and Shotter, D. C. A. 2005 Two Roman milestones from the Penrith area, *Transactions of the Cumberland and Westmorland Antiquarian and Archaeological Society* ser. 3, 5, 65–79.

Society North of the Wall

Huckhoe: Jobey, G. 1959 Excavations at the native settlement at Huckhoe, Northumberland, 1955–7, *Archaeologia Aeliana* ser. 4, 37, 217–78. **Pollen evidence:** Young, R. 2004 Peat, pollen and people: palaeoenvironmental reconstruction in Northumberland

National Park, in P. Frodsham 2004 *Archaeology in Northumberland National Park* (CBA Res. Rep. 136), York, 156–70. **Broxmouth:** Armit, I. and McKenzie, J. 2013 *An Inherited Place: Broxmouth Hillfort and the South-east Scottish Iron Age*, Edinburgh. **Traprain:** Hunter, F. 2009 Traprain Law and the Roman World, in W. S. Hanson (ed.), *The Army and Frontiers of Rome*, Portsmouth, RI, 225–40. **Changes in society in Scotland, and in uptake of Roman objects:** Hunter, F. 2005 Rome and the creation of the Picts, in Visy Z. (ed.) *Limes XIX: Proceedings of the XIX International Congress of Roman Frontier Studies*, Pécs, 235–40; Hunter, F. 2007 *Beyond the Edge of the Empire – Caledonians, Picts and Romans*, Rosemarkie. **Birnie:** Holmes, N. 2006 *Two denarius hoards from Birnie, Moray, British Numismatic Journal* 76, 1–44. **Denarius subsidies and hoards:** Hunter, F. 2009 *Denarius* hoards beyond the frontier. A Scottish case study, in A. Morillo, N. Hanel and E. Martin (eds) *Limes XX* (Anejos de *Gladius* 13), Madrid, 1619–30; Reece, R. 2008 Roman silver goes abroad, in *Roman coins outside the empire: ways and phases, contexts and functions* (Proceedings of the ESF/SCH Exploratory Workshop Radziwill Palace, Nieborów (Poland), 3–6 September 2005), Institute of Archaeology, University of Warsaw, Wetteren, 59–73. **The 'loca' debunked:** Rivet, A. L. F. and Smith, C. 1979 *The Place Names of Roman Britain*, London, esp. 212.

5 THE WALL IN THE LATER EMPIRE: AD250–369

Events

Dereliction and poor maintenance at Birdoswald: RIB 1912; Wilmott, T. 1997 *Birdoswald, Excavations of a Roman fort on Hadrian's Wall and its successor settlements: 1987–92*, London, 198–202. **Constantine takes troops from Britain and outpost forts abandoned in 312:** Casey, P. J. 1978 Constantine the Great in Britain – the evidence of the coinage of the London mint, ad312–14, in J. Bird, H. Chapman and J. Clarke (eds) *Collectanea Londiniensia*, London, 181–93. **Overview of sources:** Birley, A. R. 2005 *The Roman Government of Britain*, Oxford, 411–12. **Latest excavated coin from the outpost forts:** Gillam, J. P., Jobey, I. M. and Welsby, D. A. 1993 *The Roman Bath-house at Bewcastle, Cumbria* (Cumberland and Westmorland Antiquarian and Archaeological Society Research Series 7), Kendal, 27–8. **Old unit in 276–82 at Birdoswald:** RIB 3438; **Vindolanda:** RIB 1710. **Diocletianic rebuilding at Birdoswald:** RIB 1912; **Housesteads:** RIB 1613; **Milecastles:** Casey, P. J. 1984 The Coins, in D. Haigh and M. Savage, Sewingshields, *Archaeologia Aeliana* ser. 5, 12, 33–147, at 133–6; **South Shields:** Bidwell, P. and Speak, S. 1994 *Excavations at South Shields Roman Fort vol. 1*, Newcastle upon Tyne, 40–3.

The Fourth-Century Army of the Wall

The *Notitia Dignitatum*: Text: ed. O. Seeck, Berlin 1876. **General:** Jones, A. H. M. 1964 *The Later Roman Empire 284–602*, Oxford, Appendix II, 1429–50; **British section:** Rivet, A. L. F. and Smith, C. 1979 *The Place Names of Roman Britain*, London, 216–25. **Reflects situation on Wall in late fourth century:** Hodgson, N. 1991 The Notitia Dignitatum and the Later Roman Garrison of Britain, in V. A. Maxfield and M. J. Dobson (eds) *Roman Frontier Studies 1989*, Exeter, 84–92.

The Reformed Late Roman Army

Recent research points to completion under Constantine: Nicasie, M. J. 1998 *Twilight of Empire: the Roman army from the reign of Diocletian until the battle of Adrianople*, Amsterdam, 16–41. **Late Roman style of replanning at South Shields:** Bidwell, P. 1996 Some aspects of the development of later Roman fort plans, *Arbeia Journal* 5, 1–18; Bidwell, P. and Speak, S. 1994 *Excavations at South Shields Roman Fort vol. 1*, Newcastle upon Tyne, 40–2. **Binchester:** Ferris, I. 2010 *The Beautiful Rooms are empty: excavations at Binchester Roman Fort, County Durham 1976–81 and 1986–1991*, Durham; cf. review by N. Hodgson in *Britannia* 44 (2013), 409–10.

Numbers of Troops on the Fourth-Century Wall

Old belief that each 'chalet' occupied by a single soldier and his family: Daniels, C. M. 1980 Excavations at Wallsend and the fourth-century barracks on Hadrian's Wall, in W. S. Hanson and L. J. F. Keppie (eds) *Roman Frontier Studies 1979*, BAR Int. Ser. 71, Oxford, 173–93. **Standard barrack arrangements continue in fourth century:** Bidwell, P. 1991 Later Roman Barracks in Britain, in V. A. Maxfield and M. J. Dobson (eds), *Roman Frontier Studies 1989*, Exeter, 9–15; Hodgson, N. and Bidwell, P. 2004 Auxiliary barracks in a new light: recent discoveries on Hadrian's Wall, *Britannia* 35, 121–57, esp. 147–54. **Hexarchus:** Grosse, R. 1920 *Römische Militärgeschichte von Gallienus bis zum Beginn der byzantinischen Themenverfassung*, Berlin, 109–10. **Late Roman frontier units not all of very small size:** Hodgson, N. 1999 The late Roman plan at South Shields and the size and status of units in the late Roman army, in N. Gudea (ed.) *Roman Frontier Studies VXII/1997*, Zalau, 547–54. **Areani:** Ammianus Marcellinus 28.3.8. **Similar secret agents on Chinese frontier:** Serruys, H. 1982 Towers in the northern frontier defenses of the Ming, *Ming Studies* 14 (Spring), 9–76, esp. 47–53.

The Operation and Maintenance of the Wall in the Late Roman Period

Late activity in Milecastle 9: Birley, E. B. 1930 Excavations on Hadrian's Wall west of Newcastle upon Tyne in 1929, *Archaeologia Aeliana* ser. 4, 7, 143–74. **Milecastle 35:** Haigh, D. and Savage, M. 1984 Sewingshields, *Archaeologia Aeliana* ser. 5, 12, 33–147. **Milecastle 39:** Crow, J. G. 1989 Milecastle 39 Castle Nick, in C. M. Daniels (ed.) 1989 *The Eleventh Pilgrimage of Hadrian's Wall* Newcastle upon Tyne, 52–3. **Maintenance of the Wall in later times at Wallsend:** Report in preparation. **West Denton, with explanation of outsets and insets west of Housesteads:** Bidwell, P. T. and Watson, M. 1996 Excavations on Hadrian's Wall at Denton, Newcastle upon Tyne, 1986–89, *Archaeologia Aeliana* ser. 5, 24, 1–56. **Birdoswald:** Simpson, F. G. and Richmond, I. A. 1934 Report of the Cumberland Excavation Committee for 1933, *Transactions of the Cumberland and Westmorland Antiquarian and Archaeological Society* ser. 2, 34, 134–7, esp. 127–29 and Fig. 2.

The Life of the Soldiers

Origins and appearance: hereditary service and annual regular conscription: Jones, A. H. M. 1964 *The Later Roman Empire 284–602*, Oxford, 615. **Egyptian soldiers sprung from local society:** Alston, R. 1995 *Soldier and Society in Roman Egypt*, London.

Pay and Status

Late Roman military pay and donatives paid to *alae* and cohorts at 20 per cent rate: Jones, A. H. M. 1964 *The Later Roman Empire 284–602*, Oxford, 623–4; 1257–9, n. 31–3. **Argument that accession donatives paid to *alae* and cohorts is at the same rate as field armies:** Brickstock, R. J. 2010 Coins and the frontier troops in the fourth century, in R. Collins and L. Allason-Jones (eds) *Finds from the Frontier: material culture in the 4th–5th centuries*, York, 86–91.

The Commanding Élite

Late Roman commanding officers: Jones, A. H. M. 1964 *The Later Roman Empire 284–602*, Oxford, 636–46. **Abinnaeus:** Bell, H., Martin, V., Turner, E. and van Berchem, D. (eds) 1962 *The Abinnaeus Archive: papers of a Roman Officer in the reign of Constantius II*, Oxford. **South Shields late Roman *praetorium*:** Hodgson, N. 1996 A late Roman courtyard house at South Shields and its parallels, in P. Johnson with I. Haynes (eds) *Architecture in Roman Britain*, York,

135–51. **Vindolanda *praetorium*:** Birley, R., Blake, J. and Birley, A. 1998 *The 1997 Excavations at Vindolanda Praetorium Site interim report*, Carvoran; Birley, R., Blake, J. and Birley, A. 1999 *The 1998 Excavations at Vindolanda Praetorium Site interim report*, Carvoran.

Wives and Relationships

Women in forts: Hodgson, N. 2014 The accommodation of soldiers' wives in Roman fort barracks – on Hadrian's Wall and beyond, in R. Collins and F. McIntosh (eds) *Life in the Limes: studies in the people and objects of the Roman frontiers*, Oxford, 18–28. **'The village of his wife':** *The Abinnaeus Archive* no. 37.

The Religion of the Fourth-Century Soldiers

Fall-off in religious dedications after 250s: Lane Fox, R. 1986 *Pagans and Christians*, London, 572–85, esp. 582–3. **Destruction of Carrawburgh mithraeum:** Richmond, I. A. and Gillam, J. P. 1951 The Temple of Mithras at Carrawburgh, *Archaeologia Aeliana* ser. 4, 29, 1–44, esp. 39–44. **Temples at Corbridge:** Hodgson, N. 2010 Roman architectural fragments at Corbridge: a survey and study, *Arbeia Journal* 9, 1–41, esp. 29–30. **Christian objects:** Mawer, F. *Evidence for Christianity in Roman Britain*, BAR Brit. Ser. 243, Oxford. **Co-existence:** Bell, H., Martin, V., Turner, E. and van Berchem, D. (eds) 1962 *The Abinnaeus Archive: papers of a Roman Officer in the reign of Constantius II*, Oxford, 30–3. **Beckfoot cremations:** Caruana, I. 2004 The cemetery at Beckfoot Roman fort, in R. J. A. Wilson and I. D. Caruana (eds) 2004 *Romans on the Solway*, Kendal, 134–73, esp. 165 no. 46.

The Civilians of the Wall in the Later Empire

The abandonment of the *vici*: Bidwell, P. 1991 Later Roman Barracks in Britain, in V. A. Maxfield and M. J. Dobson (eds) *Roman Frontier Studies 1989*, Exeter, 9–15, esp. 14; Bidwell, P. T. 1999 *Hadrian's Wall 1989–1999*, Carlisle, 29–30; Hodgson N. (ed.) 2009 *Hadrian's Wall 1999–2009: A Summary of Recent Excavation and Research*, Kendal, 35–6; 95–7; Bidwell, P. and Hodgson, N. 2009 *The Roman Army in Northern England*, Newcastle upon Tyne, 33–4. **Vindolanda *vicus* coin list:** Casey, P. J. 1985 The coins, in Bidwell, P. T., *The Roman Fort of Vindolanda*, London, 103–16. **Housesteads:** Daniels, C. M. 1980 Excavations at Wallsend and the fourth-century barracks on Hadrian's Wall, in W. S. Hanson and L. J. F. Keppie (eds) *Roman Frontier Studies 1979*, BAR Int. Ser. 71, Oxford, 173–93, esp. 190. **Detailed publication of dating evidence for abandonment at South Shields:** Snape, M. E., Bidwell,

P. T. and Stobbs, G. C. 2010 Excavations in the military *vicus* south-west of the Roman Fort at South Shields in 1973, 1988 and 2002, *Arbeia Journal* 9, 43–132; **Burgh-by-Sands:** Breeze, D. J. and Woolliscroft, D. J. (eds) *Excavation and Survey at Roman Burgh-by-Sands* (Cumbria Archaeological Research Reports 1), Carlisle; **Greta Bridge:** Casey, P. J. and Hoffmann, B. 1998 Rescue excavations in the *vicus* of the fort at Greta Bridge, C. Durham, *Britannia* 29, 111–83. **Other *vici* south of the Wall:** Alphabetically in Bidwell, P. and Hodgson, N. 2009 *The Roman Army in Northern England*, Newcastle upon Tyne. **Radiate coinage at Corbridge:** Casey, P. J. 1988 The Coins, in M. C. Bishop and J. N. Dore, *Corbridge: excavation of the Roman fort and town 1947–80*, London, 142–58, esp. Table 13.

Markets at Forts

Wallsend: Hodgson, N. 2003 *The Roman Fort at Wallsend: excavations in 1997–8*, Newcastle upon Tyne, 166–7. **Newcastle:** Snape, M. E. and Bidwell, P. T. 2002 Excavations at Castle Garth, Newcastle upon Tyne, 1976–92 and 1995–6: the excavation of the Roman fort, *Archaeologia Aeliana* ser. 5, 31, 1–249, esp. 275. **Vindolanda:** Birley, A. 2013 *The Vindolanda Granary Excavation*, Greenhead, 44–46. **Carlisle:** Zant, J. 2009 *The Carlisle Millennium Project: Excavations in Carlisle 1998–2001, volume 1: stratigraphy*, Lancaster, 463–4.

The Towns

Local government: Breeze, D. J. 2008 Civil government in the North: the Carvetii, Brigantes and Rome, *Transactions of the Cumberland and Westmorland Antiquarian and Archaeological Society* ser. 3, 8, 63–72. **Civitas Carvetiorum:** Edwards, B. J. N. and Shotter, D. C. A. 2005 Two Roman milestones from the Penrith area, *Transactions of the Cumberland and Westmorland Antiquarian and Archaeological Society* ser. 3, 5, 65–79. **Crindledykes milestones:** RIB 2299–2305. **Corbridge defences:** Salway, P. 1965 *The Frontier people of Roman Britain*, Cambridge, 56–9.

Everyday Life: the Indigenous People

Settlement south of the Wall, west of the Pennines: Blake, B. 1959 Excavations of Native (Iron Age) Sites in Cumberland, 1956–58, *Transactions of the Cumberland and Westmorland Antiquarian and Archaeological Society* ser. 2, 59, 1–14. **Settlement south of the Wall east of the Pennines**: Sherlock, S. J. 2012 *Late Prehistoric settlement in the Tees valley and north-east England* (Tees Archaeology Monograph 5), Hartlepool, esp. 113–6 and Appendices 1, 2 and 4. **Wattle Syke:**

Martin, L., Richardson, J. and Roberts, I. 2013 *Iron Age and Roman Settlements at Wattle Syke*, Leeds.

Society North of the Wall

End of silver denarius subsidies: Hunter, F. 2007 *Beyond the Edge of the Empire – Caledonians, Picts and Romans*, Rosemarkie; Hunter, F. 2009 *Denarius hoards beyond the frontier. A Scottish case study*, in A. Morillo, N. Hanel and E. Martín (eds) *Limes XX: estudios sobre la frontera Romana* (3 vols) (Anejos de *Gladius* 13), Madrid, 1619–30. **Picts, occurrence in sources and meaning of name:** Rivet, A. L. F. and Smith, C. 1979 *The Place Names of Roman Britain*, London, 438–40. **Social change in Scotland triggered by empire:** Fraser, J. E. 2009 *From Caledonia to Pictland: Scotland to 795*, Edinburgh, esp. 35–6. **Application of 'prestige goods system model' to Scotland:** Ingemark, D. 2014 *Glass, alcohol and power in Roman Iron Age Scotland*, Edinburgh, esp. 187. **Diplomacy and trade on Russian steppe:** Khodarkovsky, M. 2002 *Russia's steppe frontier: the making of a colonial empire, 1500–1800*, Bloomington IN. ***Pictos victos* dice tower:** Horn, H. G. 1989 Si per me misit, nil nisi vota feret. Ein römischer Spielturm aus Froitzheim, *Bonner Jahrbuch* 189, 139–60. **Archaeological traces:** Hunter, F. 2010 Beyond the frontier: interpreting late Roman Iron Age indigenous and imported material culture, in R. Collins and L. Allason-Jones (eds) *Finds from the Frontier: material culture in the 4th–5th centuries*, York, 96–109. **Aldclune:** Hingley, R., Moore, H. L., Triscott, J. E. and Wilson, G. 1997 The excavation of two later Iron Age fortified homesteads at Aldclune, Blair Atholl, Perth and Kinross, *Proceedings of the Society of Antiquaries of Scotland* 127, 407–66; **Black Spout:** Strachan, D. 2013 *Excavations at the Black Spout, Pitlochry*, Perth and Kinross Heritage Trust. **Late Roman objects in Scotland and their distribution:** Hunter, F. 2007 *Beyond the Edge of the Empire – Caledonians, Picts and Romans*, Rosemarkie, esp. 26, Figs. 9, 33, Figs. 14 and 35, Fig. 15. **Traprain hoard:** Hunter, F. and Painter, K. (eds) 2013 *Late Roman silver: the Traprain treasure in context*, Edinburgh. **Erickstanebrae brooch:** RIB 2421.43. **Settlements in the vicinity of Traprain Law:** Haselgrove, C. (ed.) 2009 *The Traprain Law Environs Project: Fieldwork and Excavations 2000–2004*, Edinburgh, esp. 230–1; cf. Hodgson, N., McKelvey, J. and Muncaster, W. 2012 *The Iron Age on the Northumberland Coastal Plain*, Newcastle upon Tyne, 215. **Idea of buffer states in southern Scotland:** Hunter, F. 2007 *Beyond the Edge of the Empire – Caledonians, Picts and Romans*, Rosemarkie, 44; Hunter, F. 2010 Beyond the frontier: interpreting late Roman Iron Age indigenous and imported material culture, in R. Collins and L. Allason-Jones (eds) *Finds from the Frontier: material culture in the 4th–5th centuries*, York, 96–109, esp. 99–100. **Dynasties founded by the Romans:** Richmond, I. A. 1940 The Roman in Redesdale, in *Northumberland County History* vol. 15, 63–159, esp. 112–16. **Against:** Mann, J. C. 1974 The Northern frontier after AD369, *Glasgow Archaeological Journal* 3, 34–42; Jackson, K. 1955 The Britons in southern Scotland, *Antiquity* 29, issue 114, 77–88, esp. 80. **Latest coin from the Wall found at Great Whittington:** Collins, R. 2008 The Latest Roman Coin from Hadrian's Wall: a small fifth-century purse group, *Britannia* 39, 256–326.

6 WHAT WAS THE PURPOSE OF HADRIAN'S WALL?

The General Idea behind the Wall – The Security of the Provincial Population

Hadrian's Wall as a policy to aid provincial economic development: Birley, E. 1956 Hadrianic Frontier Policy, in Swoboda, E. (ed.) *Carnuntina*, Graz-Cologne, 25–36. **Tacitus on land and river boundaries of empire:** *Agricola* 41.2. **Wall termed *limes* in Antonine Itinerary:** Iter I 464.1; Rivet, A. L. F. and Smith, C. 1979 *The Place Names of Roman Britain*, London, 155. **Ordered inner space separated by the Wall from an area of external control:** Whittaker, C. R. 1994 *Frontiers of the Roman empire: a social and economic study*, Baltimore, 10–30 (Cap. 1). **Robert Spence's painting *The Night Attack*:** Hingley, R. 2012 *Hadrian's Wall: a Life*, Oxford, 48, 224–5.

The Non-Military Interpretation

1921 influential essay: Collingwood, R. G. 1921 The Purpose of the Roman Wall, *Vasculum* 8, 4–9. **'Groundswell of opinion':** Lucy Mangan, *The Guardian Weekend* 23.01.2010. **Wall portrayed as a customs and passport barrier:** Birley, E. 1956 Hadrianic Frontier Policy, 33. **Doubts about the existence of the Wall walk:** Breeze, D. J. and Dobson, B. 1972 Hadrian's Wall: Some Problems, *Britannia* 3, 182–208, at 187; Breeze, D. J. and Dobson, B. 1976 *Hadrian's Wall*, London, 39; Johnson, S. 1989 *Hadrian's Wall*, English Heritage, London, 62. **Use of milecastles as civilian checkpoints as well as for military movement:** Breeze, D. J. and Dobson, B. 1976 *Hadrian's Wall*, London, 37–8; 51; Jones, G. D. B. and Woolliscroft, D. 2001 *Hadrian's Wall from the Air*, Stroud, esp. 76–7.

A Barrier For Economic Regulation?

The social and economic explanation: Whittaker, C. R. 1994 *Frontiers of the Roman empire: a social and economic study*, Baltimore. **Restrictions on movement of goods out of empire:** Erdrich, M. 2000 *Rom und die Barbaren: das Verhältnis zwischen dem Imperium Romanum und den Germanischen Stämmen vor seiner Nordwestgrenze von der späten römischen Republik bis zum Galischen Sonderreich*, Mainz. **Prevention of raiding recently stressed more than economic regulation:** Breeze, D. J. 2011 *The Frontiers of Imperial Rome*, Barnsley, esp. 203–5.

The Context in which the Wall was Built

'Displacement activity' and 'Neither strategic nor tactical value': Mann, J. C. 1974 The Frontiers of the Principate, *Aufstieg und Niedergang der römischen Welt* 2 (I), 508–33. **British cavalry in Vindolanda tablet:** Bowman, A. K. and Thomas, J. D. 1994 *The Vindolanda Writing Tablets (Tabulae Vindolandenses II)*, British Museum, London, no. 164. ***Latrunculi:*** CIL 3385 = ILS 395. **Caesar on *latrones*:** *Bellum Gallicum* 3.17. **Size of Scots force under Edward II:** Rogers, C. J. 2000 *War Cruel and Sharp: English Strategy under Edward III, 1327–60*, Woodbridge. **Early medieval war bands:** Aitchison, N. 2003 *The Picts and the Scots at War*, Stroud.

The Form of the Wall as Evidence for its Function

Evidence for the Wall walk and crenellations: Bidwell, P. T. 2008 Did Hadrian's Wall have a Wall walk?, in P. Bidwell (ed.) *Understanding Hadrian's Wall*, Kendal, 129–43. **The counter view:** Breeze, D. J. 2006 *J. Collingwood Bruce's Handbook to the Roman Wall* (14th edn), Newcastle upon Tyne, 109–10. **Caesar's explicit authority:** *BG* 7.81–2. **Use of defensive weapons; Walk walk wide enough to fight from:** Bidwell, P. T. 2005 The systems of obstacles on Hadrian's Wall: their extent, date and purpose, *Arbeia Journal* 8, 53–76.

The Military Functions of the Wall Curtain

Raid on Egyptian *praesidium*: Cuvigny, H. 2005 *Ostraca de Krokodilô: la correspondence militaire et sa circulation*, Cairo (*O. Krok.*), no. 87.

Changes in the Function of the Wall over Time

Peel Gap: Crow, J. G. 1991 A review of current research on the turrets and curtain of Hadrian's Wall, *Britannia*

22, 51–63, esp. 53. **Procopius:** *Wars* 8.20.42–6; Crow, J. G. 2004 The Northern Frontier of Britain from Trajan to Antoninus Pius: Roman Builders and Native Britons, in M. Todd (ed.) 2004 *A Companion to Roman Britain*, Oxford, 114–37, esp. 114–125.

The Purpose of the Wall in the Light of other Long Walls in Antiquity

Other long walls of antiquity: Crow, J. G. 1986 The Function of Hadrian's Wall and the Comparative Evidence of Late Roman Long Walls, in *Studien zu den Militärgrenzen Roms III*, Stuttgart, 724–9; Crow, J. G. and Ricci, A. 1997 Investigating the hinterland of Constantinople: interim report on the Anastasian Long Wall, *Journal of Roman Archaeology* 10, 235–63. **Greek tradition of defensive long walls familiar to Hadrian and Platorius Nepos:** Crow, J. G. 2004 The Northern Frontier of Britain from Trajan to Antoninus Pius: Roman Builders and Native Britons in M. Todd (ed.) 2004 *A Companion to Roman Britain*, Oxford, 114–37, esp. 129–30. **Gorgan Wall:** Sauer, E. W., Rekavandi, H. O., Wilkinson, T. J. and Nokandeh, J. 2013 *Persia's Imperial Power in Late Antiquity: the Great Wall of Gorgan and the Frontier Landscapes of Sasanian Iran,* Oxford. **Gao Lü:** Quoted in Lovell, J. 2006 *The Great Wall: China against the World*, London, 110. **Towers on Han and Ming walls of China:** Serruys, H. 1982 Towers in the northern frontier defenses of the Ming, *Ming Studies* 14 (Spring), 9–76. **Russian fortification walls:** Khodarkovsky, M. 2002 *Russia's steppe frontier: the making of a colonial empire, 1500–1800*, Bloomington IN, esp. 126–66; 215–16; Moon, D. 2014 *The Russian Peasantry 1600–1930: The World the Peasants Made*, London, esp. 46. **Roman siege works seen as precursors of Hadrian's Wall:** Petrikovits, H. v. 1967 Über die Herkunft der Annäherungshindernisse an den römischen Militärgrenzen, in *Studien zu den Militärgrenzen Roms*, Graz-Cologne, 215–20. **Defences against Vitellius:** Tactitus, *Hist.* 2.19. **Concealed trenches at battle of Lugdunum:** Cassius Dio 76.6.

A Final Mystery: The Purpose of the Vallum

Reviews of the evidence: Breeze, D. J. 2015 The Vallum of Hadrian's Wall, *Archaeologia Aeliana* ser. 5, 44, 1–29; Woolliscroft, D. J. 1999 More thoughts on the Vallum, *Transactions of the Cumberland and Westmorland Antiquarian and Archaeological Society* ser. 2, 99, 53–65, esp. 61 (stresses obstacle to raiders returning with stolen cattle etc.). **Aelius Aristides:** *Roman Oration* 84. **Triumphal arches at ends of empire:** Tacitus, *Ann.* 2.83. **Balbus the surveyor:** *Balbi ad Celsum Expositio*

et Ratio Omnium Formarum, translation in F. Fodorean 2011 Review of Richard J. A. Talbert: Rome's World. The Peutinger map reconsidered (2010), *Plekos* 13, 9–19 (http://www.plekos.uni-muenchen.de/2011/r-talbert.pdf).

7 THE LAST DAYS OF THE ROMAN WALL: AD367–?

Events

Chronology: Birley, A. R. 2005 *The Roman Government of Britain*, Oxford, 430–65. **Rescript of Honorius:** ibid., 460–61. **Drafts from Continental field army into hinterland forts after 367:** Hoffmann. D. 1969 *Das spätrömische Bewegungsheer und die Notitia Dignitatum*, Düsseldorf, esp. 339–50.

The Wall Forts after *c.* 370

Corbridge granaries: Knowles, W. H. and Forster, R. H. 1909 Corstopitum: report on the excavations in 1908, *Archaeologia Aeliana* ser. 3, 5, 305–424, esp. 323. **Stanegate:** Wright, R. P. 1941 The Stanegate at Corbridge, *Archaeologia Aeliana* ser. 4, 19, 194–209. **Yorkshire coast signal stations:** Bidwell, P. and Hodgson, N. 2009 *The Roman Army in Northern England*, Newcastle upon Tyne, 172–6. **Filey:** Ottaway, P. 2000 Excavations on the site of the Roman signal station at Carr Naze, Filey, 1993–4, *Archaeological Journal* 157, 79–199. **South Shields commanding officer's house:** Bidwell, P. and Speak, S. 1994 *Excavations at South Shields Roman Fort vol. 1*, Newcastle upon Tyne, 44. **Granaries:** Collins, R. 2015 Economic reduction or military reorganization? Granary demolition and conversion in later fourth-century northern Britannia, in R. Collins, M. Symonds and M. Weber (eds) *Roman Military Architecture on the Frontiers: Armies and their Architecture in Late Antiquity*, Oxford, 18–31. **Barracks:** Hodgson, N. and Bidwell, P. T. 2004 Auxiliary barracks in a new light: recent discoveries on Hadrian's Wall, *Britannia* 35, 121–58, esp. 153–4; Hodgson, N. 2014 The accommodation of soldiers' wives in Roman fort barracks – on Hadrian's Wall and beyond, in R. Collins and F. McIntosh (eds) *Life in the Limes: studies in the people and objects of the Roman frontiers*, Oxford, 18–28. **Late style of paving:** Zant, J. 2009 *The Carlisle Millennium Project: Excavations in Carlisle 1998–2001, volume 1: stratigraphy*, Lancaster, 329–31; Forster, R. H. and Knowles, W. H. 1912 Corstopitum: report on the excavations in 1911, *Archaeologia Aeliana* ser. 3, 8, 137–263, p.165; Snape, M. E. and Bidwell, P. T. 2002 Excavations at Castle Garth, Newcastle upon Tyne, 1976–92 and 1995–6: the excavation of the Roman fort, *Archaeologia Aeliana* ser. 5, 31, 1–249, esp. Figs 3.8; 8.6; 9.1; Ferris, I. 2010 *The Beautiful Rooms are empty: excavations at Binchester Roman Fort, County Durham 1976–81 and 1986–1991*, Durham, 82–91. **Late ramparts at Housesteads and Vindolanda:** Rushworth, A. 2009 *Housesteads Roman Fort – the Grandest Station*, Swindon, 136–40; Bidwell, P. 1985 *The Roman fort of Vindolanda*, London, 46.

The Wall Forts after *c*. 410

South Shields: Bidwell, P. and Speak, S. 1994 *Excavations at South Shields Roman Fort vol. 1*, Newcastle upon Tyne, esp. 44–7; Hodgson N. (ed.) 2009 *Hadrian's Wall 1999–2009: A Summary of Recent Excavation and Research*, Kendal, 71–2. **Newcastle:** Snape, M. E. and Bidwell, P. T. 2002 Excavations at Castle Garth, Newcastle upon Tyne, 1976–92 and 1995–6: the excavation of the Roman fort, *Archaeologia Aeliana* ser. 5, 31, 1–249. **Housesteads:** Rushworth, A. 2009 *Housesteads Roman Fort – the Grandest Station*, Swindon, esp. 314–22. **Vindolanda:** Jackson, K. 1982 Brigomaglos and St Briog, *Archaeologia Aeliana* ser. 5, 10, 61–6. **Christian symbol stone disputed:** Notes to RIB 3370 and 3448. **Castlesteads:** RIB 2331. **Birdoswald:** Wilmott, T. 1997 *Birdoswald, Excavations of a Roman fort on Hadrian's Wall and its successor settlements: 1987–92*, London; Wilmott, T. (ed.) 2009 *Hadrian's Wall. Archaeological Research by English Heritage 1976–2000*, Swindon. **Same type of very late paving at Birdoswald and South Shields:** compare *Birdoswald*, Plate 8, with Hodgson, N. 2008. After the Wall periods: what is our historical framework for Hadrian's Wall in the twenty-first century?, in P. Bidwell (ed.), *Understanding Hadrian's Wall*, Newcastle upon Tyne, 11–23, p. 20, Fig. 7. **Binchester:** Ferris, I. 2010 *The Beautiful Rooms are empty: excavations at Binchester Roman Fort, County Durham 1976–81 and 1986–1991*, Durham; cf. review by N. Hodgson in *Britannia* 44 (2013), 409–10. **Binchester Post-420 radiocarbon dates:** Petts, D. 2015 Late Roman Military Buildings at Binchester, in R. Collins, M. Symonds and M. Weber (eds) *Roman Military Architecture on the Frontiers: Armies and their Architecture in Late Antiquity*, Oxford, 33–45.

Explaining the Fifth-Century Archaeology

St Severinus: Eugippius, *Vita*; E. A. Thompson 1982 *Romans and Barbarians: the decline of the Western Empire*, Madison, 113–33.

Collapse or Transition?

War-band theory: Casey, P. J. 1993 The end of garrisons on Hadrian's Wall: a historic-environmental model, in D. F. Clark, M. Roxan and J. J. Wilkes (eds) *The later Roman empire today*, London, 69–80; Wilmott, T. 2000 The late Roman transition at Birdoswald and on Hadrian's Wall, in T. Wilmott and P. Wilson (eds) *The Late Roman Transition in the North* (BAR Brit. Ser. 299), Oxford, 13–23; Collins, R. 2012 *Hadrian's Wall and the end of empire*, London; **late fourth-century/early fifth-century date of changes to granaries at Birdoswald:** Bidwell, P. and Croom, A. 2010 The supply and use of pottery on Hadrian's Wall in the fourth century ad, in R. Collins and L. Allason-Jones (eds) *Finds from the Frontier: material culture in the 4th–5th centuries*, York, 20–36, p. 30; Bidwell, P. 2005 The dating of Crambeck Parchment Ware, *Journal of Roman Pottery Studies* 12, 15–21.

When were the Wall Forts finally Abandoned?

Late sequences: *See* individual site reports above; **Carlisle:** McCarthy, M. R. 1990 *A Roman, Anglian and Medieval site at Blackfriars Street, Carlisle*, Kendal; McCarthy, M. R. 2002 *Roman Carlisle and the lands of the Solway*, Stroud, 131–54; **Pollen evidence:** Dark, K. and Dark, P. 1996 New archaeological and palynological evidence for a sub-Roman reoccupation of Hadrian's Wall, *Archaeologia Aeliana* ser. 5, 24, 57–72; cf. Collins, R. 2012 *Hadrian's Wall and the end of empire*, London, 134–7; Huntley, J., Gates, T. and Stallibrass, S. 2009 Landscape and Environment, in M. F. A. Symonds and D. J. P. Mason (eds) 2009 *Frontiers of Knowledge: a research framework for Hadrian's Wall*, Durham, 108–18, p.113; **Camlann:** Dumville, D. N. 1977 Sub-Roman Britain: History and Legend, *History* 62, 173–92, 187–8.

Anglo-Saxons

Royal site at South Shields: Wood, I. N. 2008 *The origins of Jarrow: the monastery, the slake and Ecgfrith's minster*, Bede's World: Jarrow; **Newcastle, Corbridge, Carlisle:** *see* references above; **Other finds:** Miket, R. 1978 Two early Anglo-Saxon brooches from Chesters and Chesterholm, *Archaeologia Aeliana* ser. 5, 6, 177–80; **Wilfrid:** Bidwell, P. 2010 A survey of the Anglo-Saxon crypt at Hexham and its reused Roman stonework, *Archaeologia Aeliana* ser. 5, 39, 53–145; **St Cuthbert at Carlisle:** *Anon. Life of St Cuthbert*, 8.

The Wall in Later Times

'**The wayfarer may pass through them without knowing it**': Bruce, J. Collingwood 1851 *The Roman Wall*, Newcastle upon Tyne, 58.